# MANDEVILLE'S TRAVELS

---

EARLY ENGLISH TEXT SOCIETY
No. 319
2002

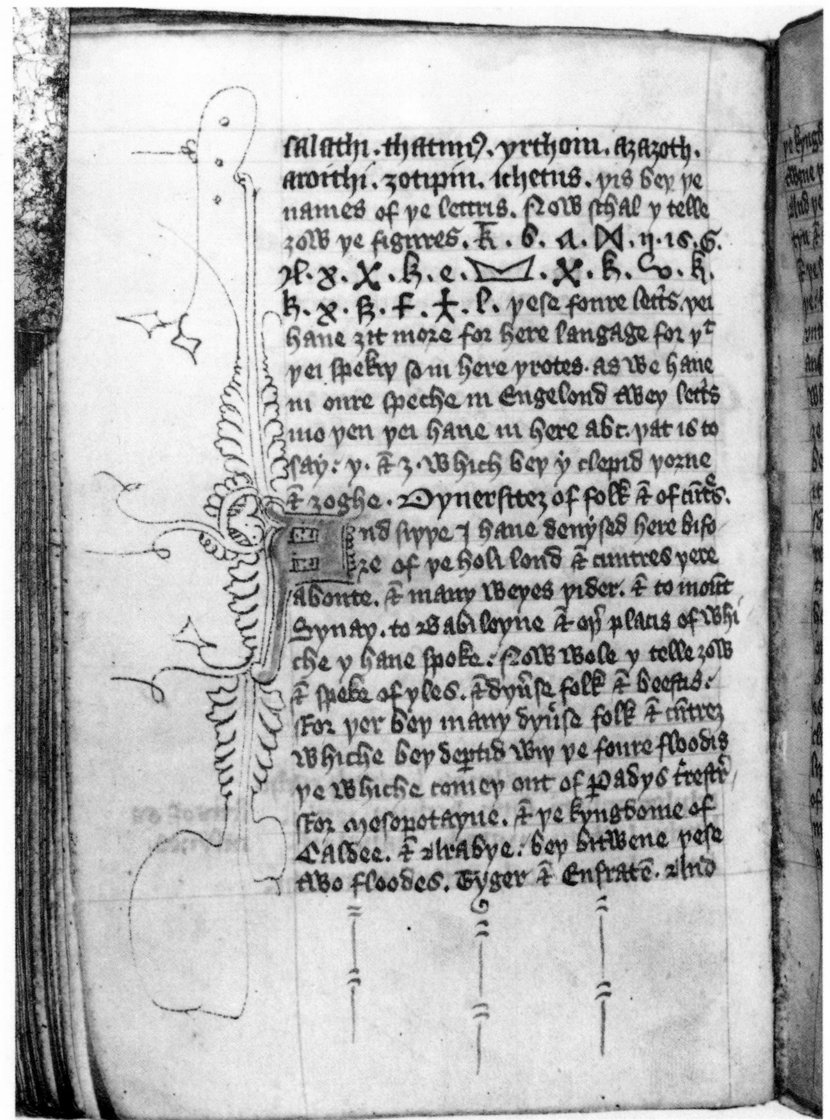

salathi. thatanu. yrthom. azazoth.
aroithi. zotipin. ichetus. yis ben ye
names of ye lettris. Now schal y telle
ȝow ye figures.
yese foure lettris yei
haue ȝit more for here langage for yt
yei speken sum here protes. As we haue
in oure speche in Engelond two lettris
mo yen yei haue in here abc. yat is to
say: y. & ȝ. which ben y clepid yorne
& ȝoghe. Dyuersitez of folk & of cuntrees.
And siyye I haue deuysed here bifo
re of ye holi lond & cuntrees yere
aboute. & many weyes yider. & to mount
Synay. to Babiloyne & oyer plaas of whi
che y haue spoke: Now wole y telle ȝow
& speke of yles. & dyuerse folk & beestis.
For yer ben many dyuerse folk & cuntrez
whiche ben departid wiy ye foure floodis
ye whiche comey out of paradys terestre.
For Mesopotamye. & ye kyngdome of
Caldee. & Arabye. ben bitwene yese
two floodes. Tyger & Eufrate. And

The Queen's College, Oxford, MS 383, f. 77v

men. nun. Samech. ey. phe. sad. corth
sir. sinn. thau. lowis. Now shal ye have
þe figures of þe iewis lettre. [illegible]
[illegible]
[illegible] And fro
þis cuntre þat I have spoke of: men goþ
þurȝ Galile. & leveþ þe hillis at þe on sy
de. And Galile is of þe prouince of þe lond
of promission. And in þat prouince: is þe
lond of Naym & Capharnaum & Corosaym
& Bethsayda. And of Bethsayda: was
seynt Petir y bore. & seynt Andrew. Al
so & of Corosaym: shal Antecrist be bore.
And some seiþ: he shal be bore in Babi
loyne. And þerfore seiþ þe prophete þus.
De babilonia exiet coluber qui totum
mundum devorabit. þat is to say: of Ba
bilonye shal a worme come out. þat shal
swolewe al þe world. And þis antecrist
shal be nourishid in Bethsayda: & he
shal regne in Corosaym. And þerfore seiþ
holy writ of hem þus. Ve tibi corosay
me. ve tibi bethsayda. ve tibi capharna
um. þat is to say: woo be to þee. Corosay.

The Queen's College, Oxford, MS 383, f. 55r

# THE DEFECTIVE VERSION OF MANDEVILLE'S TRAVELS

EDITED BY
M. C. SEYMOUR

*Published for*

THE EARLY ENGLISH TEXT SOCIETY

*by the*

OXFORD UNIVERSITY PRESS

*Published for*
THE EARLY ENGLISH TEXT SOCIETY
*by the*
OXFORD UNIVERSITY PRESS
2002

OXFORD
UNIVERSITY PRESS

Great Clarendon Street, Oxford OX2 6DP

Oxford University Press is a department of the University of Oxford.
It furthers the University's objective of excellence in research, scholarship,
and education by publishing worldwide in

Oxford New York
Athens Auckland Bangkok Bogotá Buenos Aires Cape Town
Chennai Dar es Salaam Delhi Florence Hong Kong Istanbul Karachi
Kolkata Kuala Lumpur Madrid Melbourne Mexico City Mumbai Nairobi
Paris São Paulo Shanghai Singapore Taipei Tokyo Toronto Warsaw

with associated companies in Berlin Ibadan

Oxford is a registered trade mark of Oxford University Press
in the UK and in certain other countries

Published in the United States
by Oxford University Press Inc., New York



First published 2002



British Library Cataloguing in Publication Data
Data available

Library of Congress Cataloging in Publication Data
Data applied for

ISBN 0-19-722322-2

1 3 5 7 9 10 8 6 4 2

Typeset by Joshua Associates Ltd., Oxford
Printed in Great Britain
on acid-free paper by
Print Wright Ltd., Ipswich

TO
ELIZABETH

# PREFACE

This third volume in the projected series of four English editions of *Mandeville's Travels* was scheduled to appear in 1983. The disappearance of the typescript after the death of J. A. W. Bennett in 1981 when many of his papers in Cambridge were discarded required its reconstruction, which had to be postponed because of other commitments. This delay enabled me to take note of more recent publications and discoveries and so to present it here to the Society, as it were, in a second edition.

I record my gratitude to Professors Norman Davis, Eric Dobson, Jack Bennett, Robert Burchfield, and John Burrow who read and commented on the typescript. To them and their colleagues on the Council much is owed. The custodians and owners of Mandeville manuscripts throughout the world have shown me every courtesy. I am particularly indebted to the late Colonel Bradfer-Lawrence for the loan of his manuscript (now in Japan), and to the librarians of the Pierpont Morgan Library and the Corning Museum of Glass for their gifts of microfilm. And the scholarship and personal kindness of other workers in the field, particularly those concerned with the non-English versions of the book and with Middle English dialects and manuscripts, have been of great benefit.

The Provost and Fellows of the Queen's College granted me the courtesy of their magnificent library and the kindness to print one of their manuscripts and to reproduce two pages therefrom. The Librarian and staff of the Bodleian Library have again given invaluable assistance. And lastly, I thank Joshua Associates for their patient conversion of a foul typescript into a fair copy.

*8 December 2000* M.C.S.

# CONTENTS

# INTRODUCTION

*Mandeville's Travels* was written in French on the Continent *c.*1356 by an unknown author, a Benedictine in an abbey in northern France.[1] A copy of this primary version of the book, known as the Continental Version and extant in thirty-two manuscripts, was carried into England before *c.*1365 and there developed a separate scribal tradition, known as the Insular Version and extant in twenty-three manuscripts.[2] This Insular Version, written in Anglo-French and distinguished by the presence of a paragraph describing the seven climates of the world and by numerous other small characteristics,[3] is the origin of all other versions of *Mandeville's Travels* (four in English, four in Latin) made in England. Its manuscripts group themselves into three major divisions: subgroup A, most easily distinguished by an interpolated dedication to Edward III (d. 1377) and extant in ten manuscripts; subgroup B, extant in four manuscripts; subgroup C, which developed in France, its lost archetype having been carried there before 1402, and extant in nine manuscripts in French hands.[4]

The Defective Version is the oldest English translation of the Insular Version. Its name derives from the loss of the second quire in the Insular manuscript (or a predecessor) from which it was translated, containing part of the description of Egypt.[5] This 'Egypt Gap' occurs in this edition on page 22 line 12. In spite of

[1] M. C. Seymour, *Sir John Mandeville* (Aldershot, 1993), pp. 1–24 , and p. 173 below.

[2] Ibid., pp. 38–9, 42–3. A Continental manuscript, not reported there, is Bibl. Nationale MS nouvelles acq. fr. 14313, described by S. Röhl in *Codices Manuscripti* 27/28 (1999), 55–6.

[3] G. De Poerck, 'La tradition manuscrite des *Voyages* de Jean de Mandeville', *Romanica Gandensia* 4 (1956), 125–58.

[4] Seymour, 'The scribal tradition of *Mandeville's Travels*: the Insular Version', *Scriptorium* 18 (1965), 38–48. The version is edited by G. F. Warner, *The Buke of Iohn Maundeuill*, Roxburghe Club (Westminster, 1889). A modernized edition of another manuscript of this version, BL MS Harley 212, is *Jean de Mandeville. Voyage autour de la terre*, ed. C. Deluz, Les Belles Lettres (Paris, 1993).

[5] E. W. Nicholson, 'Sir John Mandeville', *Encyclopaedia Britannica* (1883 edition) speaks of the loss of many pages. The matter lost is approximately of the same length as that which precedes the omission, hence the deduction of a missing quire. A comparable omission is evident in another Insular manuscript, MS Harley 204 f. 13$^r$ where the reading *la terre de Prestre Iohan ce nes mie loin qe ces sont lies griniers Ioseph* abridges Warner's edition pp. 21/44–27/33.

this loss of text the Defective Version established itself as the dominant form of the book in England. It is extant in thirty-three manuscripts and six fragments and extracts.[1] It is the base text of two conflations, the Cotton Version and the Egerton Version.[2] And it was printed in the *editio princeps* by Richard Pynson *c.*1496, whose text remained the basis of all English printed editions until 1725.[3]

The extant Defective Version is a slightly abridged translation of the Insular Version which featured the major lacuna of the 'Egypt Gap'. It is not possible to say whether its abridgement was already present in the translator's copy-text. No extant Insular manuscript is editorially abridged, whereas both major states of the Defective Version (subgroups 1 and 2) show some characteristically different omissions from the common substance. It may be that the English translator followed his Insular copy-text in full, lacking only the 'Egypt Gap', and that the extant manuscripts of his translation variously reflect an early scribal abridgement. On the other hand, the translator sometimes condenses and paraphrases the sense of the Insular text, and this approach may have prompted an editorial rather than a literal approach to translation. This proneness of the Defective Version to shrink as it is copied is evident in all subgroups and in many individual manuscripts and appears more commonly in the second half of the book after the description of Jerusalem and the Holy Land. Such emphasis on the biblical rather than the fabulous appears in the epitome and the extracts and says something about the appeal of the book.

There is no way of knowing how soon after the composition of the book *c.*1356 the translation was made. A manuscript of a Latin translation of the Insular Version was written at Abingdon in 1390 (Leiden MS Vulcan 96). The two English conflations based on the Defective Version, the Cotton and the Egerton Versions, survive in

[1] Seymour, 'The English manuscripts of *Mandeville's Travels*', *Trans. Edinburgh Bibl. Soc.* 4 (1966), 169–210, which overlooked Bodleian Library, MS Rawl. D 652 and the fragment MS Lat. misc. e 85.

[2] The edition of the Egerton Version cited above in footnote 4 is an accurate transcription but unaware of the precise components of its text. A new edition is forthcoming. The edition of the Cotton Version, ed. P. Hamelius, EETS OS 153 (London, 1919), is inaccurate; there are large lacunae, e.g. p. 18/34 omits 14 words, p. 19/27 omits 20 words, and there are innumerable misreadings, e.g. p. 121/14 *as*, 17 *dwellyn*, 34 *right* for MS *als*, *dwellen*, *pight*. My edition (Clarendon Press, 1967) modernizes *þ* and *ȝ*.

[3] Seymour, 'The early English editions of *Mandeville's Travels*', *The Library*, 5th ser. 19 (1964), 202–7. A facsimile of Pynson's edition was printed by Exeter University Press in 1980; after sig. gvii recto two pages are misplaced.

unique manuscripts that date from *c.*1400 and have no evident prior scribal tradition. No extant Defective manuscript was certainly written before 1400, and the interpolation at the end which claims that the book was submitted to the Pope at Rome certainly could not have been written before his return from Avignon in 1377. The echoes of *Mandeville's Travels* in the *Pearl* and Chaucer's Squire's Tale are likely to come from the Insular Version. At a guess, therefore, the Defective Version was translated (if the interpolation is not a later addition) after 1377, perhaps *c.*1385.

Equally there is no way of knowing how closely the chapter divisions of the translator's text are preserved in the extant manuscripts. One Insular manuscript (BL MS Royal B. x) has a table of contents and thirty-six numbered chapters which sometimes agree with the chapter divisions of the manuscripts of subgroups 1 and 2. The loss of matter in the 'Egypt Gap' obviously prevents a complete correspondence of chapter divisions between the Insular and Defective Versions. With some variation the extant English manuscripts of subgroups 1 and 2 preserve a sequence of twenty-four chapters (twenty-one in subgroup 2), sometimes rubricated without numbers, sometimes marked merely by a large initial letter. Uniquely MS Royal 17 C. xxxviii, which derives from the lost archetype of the Defective Version independently, has a tabula and twenty-two numbered and rubricated chapters, and Pynson's *editio princeps*, which belongs to subgroup 2, has eighteen unnumbered and unrubricated major divisions. The subgroups which develop from subgroup 2 generally show a decline in the number of chapters and their rubrication which at their most degenerate disappear altogether. As the number of chapter divisions decreases, so the places at which the chapters begin and the rubrics where they survive differ from those in subgroups 1 and 2. Such variations give a crude indication of classification and affiliation. Since the divisions of subgroups 1 and 2 agree with minor variation,[1] it seems likely that they reflect the translator's chapters and rubrics. The numbering found in some manuscripts may not, however, depend on him. Of the two conflations based on the Defective Version, the Cotton Version has

[1] Only MS Douce 33 (stolen from the Society of Antiquaries after 1793) of subgroup 1 preserves the rubric 'þe land of Ynde' which corresponds to Chapter 15 of subgroup 2. With this exception there is an exact correlation of chapter division between subgroups 1 and 2 until Chapter 18 'Why he is yclepid þe greete Chan' which is not marked in subgroup 2; the latter subgroup also does not mark the final two chapters.

a tabula and Prologue and thirty-five rubricated chapters which follow the Insular manuscript used by the conflator, cf. MS Royal B. x mentioned above; and the Egerton Version has a Prologue and 162 unrubricated chapters. Neither conflation numbers its chapters, and neither has a sequence of chapter divisions which closely reflects that of the Defective Version.

## A STATEMENT OF AFFILIATION

The prime tasks which face an editor of the Defective Version are to determine as far as possible the nature of the Insular manuscript used by the translator, and to discover by collation, supported by reference to the Insular manuscripts, coherent boundaries of subgroups for the thirty-three extant English manuscripts. Since these determinations depend on close textual argument and concern numerous variant readings reported in the collations printed below the text and in the Textual Commentary and the Appendix, the reader who comes fresh to the Defective Version may find it useful to have at the outset a simplified statement of affiliation before the justification of its details.

No Insular manuscript with the 'Egypt Gap' survives. From readings recorded in the Textual Commentary it is clear that the translator's copy-text belonged to subgroup B of the Insular Version, and was superior to any of the four manuscripts of that subgroup which are extant or to the lost manuscripts which lie behind the three Latin translations known as the Harley, Ashmole and Leiden versions;[1] the fourth Latin version depends on subgroup A. The extant manuscripts closest to the translator's copy-text are MSS Sloane 1464 at London and Additional C. 280 at Oxford.

One of the two English manuscripts in private hands, the Sneyd manuscript of an inferior subgroup, is not available for study.[2] Another, MS Royal 17 C. xxxviii, derives independently from the lost archetype of the Defective Version and preserves at least one superior reading, but it is a robustly edited text, abridging matter

[1] The Harley Version is printed in part by Seymour, *The Metrical Version of Mandeville's Travels*, EETS 269 (London, 1973), pp. 148–92.

[2] Last seen at Sir Leicester Harmsworth's sale (Sotheby S.C. Oct. 1945, lot 2023) when it was purchased by Maggs for £100. The date in its prologue is 1300, characteristic of subgroups 3, 4, and 5.

and altering or curtailing scribal errors in its exemplar according to its editor's judgement.[1] The remaining thirty-one manuscripts of the Defective Version can be classified into five subgroups in which there are four instances of conflation. The first occurs in CUL MS Gg. 1. 34 (subgroup 4) where the initial leaves give the text of subgroup 1, presumably due to the replacement of the lost beginning in an ancestor. The second occurs in Princeton MS Taylor 10 (also subgroup 4) where the interpolated Latin letter of Dindymus in the account of Alexander has been adopted from subgroup 5. The third occurs in MS Sloane 2319 (subgroup 5) where the first sixteen leaves follow the text of subgroup 4. And the fourth occurs in the Rugby School MS (subgroup 3) where ff. 33–7 follow subgroup 1. Classification of manuscripts into subgroups is, of course, an academic exercise. The boundaries of the subgroups of the Defective Version, however, seem clear except for subgroup 3 where two manuscripts at the beginning of its tradition (TCC MS R. 4. 20 and the Rugby School MS) could be placed at the end of the tradition of subgroup 2; since the subgroups are dependent, the allocation has little practical distinction. With these caveats a simplified statement of affiliation and major distinguishing features may be made.

subgroup 1 (nine manuscripts) gives the most substantial text but lacks part of the Alexander legend.

subgroup 2 (five manuscripts and Pynson's *editio princeps*) derives independently from the lost archetype and lacks the account of the rotundity of the world.

subgroup 3 (seven manuscripts) derives from a lost manuscript of subgroup 2 and lacks the Hebrew alphabet.

subgroup 4 (five manuscripts) derives from a lost manuscript of subgroup 3 and gives a distinctly corrupt reading at the 'Egypt Gap'.

subgroup 5 (five manuscripts) derives from a lost manuscript of subgroup 4 and interpolates a Latin translation of the letter of Dindymus to Alexander.

Most manuscripts of the Defective Version were written in the first half of the fifteenth century, and none was certainly written before 1400, although the earliest manuscripts of subgroup 1 (including the base manuscript of this edition) may have been written about then. Subgroup 5 was in existence by 1425. Several manuscripts now lost

[1] Predominantly a manuscript of subgroup 2, it is described more fully below.

are recorded in fifteenth-century sources.[1] At a guess over one hundred manuscripts of the version and perhaps many more were written before Pynson's *editio princeps c.*1496.

The base manuscript of this edition, Queen's College MS 383, and its affiliates in subgroup 1 do not, on analysis of their detectable inherited scribal errors, lie at a great remove from the translator's holograph. At three critical points where later manuscripts are corrupt they preserve an unblemished text: at the 'Egypt Gap' they give the French words *roys ils* which span the lacuna, and they have uncorrupted the names and characters of the Saracen and Hebrew alphabets. The degree of minor scribal error which these manuscripts show, on comparison for sense with the Insular Version, is consistent with a prior scribal tradition of three copying stages between their immediate common ancestor (now lost) and the original translation.[2]

The linguistic evidence of subgroup 1 is less clear. Its nine manuscripts are predominantly of northern or western dialects, and there are faint signs of a Lincolnshire underlay which may mark the geographical location of the translator and so would make such a dialectal distribution feasible. Subgroup 2 is diffuse in its linguistic spread. Subgroup 3 has a distinctive scribal corruption (Appendix reading 5), *þe falle of þe deede see* from the better *ȝe schal wite of þe deede see*, which could only have arisen from the presence of the northern form *sal* in the archetype of the subgroup, which was thus arguably of northern provenance.

## AN ABSTRACT OF EVIDENCE OF AFFILIATION

The readings on which the affiliations of the manuscripts are based are given more fully in the apparatus printed below the text and in

[1] In addition to the records cited in *Trans. Edinburgh Bibl. Soc.* noted above are: John Blair who wrote out for James III (1452–88) 'a boke called Mandvile' [J. Durkan, *The University of Glasgow, 1451–1577* (1977), p. 178]; John Capgrave, *Ye solace of pilgrimes*, MS Bodley 423 f. 355, refers to 'Iohn maundevyle . . . a book ful solacious on to his nacyoun'; John Tittleshall, Master of Corpus Christi College, Cambridge gave to the college in 1446 a book *de terris orientalibus*, sec. fol. *the ouertwert dale* cf. p. 7/24 below. In 1488/9 Thomas Richard of Prittewell, Essex bequeathed a copy to the Benedictines at Wallingford [*Essays in Arts and Science* 5. 286].

[2] Further copying stages between that lost common ancestor and the base manuscript are evident; using sigla explained below, the common ancestors of DQ, of BDQ, and of ABDQ, and an immediately superior copy.

the Appendix. The manuscripts are given sigla which are used throughout the edition. An asterisk after a folio abbreviation indicates that the relevant leaf is lost.

### *Subgroup 1*

The nine manuscripts of subgroup 1 have in common these features among many others:

1. they omit the phrase *by the ile towun that is toward the ende of Hungrye* 6/15–16 [Appendix reading 2]
2. they suppress a reference to Lot's incest 42/14–18 and misplace the previous paragraph at 42/2 and another at 114/25
3. they omit the descriptions of *Tourmagute* 69/9–12 and *Thomare* 67/28–68/6
4. they corruptly read *holy* 34/27 and *aples* 53/6 instead of the better *barly* and *alpes*
5. they omit part of the Alexander legend [Appendix reading 11].

These manuscripts with the relevant folio references are:

A Bodleian MS Douce 33 ff. $4^{r}$, *, $74^{r}$, $45^{v}$, $54^{v}$, $138^{r}$
B Balliol College MS 239 ff. $93^{rb}$, $108^{vb}$, *, $105^{vb}$, $113^{rb}$, *
C Corning Museum of Glass, New York MS 6 ff. $2^{r}$, $28^{v}$, $48^{v}$, $23^{v}$, $36^{v}$, $91^{v}$
D CUL MS Dd. 1. 17 ff. $33^{ra}$, $39^{rb}$, $43^{ra}$, $38^{ra}$, $40^{vb}$, $52^{ra}$
E Bodleian MS e Musaeo 124 ff. *, *, $3^{v}$, *, *, $22^{v}$
F CUL MS Ff. 5. 35 ff. $2^{r}$, *, $26^{r}$, *, $21^{v}$, $45^{v}$
M Cambridge, Magdalene College, MS Pepys 1955 ff. $3^{r}$, $26^{v}$, $41^{v}$, $22^{r}$, $32^{v}$, 71[1]
Q Queen's College, Oxford MS 383 ff. $17^{v}$, $52^{r}$, $75^{v}$, $45^{v}$, $61^{v}$, $124^{v}$
R Bodleian MS Rawlinson D. 101 ff. $3^{r}$, $31^{r}$, $51^{r}$, $26^{r}$, $39^{r}$, $102^{r}$.

These nine manuscripts show two lines of descent from their lost common ancestor. These internal affiliations with some characteristic readings are:

QABD read *somme men* 26/16 and *men* 72/18 instead of the better *samen* and *menys balokys*. D and Q, as evident in the apparatus printed below the text, are close affiliates, and B is nearly derived. R is slightly abridged, omitting the two cited corruptions, and depends

[1] Extracts are printed in *Éigse* 12 (1967), 29–36.

so closely on B in textual and linguistic transmission that it is can only be a direct copy or a copy of a very close affiliate.[1]

EF share a large number of minor scribal errors and omissions not found in QABD, but they preserve the characteristic readings and omissions of that group, reported above and in the apparatus printed below the text, with one exception noted below, and they avoid the individual variant readings of each of those manuscripts. They also avoid minor interpolations and omissions common to QBD but avoided by A; e.g. *many kyngdomes and* 113/24. The lost common ancestor of EF would thus appear to derive independently from the lost common ancestor of QABD. Their text is imperfectly preserved: E lacks thirty-two leaves before f. 1 and eight leaves after f. 8, i.e. over half the text (3/1–63/6 and 79/31–96/5); and F lacks eight leaves after f. 8 (22/18–42/25). The most easily observed distinguishing features of their text is the uniquely corrupt date of 1302 in the Epilogue and a number of minor omissions marked by blank spaces in E (but not in F): *his vndoynge for gret pruyde* 66/13, *in þe merueyl* 66/16, *for he hadde grete desire to go vppon þat hulle and he aforsed hym þerto* 87/3, *yn Assye* 106/25, *þat men clepiþ lonhorans* 124/29. There are a number of other omissions not marked by blanks in E: e.g. *And so hit lackiþ but iiii. score and foure degreez and nere half a degre þan Y haue seen alle þe firmament* 79/29–30, *and eueriche bringeþ a white steede oþer a white hors and makiþ presaunt to þe emperour* 100/22–24. E and F derive independently from their common ancestor which lacked these phrases and clauses, as may be demonstrated by comparison of their readings at:

E f. 9v þe sel of emperour of alle [f. 10r] men *Dei fortitudo hominum Imperatoris sigillum* þat ys to say strengþe of god seel of emperour of alle men

F f. 36v þe sel of þe emperour of alle men His preuy sel seith þus *Dei fortitudo hominum imperatoris sigillum* þat is to say strenkþe of god sel of þe men of þe emperour.

Here both E and F omit *omnium* before *hominum*; F alone inserts *His preuy sel seith þus*, not found elsewhere in subgroup 1 and presumably a scribal contextual addition which in general terms parallels the

[1] Every otherwise unique variant reading in B recorded in the apparatus below (e.g. *prioures dowȝter 21/30, wifes and husbondes* 85/25) is reproduced in R unless the word or phrase or clause is omitted there. The language of the scribe of R, who also wrote MS Royal 18 B. xxiii, is Berkshire, which is the underlay of the language of B, Warwickshire.

reading of subgroup 2 *And þe wrytyng aboute his pryue seal is þus*; F alone misreads the last phrase. Another demonstration by comparison is offered at the end of chapter 19 where the last phrase *þe grete* [*see*] *of Spayn* has become confused with the following rubric *þe lond of Caldilhe* 110/25–6:

E f. 15^v^ And it lasteþ to þe gret kyngdom of Caldyhylle *Of londes and yles and contrees byȝond Catay*
E f. 40^v^ and it lastiþ to þe gret kyngdom of Caldyhille *See of Spayne*

Both manuscripts have the confusion and the distinct form *Caldyhille*. E invents its following rubric where F preserves the misplaced relic of the earlier line. Finally, at a place where the common ancestor of subgroup 1 omitted or garbled a detail of the Great Khan's procession 102/27 leaving subsequent scribes to attempt individual repair, E f. 12^r^ reads *rydeþ or schal come* which preserves part of the original (cf. A and D) and F f. 38 reads *rideþ*. In sum, E and F are independent derivatives of a comparatively corrupt copy descended from the lost ancestor of QABD, and neither offers a text as good as QABD.

CM interpolate the phrase *þat men call seynt Iohan wiþ þe gilden mowþe* 10/29 and 37/16 and omit the verse *Iesus Cristus nascetur de virgine Maria et credo in eum* 12/12, and share over 200 other distinctive readings recorded in the collations printed below the text, which show that they are independent copies of an exemplar which derived from the archetype of the sub-group separately from the ancestor of QABD.

The conflators of the Cotton and Egerton Versions both used lost manuscripts of the Defective Version as their base which were affiliated to the text of a manuscript superior to the common ancestor of QABD of this group.

*Subgroup 2*

The five manuscripts of subgroup 2 and the Pynson print avoid all the features of subgroup 1 listed above, and in their turn have numerous characteristic readings, as reported in the textual apparatus, including these omissions:

1. part of the account of the Saracen beliefs 58/7–24
2. the reference to *Croke* 65/17–18

3. the account of the rotundity of the world 78/21–82/13 [Appendix reading 9]
4. the description of elephants 84/4–8
5. the account of *Sylha* 87/28–88/23
6. part of the account of the Great Khan 100/15–101/12.

These manuscripts and print with the relevant folio and signature references are:

2A BL MS Arundel 140 ff. 21$^{r}$, 23$^{r}$, 27$^{r}$, 27$^{v}$, 28$^{v}$, 32$^{r}$
2B BL MS Royal 17 B. xliii ff. 52$^{v}$, 57$^{v}$, 70$^{r}$, 72$^{r}$, 75$^{v}$, 86$^{r}$
2D BL MS Harley 2386 ff. 105$^{r}$, 107$^{v}$, 112$^{v}$, 113$^{r}$, 115$^{r}$, 119$^{v}$
2H BL MS Harley 3954 ff. 26$^{r}$, 28$^{v}$, 38$^{r}$, 39$^{v}$, 42$^{v}$, 48$^{v}$
2M Huntington Library, San Marino MS HM 114 ff. 155$^{r}$, 157$^{v}$, 161$^{v}$, 163$^{r}$, 164$^{v}$, 168$^{v}$
2P Pynson sigs. eii. ev$^{v}$, fiv$^{v}$, fv$^{v}$, fvii, gv

Each of these manuscripts and Pynson's copy-text derives from their lost common ancestor independently of its affiliates within its subgroup, as these specimen readings show:

2A uniquely omits the account of *Tracota* 85/16–22 and part of the Epilogue 135/29–31 [Appendix reading 12]

2B uniquely interpolates an account of *þe ile of Hogge* at 82/20, omits the description of Carnaa 67/23, and corrupts the reference to Jonas the widow's son 18/28

2D uniquely omits the description of the Saracen alphabet 63/21–27 and the account of Alexander and the Brahmans 125/1–127/29

2H, a holster book with many tinted drawings extending across the page, often abridges the text to end a page with a completed paragraph, thus uniquely omitting references to *þe bokis of þe fader lyf* 30/29 and *herode þe kyng* 36/23 and curtailing the account of *symylacris* 73/8

2M is so idiosyncratic in its copying that at times, as in the account of the sultan's strictures on Christian living 60/7, it is more a paraphrase than a copy[1]

2P omits the rest of chapter 15 after the common loss of the account of *Sylha* noted above.

[1] Seymour, 'The scribe of Huntington Library MS. HM 114', *Medium Aevum* 43 (1974), 139–43.

This lack of close affiliation within the subgroup suggests that the extant manuscripts are a small remnant of a once much wider dissemination of their common text.

Associated with this subgroup is MS Royal 17 C. xxxviii. It has four of the five characteristic features of subgroup 2 noted above but includes the account of the rotundity of the world; with this exception it avoids all the features of subgroup 1 listed above. The siglum and relevant folio references are:

2C BL MS Royal 17 C. xxxviii ff. $32^{ra}$, $35^{ra}$, $40^{ra}$–$41^{vb}$, $42^{va}$, $44^{ra}$

This association with subgroup 2 is supported by numerous other common readings and lacunae, and it seems clear that the manuscript derives from an exemplar which contained the passage about the rotundity of the world while otherwise having the features of subgroup 2 listed here, i.e. from a place in the scribal tradition immediately superior to the common ancestor of the five manuscripts of subgroup 2. There is little evidence elsewhere to support the possibility of conflation with a manuscript of subgroup 1, but they do share some omissions and see Textual Note 50/23.

Further evidence for independent derivation is perhaps provided by two readings, *Sampson þe fort* 20/23 and *onices* 93/26 on ff. $15^{va}$ and $46^{ra}$ which more closely reflect the Insular text than the more common *Sampson the strong* and the universal *quyces*. Both readings are apparently relics of the translation rather than later alterations. A similar degree of affiliation with an exemplar superior to that of the common ancestor of the subgroup is noted for two manuscripts of subgroup 3 and one of subgroup 4 below.[1]

The manuscript is uniquely abridged, e.g. in accounts of Menke 91/12, grief at birth 123/6, and Taprobane 129/7 on ff. $45^{ra}$, $56^{vb}$, $59^{vb}$. It uniquely alters or avoids by omission several corrupt phrases (e.g. Appendix readings 1, 3, 6, 8) and gives numerous other individual readings. It thus stands apart from the main scribal tradition of subgroup 2 and its dependents.

## *Subgroup 3*

The seven manuscripts of subgroup 3 avoid the features which characterize subgroup 1 and share those which characterize subgroup 2, but do not reflect any of the unique features of any one manuscript

[1] The reading *þe fort* recurs in the Egerton Version (ed. Warner 17/2) and MSS Douce 109 f. $10^{v}$, Gg. 1. 34 f. $14^{r}$, Additional 33758 f. $10^{v}$.

of that subgroup. Therefore it would appear that subgroup 3 derives from a lost manuscript of subgroup 2. The subgroup is not homogeneous. The imperfect and conflated Rugby School manuscript and TCC MS R. 4. 20 only partly reflect the characteristic features of this subgroup noted below and so presumably derive from copies anterior in the scribal tradition to the lost common ancestor of the other five manuscripts of the subgroup. These manuscripts have these distinctive features:

1. they omit the Hebrew alphabet [Appendix reading 7]
2. they corrupt the date in Prologue and Epilogue [Appendix readings 1 and 12]
3. they variously corrupt the phrase *wel lowe in Ethiope* 30/26 [Appendix reading 4]
4. they corrupt an earlier *ȝe schal wite þat þe deed see* 41/23 to *þe falle of þe deed see* and omit by eyeskip the next sentence *and þat see lastiþ fro Sora to Arabie* [Appendix reading 5].

These manuscripts with the relevant folio references are:

3A BL MS Additional 33758 ff. $22^{r}$, $3^{v}$, $50^{v}$, $15^{v}$, $20^{r}$
3B Bodleian MS Rawlinson B 216 ff. $143^{ra}$, $131^{va}$, $161^{ra}$, $138^{rb}$, $141^{ra}$
3C Bodleian MS Rawlinson D 100 f. $22^{v}$, *, *, $10^{v}$, $19^{r}$
3D Bodleian MS Douce 109 ff. $27^{r}$, $1^{r}$, $72^{v}$, $18^{r}$, $24^{r}$
3L Takamiya MS 63 ff. $28^{v}$, $2^{v}$, $116^{r}$, $25^{v}$, $35^{r}$
3R Rugby School MS ff. $9^{r}$, $1^{v}$, $36^{v}$, *, *
3T Cambridge, Trinity College, MS R. 4. 20 ff. $32^{v}$, $2^{r}$, $86^{v}$, $22^{r}$, $29^{v}$.

The two aberrant manuscripts, 3R and 3T, give different dates in Prologue and Epilogue: 3R has 1300, the common corruption, and 1356, the palmary reading; 3T has 1332 and 1366, as in subgroups 1 and 2; 3T avoids the corruptions numbered 4 above; 3R lacks the leaf. Both manuscripts lack the extended initial rubric found in 3A and 3B (3C and 3D lack leaf); avoid corrupt forms of names, like *Steven* for the better *Sophe* at 6/29, which occur elsewhere in the subgroup; and avoid the *ile turne* corruption and give the Epilogue in full [Appendix readings 1, 12]. Uniquely in its subgroup 3R is conflated with subgroup 1 for its last four leaves, ff. 33–7 [Appendix readings 11 and 12].

Each of the five remaining manuscripts of the subgroup has

unique features, for example in Appendix readings 4 and 8 and in the following places:

3A omits the characters of the Saracen alphabet f. 29$^{r}$, leaving a blank half-line

3B preserves the twenty-one chapter divisions of subgroup 2 and has a large interpolation about the abbey of St Katherine and a smaller interpolation about Vespasian ff. 135$^{v}$, 138$^{v}$, printed in the Appendix

3C gives a good text in general, sharing many of the variant readings of 3D while avoiding its unique excesses, but has many unique minor errors: e.g. f. 9$^{v}$ repeats *in þe same place* after *roche* 29/17, f 64$^{r}$ *lond* for *kyngdome* 108/27, f. 68$^{r}$ adds at end of chapter 21 *as I herde men þer sey of þe same contre*

3D has unique corruptions, printed in Appendix readings 6, 7, 8, and f. 37$^{v}$ makes a special chapter division for *Athanas* 64/29 and adds *but y telle it for a marveyle* 66/17, and f. 46$^{r}$ uniquely omits *whiche blood þei clepiþ God* 85/12

3L gives unique corruptions, printed in Appendix readings 4, 5, 6, f. 27 reads *Vauntz* instead of the better *Vatynz* 32/12, and f. 57$^{v}$ adds *hade wifes* after *dwellyng* 68/21.

### *Subgroup 4*

The five manuscripts of subgroup 4 avoid the features which characterize subgroup 1 and share those which characterize subgroups 2 and 3. Their lost common ancestor derived from a manuscript of subgroup 3 no longer extant. Its text showed an advanced state of deterioration in which some attempt to make sense of garbled readings is evident. Two distinctive examples are the readings *among these iles and valeyes* at the 'Egypt Gap' and *þe feld lawe*, printed in Appendix readings 3 and 4. Chapter division is without rubrics or numbers, and except in 4C there is little uniformity of division compared with earlier subgroups. The opening sentence of its text (except 4G which follows subgroup 1 in its Prologue) is *Here bygynneth the boke of Maundvile* followed by a descriptive passage; in 4A and 4T this is written in rubric, preserving its evident origin as the scribal title and description that appears first in 3A and 3B; it does not recur in any manuscript of subgroup 5.

These five manuscripts, with the relevant folio references are:

4A Bodleian MS Additional C 285 ff. 12$^{r}$, 17$^{r}$
4C Manchester, Chetham's Library, MS 67114 ff. 14$^{rb}$, 21$^{ra}$
4G CUL MS Gg. 1 34 part 3 ff. 15$^{r}$, 21$^{r}$
4P Princeton University MS Taylor 10 ff. 8$^{ra}$, passage omitted
4T Bodleian MS Tanner 405 ff. 12$^{r}$, 17$^{v}$

Each of these manuscripts, which collectively show an advanced state of textual deterioration, has unique features.

4A has many unique forms of exotic names, e.g. f. 7$^{v}$ *choutot*, 14/14, f. 8 *gossos* 15/8, f. 29$^{r}$ *glebris* 53/5, f. 45$^{r}$ *bygod* 89/26.

4C has an extensive lacuna at f. 78$^{rb}$ mid-column, perhaps due to the loss of a quire in an ancestor, cf. 123/30–135/18.

4G, much given to the omission of garbled phrases, omits the sentence before the loss of the Hebrew alphabet, the references containing the corruptions of *yle towun* and *wel lowe in Ethiope*, and uniquely creates two castles *Carras and Sermoys* at Mont Royal [Appendix readings 2, 4, 6, 7]. It also has most of its Prologue from subgroup 1.

4P omits the Saracen alphabet in a larger lacuna f. 20$^{vb}$ and interpolates from subgroup 5 the Latin version of the letter to Alexander 125/23 while preserving the English text which avoids the later scribal contaminations reflected in the translation.

4T, very imperfect and much abridged, considerably shortens the account of the two Alexander stories f. 38 and adds at the end f. 41$^{v}$ an account of exotic funeral rites. It shares some readings with 4G.

*Subgroup 5*

The five manuscripts of subgroup 5 share the characteristic features of subgroup 4 and are further distinguished by the phrase *sothe to saie* at the 'Egypt Gap' and by a Latin translation of the letter to Alexander. With the exception of MS Sloane 2319 which is conflated at these points, they also give corrupt readings *þe feldlawe* and *þe falle of the depe see* at two critical points [Appendix readings 4, 5]. These manuscripts with their folio references are:

5D Dublin, Trinity College, MS E.5.6 ff. 11$^{v}$, 16$^{r}$, 21$^{r}$, 51$^{v}$
5E National Library of Scotland MS Advocates 19. i. ii ff. *, 14$^{v}$, 21$^{r}$, 67$^{v}$

5L Bodleian MS Laud misc. 699 ff. 12$^{v}$, 18$^{r}$, 25$^{r}$, 70$^{r}$
5R Bodleian MS Rawlinson D 652 ff. 6$^{v}$, 9$^{v}$, 12$^{v}$, *
5S BL MS Sloane 2319 ff. *, 1$^{v}$, 8$^{r}$, 42$^{r}$

The anomalous MS Sloane 2139 is very imperfect and the text of the first sixteen leaves derives from a manuscript of subgroup 4, similar to MS Gg 1. 34, which included the names and figures of the Saracen alphabet. It has a unique lacuna at 71/26.

5D has the text closest to the lost archetype of subgroup 4 which did not contain the introductory rubric that is found there.

5E and 5L are related; for example, they both omit the clause *and þen er þai eten* [Appendix reading 9] found in 5D and 5R; but they are not immediate copies of one exemplar. 5E has numerous unique lacunae; for example, at f. 47$^{r}$ it omits a sentence 75/21–23.

5L has some minor interpolations; for example, at f. 45$^{v}$ it adds *as I haue don* 83/4.

## EXTRACTS AND FRAGMENTS

There are four collections of discontinuous extracts and two fragments of lost manuscripts of the Defective Version. None is of textual importance, and it will suffice here to record their location and affiliation.

BL MS Additional 37049 ff. 3–9: an epitome printed by M. C. Seymour in *Anglia* 84 (1966), 27–58. Subgroup 5. West Riding. Possibly written at the Carthusian abbey at Axholme.

Ripon Cathedral, parchment cover of a printed book, *Petri Carpentarii Epistola* 1573: a bifolium (3 + 6 of a quire of 8) printed by A. C. Cawley in *English Studies* 28 (1957), 262–5. Subgroup 4. Lichfield.

Bodleian MS Ashmole 751 ff. 48–50, 142–3: extracts printed by M. C. Seymour in *English Studies in Africa* 4 (1961), 148–58. Subgroup 1. Borders of Yorkshire and Lincs.

Bodleian MS Latin misc. e. 85 ff. 85–91 (misbound, correct order being 86/87/84/85/90/91/88/89) one quire, text beginning at 49/30. Subgroup 3. East Midlands. Transcription available.

Bodleian MS Digby 88 f. $28^{r}$: extracts printed by P. J. Horner in *Manuscripta* 24 (1980), 171–5. Subgroup and dialect undetermined.

Oxford, Trinity College, MS 29: scattered extracts within a larger text. Subgroup undetermined. Berks. Possibly written at the Augustinian house at Bisham Montague.

Bodleian MS Douce ff. $118^{v}$–$19^{v}$: copies of Latin letters to Pope John XXII and Alexander. Subgroup 5.

The extracts from *Mandeville's Travels* appended to Sir Richard Torkington's account of his travel to the Holy Land in 1517, virtually transcribed verbatim from the *Pylgrymage of Sir Richard Guildeforde* (Pynson, 1495), are taken from an edition of Wynkyn De Worde (1499, 1503, *c.*1510). All subsequent extracts in sixteenth-century sources derive from early prints of De Worde or Thomas East (1568, 1582); East conflated his copy-text of De Worde, perhaps imperfectly preserved, with a manuscript of subgroup 3. See M. C. Seymour in *The Library*, 5th series, 19 (1964), 202–7 and *Bodleian Library Record* 13 (1990), 341–2.

## EDITORIAL PROCEDURES

The aim of this critical edition is to recover as far as possible the substance of the earliest extant Middle English translation of *Mandeville's Travels*. It is not possible to recover the forms of the translator or even to be certain of his reading where the manuscripts have differences of synonym (e.g. *clepe* and *calle*, *graue* and *toumbe*, *apposid* and *examyned*) or word-order (e.g. of pairs of adjectives or nouns, or of sequence of subject and verb) or syntax. All such differences are unresolvable by reference to the Anglo-French source. Though one may suppose that the translator regularly used older words such as *clepe*, *graue*, *apposid* which scribes then modernized, such preference must always be guesswork, and the French word-order and syntax can never be a certain guide to the shape of their Middle English translation. In these circumstances of ignorance the wisest course seemed to be to follow the language of the base manuscript in its entirety unless there was good textual reason for emendation, and so to let the edition stand as a critical edition of the base manuscript rather than attempt an academic linguistic reconstruction of the lost holograph of the translator.

The choice of the base manuscript was thus a matter of some nicety. Subgroup 1 gives the least incomplete text and contains two manuscripts which are not disfigured by accidental loss of leaves, MSS Queen's 383 and Pepys 1955. The first offers a text free from the many minor idiosyncrasies of the other, has three close associates (which enables an editor to discover its immediate scribal distortions with some hope of the accuracy), probably lies at fewer removes from the archetype, and is one of the earliest (if not the earliest) of the extant manuscripts. On the other hand, its dialectal colouring is South-West Midlands with a Northern underlay and not very close to the dialect of the translator.[1] Despite this drawback, MS Queen's 383 is in the editor's judgement the best choice for the base of this edition.

Subgroup 1 omits a number of phrases and sentences and sometimes larger passages from the extant translation. In the first quarter of the text, concerning the Holy Land, these omissions are minor, totalling less than a printed page, but thereafter they are larger and more numerous. A similar pattern of omission is observable in subgroup 2 when compared with subgroup 1. For the repair of such omissions in the printed edition it is clearly preferable to use one manuscript of subgroup 2. Each lacks one or more leaves and has unique minor omissions.

2A lacks one leaf after ff. 5 and 15. Both language (North Essex) and early date (before 1425) are suitable. The text is good.

2B lacks final paragraph only. But its scribe modernizes and expands his text, occasionally with large interpolations, and his language (Hereford–Monmouth borders) and attitude to copy are provincial.[2]

2C is uniquely edited, with many minor and major abridgements, and untypical. Hants or West Sussex. Before 1425.

[1] For example, in Appendix reading 1 the phrase *if al it be þat* found in subgroups 1, 2, and 3, like the older forms quoted above, is consistent with a Lincolnshire origin *c.*1385. Further analysis is needed. In linguistic terms MS Arundel 140, the superior text of subgroup 2, might have been the better choice as a base, but it has lost two large leaves, has the larger omissions, and lacks immediate affiliates. The linguistic differences between it and the base manuscript are numerous, and there is no way of telling which reflects more closely the translator's holograph. However, 2C is closer to the base manuscript than to 2A linguistically.

[2] Cf. Warner, op. cit., p. 61, n. 3, 'The readings of this ms. are very inferior and seldom worth quoting.'

2H is an illustrated holster-book where the text is abridged to accommodate the tinted drawings. Apart from the extensive omissions its text is fairly good. South Norfolk, after 1425.

2D has several unique lacunae and was written in Devon after 1470.

2M is almost a paraphrase rather than a copy, and its idiosyncratic phrasing makes it unsuitable for recension. South Essex. *c.*1425.[1]

2P is the unique copy of Pynson's print *c.*1496, lacks three leaves of text and has some editorial omissions and modernized language.

Despite losses 2A (MS Arundel 140) is the superior text and is chosen as the main source from which the scribal omissions observable in subgroup 1 are repaired in this edition. Where its text has gone on leaves lost after ff. 5 and 15 (4/11–6/31 and 38/1–40/31 below) the omissions are repaired from 2B (MS Royal 17 B. xliii), which is a full affiliate within its subgroup; 2H is perhaps closer in text as in dialect but it is abridged.

The apparatus below the text records readings rejected from the base manuscript (Queen's College MS 383) and variations of substance from the manuscripts of the two major subgroups 1 and 2 chosen for collation. A work of late Middle English prose extant in thirty-three manuscripts is so diverse in its record of every sentence that to print a full collation here is impractical.[2] The collations printed in this edition are the substantial variant readings of the chosen referrants but generally not their linguistic variations nor their forms of exotic names. These chosen manuscripts are:

subgroup 1, ABCDM (i.e. with the base, six of the extant nine copies, with R being an abridgement of B and EF being corrupt copies of the ancestor of QABD)

subgroup 2, 2A, 2B, 2C (i.e. three of the extant six) and 2P (Pyson's print *c.*1496).

In addition, the collation records textual features (variant readings and omissions) which are common to individual subgroups. The sigils for these collective collations are G1, G2 and so on, and do not

[1] See p. xx, n. 1 above.

[2] Cf. the collations of French manuscripts printed by De Poerck, op. cit., pp. 143–54. As an example, most of the readings of C and M which are given here in the apparatus are scribal variants without value in establishing a critical text except those few which agree with subgroup 2 against QABD and so support emendation. Likewise the readings of 2B are often idiosyncratic, as Warner noted, loc. cit.

notice individual lacunae and scribal singularities, as in 2H and 2M. In all collations the forms cited are those of the manuscript whose sigil begins the record or occurs first in the subgroup, i.e. 2A..

Several manuscripts have marginalia which act as *notae* or sub-headings but without established patterns in subgroups 2–5. All appear scribal embellishments in origin, and none is recorded. The rubrics of the base manuscript are not generally found outside subgroup 1 and (irregularly and abridged) subgroup 2, and their absence from other manuscripts and the presence there of other rubrics (which are generally brief and uncommon) are not recorded. Chapter numbers, based on those of subgroup 2, are added for convenience of reference.

In the transcription suspended letters and abbreviations except roman numerals are silently expanded. Initial *ff-* is printed as *f* or *F*, and minuscule *z* is distinguished from the scribe's identical graph of minuscule *ȝ*. Punctuation is editorial. Word-division follows modern usage, with slight modification of spellings like *therupon* for scribal *ther vpon*. Within the printed text editorially altered letters are italicized and added letters and words are set within square brackets. Scribal corrections are accepted without notice.

Each emendation of the base manuscript was made on the evidence of collation without resort to formula. Each emendation of substance (excluding those wholly of a linguistic nature of Middle English forms) has as its ultimate justification the relevant word, phrase, or sentence in the Insular Version. This version was consulted both in the printed edition (ed. Warner, Roxburghe Club, 1889) and in the extant manuscripts, especially those two manuscripts (Bodleian Library MS Addition C 280 and British Library MS Sloane 1464) which are the closest surviving affiliates of the lost manuscript from which the translator worked.

The sequence of collation of the Middle English manuscripts was threefold. First, the immediate affiliates of the base (ABDR) were consulted, and then the rest of subgroup 1 (first EF; then CM which record a later and slightly different descent from the lost archetype of the subgroup). Secondly, the six manuscripts of subgroup 2 and the affiliated Pynson print were collated; collectively they preserve phrases, sentences, and paragraphs of the translation which have been omitted or distorted in subgroup 1. Thirdly, the manuscripts of subgroups 3, 4, and 5 were collated. These three subgroups record successive stages in the copying of the text of subgroup 2, and while they confirm the nature of that text they do not offer independent evidence towards the establishment of a critical edition. They do, of course, offer a great deal of information about scribal transmission and linguistic change within the fifteenth century, but for the present purpose their collation proved of marginal value.

In accordance with the stated editorial preference for the base manuscript and its affiliates within subgroup 1, the printed text has these features:

1. five sentences and the account of Sylha 87/28–88/23 which are out of sequence compared with subgroups 2-5 and the Insular Version are printed in their dislocations (42/2–7, 104/4–5, 114/25–115/2, 118/18–20, 127/30–128/5) which are noted in the apparatus and the Textual Commentary.
2. those phrases and clauses which have no equivalent in subgroups 2–5 or the Insular Version but which (in the editor's judgement) may be part of the translation are allowed to stand and their absence in other subgroups noted in the apparatus. Conversely, such readings which (in the editor's judgement) are scribal additions are rejected from the printed text and reported in the apparatus.
3. where a word or phrase in the base manuscript and its affiliates offer one possible translation of the reading in the Insular Version and where manuscripts of subgroup 2 offer a variant reading which is also a valid translation, the reading of the base and its affiliates is retained in the text and the variant reading reported in the apparatus.

With these qualifications, the printed text is a substantial (but not linguistic) reconstruction of the archetype of the extant manuscripts of the Defective Version and of parts of that version visible in the Cotton and Egerton conflations. This reconstruction shows very few scribal distortions of meaning when it is compared with the Insular Version (as reported in the Textual Commentary), and this low incidence of error suggests that there were very few intermediary copies between the stage in the scribal tradition which it represents and the original translation. But it is impossible to say on present evidence whether or not the printed text is an abridgement of that translation.

# MANDEVILLE'S TRAVELS
# THE DEFECTIVE VERSION

# CHAPTER 1 PROLOGUE

| For as myche as þe lond ouer þe see, þat is to say þe holi lond þat [f. 15r] men calliþ þe lond of biheest, among alle oþer londis þat is moost worþi lady and souereyn of alle oþere londis, and it is blessid and halewid [and sacred] of þe precious blood of oure lord Ihesu Crist; in þe whiche lond it likeþ hym to take fleisch and blood of þe virgyne Marie and to enuyroun þat lond wiþ his blesside feet. And þere he wolde do many myraclis and preche and teche þe feiþ and þe lawe of vs cristene men as to his children. And þere he wolde suffre many repreuys and scornys for vs. And he þat was kyng of heuene and of erþe, of eir, of see, and of alle þinges þat beþ conteyned in hem, wolde al only be clepid kyng of þat lond when he seyde þus, *Rex sum Iudeorum*, þat is to say, I am kyng of Iewis, for þat tyme was þat lond [of] Iewis.

And þat lond hadde he chose bifore alle oþere londis as for þe beste [and most vertuous] and þe moost worþi of þe world, | for as þe [f. 15v] philosofir seiþ, *Virtus rerum in medio consistit*, þat is to say, þe vertu of þinges is in þe myddel. And in þat lond he wolde lede his lyf and suffre passioun and deeþ of þe Iewis for vs and for to bye vs and delyuere vs fro þe paynes of helle and fro deeþ wiþouten ende, þe whiche was ordeynd to vs for þe synne of oure fader Adam and for oure owne synnes also; for hymself he hadde noon yuel deserued, for he þou3te neuer yuel and he dide neuer yuel. And he þat was kyng of glorie and of ioi3e mi3t best in þat place suffre deeþ; for he þat wol do ony þing þat he wole be knowen openly by, he wole do crie it openliche in þe myddel place of a cite oþer of a toun, so þat yt may be wel knowe to alle þe parties of þe cite. And þerfore he þat was

1–23 For . . . þou3te] A *out* 2 þat] 2C hit 4 lady] 2B lad *and space*; 2C *om.*; 2P lande; G3–G5 londe 5 and sacred] G1 *om.* 7 to] M also enuyroun] 2C honoure lond] C lond abowt blesside] 2P owne þere] CM þat 9 his] 2C his dere 10 was] 2C *om.* 11 of eir . . . hem] M *om.* 12 wolde] 2C he wolde 13–14 for þat . . . Iewis] M *om.*; C and þat time þe lond of Iewis was callid a good lond 14 of] QD *om.* 15–16 as for þe beste] 2C *om.* 16 and most vertuous] QCDM *om.* 19 and deeþ] M *om.* 19–20 for vs . . . ende] M and dey for vs 19 for vs and] 2C *om.* 21 fader] 2C forme fader 23 he þou3te neuer yuel and] 2C *om.* and he dide neuer yuel] G3–G5 *om.* 23–24 of glorie and] 2C *om.* 25 þat he wole be knowen] 2B *om.* 26 of a cite oþer] 2C *om.* oþer] D *om.* 27 wel] G2–G5 *om.* was] 2B was and ys kyng of al þe world wolde suffre deeþ at Ierusalem for þat is in þe myddel of þe world, so þat it miȝt be knowe to men of alle partyes of þe world how dere he bouȝte man þat he made to his owne likenes f. 16r for [þe grete] loue þat he hadde to vs, for more worþi catel | miȝt he not haue yset for vs þan his owne [blyssyd body and his owen] precious blood, þe whiche he offrid for vs.

A dere God, what loue he hadde to his sugetis whanne he þat hadde ydo no trespas wolde for trespassouris suffre deeþ! Riȝt wel auȝte men to loue and worschipe and drede and serue siche a god and a lord, and worschipe and preyse siche an holy lond þat brouȝt forþ siche fruyt, þurȝ þe whiche eche man is sauyd but it be his owne defaute. Þis is þe lond hiȝt til vs in heritage, and in þat lond he wolde deiȝe as cesid þerynne to leue it to his children; for þe whiche eueryche [good] cristen man þat may and haþ wherof schulde strengþe hym for to conquere oure riȝt heritage and cacche out þereof hem þat beþ yuel trowyng. For we beþ clepid cristen men of Crist oure fader, and ȝif we be þe riȝt children of Crist, we owe to calenge þe heritage [þat] oure fader left to vs and do it out of straunge men hondis.

But now pruyde, enuye, and couetise haþ so enflawmed þe hertis of lordis of þe world þat þei beþ more besy for to disherite here f. 16v neiȝeboris þan for to | calenge or conquere here riȝt heritage biforeseid. And þe comyn puple þat wolde putte here bodies and catel for to conquere oure heritage, þei may not do wiþoute lordis, for assemble of þe puple wiþoute [a chief] lord*e* þat may gouerne hem is as a flok of scheep þat haþ no scheephurd, þe which is departid asunder and woot neuer whider þei schulde go. [But] wolde God þat þe wordly lordis were at goode acord and wiþ oþer of here comyn puple wolde take þis holy viage ouer þe see, I trowe wel þat

1 wolde suffre] 2C only for our trespas suffred 3 made] 2B 2P had made 4 þe grete] Q *om.* 5 blessyd body and his owen] QA *om.* blessyd] M precyous owen] 2C *om.* 7 his] A vs; M vs þat beth his 8 wolde . . . suffre] C sufferid; 2C only for our trespas suffred 9–10 and drede . . . worschipe] C *om.* 9 men] A we and serue] 2C *om.* 9–10 god and a lord] M lorde god and man 11–6/31 eche man . . . appul] 2A *out* 12 hiȝt til vs in] 2C that longeth to oure 13 as cesid] C and assesid; 2C and seysid to leue hit þerynne] 2B 2P *om.* 14 good] G1 *om.* 15–5/24 strengþe . . . þe name] C *out* 16 þereof] M 2P *om.* yuel trowyng] D ille and trowand ille cristen] *om.* 18 þat] QA of left to vs] 2C *om.* 20 pruyde] M pride wrathe 21 lordis] 2C londes 22 riȝt] M *om.* 23 putte] M spende 25 a chief lorde] G1 lordis 26 is] D *om.* 27 But] QA ffor 28 were at] A with here wiþ oþer of here] M þe; 2C eche of hem other and also 29 wolde] 2C that they wolde ouer þe see] A to þe haly land wel] A *om.*; 2C then

wiþynne a litel tyme oure ri3te heritage biforeseid schulde be reconciled and yput in þe hondis of þe ri3t eires of Ihesu Crist.

And for as myche as it is long tyme passid þat þer was no generale passage ouer þe see, and [many] men coueiteþ to hure speke of þat lond and cuntreys dyuerse þereaboute and þerof þei haue grete solace and comfort; I Ioon Maundeuyle kni3t, if al it be þat Y be not worþi, þat was ybore in Engelond in þe toun of seynt Albanes, and passid þe see in þe 3ere of oure lord Ihesu Crist a þowsand þre hundrid and two and þirty on Mi3ghelmasday | and siþþe hiderward f. 17r
haþ be long tyme ouer þe see; and haþ seye and go þur3 manye kyngdomes and londes and prouynces and yles, and haþ pasid þur3 Turkye and Ermonye þe litel and þe grete, Tartarie, Perse, Syrie, Arabye, Egipt þe hi3e and þe lowe, Lybye, Caldee, and a grete partye of Ethiope, Amazoyne, Ynde þe lasse and þe more a grete partye, and þur3 many oþere yles þat beþ aboute Ynde, whare þat dwelliþ many dyuerse of folk of dyuerse lawis and schappis; of which londis and yles Y schal speke more plenerliche. And I schal deuyse a partye of þingis what þei beþ when tyme schal be, aftir þat it may come to my mynde, and specialy for hem þat wol and beþ on purpos to visity þe holy cite of Ierusalem and þe holi places þat beþ þereaboute. And Y schal telle þe way þat þei schul holde þidere, for Y haue many times passid and riden it wiþ [good] cumpenye of lordis.

# CHAPTER 2 A WAY TO IERUSALEM

[I]n þe name of God almi3ty, he þat wole passe ouer þe see, he may go many weies, boþe on see and lond, aftir þe cuntreys þat he comeþ fro, and many of hem comeþ alle to on ende. | But trowiþ not f. 17v

2 þe[1]] QABDM þe ri3t 3–6 it is long tyme . . . comfort] 2C men desireth to hyr speke of the holy lond and they haue therof greet solas sport and comfort I shal telle somewhat that I haue sey 3 passid] 2P *om.* 4 see] G1 *add* in to þat holy londe many] G1 *om.* men] M *om.* 8 of] G2–G5 of the yncarnacion of (see Appendix 1) 9 and two and þirty] G3–G5 *om.* (see Appendix 1) siþþe] 2B 2P *om.* 11 kyngdomes . . . yles] 2C londes and yleygh in many prouinces and kyngdomes and londes and] A *om.* 13 Arabye] D *om.* 16 of [1]] DM *om.* A manere of of folk of] 2C folk of maneris of 17 plenerliche] 2B openly 29 wol and] M *om.* and beþ on] B *om.* 21 Y schal telle þe way] 2C weyes þei] B ye 22 and riden it] 2B yn rydyng good] QAD grete; 2C *om.* cumpenye of lordis] M lordys and oþere goode companye of lordis] 2B and of many lordys; 2C of greet lordes and other good companye; 2P and of many lordes (see Appendix 2) 24 In] Q N 25 boþe on see and lond] 2C *om.* 26 not] 2B *om.*

þat Y wole telle alle þe townus and citees and castels þat men schul go by, for þan schulde Y make to long tale, but al onelich somme cuntrez and most principale stedis þat men schul go þurȝ to go þe riȝt way.

F*er*[st] if a man come fro þe west syde of þe world as Engelond, Irlond, Walis, Scotlond, Norþway, he may yf he wol go þurȝ Almayne and þurȝ þe kyngdome of Hungry þat marchiþ to þe lond of Peyaline and to þe lond of Pannonye and of Alleseye.

And þe kyng of Hungrie is a ful grete lord and ful miȝti and holdeþ grete and myche lond, for he holdiþ þe lond of Hungrie, Sauoye, C*o*mayne, a grete part of Bu*l*garie þat men clepiþ þe lond of Bugers, and a grete partye of þe kyngdome of Rosse, and þat lastiþ to þe lond of Neuelond and marchiþ to Pruyse. And men goþ þurȝ þe lond of Hungery to a cite þat men clepiþ Chippron and þurȝ þe castel of Newburȝ [and by the ile towun that is toward the ende of Hungrye]. And men passiþ by þe ryuer of Damuby þat is a ful grete ryuer and goþ into Almayn vndir þe hullis of Lumbardye, and it f. 18r takiþ into hym fourty oþer ryueris | and it renneþ þurȝ Hungrie, *G*resses, and Trachie and gooþ into þe see so staleworþly and wiþ so grete strengþe þat þat water is freisch twenty myle wiþynne þe see.

And aftirward men goþ to Belgraue and entriþ into þe lond of Bugrys, and þer passiþ men a brigge of stoon þat is ouer þe ryuer of Marrok. And men passiþ þurȝ þe lond of Pynceras and comeþ to Grece to þe cite of Sternes and to þe cite of Affympayne and siþþe to þe cite of Bradenople and siþþe to þe cite of Constantynople þat was somtyme yclepid Bessamozoun, and þere dwelliþ comynliche þe emperour of Grece.

þere is þe beste chirche of þe world and þe fairest, and it is of seynt Sophe. And bifore þe chirche is an ymage of Iustynyan þe emperour [y]gildid, and hit is made sittyng vpon an hors ycrowned. And hit was woned to holde a round appul in his hond, for þe appul

1 townus] M *adds* names castels] 2B *adds* and moost pryncypal stedes 2 al onelich] 2C *om.* 3 stedis] QD somme stedis; B of cyteis 5 Ferst] G1 ffor 9 a ful grete lord] 2C right a greet londe; 2B 2P *om.* ful 10 and myche] 2B *om.* 11 Comayne, Bulgarie] Q Cemayne, Burgarie 12 kyngdome of] C kingis land Rosse] 2C Rome 14 to] 2P thorough Chippron] QB Chipproner 15–16 and by . . . Hungrye] G1 *om.* (see Appendix 2) 15 ile] 2C same 16 passiþ] 2P *om.* 19 Gresses and] QABD Cresses; 2P thorowe Gresses and thoroughe 19–20 staleworþy and with so grete strenþe] 2C *om.* 21 of[1]] 2P *om.* 25 Bradenople and siþþe to þe cite of] 2P *om.* 30 ygildid] QBD gildid it; M ygylde with fyne golde made sittyng] 2B 2P *om.* ycrowned] 2P and crowned 31 round] C *om.* 31–7/1 for þe appul . . . hond] G1 *after* lordschip

is yfalle out of þe ymagis hond. And men saye þer þat it is a tokene þat þe emperour haþ lost a grete partye of his lordschip. For he was ywoned to be emperour | of Romayne, of Grece, Assye þe lasse, of f. 18v Surrye, of þe lond of Iudee in þe whiche Ierusalem is, of þe lond of Egipt, of Perse and Arabye; but he haþ lost al saf Grece, and þat lond holdeþ he al oneliche. And men wold many tymes haue yput þe appul into þe ymagis hond aȝen, and it wol noȝt holde it. Þis appul bitokeneþ þe lordschip þat he hadde ouer alle þe world. And þe oþer hond he holdiþ vp aȝens þe west in tokene for to manase þe mysdoers. Þis ymage stondiþ at Constantynople on a pilour of marbel.

And þer is þe spounge and þe reod þat þe Iewis ȝaf oure lord to drinke wiþ whenne þat he was on þe croys. And þere is one of þe nayles þat Crist was nailed wiþ to þe cros. Somme men trowe þat half þe crois of Crist be in Cypre in an abbey of monkis þat men clepiþ hille of þe holy crois; but it is not so, for þat croys þat is in Cypre is þe croys of whiche Dismas þe goode þeof was hongid. But al men knowiþ not þat, and þat is yuel ydo for, for getyng of offrynges, þei sey þat þat is | þe croys of oure lord Ihesu Crist. f. 19r

And ȝe schul vndirstonde þat þe croys of oure lord Ihesu Crist was made of foure manere of trees, as it is yconteyned in þis vers, whiche is here ywrite þus, *In cruce sit palma, cedrus, cypressus, oliua*. For þe pece þat went vpriȝt fro þe erþe vnto þe heed was of cipres; and þat pece þat went ouertwert, to þe whiche his hondis was nayled, was of palme; and þe stok þat stode in þe erþe, to which was made a mortays, was [of] cedre; and þe table abouen his heed was of olyue; and it was a foot and an half long, in þe whiche þe title was writun in Ebrewe, Grewe, and Latyn.

And þe Iewis made þis croys of þese [foure] manere treez for þei trowid þat oure lord Ihesu Crist schulde haue hongid vpon þat crois

2 lordschip] 2P londe 5–6 and þat . . . oneliche] 2C *om.* 6 oneliche] CM *om.* haue] 2B 2P *om.* 7 aȝen] 2B 2P *om.* 7–8 þis appul . . . þe world] 2C *om.* 8 þay he hadde] 2B *om.* 9 vp] 2P lyfte vp 10 at Constantynople] 2C *om.*; G2–G5 *after* marbel 12 reod] 2B *blank* 13 wiþ whenne þat he was] G2–G5 galle 13–14 And þere . . . cros] 2C *om.* 17 þe goode] B goddis 18 for[1]] AB *om.*; C 2P but 19 offrynges] BD frendes 21 foure manere of] C diuersis yconteyned] D conceyued 21–22 whiche is here ywrite þus] M G2–G5 *om.* 22 þus] B *om.* 23 fro þe erþe] D fro the herte; M *om.* 24 hondis] 2B hedde 25 stok . . . made a] 2C *om.* 25–26 to which . . . mortays] M *om.* 26 of[1]] QA *om.* was of olyue] ABCM G2–G5 *after* Latyn 28 Latyn] QD *add* and it was on englische Ihesu of Nazareth kyng of Iewis 29–30 þis croys . . . trowid þat] C *om.* 29 foure] G1 *om.*

as long as þat cros mi3t laste. And þerfore þei made þe foot of cedre, for þat may not rote in erþe noþer in watir, for hy wolde þat it schulde haue long last. And for þei trowid þat Cristis body schulde f. 19[v] haue stonke, þei ma|de þat pece þat wente fro þe erþe vpward, on whiche his body heng, of cypres, for it is wel smellyng, so þat þe smel of his body schulde not greue to men þat come forþ by. And þat ouertwert, to whiche his hondis were nayled, was of palm, for in þe olde testament it was yordeyned þat whenne ony man hadde þe victorie of his enemye he schulde be crowned wiþ palm, and for þei trowid þat þei hadde þe victorie vpon Ihesu Crist, þei made þe ouertwert of palme. And þe table of þe title was made of olyue for olyue bitokeneþ pees, as þe storie of Noe beriþ witness whenne þe dowfe brou3t þe braunche of olyue þat tokenyd pees ymade bitwene God and man; and so trowid þe Iewis to haue pees when Crist was deed, for þei seide þat he made stryf among hem.

And 3e schul vndirstonde þat oure lord was nayled to þe croys liggyng, and þerfore he suffride more peyne. A[l]s Grecis and cristen men þat dwelliþ ouer þe see seye [þat] þe tree of þe croys þat we f. 20[r] clepe cipresse was of | þe tree þat Adam eet þe appul, and so þei fynde ywrite. And þei seye also þat here scripture seiþ þat Adam was seeke and seyde to his sone Seth þat he schulde go to paradys and preie þe aungel þat kepiþ paradys þat he wolde sende hym of þe tree of mercy oyle for to anoynte [wiþ] his membris, þat he mi3t haue hele. And Seth wente, but þe aungel wolde not lete hym yn but seyde to hym þat he mi3t not haue of þe oile of mercy. But he toke to hym foure graynes of þat same tree þat his fader eet of þe appul, and bade hym, also soone as his fadir were deed, þat he schulde putte þilke graynes vndir hys tunge and bury hym so. [And he dide so.] And of þilke foure graynes sprang trees, as þe aungel seide, þat schulde bere a fruyt þur3 which fruyt Adam schulde be saued.

1 cedre] C *adds* and of non oþir 2–3 for hy wolde . . . last] 2C *om.* 3 long] D *om.* 4 þei made] 2P *om.* 4–5 þat wente . . . heng] 2P *om.* on whiche his body heng] G2–G5 *om.* 5 is] D *om.* 6 to men] A hem 7, 11 ouertwert] CM *add* tre; 2C *adds* peece 7 to whiche his hondis were nayled] G2–G5 *om.* hondis] CM *add* and his armis 8–9 for in þe olde . . . palm and] D *om.* 9 of his enemye] G2–G5 *om.* 10 Crist] 2P *adds* therfore 13 ymade] C *om.* 14 and so] 2P Also 15 for þei . . . hem] B *om.* 15 stryf] 2P discorde and stryfe hem] 2B hem alle 17 liggyng] C *adds* on þe erþe Als] QABD 2C as Grecis] C in Gres 18 þat[2]] Q and 20 ywrite] CM *add* yn þer bokis also] 2P as here] C *om.* 21 þat he schulde] C *om.* 22 of þe tree] M *om.* 23 wiþ] QD *om.*; 2C therwith 24 wente] C went forþe yn] G2–G5 *add* at that dore 26, 28 graynes] 2P braunches 28 And he dide so] QAB *om.*

And whanne Seth come aȝen he fond his fader nyȝ deed, and he dide wiþ þe graynes as þe aungel bade him; of whiche [sprang iiii. treys of whilk] a croys was made þat bare good fruyt, Ihesu Crist, þurȝ which Adam and al þat come of hym were ysaued and delyuered fro deeþ wiþouten ende, but it be here owne defaute.

Þis holy | croys hidde Iewis vndir erþe vndir þe roche of mount f. 20v
Caluarie, and it lay þere two hundrid ȝere and more vnto þat tyme þat seynt Elyn fond it; þe whiche seynt Elyn was moder of Constantyn emperour of Rome, and heo was douȝter of kyng Collo þat was kyng of Engelond, þat was þat tyme yclepid þe Grete Brutayne, wham þe emperour toke to wyf for hure fairenesse whan he was in þat cuntre. And ȝe schul vndirstonde þat þe croys of oure lord Ihesu Crist was of lengþe eiȝte cubetis, and þat þat was ouertwert hadde yn [lengþe] þre cubetis and an half.

A partie of þe crowne of oure lord wharewiþ he was ycrowned and oon of þe nayles and þe sperheed and many oþer relikes beþ in Fraunce in þe chapel of þe kyng. And þe crowne liþ in a vessel of crestal wel ydiȝt and richeliche, for a kyng of Fraunce bouȝte þese relikes of þe Iewis whom þe emperour leide hem to wedde for a grete somme of gold. And þouȝ it be so þat men seye þat his crowne be of þornes, ȝe schul vndirstonde þat it is of ionqes | of þe see, þat is to f. 21r
seie ruysches, þat were white þat prickid as scharply as þornes. For Y haue yseie and biholde many a tymes þat of Parys and þat of Constantynople, for þei were boþe of oon ymade of ionqes of þe see, but men haueþ departid hem in twey parties, of whiche o partye is at Parys and þat oþer partie is at Constantynople. And I haue a poynt þerof þat semeþ a white þorn, and þat was ȝeue me for grete frendschip, for þer ys many of hem tobroke and falle into þe vessel þere þat crowne is as þei breke when men remewiþ þe vessel to schewe to grete lordis þat comeþ þedir.

And ȝe schul vndirstonde þat oure lord, in þat niȝt þat he was

1–3 And whanne . . . whilk] 2C of which trees 1 aȝen] C hom aȝeyne from paradis 2 sprang] 2P came 2–3 sprang . . . whilk] Q *om.* 5 but it be here owne defaute] C *om.* 6 vndir þe roche] 2B *om.* 9–10 heo was . . . kyng] A he was a kyngis doghter 9 Collo] C All; C Colle; 2B Coyle; 2C *om.*; 2P Alle 11 wham] 2B whanne 12 he] D sche 13 þat was] 2P *om.* 14 lengþe] Q *om.* 15 A] C men sayn þat o 16 oon] 2P *om.* 17 kyng] 2P *adds* of fraunce 18–20 for a kyng . . . gold] A *om.* 20 gold] 2P syluer 21 schul] CM *add* welle 21–22 þat is to seie ruysches] G2–G5 *om.* 22 were white] 2C beth white wede prickid . . . þornes] C had pryckys lyke þornes; M had prykels 24 for þei] M *om.* ymade] 2B and made þe see] C þes 28 frendschip] CM loue and gret frenschyppe; 2C loue 29 þere þat . . . vessel] 2P *om.* 30 þat] 2B that alle day ytake, he was lad into a gardyn and þere he was apposid scharply. And þere þe Iewis scorned hym [and made hym a croune of braunches of albespine þat grewe in þe same gardyn] and sette [it] on his heed so faste þat þe blood ran doun by many placis of his visage and his necke and his schuldris, and þerfore haþ albespyne many vertues. And he þat beriþ a braunche of it vpon hym, no f. 21v þonder noþer no maner of tempest | schal dere hym, noþer no hows þat hit is ynne may none yuel goost come noþer in þe place where it is. And in þat same gardyn seynt Petir forsook oure lord þries.

Aftirward was oure lord ylad bifore þe byschop and officeris of þe lawe in anoþer gardyn of Anne, and þere he was aposid also and yscorned and ycrowned eftsoones wiþ a whyt þorn þat men clepiþ barbarynes þat growid in þe gardyn, and þat also haþ many vertues. And after he was lad into a gardyn of Cayphas, and þere he was ycrowned wiþ engle[n]tere. And siþþe he was lad into þe chambre of Pylat, and þere he was apposid and crowned. And þe Iewis sette h*y*m [in] a chaire and cloþid hym in a mantel, and þanne made þei þe crowne of ionqes of þe see, and þei knelid to hym and [s]c*o*rned hym þerwiþ and seide *Aue rex Iudeorum*, þat is to say, Hayl kyng of Iewis. And þis crowne, whiche on half is at Parys and þat oþer half at Constantynople, hadde Crist vpon his heed whan he was don vpon þe croys. And þerfore men schul most worschipe hit and holde it f. 22r more worþi þan ony of þe oþere. | And þe sperschaft haþ þe emperour of Almayn, but þe heed is at Parys. And many tymes seiþ þe emperour of Constantynople þat he haþ þe sperheed; and Y haue ofte yseie þat þat he haþ, but it is grettere þan þat of Parys.

Also at Constantynople liþ seynt Anne our lady moder, wham seynt Elyn dide bringe fro Ierusalem. And þer liþ also þe body of Ion Crisostom þat was byschop of Constantynople. And þere liþ seynt Luke þe euangelist, for his bones were ybrouȝt fro B*e*tayne where he was yburied. And many oþer relikis beþ þere, and þere beþ þe

1 þere] B *om.* 2–3 and made . . . gardyne] G1 *om.* 3 it] G1 a crowne 5 schuldris] G1 *add* and þat crowne was maad of braunchis of albespyne 6 beriþ] CM *add* þe albespyn vpon hym þat ys to say of it] 2C *om.* 8 come] C have powyr to cum þeder in 11 lawe] 2B *om.* of Anne] M *om.* 12 ycrowned eftsoones] 2P after whyt] G3 (*ex* 3R) G4 G5 swete 15 englentere] Q engletere 16 crowned] CM squornid 16–17 hym in] Q hem 18–19 and scorned . . . seide] 2P saynge 18 scorned] G1 crowned 23 more] M *adds* precyous and more sperschaft] M sperehed 24–25 but . . . sperheed] M *om.* 24 tymes] A men 26 þat þat he haþ] 2P it 29 Crisostom] CM *add* þat men call seynt Iohan wiþ þe gilden mowþe 30 Betayne] Q Brutayne

vessels of ston as it were marbul, which men clepiþ *idriouns*, þat euermore droppiþ water and fulliþ hemself eche ȝere aȝen.

And Y do yow to wite þat Constantynople is riȝt a faire cite and a good and wel ywallid and it is þre cornerd. And þer is an arm of þe see þat men clepiþ Hellespounte, and somme clepiþ it þe bouche of Constantynople, and somme clepiþ it þe brache of seint George. And þis water encloseþ two parties of þe cite. And vp toward þe see vpon | þe same watir was woned to be þe grete cite of Troye in a wel faire f. 22v playn, but þat cite was destruyed wiþ hem of Grece.

And þere beþ many yles þat men clepiþ þus: Calcas, Calastre, Ceytige, Tesbiria, Armona, Faxton, Molo, Carpate, Lempne. And in þis yle is þe mount Athos þat passiþ þe clowdes. And þer beþ many spechis and many cuntreys þat beþ obeschaunt vnto þe emperour, þat is to sai, Turcople, Princynard, Comange, and many oþere, Trache, Macydoyne of which Alisaundre was kyng.

In þis cuntre was Aristotel bore in a cite þat men clepiþ Strages a litel fro Trachis, and at Strages liþ Aristotel. And þere is an autere vpon his toumbe, and þere makiþ þei a grete feste eche ȝere as he were a seint. And vpon his autre þei holdeþ here grete counseils and assemblez, and þei trowiþ þat þurȝ inspiracoun of God and hym þei schulde haue þe better counseil.

In þat cuntre beþ riȝt grete hullis, and toward þe ende of Macidoyne is a grete hulle þat men clepiþ Olympne þat departiþ Macidoyne and Trache and it is hiȝ vp to þe clowdes. And anoþer | hulle is þer þat men clepiþ Athos, and þat is so hiȝ þat þe schadewe f. 23r of hym rechiþ vnto Olymphus þat is nere lxxvii. myle bitwene. And aboue þat hulle is þe eir so clere þat men may fele no wynd þare, and þerfore may no beest lyue þere, so ys þe eir drie. And men seiþ in þilke cuntres somtyme went vpon þese hullis philosofris and helde to here noses a spounge moyst wiþ water for to haue eir, for þe eir was so drie þere. And also aboue in þe poudre of þe hulle þei wroote lettris wiþ here fyngris, and at þe ȝere ende þei come aȝen and fonde þe same lettris þe whiche þei hadde ywrite in þe ȝere bifore wiþoute

1 marbul] 2B fyne marbel 6 þe brache of] C le braunche de; G2 (*ex* 2P) le brace de 8 same] 2P *om.* a wel] B *om.* 9 hem] M men 11–12 Faxton . . . Athos] 2B *om.* 12 þe mount] D *om.* 12–13 many spechis and] AB *om.*; CM *add* and diuerys langagis 14 and many oþere] G1 *after* kyng 16–17 a litel . . . Aristotel] C and þer he is yberid 17 Trachis . . . Aristotel] A Stragis 19 a] C a grett 22 grete] 2A hye and] 2P *om.* 25 is þer . . . and þat] 2P *om.* 30 moyst] CM *om.*; 2B weete 30–31 to haue . . . þere] 2B þe drynesse of þe ayre 31 also] 2P *om.* 33 þe same] 2P those ȝere] C erþe

ony defaute. þerfore it semeþ wel þat þese hullis passen þe clowdes to þe pure eir.

And at Constantynople þe emperouris paleys is ri3t faire and wel ydi3t. And þer is ynne a faire paleys for ioustyng, and þer beþ stagis ymade þat men may sitte yn and se and no man dere oþer. And vndir þe stagis beþ stablis vowtid for þe emperours hors, and alle þe pilers beþ of marbel.

fo. 23v And wiþynne þe chirche of | seynt Sophe an emperour wolde haue leid þe body of his fadir when he was deed. And as þei made a graue þei fond a body in þe erþe, and vpon þe bodye lay a grete plate of gold and þerupon was write [in] Ebrew, Grew, and Latyn [lettres þat seyde] þus, *Ihesus Cristus nascetur de virgine Maria et ego credo in eum*, þis is to say, Ihesu Crist schal be bore of þe virgyne Marie and I beleeue in him. And þe date when þis was ywrite and þis was leid in þe erþe was two þousand 3ere bifore our lord was ybore. And 3it is þat plate in þe tresorie of þe chirche, and men seiþ þat it was Ermogynes þe wise man.

And yf al it be so þat men of þe lond of Grece be cristene, 3it hy varieþ fro oure feiþ; for þei seiþ þat þe holi goost comeþ not out of þe sone but onliche out of þe fadir, and þei beþ no3t obeschaunt to þe chirche of Rome noþer to þe pope, and þei seiþ þat þe patriark haþ as myche power by3onde þe see as þe pope haþ on þis side þe f. 24r see. And þerfore þe pope Ioon þe two | and twentyþe sent lettris to hem how cristen feiþ schulde be al oon and þat þei schulde be obeschaunt alle to a pope þat is Cristis vikery in erþe, to whom God 3af ful power for to bynde and to asoile, and þerfore þei schulde be obedient to hym. And þei sent to hym many ansueris, and among oþere þey seide þus: *Potenciam tuam circa tuos subiectos firmiter credimus. Superbiam tuam summam tollerare non possumus. Auariciam tuam summam saciare non intendimus. Dominus tecum sit quia Dominus nobiscum est. Vale*. þis is to saye, We trowe wel þi power is [grete] vpon þi sugetis. We mowe not suffry þi grete pruyde. We beþ not in purpos to staunche þi grete couetise. Lord

3 paleys] D *om.* 4 ynne] 2A *om.* 5 and se] A *adds* þe iustynge; B ther see; D sete; M *adds* þe reuelle 4–5 þer . . . yn and] G2–G5 it is on stages þat iche man may well 6 vowtid] C ybiggid 9 fadir] G1 *add* in þe erþe he] B is fader 10 grete] 2A *om.* of] G2–G5 of fyn 11 in] QB *om.* lettres þat seyde] G1 *om.* 13 þus . . . to say] CM *om.* 14 ywrite and þis was] A ywrite and; C wrytyn þis; 2A foundyn; 2B 2P *om.* 15 And] C *om.* 16 was] G1 *add* þe body of 18 cristene] C cristynid as we ben 21 pope] A *deleted passim* 23 lettris] C on 28 þey] G1 *add* sent and 28–15/6 *tuam . . .* growiþ] C *out* 32 grete] G1 *om.*

be wiþ þee, [for þe] lord is wiþ vs. Farewel. And oþer ansuere hadde he not of hem.

And also þei makiþ þe sacrament of þe autere of þerf breed for oure lord made it of þerf breed whenne he made his maunde. And on schere þorsday þei makiþ here þerf breed in tokenyng of þe maunde and drieþ it at þe sonne and kepiþ it al þe | ȝere and ȝeueþ it to sike (f. 24v) men in stede of Goddus body. And þei makiþ but on vnccioun when þei cristeneþ children. And þei anoynteþ none sike men. And þei sey þat þer is non purgatorie and þat soulis schul n*oþ*er haue ioiȝe ne payn vnto þe day of dome. And þei seiþ þat fornicacoun is no dedly synne bote a kyndely þing, and þat men and wymmen schal not be weddid but onys, and who so weddiþ more þan onys here children beþ bastardis and gete in synne. And here prestis also beþ yweddid. And þei seiþ þat oker is no dedly synne. And þei sille þe benefices of holy chirche, and so doþ men in oþer placis, and þat is grete sclaundre, for now is symonye kyng crowned in holi chirche. God may amende it when his wille is.

And þei seiþ þat men in þe leynten schul not synge masse but on þe satirday and on þe sonday. And þey faste not þe satirday no tyme of þe ȝere but it be ȝole eue or ellis ester eeue. And þei suffre no man þat comeþ fro þis side of þe [grete] see synge at here autres. And yf it falle þat þei do þurȝ ony hap þei waische | here auters also [sone] wiþ (f. 25r) holy water. And þey seiþ þat þer schulde but o masse be seid at on autere on a day. And ouer þat þei say þat oure lord ete neuer mete but he made token of etyng. And also þei seiþ þat we synne dedly in schauyng of oure berdis, for þe berd is tokene of man. And þei seiþ þat we synne in etyng of bestis þat were forbode in þe olde testament and þe olde lawe, as swyn and haris and oþer beestis; also þat we synneþ in etyng of fleisch in þe dayes bifore axe wendisday, and also in etyng of fleisch þe wendisday, when we ete chese or eiren in þe friday, and þei curse al þilke þat ete no fleisch on satirday. Also þe emperour of Constantynople makiþ [þe] patriark, erchebyschopis,

3 for þe] G1 *om.* lord[2]] A oure lord 2 he] 2P we 3 þerf] G3–G5 here 4 it of] B *om.* þerf] B *om.* 5 here þerf] M þere fore; 2P their; G3–G5 shrifte 6–14/16 and drieþ . . . men] 2P *out* 9 noþer] G1 neuer 13 synne] A dedly synne 15 so doþ] 2B dede 20 ȝole] B midwinter; G3–G5 cristmasse ellis] B *om.* 21 grete] G1 *om.* 22 also sone] QAB also; 2B clene after; 2C afterward; G3–G5 *om.* 26 tokene of man] M semblant and tokyn of man; 2A 2B *add* and of oure lord; 2C knowyng a man fro a womman; G3–G5 a synne 27 synne] M synne dedely 27–28 þat were . . . lawe] D *om.* 28 and þe olde lawe] A *om.* 29–30 also . . . wendisday] A G3–G5 *om.* 31 þilke] A *om.* no] AM *om.* 32 þe patriak] QB patriarkis erchebyschopis] 2B eueriche byshope

and byschopis, and he ȝeueþ alle dignites and chirches, and he priueþ þilke þat beþ worþy.

And ȝif alle it be so þat þese þinges touche not to þe way, neuerþeles þei touchiþ to þat þat I haue hiȝt to schewe a partye of customes and maners and dyuersetez of cuntreis. And for þis is þe f. 25v nexte cuntrey þat varieþ and is discor|daunt in feiþ and lettris fro oure feiþ, þerfore I haue set it here þat ȝe may wite þe dyuersite þat is bitwene oure feiþ and heris, for many men haue grete likyng and comfort to hure speke of straunge þingis.

## CHAPTER 3 AȜEN TO ÞE WAY FRO CONSTANTYNOPLE

Now come Y aȝen to þe way fro Constantynople. He þat wole go þurȝ Turkye, he goþ toward þe cite of Nyke and passiþ þurȝ þe ȝate of Chiuitot þat is riȝt hiȝ, and it is a myle and an half fro Nyke. [And] who [so] wol go by þe brache of seynt George and by þe Grete See where seynt Nicolas liþ and oþer placis, first men comeþ to þe yle of Sylo. In þat yle growiþ mastyk vpon smale trees as plumtrees or cheritrees. And þan men goþ þurȝ þe yle of Pathmos þere wroot seynt Ioon euangelist þe Apocalips. And Y do ȝow to wite whenne oure lord deide, seynt Ioon was of elde xxxii. ȝere, and he lyued aftir þe passioun of Crist lxii. ȝere.

f. 26r Fro Pathmos men goþ to Efesume, a faire cite and a ne|re to þe see, and þere deide seynt Ioon and was yburied bihynde þe auter in a toumbe. And þer is a faire chirche, for cristen men were woned to holde þat place. But in þe toumbe of seynt Ioon is no þing but manna, for his body was translatid into paradys. And Turkys holdeþ now þat cite and þat chirche and alle Assye þe lasse, and þerfore is Assye þe lasse yclept Turkye. And ȝe schal vndirstonde þat seynt Ioon lete make his graue þere in his lyf and leide hymself þerynne al quike. And þerfore somme men seiþ þat he deide nouȝt

2 worþy] M *adds* to be pryued; 2c *adds* of the pryuacion  3 way] M *adds* towarde the cytee of Ierusalem  5 þis] G1 þis lond of Grece  6 nexte] A moste; 2C fyrst  varieþ and] G2–G5 *om.*  feiþ] 2B *adds* on þis syde þe see  8 likyng] M wylle and lykyng  8–9 and comfort] G2–G5 *om.*  9 þingis] M contreis and dyuerse þynges  10–11 FRO CONSTANTYNOPLE] AB *om.*  12 Y] 2B *om.*  13 Nyke] G3–G5 Iuke  14 hiȝ] D by  15 And who so] QBD in þe way who  Grete] G2–G5 Greke  16 first] G2–G5 and fyrst  18 þan] 2A afture  24 for] M þat  25 þat place] M *om.*  30 quike] M *adds* lyuyng

but þat he restiþ þere to þe day of dome. And forsoþe þer is a ful grete merueil, for men may se þare þe erþe of þe toumbe many tymes stere and meue as þer were a quike þing vndir.

And fro Efesume men goþ þurȝ many yles in þe see into þe cite of Pateran whare seynt Nicholas was bore, and so to Marca whare he was chose to be byschope. Þere growiþ riche wyn and strong þat men clepiþ wyn of Marca. And fro þen | men may se þe yle of Grece, f. 26v þe whiche þe emperour ȝaf somtyme to Ionas. And þanne passiþ men þurȝ þe yles of Cophos and Lango, of whiche yles Ypocras was *l*or*d*.

And somme seiþ þat in þat yle of Lango is Ypocras douȝter in schap of a dragoun þat is an hundrid feet long, as men seiþ, for Y haue not yseye it. And þei of þe yles clepiþ here lady of þat cuntre. And heo liþ in an old castel and schewiþ here þries in þe ȝere, and heo doþ no man harm but yf ony man do here harm. And heo was þus chaungid fro a feire damysel to a dragoun þurȝ a god[des] þat men clepiþ Deane. And men seiþ þat heo schal dwelle so to þe tyme þat a knyȝt come þat is so hardy þat dar go to here and kisse here mouþ, and þan schal heo turne aȝen to here owne kynde and be a womman, and aftir þat heo schal not lyue longe.

And it is not longe siþen a kniȝt of Roodes þat was douȝty and hardy seyde þat he wolde kisse here. And whan he was vpon his coursere, he went in|to þe castel and entrid into þe caue. And þe f. 27r dragoun bigan to lifte vp his heed aȝens hym, and þe kniȝt sauȝ it so [hydous] he fliȝ away. And þe dragoun folewid after and toke þe kniȝt and bare hym mawgre his teeþ on a roche, and of þat roche heo cast hym into þe see, and so was þe kniȝt lost.

Also a ȝong man þat wist not of þat dragoun went out of a schip and ȝeode þurȝ þe yle til he come to þat castel, and he come into þat caue and went so long til þat he fond a chambre. And þere he sauȝ a damysel þat kembid here heed and lokid in a myrrour, and heo

1 þat he restiþ] B restiþ him 2 þare] B *om.* 3 stere] D *om.* 6 was] D *om.* 10 lord] G1 bore 12 schap] 2A 2P maner; 2B lyknesse 12–13 Y haue not yseye it] C proue is not 13 þei] 2A *om.* 14 þries] C *om.* 15 but yf . . . harm] 2P *om.* 16 fro] M *adds* the schappe of a fayre womman and to a] C to a fowle goddes] Q god 17 dwelle so] C *adds* a dragoun; M *adds* yn þe forme of a draguun 18 þat is so hardy] C *om.* go] M *om.* 20 womman] CM *add* as sche was before longe] CM *add* agon 22 seyde] C and he sayd here] 2B hure mouþe 22–23 And whan . . . caue] 2P *om.* 24 bigan to] CM *om.* 25 hydous] QBD meruelous; M *adds* and so horrible; 2C the huge beest 25–26 folewid . . . teeþ] 2A bare þe knyght maugre his; 2B bare þe knyȝt; 2P in his angre bare 30 long] M *adds* þeryn; 2A *om.* fond] C come to 31 kembid] C sate komyng

hadde myche tresour aboute here, and he trowid þat heo hadde be a comyne womman þat dwellid þere to kepe men. And he abode vnto þe damysele sauȝ þe schadewe of hym in þe mirrour, and þen heo turned here toward hym and askid what he wolde. And he seide þat wolde be here paramour oþer lemman. And heo askid hym if he were f. 27[v] a kniȝt, and he seide nay. And heo seide þan miȝt he | not be hure lemman. But heo bade hym go aȝen vnto his felawis and make hym kniȝt and come aȝe[n] on þe morwenyng, and heo schulde come out of þe caue, and bade hym þat he schulde kisse here þanne on þe mouþ. And heo bade hym haue no drede, for heo schulde do hym non harm yf al hym þouȝt þat heo were [hidous] to se. Heo seide it was don by enchauntement, for heo seide þat heo was siche as he sauȝ here þanne. And heo seide ȝif he kissid here, he schulde haue al þe tresour and be lord of here and of þese yles.

And he departid fro hure and went to his felawis to þe schip and made hym kniȝt and come aȝen vpon þe morwe to kisse hure. And when he sauȝ here come out of þe caue in likenes of a dragoun, he hadde so grete drede þat he fliȝ to þe schip. And heo folewid hym, and when heo sauȝ he turned not aȝen, heo bigan to crie as a þing þat hadde grete sorwe, and heo turned aȝen. And als soone þe kniȝt deide.

f. 28[r] | And siþþe hiderward miȝt no kniȝt se here þat he ne deide riȝt soone. But when a kniȝt comeþ þat is so hardy to kisse here, he schal not deiȝe but he schale turne þat damysele into here riȝte schap, and he schal be lord of here and þe yles biforeseid.

And fro þenne [men] come to þe yle of Rodis, þe whiche Hospiteleris holde [and] gouerne, and þat toke þey somtyme fro þe emperour. And þat yle was woned to be clepid Colles, and so calliþ þe Turkys ȝit. And seynt Poule in his pistels wroot to hem of þat yle *Ad Collosenses*. Þis yle is nere viii.[c] myle fro Constantynople.

2 to kepe men] 2B on þat manere abode] 2P obeyde 3–4 þe schadewe . . . toward] B *om.* 4 askid] BC *add* him 6 he not be hure] C not ȝe be my 7 aȝen] G1 *add* to þe schip 8 aȝen] Q aȝe 9–10 and bade . . . mouþ] C *om.* 9 hym] C *om.* þanne on þe] B *om.* 11 hidous] QBD meruelous; M *adds* and dredeful 12–13 heo seide . . . þanne] C I am soche as thu seyst now 14 tresour] M *adds* þat he saw abowte here lord of here and] G2–G5 here lorde and lorde of 16 made] M tolde þem that case and þey made to kisse hure] M *om.*; G2–G5 to kysse þe damsele 17 likenes] G2–G5 fourme dragoun] M *adds* so lothely and so horryble 18 fliȝ] M turnyd hym aȝen and fledde 23 But . . . þat is] C *om.* 25 here and þe yles] G2–G5 þe contrees (2B þat contre) biforeseid] CM *om.* 26 men] G1 *om.* come] M go men 27 and[1]] QD in 27–28 and gouerne . . . emperour] 2C *om.* 28 þat yle] 2P it 30 *Ad*] 2P of þis yle] M *adds* of Rodys myle] G2–G5 myle longe fro] 2B and for

And fro þis yle of Rodes men goþ to Cypre whare beþ many vynes þat first beþ reede and after a ȝe[r] waxiþ white. And þese vynes þat beþ most white beþ most clere and best smellyng. And men passe by þis way by a place whare was woned to be a grete cite þat men clepiþ Sathalay.

And alle þat cuntre was lost þurȝ þe foly of a ȝong man, for | þer f. 28$^{v}$ was a faire damysele þat he loued wele, and heo deide sodenly and was [put] in a graue of marbel. And for þe grete loue þat he hadde to here, he went on a nyȝt to here graue and openyd it and went yn and lay by here and ȝeode his way. And when it come to þe ende of þe ix. monþis, a vois come to hym on a nyȝt and seyde, Go to þe graue of þat womman and open it and bihold what þou hast gete of here, and if þou go nouȝt, þou schalt haue grete harm. And he ȝeode and openyde þe graue, and þer flowe out an he*d*e riȝt [hidous] to se, þe whiche alsoone flowe aboute þe cite and þe cuntre, and als soone þe cite sank doun. And þere beþ many perilous passagis.

Fro Rodis to Cypre is nyȝ v.$^{c}$ myle [and more] but men may go to Cypre and come not at Rhodes. Cypre is a gode yle and a grete, and þer beþ many gode cites. And þer is an erchebyschop at Nichosye, and foure oþer byschopis beþ in þat lond. And at Famagost is [one of] þe beste hauen on þe see þat is in þe world, and þer beþ ynne cristyne men and sarasyns and | men of alle naciouns. And in Cipre is f. 29$^{r}$ þe hulle of þe holi croys [and þere is an abbay of mounkes and þere is þe crosse] of þe gode þeof Dismas, as Y haue yseid bifore. And somme trowe þat þer is þe half of þe croys of oure lord, but it is nouȝt so, and þei do wrong to make men to [trowen] so.

In Cipre liþ seynt Genenoun, of whom men of þat cuntre makiþ grete feeste. And in þe castel of Amours liþ þe body of seynt Hillarion, and men kepiþ it riȝt worschipfully. And biside Famagost was seynt Bernard bore. In Cipre men huntiþ wiþ paupiouns þat beþ

1 yle] 2A *om.* 2 þat first] C þe whiche a ȝer] QD aȝe; B thei white] G2–G5 all whyte (2B alle ryȝt whyte) þese] 2B as 3 most clere] C most cherfull and; M holden smellyng] M *adds* of Tarage And] C 2P and as 4 way] C way þay go 6–7 þer was] G2–G5 he hadde (2A *deleted*) 8 put] Q *om.*; G2–G5 don marbel] M *adds* stone 11 on a nyȝt] 2P *om.* seyde] 2P *adds* in this manere of wyse 12 womman] 2P same woman that thou haste lyne by 12–13 and . . . harm] C *om.* 13 ȝeode] C *adds* þedyr 14 hede] Q hete hidous] QBD meruelous 15 alsoone] B *om.* cite] C fayre cite 17 and more] G1 *om.* 20–21 one of] G1 *om.* 21 on þe see] B *om.* on] CM of world] B *adds* that is of eny see 23 hulle] A half; M bulle 23–24 and þere . . . crosse] G1 *om.*; 2A *om.* is$^{1}$ 25 þer . . . but] 2B *om.* 26 and þei . . . so] 2C *om.* trowen] QBD do 28 feeste] G2–G5 solemnite 29 Hillarion] M *adds* and at Famagost was seynt Bernard buryed 30 In Cipre] 2P *om.*

like to leopardes. And þei beþ somme wel more þan lyouns, and þei take wilde beestis riȝt wel and beter and more felliche þan houndis.

In Cipre is a maner þat lordis and oþer alle ete vpon þe erþe, for þei make dichis in þe erþe al aboute þe halle deope to þe knee, and þei do pauy hit. And when þei wole ete, þei goþ þerynne and sittiþ þere; and þis is here cause, for to be þe more fresch, for þat lond is more hoot þan it is here. And at grete festis and for straunge men þat comeþ | f. 29v þei sette bordis and foormes as men doþ in þis cuntre, but hem were leuer sitte on þe erþe.

Fro Cypre men goþ by londe to Ierusalem and by þe see also. And in a day and in a nyȝt he þat haþ good wynd may come to þe hauen of Tyre þat now is callid Sure, and hit is at þe entre of Surrye. Þer was somtyme a faire cite of cristene men, but Sarasyns haueþ destruyed hit a grete partye and þei kepe þat hauen riȝt wel for drede [þat þei haue] of cristene men. Men miȝte go more riȝt to þat hauen and come not at Cypre, but þei goþ gladlich to Cypre to rest hem on þat lond or ellis to bye þingis þat þei haue neode to here lyuyng.

Vpon þat see side men may fynde many rubies. And þere is þe welle of whiche holi writt seiþ þus, *Fons ortorum et puteus aquarum uiuencium*, þat is to say, Welle of gardines and diche of watirs lyuyng. And to oure lord seide a womman in [þe cyte of] Tyre þus, *Beatus uenter qui te portauit et ubera que succisti*, þat is to say, Blessid be þe body þat þee bare and þe tetys | f. 30r þe whiche þou sowkedist. And þer oure lord forȝaf to þe womman of Canane here synnes. And bifore Tyre was ywoned to be þe ston on whiche oure lord sate and prechid, and in þat stoon was foundid þe chirche of seynt sauour. Vpon þat see is þe cite of Saphen oþer Sarepte oþer Sydonis, þere was Helyas þe prophet woned to dwelle and Ionas þe prophete rerid þere þe wydow s*o*n.

And v. myle fro Saphen is þe cite of Sydonour, of whiche cite

1 And þei beþ . . . lyouns] G1 *after* houndis 3 alle] C *om.* 4 halle] M *adds* withyn 5 pauy hit] 2P peyne them 6 þere] M *adds* at mete cause] G2–G5 manere 7 here] CM in odyr londis 7–8 þat comeþ] G2–G5 *om.* 9 erþe] CM *add* in þer owin maner 10 goþ] C *om.* also] G2–G5 *om.* 11 may] C and many 12 and] 2P and also of[1]] C þat 15 þat þei haue] G1 *om.* men] C *om.* riȝt] C *om.* 16 and come not at Cypre] C *om.* gladlich] C more 17 þingis] M *adds* or vytayles 17–18 to here lyuyng] CM *om.* 19 see] C same se 22 þe cyte of] G1 *om.* 24–25 þer oure lord forȝaf] M oure lord þerfore ȝaf 26 Tyre] 2P *om.* 26–27 on whiche . . . stoon] 2B *om.* 28 Sydonis] G2–G5 Sodomys 28–29 þere was . . . rerid] 2B *om.* 30 wydow son] Q wyndowsen; C wydow sum; D wysdom

Dydo þat was Eneas wyf after þe distruccioun of Troye was. And heo foundid þe cite of Cartage in Aufryk, and now it is yclepid *S*ydonsayto. And in the cite of Tyre regned [Agenor] Dido fader. And xviii. myle fro *S*idon is Beru*t*h, and fro Beru*t*h to Sardona is iii. iourneys, and fro Sardona is v. myle of þat lond to Damas.

## CHAPTER 4 A WEY LENGERE [ON þE SEE] TO IERUSALEM

And who so wole go lengere tyme on þe see and come nere to Ierusalem, he schal go fro Cypre to port Iaff by see, for þat | is þe f. 30v nexte hauene to Ierusalem, for fro þat hauen is nouȝt but a daies iourney and an half to Ierusalem. And þe hauen is callid Iaffe and þe toun Affe aftir one of Noe sones þat men clepiþ Iaphath þat foundid it and now is it called Ioppe]. And ȝe schul vndirstonde þat it is þe eldeste toun of þe world, for it was made bifore Noes flode. And þer beþ bones of a geauntis side þat was fourty feete long.

And who so comeþ to lond at þe firste hauen of Tyre oþere of Surrey [byforesayde] he may go by londe yf he wole to Ierusalem, and he schal go to þe cite of Aco*un* in a day, þat was somtyme yclepid Tolomayda. Hit was a cite of cristene men somtyme, but it is now destruyd [and it is on þe see]. And fro Venys to Aco*un* is by see ii. m$^{l}$. and iiii.$^{xx.}$ myle of Lumbardy. And fro Calabre oþer fro Cicyle is to Aco*un* a m$^{l}$. and ccc. myle [of Lombardy], and þe yle of Grece is ynne riȝt þe mydway.

And biside þe cite of Aco*un* toward þe see at vi. [score] furlongis on þe [riȝt] side toward þe souþ is þe hulle of Carme whare Helyas þe prophete dwellide, and þere was þe order of frere Carmes first | foundid. þis hille is nouȝt riȝt grete ne hiȝ. And at þe fote of þis hille f. 31r

1 was$^{2}$] A *adds* founder, BQ bigynnere, CM lady 2 heo] Q *adds* also 3 Sydonsayto] QBD G2–G5 Dydonsayto Agenor] G1 *om.*; 2A Ateles; 2B Ateldes; 2C Achiles; 2P *om. sentence* 4 Sidon] QBD Didonsayto Beruth . . . Beruth] Q Beruch . . . Beruch 5 of þat lond] M *om.* 6–7 ON þE SEE] Q *om.*; CM *om. rubric* 10 nouȝt] A *om.* 12 Affe] M also 13 and now . . . Ioppe] G1 2C *om.*; 2A *om.* now Ioppe] 2A Ioppse; 2B Iospys; 2P Iope 15 beþ] C *om.* 16 hauen] C *om.* 17 byforesayde] G1 *om.* 18, 20, 22, 24 Acoun] Q Acon' 19 Tolomayda] C þe Lomoda somtyme] M *om.* 20 and it is on þe see] G1 *om.* 21 m$^{l}$. and iiii.] 2B myle þat ys 22 of Lombardy] G1 *om.* 23 riȝt] BC *om.* 24 And] M and also score] G1 *om.* 25 riȝt] G1 *om.* souþ] 2P North 26 first] G1 *add* ordeyned and

was somtyme a gode cite [of crysten men] þat men clepide Cayphas, for Cayphas foundid it, but it is now al waast. But at þe lyft side of þe hulle is a toun þat men clepiþ Saffre, and þat is set vpon anoþer hulle. Þere was seynt Iame and seyn Ioon ybore, and in þe worschip of hem þer is a faire chirche.

And fro [Tholomaida þat men calle now] Aco*un* to a grete hulle þat men clepiþ *Scale de Tyreys* is a C. furlonges. And biside þe cite of Aco*un* renneþ a litel ryuer þat men clepiþ Belyon. And þer nere is þe fosse of Mynoun al round þat is nere an C. schaftmountes large, and it is al ful of grauel schenyng of which men makiþ goode glas and clere. And men comeþ fro fer wiþ schippis and wiþ cartis bi londe to take of þat grauel. And þouȝ yf þer be neuer so myche ytake on o day, on þe morwe it is as ful as euer it was, and þat is a grete merueyl. And þer is euermore grete wind in þat fosse þat steriþ alway þe grauel | f. 31v and makiþ it trowble. And yf a man do þerynne ony metal, hit turneþ als soone into glas. And þe glas þat is made of þis, yf it be put aȝen into þe grauel, hit turneþ to grauel aȝen as it was first. And somme seiþ þat it is a swolough of þe see grauely.

And fro Aco*un* biforseid men goþ iii. iourneys to þe cite of Philistien þat now is yclepid Gaza [þat ys to sey cite ryche] and it [is] ful feire and ful of folk [and it is a lytylle on þe see]. And fro þis cite brouȝte Sampson þe strong þe ȝatis [opon a hegh londe] when he was ytake in þat cite, and þer he slowe þe kyng yn his paleys and many [þousande] wiþ hym, for he made an hous falle vpon hem. And fro þen schal men go to Cesare and so to þe castel of Pillerynes, and so to Askaloun, and þanne to Iaphet, and so to Ierusalem.

1 gode] M grete of crysten men] G1 *om.* 2 lyft] CM est 5 chirche] 2B *adds* and a ful ryal 6 Tholomayda . . . now] G1 *om.* 6, 20 Acoun] Q Acon' 9 round] 2B *adds* as a whole nere] 2P *om.* C.] G2–G5 c. cubytes or 10 large] B G2–G5 longe; C longe þat is large al] B *om.* of which men] B þe which 11 glas] G2–G5 verres wiþ[1]] D *om.* 13 ytake] QA *add* of þat grauel on o day] 2B þereof ful as] D *om.* is a] 2A *om.* 14 grete[2]] 2P *om.* 15 alway] B away 17 þis] G2–G5 þis grauelle 19 grauely] 2B *om.* 20 And] G2–G5 Also 21 þat ys . . . ryche] G1 *om.* cite riche] 2C a riche cite 22 is] Q *om.* ful feire] M *om.* and it . . . see] G1 *om.* 22–24 fro . . . slowe] 2C þer slow Sampson þe fort 23 þe strong þe ȝatis] Q þe ȝatis strong; D þe ȝatis; 2P the stronge gates opon a hegh londe] G1 *om.* 25 þousande] G1 oþer (M *adds* of his men þat were) 25 þen] C Gaza to] G2 to þe citee of 27 so to] C þan to þe cite of

# CHAPTER 5 þE WAY TO BABILOYNE FRO GAZA

[And who so] þat wole go bi londe to Babiloyne whare þe sowdan dwelliþ to haue leue to go more sikerly þurȝ þe cuntreez, and for to go to mount Synay bifore he come to Ierusalem and þanne turne aȝen by Ierusalem, he schal go fro Gaza to | f. 32r þe castel Dayre. And aftir þat a man comeþ out of Surrye and goþ into wildernesse whare þe wey is ful sondy, and þat wildernesse lastiþ viii. iourneys, whare men fynden al þat hem nediþ of alle vitailes. And men clepiþ þat wildernesse Achellek. And whan a man comeþ out of þis desert, he entriþ into Egipt. And þei clepiþ Egipt Canopater, and in anoþer langage it is yclepid Mersyne. And þe firste good toun þat men fynde is yclepide Beleth, and it is in þe ende of þe kyngdom of Alaphe. and fro Alaphe men comeþ to Babiloyne and to Kayre.

And [in Babiloyne] is a faire chirche of oure lady whare heo dwellid vii. ȝere when heo fliȝ out of þe lond of *I*udee for drede of kyng Herode. And þer liþ þe body of seynt Barbara virgine. And þer dwellid Ioseph when he was ysold of his breþeren. And þere made Nabugodonosore [put] iii. children in *f*yre for þei were in riȝt treuþe; þe whiche children men clepid Anania, Azaria, Misael as þe psalme of þe Benedicite seiþ. But Na| f. 32v bugodonosore clepid hem þus, Sydrak, Misaak, Abdenago, þat is for to say, God glorious, God victorious, God ouer alle kyngdomes; and þat was for myracle þat he made, as he seide, God sonne go wiþ þese children þurȝ þe fuyre.

At Babiloyne dwelliþ þe sowdan, for þer is a faire castel and strong and wel ysett vpon a roche. In þat castel is dwellyng alwey, to kepe þe castel and to serue þe sowdan, mo þan viii. m[l]. men þat takiþ alle here necessaries of þe court of þe sowdan. I schulde wel wite for Y dwellid sawdeour wiþ hym [in his werrys a grete while] aȝenst Bedoynes. And he wolde þat I hadde weddid a grete princis

2 FRO GAZA] AD *om.*; CM *om. rubric* 3 And who so] G1 he 4 þe] 2P the churches and 6 he] C *om.* Dayre] B there 10 þis] M þat selfe 14 Alaphe] 2A thyne to] ACM at 15 in Babiloyne] G1 þer 16 vii.] G1 viii. fliȝ] G2–G5 was Iudee] QABD Audee 17 þe body of] C *om.* 19 put] QBD *om.* fyre] QD Syre; C ryȝt fayþe 21 But] M and þe same 22 victorious] 2A vertuouse 24 sonne] Q sonn' 25 At Babiloyne] G2 þere faire] G2 *add* see in a 27 men] G2–G5 persones of folke 28 of þe court] AD *om.* 29 Y dwellid sawdeour] C sowd; 2B I dwelled in his . . . while] G1 *om.* 30 princis] B priours

doughter and riche of his londe, so þat I wolde haue forsake my treuþe.

And ȝe schal vndirstonde þat þe sowdan is lord of fyue kyngedomes, þe whiche he haþ conquerid and ygete to hym by strengþe, and þis beþ þei: Canopater þat is Egipt; and þe kyngdome of Ierusalem, of whiche Dauid and Salomon were kynges; [þe kyngdome of] Surrye, of whiche þe cite of Damas was cheef; þe
f. 33r kyngdome of Analpe in | þe lond of Dameth; and þe kyngdome of Arabye, of whiche on of þe þre kynges þat made offeryng to oure lord whan he was ybore was kyng. And many oþer londes he holdeþ on his hond, and he holdeþ Calaphes, þat is a grete þing to þe sowdan, þat is to say among hem *Roys yles*.

And it is a valey þat is riȝt cold. And þan men goþ vpon þe mount of seynt Katerine, and it is myche hiȝere þan þe mount Moyses. And þer as seynt Kateryne was grauen is no chirche noþer chapel noþer oþer dwellyng place, but þer is an hulle of stones gederid samen aboute þe place þere heo was grauen of aungels. Þere was woned to be a chapel, but it is cast adoun and ȝit liþ þe stones þere. And if al it be so þat þe colect of seynt Katerine seiþ þat it is alle a place whare oure lord ȝaf þe lawe vnto Moyses and þer seynt Katerine was grauen, ȝe schal vndirstonde þat it is alle a cuntre oþer ellis [o] stede þat beriþ boþe o name, for þei beþ boþe yclepid mount Synay, but it is a grete wei bitwene hem [and a grete valay].

## f. 33v | CHAPTER 6 A WEY TO IERUSALEM

Now siþþe a man haþ visited þis holy place of seynt Katerine and he wole turne to Ierusalem, he schal first take his leue at þe monkis and recomaunde him specialy into here preieris. And þese monkis ȝeueþ wiþ goode wille vitailes to pilgrimes to passe wiþ þurȝ þe wildernesse to Surrey, and þat lastiþ more þan xiii. iourneis.

And in þat wildernesse dwelliþ many Arabynes þat men clepiþ

4 by] B with grete 6–7 þe kyngdome of] G1 *om.* 7 cheef] BD chosen 8 Analpe . . . of²] D *blank* 9 of which] 2A þat was to 10 And] C and also 12 *Roys Yles*] see Appendix 3 13 it is . . . riȝt] G2 þis valle is fulle (see Appendix 3) 17 þere] CM but þere as 18 cast adoun] C agon; G2–G5 alle castyn doune þe¹] 2P a greate part of the 19 þat] Q in þat seiþ] A ben sayd 21 oþer ellis] C but o stede] G1 in twey stedis 23 and a grete valay] G1 *om.* 26 he . . . he] B ye . . . ye 27 here] M *adds* goode 28 wille] M *adds* þere 29 xiii.] C xiiii 30 þat men clepiþ] 2B *om.*

Bydoynes and Ascopardes. þese beþ folk ful of alle maner yuel condicioun, and þei haueþ none howses but tentes, whiche þei make of bestis skynnes as of camels and of oþer bestis whiche þei ete, [and þereundyr þei lye]. And þei dwelle in placis whare þei may haue water as on þe Reede See, for on þat wildernesse is grete defaute of watir. And it falliþ ofte whare men fyndeþ watir o tyme, [þei] fyndeþ non anoþer tyme, and þerfore þei makiþ none howses in þat cuntre. þese men of whom Y speke tilieþ not þe lond, for þei etiþ no breed but yf it be ony þat dwelliþ nere [a] gode toun. And þei rooste al he|re fyschis and here fleisch vpon hote stonus aȝens þe sonne. And (f. 34r) þei beþ stronge men and wel fiȝtyng, and þei don nouȝt ellis but chace wilde bestis for here sustinaunce. And þei sette nouȝt by here lyf, and þerfore þei drede noȝt þe sowdan noþer none oþer prince of alle þe worlde. And þei haue ofte werre wiþ þe sowdan. And þat same tyme þat Y was wiþ þe sowdan, þei bar noȝt but a scheld and a spere for to defende here bodies wiþ. And þei hadde non oþer armour, but þei wynde here heedis and here neckis in a grete lynnen clooþ. And þei beþ men of ful yuel kynde.

And when men beþ passid þis wildernesse to Ierusalem, þey come to Bersabe, þat was somtyme a feire and a likyng toun of cristen men, and ȝit is þer somme of here chirchis. And in þat toun dwellid somtyme Abraham þe patriark. þis toun of Bersabe foundid þe wyf of Vrrye, of whom Dauid gate Salomon þe wise þat was kyng of Ierusalem and of xii. kynde of Israel, and he regned xl. ȝere.

And fro þenne goþ men to [þe vale of] Ebron, þat is fro þenne | nere xii. myle. And somme clepiþ it þe vale of Mambre, and also it is (f. 34v) yclepid þe vale of teeris for as myche as Adam gret in þat *v*ale C. ȝere for þe deeþ of his sone Abel þat Caym slow. And Ebron was somtyme þe cheef cite of Philistien, and þer dwellid geauntis. [And þere it was so free þat men toke alle þe flears of alle oþere places þat hade done ille.] In Ebron Iosue and Calophe and þer felawschip come first to aspye how þei miȝt wynne þe lond of

3 as of . . . bestis] A *om.* and of þer bestis] C *om.* 3–4 and þereundyr þei lye] G1 2C *om.* 6 men . . . þei] Q men . . . he; G2–G5 a man . . . he 7 non] B *om.* 8 of whom Y speke] C *om.* 9 a] QAD þe 10 here fyschis and] C *om.* 11 wel] M slye in 13–14 prince of alle þe worlde] C of þe lordis 15 same] M *om.* was] G2–G5 was dwellande þe sowdan] G2–G5 hym noȝt] M noon harneys 16 here bodies] 2P theym 18 ful] A *om.* 19 þis] C þis ile and þis 20 and a likyng] C *om.* 21 toun] M sayde towne 22 foundid] A *adds* somtyme 23 wise] D whilk 24 xl.] A xii. 25 þenne[1]] M Bersabe þe vale of] G1 *om.* 27 teeris] B terces vale] QBD dale 29 cheef] G2–G5 pryncipalle 30–31 And þere . . . ille] G1 2C *om.* 31–32 and þer felawschip] C *om.*

promyssioun. In Ebron Dauid kyng regned first vii. ȝere and an half, and in Ierusalem he regned xxxiii. ȝere and an half. And þer beþ [alle þe] graues of patriakis, Adam, Abraham, Iacob, and here wifes, Eue, Sare, and Rebecca, and þei beþ in hongyng of þe hulle. And vndir hem is a riȝt faire chirche [kyrnelled] as a castel, þe whiche Sarasyns kepiþ [ryȝt] wel, and þei haueþ þat place in grete worschip of þe holy patriarkis þat liggeþ þere. And þei suffre no cristen men noþer Iewis com yn þare but þei haue special leeue of þe sowdan, for þei holde cristene men and Iewis but as houndis þat schulde come in none holy place. And þei | (f. 35r) clepiþ þat place Spelunk or dowble caue or dowble graue, for on liþ on anoþer. And þe Sarasyns clepiþ it in here langage *Cariatharba*, þat is to say, þe place of patriarkis. And Iewis clepiþ it *Arbothe*.

And in þat same place was Abrahams hows, and þat was he þat sate in his dore and sauȝ þre persones and worschipid one, as holy writt witnessiþ seying *Tres vidit et unum adorauit*, þat is to say, He sauȝ þre and he worschipid one. And hym toke Abraham in his hows.

And riȝt nere to þat place is a caue in a roche whare Adam and Eue was dwellyng whenne þei were ydryue out of paradys. And þer gate þei here children. And in þat same place was Adam made as some men seiþ, for men clepid þat place somtyme þe [felde] of Damask for it was in þe lordschipe of Damasse. And fro þen he was translatid into paradys as þei saye, and aftirward he was dryuen out of paradise and put there aȝen, for þe same day þat he was put into paradys þe sa|(f. 35v)me day he was dryuen out, for als sone he synned.

þere bigynneþ þe vale of Ebron þat lastiþ nere to Ierusalem. And þe aungel bade Adam þat he schulde dwelle wiþ his wyf, and þere þei gete Seth, of whiche kyn Ihesu Crist was ybore.

And in þat vale is þe feld whare men drawiþ out of þe erþe a þing þat men clepiþ *chambille*, and þei etiþ þat þing in stede of spices. And þei beriþ it to sille. And men may not so deope ne so wide digge it þat hit nys at þe ȝere ende ful aȝen vp to þe sides þurȝ þe grace of God.

2–3 alle þe] G1 *om.* 5 kyrnelled] G1 *om.*; 2P *adds* after the facyon and maner 6 ryȝt] QBD *om.* wel and þei] B *om.* 8 leeue] B loue; G2–G5 grace 10 or[1]] B her 16 seying] CM *add* yn thys wys 21 here] B al her 22 somtyme] M by olde tyme felde] Q place; A lordschip; BCM *om.*; D *blank* 25 day] CM *om.* 30 þe feld] C a þing 31 men] 2P men in þe countre þei etiþ] D theyth 32–33 ne so . . . nys] B sow it but digge it] D *om.* 33 þat it . . . sides] C but at hit wyll be full aȝen ful aȝen . . . sides] B it is vp aȝen

And ii. myle fro Ebron is þe graue of Loth þat was Abrahams broþer. And a litel fro Ebron is þe mount Marbre, of whiche þat vale toke his name. And þer is a tree of oke þat þe Sarasyns clepiþ *dirpe* þat is of Abrahams tyme, þat men clepiþ þe drie tree. And þei say it haþ þe fro þe bigynnyng of þe world, and þat it was somtyme grene and bare leeues vnto þat tyme þat oure lord deyde, and þanne it dried. And so dide alle trees in þe world or ellis þei fay*l*|ed in here f. 36r hertes or ellis þei fadid, and ȝit beþ many of þese in þe world. And somme prophecie seiþ þat a lord, a prince of þe west side of þe world, schal wynne þe lond of promyssioun, þat is þe holy lond, wiþ help of cristene men, and he schal do synge a masse vndir þat drie tree and þanne schal þat tree wexe grene and bere fruyt and leeues. And þurȝ þat myracle many Sarasyns and Iewis schal be turned to cristene feiþ. And þerfore þei do grete worschip þerto and kepen it riȝt besily. And if alle it be drie, it beriþ a grete vertu, for certenliche he þat haþ þerof a litel vpon hym it heeliþ of þe fallyng yuel, and many oþer vertues [hit hase and] þerfore it is yholde riȝt precious.

Fro Ebron men goþ to Bedleem on an half day for it is but v. myle, and it is a perilous way þurȝ wodis ful likyng. But Bedleem is a litel cite, long and narwe and wel ywallid and enclosed wiþ a diche. And it was woned to be clepid Effrata, as holy writ seiþ, *Ecce audiuimus eum in Effrata*, þat is to say, Loo we herde hym in Effra|ta. f. 36v Toward þe ende of þat cite [towarde þe est] is a faire chirche [and a graciouse] and it haþ many touris, pynaclis, and kernels wel strongliche ymade. And wiþynne þat chirche is xliiii. pileris of marbel grete and faire.

And bitwene þis chirche and þis cite is a feld floridous. And it is callid feld florischid for as myche as a faire mayde þat was blamed wiþ wrong þat heo hadde doon fornicacoun, for whiche cause heo was demyd to be brend in þat place to whiche heo was lad. And as þe wode bigan to brenne, heo made here preieris to oure lord, as heo was not g*i*lty of þat þing, þat he wolde helpe here þat it myȝt be

1–2 is þe graue . . . Ebron] D 2A *om.* 6–7 deyde . . . so] C *om.* and þanne it dried] M *om.* 7 faylded] Q faaded 9 prophecie] 2B prophecyeþ and prince] G1 grete prince 9–10 side of þe world] A *om.* 11 do] B *om.* drie] CM *om.* 13 myracle] 2B tree þat schal schewe þat myracle 17 hit hase and] QAB 2A 2B 2P *om.* 18 day] G1 *add* iourne 19 ful likyng] B lykyng; CM lykyng and fayre But] AM *om.* 22 Loo] B *om.* 23 ende] QAB eest ende towarde þe est] G1 *om.* 23–24 and a graciouse] G1 *om.* 30 to be] G2–G5 to þe dede and to be brend] 2P buryed place] D *om.*; M felde 31 brenne] G2–G5 *add* aboute here heo made] Q *repeats* 32 gilty] Q gulty helpe] A kepen here] QBD *add* and saue here myȝt] C wolde be his wyll to knowen to alle men. And whanne heo hadde þus yseid, heo entrid þe fire, and als soone was þe fuyre oute. And þese braunchis þat were brennyng bicome reede roseris, and þese braunchis þat were not brennyng bicome white roseris ful of roses. And þese were þe firste rosis and roseris þat ony man sauȝ. And þus was þe mayde saued f. 37r þurȝ þe grace | of God. [And þerfore is þat feld calde þe felde of god florisschede for hit was fulle of roses.]

[Also] biside þe quere of þat chirche at þe riȝt side as men comeþ dounward xvii. greez is þe place whare oure lord was bore, þat is now ful wel ydiȝt [of marbylle] and richely depaynted wiþ gold and siluer and azour and oþer coloures. And a litel þen þre pases is þe crib of þe oxe and þe asse. And biside þat is þe place whare þe sterre fel þat ladde þe þre kynges, Iasper, Melchior, Baltazar; but men of Grece clepiþ þe kyngis þus, Galgath, Galgalath, Saraphy. þese þre kynges offrid to oure lord encense, gold, and mirre. And þey come togedir þurȝ [myracle of God], for þei mette s*a*men in a cite of Ynde þat men clepiþ Cassake þat is liii. iourneis fro Bedleem, and þei were in Bedleem þe ferþe day aftir þei hadde seye þe sterre.

And vndir þe cloister of þe chirche xviii. gres at þe riȝt side is þe charnel of þe innocentez whare here bones liþ. And bifore þat place whare Crist was bore is þe toumbe of seynt Ierome þat was a prest f. 37v and a cardynal, þat translatid þe | bible and þe sautere fro Ebrew into Latyn. And biside þat chirche is a chirche of seynt Nicholas whare oure lady restid here when heo was delyuered of childe. And for as myche [þat sche hade to mochelle] melk in here pappis [þat] greued here, sche melkid it out vpon þe reede stones of marbel so þat ȝit may men se þe traces white vpon þe stones.

And ȝe schal vndirstonde þat alle þat dwelliþ in Bedleem beþ cristene men. And þer beþ feire vynes aboute þe cite and grete plente of wyn, for here bookis of here lawe þat Macomet bitoke hem (whiche þei clepiþ Alkaron, and somme clepen it Massap, and

1 men] C *adds* þat was not gilty  2 oute] C quenchid; M *adds* and aquenchid  2, 3 braunchis] CM brondes  3 reede] M to reede  roseris] 2P roses  3, 4 roseris] CM roses  4 roses] C roserris; 2P whyte roses  6–7 And þerfore . . . roses] G1 (*ex* M) 2C *om.*; M and by þys cause was yt clepyd þe felde floresshed  6 god] 2B good  7 fulle] 2B ful of roseres hangyng ful  8 Also] QBD And  10 of marbylle] G1 *om.*  richely] M *om.*  depaynted] C araid and pauid  16 myracle of God] G1 goddis grace  samen] QABD somme men  19 And] DM also  21 Ierome] QAB *add* þe doctour  22 Ebrew] M grew  25 þat . . . mochelle] G1 *om.*  to] 2P so  þat] G1 (*ex* D) on  26 sche] B he  27 traces] B strakes  28 beþ] C be no  30 of here lawe] 2P *om.*  wyn] CM wynes and þey drynke no wyne but yf yt be the lesse

somme clepen it Harme) forbediþ hem to drynke wyn, for in þat boke Macomet cursiþ alle þilke þat drinkeþ wyn and alle þat sillen it. For somme men seiden onys þat he slow a gode heremyte, whiche he louede myche, in his drunkeschip, and þerfore he curside þe wyn and hem þat drinke wyne. But his malisoun be turned to hymself, as holy writ seiþ, *Et in verticem ipsius ini|quitas eius descendet*, þat is to (f. 38r) say, And into his owne heed his wickidnesse schal descende.

And also þe Sarasyns bringen forþ no grises noþer þei ete no swynes fleisch, for þei seiþ it is broþer to man and hit was forbode in þe olde lawe. Also in þe lond of Palastyne noþer in þe lond of Egipt þei etiþ but litel veel and beof but it be so old þat it may no more traueile and werche, nouȝt for it is forbode but for þei kepe hem for tilyng of þe lond.

Of þis cite of Bedleem was kyng Dauid ybore. And he hadde lx. wifes and CCC. lemmans. Fro Bedleem to Ierusalem is but ii. myle, and in þe way to Ierusalem half a myle fro Bedleem is a chirche whare þe aungel seide to þe scheephurdis of þe beryng of Crist. And in þat way is þe toumbe of Rachel þat was Ioseps modir þat was a patriark, and heo deide als soone as heo hadde ybore Beniamyn, and þere was heo grauen. And Iacob here housbande sette xii. grete stoonys on here in tokenyng þat | heo hadde ybore xii. children. In (f. 38v) þis way to Ierusalem beþ many chirches by þe whiche men goþ to Ierusalem.

# CHAPTER 7 IERUSALEM

For to speke of Ierusalem, ȝe schal vndirstonde þat it stondiþ faire among hullis, and þere is no ryuer noþer welle but water comyng by condyt fro Ebro*n*. And Y do ȝow to wite þat me clepid it first Iebus and siþþe it was yclepid Salem vnto þat tyme þat Dauid was king; and he sette þese two names togedre and clepid it Ie*b*usalem; and þan come Salamon and clepid it Ierusalem, and so hit is yclepid ȝit.

1 forbediþ] C for he forbiddis 2 alle þat sillen it] CM in all þat celle 5 be] ACDM *om.* 7 into his owne heed] G2–G5 *after* descende heed] A nekke schal] M *om.* 8 grises] C gose 8–10 And also . . . lawe] M *om.* 12 and werche nouȝt] A *om.* but] A end; C *om.* for[2]] D fro 22–23 to Ierusalem] M *om.* 24 IERUSALEM] A þe cite of Ierusalem; CM *om. rubric* 25 schal] CM *add* well 27 Ebron] QABD Ebrow Y do yow to] G2–G5 ȝe schalle 28 Salem] 2A solomee; 2B 2P Salomee 29 Iebusalem] Q 2B Ierusalem 29–30 Iebusalem . . . clepid it] C *om.* and þan . . . ȝit] 2B *om.*

And aboute Ierusalem is þe kyngdom of Surrye, and þerby is þe lond of Palastyne and Ascolon, but Ierusalem is in þe lond of Iudee; and it is yclepid þe lond of Iude for Iudas Machabeus was kyng of þat lond. And it marchiþ estward on þe kyngdome of Arabye, on þe souþ side on þe lond of Egipt, on þe west side vpon þe Grete See, and on þe norþ [side vpon þe kyngdome of Surrye and þe see of Cypre.

In Ierusalem was somtyme a patriark and erchebyschopis and
f. 39r byschopis | aboute in þe cuntre. Aboute Ierusalem beþ þe*s* citez, Ebron at vii. myle, Ierico at vi. myle. Bar[s]abe at viii. myle, Ascaloun at xviii. myle, Iaffe at xxvii. myle, Ramatha iii. myle, and Bedleem ii. myle. And toward þe souþ is a chirche of seynt Mercaritot þat was abbote þere, for whom þei made myche sorwe whan he schulde deiȝe. And ȝit is þe payntyng þere, how þei makid deol when he deide, and it is a pitous þing to beholde.

þis lond of Ierusalem haþ ybe in many dyuerse naciouns hondis, as Iewis, Chanens, Assyriens, men of Perce, Medoynes, and Massydoynes, Grekys, Romaynes, cristene men and Sarasyns, [Barbarynes and Turkes] and many oþer nacions; for Crist wole not þat it be in þe hondis of traytours and synneris, be þei cristene men oþer oþer. And now haue þe mysdoyng men holde þat lond in here hondis xl. ȝere and more, but þei schal not holde it longe if God wil.

And ȝe schul vndirstonde when men go to Ierusalem, þei goþ þe
f. 39v firste pilgrimage to | þe chirche whare is þe holy graue, þat was out of þe cite on þe norþ side, but it is now closed wiþynne þe wal of þe toun. And þer is a wel faire chirche al round opyn abo*u*e and þekkid wel wiþ leed. And on þe west side is a faire tour and a strong for bellis. And in þe myddel of þe chirche is a tabernacle as a litel hows ymade in þe manere of half a cumpas riȝt wel and richely wiþ gold and azour and oþer colouris wel ydiȝt. And on þe riȝt side is made þe sepulcre of oure lord. And þe tabernacle is viii. feet long and fyf fote wide and xi. feet hiȝ.

3 þe lond of] CM *om.* 3–29/4 Iude . . . bifore] 2P *out* 6 norþ] 2M west side] QD *om.* 8 and erchbyschopis and] C *om.* 9 aboute in þe cuntre] A *om.* þes] Q þer; C many 10 Barsabe] QAD Barabe 11 xxvii.] D v. *blank* 12 ii. myle] 2B *om.* 13 made] 2A *om.* 14 payntyng] B pauyng 17 as] B sauf as Iewis . . . Medoynes] M *om.* and[1]] G1 Turkys and 19 Barbarynes and Turkes] G1 *om.* 21 oþer oþer] 2A be þei athyn 22 xl.] B *blank* 24 schul] C *adds* wele go] B G2–G5 cum; M comyth fyrst 27 aboue] Q aboute 28–29 And on . . . bellis] B *after next sentence* 30 wiþ] G1 diȝt wiþ 31 oþer] *adds* B fyne wel ydiȝt] ABCM *om.* 32 feet] B cubites

And it is not long siþþe þe sepulcre was al opyn þat me miȝt kisse it and touche it. But for men þat come þedir payned hem to breke þe ston in pecis oþer poudre to bere wiþ hem, þerfore þe sowdan haþ lete make a wal aboute þe graue þat no man may towche hit but in þe lyft syde. On þat tabernacle is [no] wyndowe, but þer is ynne many laumpes liȝt. And þer | is a laumpe þat hongiþ bifore þe sepulcre liȝt f. 40r brennyng and euerich Friday hit goþ out by hymself, and liȝtneþ aȝen by itself on þe Soneday at þat [oure] þat oure lord roos fro deeþ to liyf.

Also in þat chirche on þe riȝt side is þe mounte of Caluarie whare oure lord was do on þe cross. And [þe cros] was set in a morteys in þe roche þat is whyt of colour and a litel reed medlid wiþ. And vpon þat roche droppid blood of þe woundis of oure lord when he was peyned on þe crosse, and þat now is yclepid Gal[g]atha. And men goþ vpon þat Gal[g]atha on greces. And in þat morteys was Adams hed yfounde after Noe flood in tokene þat þe synnes of Adam [schulde be] bouȝt in þe same place. And aboue þat roche made Abraham sacrifise to oure lord, and þer is an autere and bifore þat autere lyþ Godefray of Boloyne, Bawdewyn, and oþer þat were cristene and kingis of Ierusalem.

And þer as oure lord was don on þe cros is writun in Grew lettris seying þus |, *Otheos basilion ysmon presemas ergaste sothias oys*, þat is f. 40v to say vpon Latyn, *Hic deus rex noster ante secula operatus est salutem in medio terre*, þat is to say, Here God oure kyng bifore worldis haþ wrouȝt hele in myddel of þe erþe. And also on þe roche whare þe crois was ficchid is write þus, *Gros ginst rasis thou pestes thoy thesmoysy*, þat is to say in Latyn, *Quod vides est fundamentum tocius mundi et huius fidei*, þat is to say, þat þou seest is ground of alle þe world and of þis fey.

And ȝe schal vndirstonde þat oure lord when he deide was xxxiii. ȝere old and þre monþis. And þe prophecye of Dauid seiþ þat he schulde haue fourty ȝere or he deide when he seiþ on þis wise, *Quadraginta annis proximus fui generacioni huic*, þat is to say, Fourty

1 kisse] M see  for] C *om.*  3 to bere wiþ hem] G2–G5 *om.*  4 no] QBD a  6 And þer . . . liȝt] C *om.*  liȝt] A *om.*  8 on þe Soneday] G2–G5 *om.*  oure] G1 tyme  roos] 2A roos aȝeyne  11 And] CM that  þe cros] G1 *om.*  14, 15 Galgatha] QABD Galatha; C hill  16–17 in tokene . . . same] M and vppon þat  17 schulde be] G1 (*ex* C) was  18 bifore] 2A vndere  20 cristene and] M *om.*  21–22 lettris seying þus] A þus; C lettris thus; G2–G5 *om.*  25 wrought] B brought  26 ficchid] B *blank*  þus] G2–G5 with inne þe roche  30 xxxiii.] 2P xxxii  32 or he deide] G2–G5 *om.*

ȝere was [Y] neiȝebore to þis kynde. And þus schulde it seme þat þe prophe*cy* were not sooþ. Boþe beþ soþe, for olde tymes m*e*n [made] ȝere of ten monþis, of whiche þe monþe of Marche was þe first and | f. 41r Decembre þe last. But Gayus Cesar þat was emperour of Rome lete sette to þese twey monþis Ianuare and Feurere and ordeyned þe ȝere of xii. monþis, þat is to say, of CCC. and lxv. dayes wiþoute lepe ȝere after propre cours of þe sonne. And þerfore after acountyng of ten monþis to þe ȝere he deide in þe fourty ȝere and aftir oure ȝere of xii. monþis he hadde xxxiii. ȝere and iii. monþis or he deide.

[Also] wiþynne þe mount of Caluarie at þe riȝt side is an auter whare þe pyler liþ to whiche oure lord was bounde when he was scourgid. And þer nere beþ foure stones þat alway droppiþ water, and somme seiþ þat þilke stones wepe for oure lord[is] de*þ*e. And nere to þis autre in a place xlii. greez depe was founde þe verrey cros by assent of seynt Elyne vndir a roche whare Iewis hadde yhudde it. And it was assayed for þei fond þre crosses, on of oure lord and tweye of þe two þeofis, and seint Elyne assayed hem on a deed body þat ros als sone as þe verrey cros was leide þeron.

f. 41v And þerby in þe walle is þe place wha|re þe foure nayles of oure lord weren hud, for he hadde ii. nayles in his hond and ii. in his feet. And of on of þese nayles made þe emperour of Constantynople a bridel to his hors to bere hym into bateyl, for þurȝ vertu of þat he ouercome his enemys and wan al þese londis, Assye, Turkye, Damazyn þe more and þe lasse, Surrye, Ierusalem, Arabye, Perse, Mesopotayne, þe kyngdome of Analpe, Egipt þe hiȝe and þe lowe, and oþer kyngdomus many vnto wel lowe [in] Ethiope and vnto Ynde þe lasse þat þanne was cristine.

And þere was in þat tyme many goode holy men and holy heremytes in þilke cuntrez, of whom þe bokis of þe fader lyf

1 Y] QBD he 2 prophecy] Q prophete Boþe] A G2–G5 but boþe (2P but it is); C I say boþe; M ȝys bothe; 2B I proue þat þey 2–3 men made ȝere] G1 many ȝere were; 2P men called yeres 3 ȝere] CM *add* ȝe ȝere þe monþe of] G2–G5 *om.* 4 þat was] A *om.* 5 to þese] C in; M yn the monþis] CM *add* more ȝere] M *adds* to be 7 to say of] CM in þe ȝere and lxv.] 2A 2P *om.* 7 after] 2P *om.* þerfore] B þer 8 to þe ȝere] C in þe same ȝeris in] 2B and ȝere[2]] CM *add* of age ȝere of] CM accountes of 9 monþis] CM *add* yn þe ȝere he hadde] G2–G5 it is or he deide] G2–G5 *om.* 10 Also] QABD And wiþynne] A at 11 þe] C þe holy 12 nere] 2A 2P bysyde atte four fete 13 wepe] G1 wepte lordis deþe] QABD lord deide 14 place] C pillour 15 assent] M asay 16 for] B and 18 þeron] C on him he aros anon 19 walle] 2P vale 23 wan] 2P whan Turkye] M *om.* 26 wel lowe] AC 2C *om.*; B the low; 2A welle laugh; 2B lawthe (see Appendix 4) in] QAB 2C *om.* 29 in þilke cuntrez] G2–G5 *om.* 29–31/1 of whom . . . spekiþ] C and þes bokis þat olde faduris spekin of

spekiþ. And alle þilke londis beþ now in payems and Sarasyns hondis. But when God wol, riȝt as þese londis beþ lost wiþ synne of cristen men, so schal þei be wonne aȝen by help of God þurȝ cristene men.

And in þe myddel of þat chirche is a cumpas in whiche Ioseph of Aramathie leyde þe body of oure lord when he hadde | take hym of f. 42r þe cross. And men seyn þat þat cumpas is þe myddel of þe world. And in þe chirche of þe sepulcre on þe norþ side is a place whare oure lord was ydo yn prisoun, for he was yprisoned in many oþer placis also. [And þeire is a party of þe cheyne wythe whiche he was boundene.] And þere he apperide first to Marie Mawdeleyn when he was rise, and heo trowid þat he hadde be a gardynere. In þe chirche of þe sepulcre was woned to be chanouns of þe ordre of seynt Benet, and þere þei hadde a priour, but þe patriark was þer souereyn.

And wiþoute þe dores of þe chirche at þe riȝt side as men goþ vp xviii. degrez seide oure lord to his moder þus, *Mulier ecce filius tuus*, þat is to say, Womman se þi sone. And þanne seide he þus, *Deinde dicit disciplo, ecce mater tua*, þat is to say, þanne seide he to his disciple, Biholde þi moder. [And þis word he sayde on þe crosse. And apon þoise gresez went oure lorde when he bare þe crosse opon hys scholdre.]

And vndir þis degreez is a chapel whare prestis syngeþ, but not aftir oure lawe but aftir her owne lawe. And alway þei make þe sacrament of þe autere of breed seiyng | *Pater Noster* and oþer þinges f. 42v also, wiþ whiche þinges þei saye þe wordis of whom þe sacrament is maad; for þei knowe not of addiciouns þat many popes haue maad, but þei synge in gode deuocioun. And þer nere is þe place whare oure lord restide hym when he was wery of beryng of þe cros.

And ȝe schal vndirstonde þat bifore þe chirche of þe sepulcre is þe cite most wayke for þe grete playn þat ys bitwene þe cite and þe chirche on þe eest side. And wiþoute þe wallis of þe cite is þe vale of

1 alle þilke londis] G2–G5 þei payems] A paen; 2B peynes and Sarasyns] A *om.* 3 by] 2B by þat swete myȝtful 3–4 God þurȝ cristene men] C cristin men by þe grace of God allmiȝty 8 sepulcre] C *adds* of our Lord 9 for] CM *om.* for he was yprisoned] 2P *om.* 10 also] AC *om.* 10–11 And þeire . . . boundene] G1 *om.* 11 first] C *om.* 14 priour] C prayar a good man þer] M alle þere 16 þus] CM *om.*; BCM *add* when he was honged on the crois 17 se] G2–G5 byholde 17–18 þus . . . seide he] 2A 2P *om.* *Deinde dicit discipulo*] A *om.* 18 *dicit*] CM dixit þat is to say] C *om.* 18–19 þanne . . . disciple] A *om.* 19–21 And þis . . . scholdre] G1 *om.* 20–21 And apon scholdre] 2C *om.* 22–23 but . . . lawe] 2P *om.* 24 of þe autere] C *om.*

Iosephat *þa*t comeþ to þe wallis. In þat vale of Iosephat wiþoute þe cite is þe chirche of seynt Steuen whare he was stenyd to deeþ. And þerby is þe gildid ȝate þat may not be openyd. þurȝ þat ȝate oure lord entride on Palm Soneday vpon an asse ridyng, and þe ȝate openyd aȝens hym whenne he wolde go to þe temple. And ȝit beþ þe stappis of þe asse sene in þre places, þe whiche beþ of ful hard stones.

f. 43r Bifore þe chirche of þe sepulcre CC. pa|sis is a grete hospitale of seynt Ioon, of þe whiche þe Hospiteleris haueþ here fundacioun. And to go toward þe eest fro þe hospitale is a riȝt faire chirche þat men clepiþ *nostre dame le graunt*. And siþþe is nere anoþer chirche þat men clepiþ *nostre dame de vatyns*. And þere was Marie Cleophe and Marie Mawdeleyne and drowe þere here heer when oure lord was don to deeþ.

And fro þe chirche of þe sepulcre toward þe eest viii.$^{xx.}$ pasis is *templum domini* þat is a riȝt faire hous. And it is al round and riȝt hiȝ and helid wiþ led and it is wel ypaued wiþ white marbel. But þe Sarasyns wole suffre no cristen men noþer Iewis come þerynne, for þei seiþ þat so foul men schulde not come into so holy places. But Y come yn þare and in oþer placis whare Y wolde for I hadde lettris of þe sowdan wiþ his grete seel, and oþer men haue comynly but his signet.

And men beriþ his lettre wiþ his seel bifore hem hongyng vpon a
f. 43v spere, and þey do greete worschipe | þerto and kneliþ þere aȝens as we doþ aȝens Goddis body. For þese men þat it is sent to, bifor þei take it, þei enclyne hem first þerto and siþþe þei take it and leiþ it on here hedis, and þanne þey kisse [it], and þanne þei rede þe lettris al inclynand wiþ grete worschip, and þanne þei profre hem to do al þat þe bringer wole.

And in þis temple *Domini* were woned to be chanouns regulers and þei hadde an abbot to whom þei were obedient. And in þis temple was Charlemayn whenne þe aungel brouȝte hym þe prepoues of oure lord when he was circumsised, and aftir kyng Charlis let bere it to Parys.

1 þat] QBD hit þat comeþ . . . Iosephat] CM *om.* 4 ridyng] G2–G5 *om.* 5 ȝit] M þere 6 þre places] M þat place 11–12 *le graunt . . . dame*] 2P *om.* 11 siþþe is] B þer is nere] 2A þeire; 2B *om.* 13 þere] ACM *om.* heer] C *om.* 16 hous] M place it is] A *om.* 17 But] M and 19 into so] B therynne for it is suche; 2P into that Y] C *adds* mysilfe 21 but] M nouȝt saue 22 men beriþ] C *om.* 24 it] CM þat hys letters 26 it] G1 þe seel þe lettris] 2P *om.* 28 þe bringer wole] B he bryng; C *adds* have doun; M *adds* after the forme and þe tenowre of þe letters 32 when he was circumsised] A *om.*

And ȝe schal vndirstonde þat þis is not þe temple þat Salamon made, for þat temple lastid but a m$^{l}$., an C., and two ȝere; for Titus, Vaspasianes sone, þat was emperour of Rome, þat leid a sege aboute Ierusalem for to destruye þe Iewis, for þei hadde do Crist to deeþ wiþoute consent of þe emperour. And whenne he hadde yta|ke þe f. 44$^{r}$ cite, he lete brenne þe temple and cast it doun, and toke alle þe Iewis and dide of hem to deeþ xi. C. M$^{l}$. And þe oþer he dide in prisoun and sold of hem xxx. for a peny for þei seide þat þei hadde bouȝt Ihesu Crist for xxx. pans.

And siþþe ȝaf Iulius Apostata þat was emperour leeue to þe Iewis to make þe temple of Ierusalem, for he hatid cristene men and ȝit he was cristine but he forsoke his lawe. And whanne þe Iewis hadde made þe temple, come an erþequakyng, as God wolde, þat cast adoun al þat þei hadde made.

And siþþe Adrian þe emperour, þat was of hem of Troye, made Ierusalem aȝen and þe temple in þe same manere þat Salamon made it. And he wolde lete no Iew dwelle þere but al cristen men, for if al it were to þat he were nouȝt cristened, he loued cristen men more þan ony oþer men saue men of his owne fey. And þis emperour lete enclose and walle þe chirche of þe holy sepulcre wiþynne þe cite [þat byfore was ferre withouten þe citee], and he wolde haue | chaungid f. 44$^{v}$ þe name of Ierusalem and clepid hit Helyam. but þat name lastid not longe.

Also I do ȝow to wite þat Sarasynes do grete worschip to þe temple *domini*, and þei saiþ þat place is riȝt holy. And when þei go þider yn, þei go barfote and kneliþ many a tymes. And when my felawis and Y come þedir yn, we dide of oure schoon and come barfote, and þouȝt þat we schulde do as myche worschip þere or more þan þe mystrowand.

And þis temple is lxiiii. schaftmountis of widenesse and as myche of lengþe, and of heiȝghþe hit is vi. score [and v.] schaftmountes.

1 Salamon] M *adds* kyng 2 an c.] C ii. c. for] C tyl þat 4 destruye] G2–G5 discomfet 5 consent] 2A 2B leeue; 2P loue 6 lete brenne] C fordid 7 oþer] A alle oþer; CM of þe toþer deele þat were on lyfe 8 for$^{2}$] C and hadde] C *om.* 10 þat was emperour] G2–G5 *om.* was] M after 12 forsoke] C for 13 come] CM þere come; 2A þanne come 13 as God wolde] 2A *om.* 15 siþþe] C þan come 19 emperour] CM *add* Adryan 20–21 þat was . . . citee] QAD *om.* 23 longe] CM *add* ne endewryt but a whyle 24 Also I do ȝow to] G2–G5 And ȝe schal 25 *domini*] G2–G5 *om.* 26 go$^{2}$] M go alle barfote] 2P *adds* into the temple 28 worschip þere or] G2–G5 *om.* 28–29 or more þan] B as more as; AM or more as; C *om.* 30 lxiiii.] 2B thre score and thre 30, 31 schaftmountis] G2–G5 cubites 31 score] 2P and twenty and v.] QBD *om.*

And hit is wiþynne al aboute of pileris of marbel, and in þe myddel of þe temple is a stage of xxiiii. degreez of heiȝghþe and gode pileris al aboute. þis place þe Iewis clepid *sancta sanctorum*, þat is to say, holy of [holyes]. And in þat place comeþ noon but onliche here prelat þat makiþ here sacrifice, and þe folk stondiþ al aboute in dyuerse stagis aftir þat þei beþ of dignite and worschip.

f. 45r And þere beþ iiii. entreez to þat temple, and þe dores | beþ of cipres wel ydiȝt. And wiþynne þe eest dore oure lord seide, 'Here ys Ierusalem'. And on þe norþ side wiþynne þe dore is a stank but it renneþ noȝt, of whiche holy writ seiþ þus, *Vidi aquam egredientem de templo*, þat is to say, I sauȝ water comyng out of þe temple. And on þe oþer side is a roche þat men clepid somtyme Moriache, but siþþe it was yclepid Beleth, *or* þe arke of God wiþ relikis of Iewis. þis arke lete Tytus lede wiþ þe relikis to grete Rome whenne he hadde discomfitid þe Iewis.

In þat [arke] was þe ten comaundementis and of Aaron ȝerd and of Moyses ȝerd wiþ þe whiche he departid þe Rede See whanne folk of Israel passid ouer drie fote. And wiþ þat ȝerd he smote on þe rochis and þe water come out of hem, and wiþ þis ȝerd he dide many wondris. And þer was a vessel of gold ful of manna and cloþyngis and o*r*nementis [and] þe tabernacle of Aron. And þere was a table f. 45v square of gold wiþ xii. preciouse stones, and a beost of iasper | grene wiþ iiii. figures and viii. names of oure lord wiþynne, and vii. candelstikkis of gold, and xii. pottis of gold, and iiii. ensensours of gold, and an autre of gold, and iiii. lyouns of gold vpon whiche þei hadde a cherubyn of gold xii. spanne long, and a tabernacle of gold, and xii. trumpes of siluer, and a table of siluer, and vii. *bar*ly loofes, and alle oþer relikes þat were bifore þat Crist was bore.

And also vpon þis roche slepte Iacob when he sauȝ angels go vp and doun by a stiȝe and seide, *Vere locus iste sanctus est et ego*

1 al] C and all 2 is] Q it is xxiiii.] 2P xxiii 3 al . . . Iewis] CM round abowut þat plase and þe Iuis callis it 4 holyes] QD seyntes; 2A halowes; 2B hoolynesse 6 dignitee] C degre 7 entreez to] M awters yn 9 stank] CM *add* of water 10 seiþ] G2–G5 spekys and says 13 or] QABD whare; C and there arke] 2A 2P Arke or huche God] 2A goode relikis of Iewis] C polekis and iewellis 13–14 wiþ relikis . . . lede] 2B *om.* 13 Iewis] G1 *add* stoode arke] 2P arke or hutche 15 discomfitid] CM destroyed þe[1]] G2–G5 alle þe 16 arke] QBD *om.*; 2A Arke or hache; 2P same arke 18 ouer] CM thorow; G2–G5 þorgh on 18[1]–19 he smote . . . ȝerd] 2P *om.* 19 of hem] B on hem M *om.* 21 ornementis] Q oynementis and] QBD to 22 square] 2A qware beost] AB best; CM box grene] CM ygrauyn 25 autre] 2B evere 26 a tabernacle of gold] 2A *before* iiii. lyouns 27 vii.] 2C viii barly] G1 holy 28 alle] M meny þat Crist was bore] G2–G5 þe natiuite of cryste 30 stiȝe] B him; 2A lethare

*ignorabam*, þat is to say, Forsoþe þis place is holy and I wiste no3t. And þere Iacob held stille þe aungel þat chaungid his name and clepid hym Israel. And in þat place sau3 Dauid þe aungel þat smot þe folk wiþ a swerd and put it al blody in þe scheþe. [And in þis roche was seynt Symeon when he reseyuede oure lorde into þe temple.]

And on þis roche oure lord sette hym when þe Iewis wolde haue stenyd hym, and þe roche clef atwo and in þa[t] clyft he hidde hym and a sterre came doun and 3af hym li3t. And on þys roche sate oure lady and lerid here sautere. | And þere oure lord for3af synnes to þe f. 46r
womman þat was ytake in avowtrie. And þere was Crist circumcided. And þer þe aungel schewid first of þe natiuite of seynt Ioon baptyst. And þere offrid [first] Melchisedech breed, wyn, and water to oure lord in tokene of þe sacrament þat was to come.

And þere fel Dauid preiyng to oure lord þat he wolde haue mercy of hym and of þe folk, and oure lord herde his preiere. And þer wolde he make þe temple in þat place, but oure lord forbade hym by an aungel, for he hadde do tresoun when he slow Vrrie, a good kni3t, to haue his wyf. And þerfore al þat he hadde ordeyned to makyng of þe temple, he toke it to Salamon [his] sone, and he made it. And he preied oure lord þat alle þilke þat preied in þat place deuouteliche and wiþ good herte þat he wolde hure here preiere and graunte þat þei askide ri3tfulliche, and oure lord grauntid hit. And þerfore Salamon clepid it temple of counseyl and helpe of God. | Wiþoute f. 46v
þe dores of þe temple is an auter whare Iewis were woned to offre dowfes and turtlis. And in þat temple was Zacharie slawe. [And on þe pinacle Iewes set seynt Iame in þe erthe þat first was bysschope of Ierusalem.]

A litel fro þis temple on þe ri3t side is a chirche helid wiþ led þat is clepid þe scole of Salamon. And toward þe sowþ is þe temple

3 smot] 2A keruyd; 2B 2P schare  4–6 And . . . temple] G1 2C *om.*  7 oure lord] G2–G5 he  8 hym] C him to deþe  clef . . . clyft] G2–G5 roofe . . . ryft  þat] Q þa  hidde] C dide  10 lerid] 2P serued  11 ytake] 2P founde and taaken  Crist] C *om.*  12 schewid first] G2–G5 denoncied  13 first] QAB *om.*  14 þat was to come] C *om.*  15 lord] 2P *adds* and the aungell  16 and of þe folk] B and of al þe peple; C *om.*  lord] 2P *adds* anon  þer] 2P therfore  17 forbade] C bad  18 tresoun] M trespasse  slow] G2–G5 dide scle  20 Salamon his] QAB Salamones (Q his *in margin*); M kyng Salamon; 2B Salamon þe wyse þat was  22 herte] 2B wylle and hert  24 God] G1 *add* and of þe grace of god  24–26 Wiþoute . . . turtlis] 2C *om.*  26–27 And on . . . Ierusalem] G1 *om.*  26–30 And on . . . Salamon] 2C *om.*  30–35/1 And toward . . . Salamon] M *om.*

Salamon þat is ful fayr and a grete place. And in þat place dwelliþ kniȝtes þat men clepiþ Templeris, and þat was fundacioun of Templeris and of here order. And in þat temple *domini* dwelliþ chanouns.

Fro þis temple toward þe eest at vi. score pas in an hurne of þe cite is þe baþ of oure lord, and þis baaþ was woned [to] go into paradise [and besyde is oure lady bedde]. And nere þer is þe toumbe of seint Symeon. And wiþoute [þe cloystre of] þe temple toward þe norþ is a riȝt faire chirche of seynt Anne oure lady moder þer was oure lady conseyued. And bifore þat chirche is a [grete] tre þat bigan to growe þat same niȝt.

And as men goþ doun fro þat chirche xxii. greez liþ Ioachim oure
f. 47r lady fader in a toumb of stoon. | And þer lay somtyme seynt Anne, but seynt Elyn lete translate hure to Constantynople. In þis chirche is a wel in maner of a cesterne þat is yclepid *probatica pissina* þat hadde fyue entrees. And in þat cesterne was woned an aungel to descende and stere þe water. And what man þat first baþed hym þerynne aftir þe steryng of þe water, he was made hool what sikenesse so he hadde. And þer was þe man [in the palsye] made hole þat was sike xxxviii. ȝere, and þere oure lord seide to hym, *Tolle grabatum tuum et uade*, þat is to say, Take þi bed and go. [And þeire bysyde was þe hous of Pylat.]

And a litel þenne was þe hows of Herode þe kyng þat lete sle þe innocentez. Þis Herode was a fulle wickid man and fel, for he lete sle his wyf þat he loued wel. And for þe grete loue þat he hadde to here when heo was ded, he bihelde here and he went out of his wit [and so was he longe. And sythen he come aȝeyne to his wyt] and þanne he lete slee þe children, þat he hadde gete of here, and þanne he lete slee [þe] oþer [of his wyues] and a sone þat he hadde of here. [And he dide alle þe ille þat he myght.]

1 þat[1]] 2A 2B 2B þes 3 Templeris] 2P *om.* here order] C odir 3–8 And in . . . Symeon] 2C *om.* 5 vi. score] 2P xxvi 6 to] Q *om.* 7 and besyde . . . bedde] G1 *om.* nere] B *om.* 8 þe cloystre of] G1 *om.* 9 þer] M and þere 10 grete] G1 *om.* 11 niȝt] M *adds* þat oure lady was conceyued 13 þer] G2–G5 þeire nere Anne] D *om.* 14 lete] AC *om.* hure] B her tombe 15 *pissina*] Q Pissima 15–16 þat hadde] C þat is to say it had 18–47/7 þe steryng . . . *lapis*] A *out* 18 of þe water] 2A *om.* hool] 2P *adds* that was syke 19 so] C þat euir in the palsye] G1 *om.* 21 say] 2P say in englysshe and go] C *om.* 21–22 And þeire . . . Pylat] G1 2C *om.* 23 þe] QBD þese 24 fulle] 2B foule lete] 2P dyd first and formest 26–27 and so . . . wyt] Q *om.* 27 his wyt] 2A 2P hym selfe 28 lete] C *adds* schamfully þe] 2P his owne children here] 2A 2B 2P þat wyfe 29 þe oþer of his wyues] G1 his oþer wyf 29–30 And he dide . . . myght] G1 2C *om.*

And when he sauȝ þat he | schulde deiȝe he sent for his suster and for alle þe grete lordis of his lond. (f. 47v) And when þei were alle ycome, he lete do alle þe lordis in a tour and seide to his suster, he wist wel þat men of þe lond schulde make no sorwe for hym when he were deed; and þerfore he made here to swere þat heo schulde let smyte of þe hedis of alle þe lordis als soone as he were deed, and þanne schulde alle þe cuntrey make sorwe for his deeþ, and ellis nouȝt. And þus he made his testament. But his suster fulfild not hit for als soone as he was deed heo delyuerid hem out of þe tour and told to hem here broþer wille and lete echon go whar þei wolde.

And ȝe schul vndirstonde þat þer were þre Herodes of grete name, and þes of whom Y spake men clepid Herode Ascolonete. And he þat lete smyte of seynt Ioon baptystis heed was [Heraude] Antipa. And Herode Agrippa let sle seynt Iame.

And ferþermore in þe cite is þe | chirche of þe sauyour, and þer (f. 48r) is þe arm of seynt Ioon Crisostom, and þer ys þe more partye of seynt Steuenys heed. And in þe oþer side toward þe souþ, as men goþ to mount Syon, is a faire chirche of seynt Iame whare his heed was smyte of, and þan is mount Syon. And þer is a faire chirche of God and oure lady whare heo was dwellyng and deyde. And þer was somtyme an abbey of chanouns regulers. And fro þat place was heo bore wiþ þe apostlis to þe vale of Iosephat. [And þere is the stone þat the aungel bere to oure lady fro mont Synay, and it is of þat colour þat þe roche of seynt Kateryne is. And þere bysyde is þe ȝate wheyre oure lady when she was with childe went to Bedlem.]

Also in þe entre of mount Syon is a chapel, and in þat chapel is þe ston grete and large wiþ þe whiche þe sepulcre was keuered whan

1 And] 2B and eueremore deiȝe] CM dy himsilf 2 alle ycome] 2A þeire 5 to] B do þe hedis of alle] CM all þe heddis 7 alle] 2P men of all his deeþ and ellis nouȝt] C him as wele as for hem 8 testament] G1 *add* and deyde hit] C his wyll; M alle hys wylle; 2P *adds* that thynge that parteyned vnto the lordys 9 heo] B *adds* lete and; 2P the lorde hem owt of þe tour] CM lordis hole out of prisuun; G2–G5 alle þe lordes oute of þe toure and sent ilkone home til here houses 10 wille and lete] B wolde that thei were deliuered vcchone wille . . . wolde] 2A 2B wolde have done with hem whar þei wolde] CM þer way 11 þat] G2–G5 *add* in þat tyme 13 of . . . heed] D saynt Ion baptist Heraude] G1 clepid 14 Agrippa] 2B *adds* was he þat Iame] C *adds* of Galis; M *adds* versus. Occidit pueros Herodes Ascolonita. Antipas Herodes baptistam decapitauit. Agrippa Iacobu, Petrumque in carcere trusit 15 And] G2–G5 Also 16 seynt] CD *om.* Crisostom] CM *add* þat men call Iohan wiþ þe gildyn mowþe 22–26 And þere . . . Bedlem] G1 *om.* 23 aungel] 2A *om.* 24 is] 2A *om.* 24–26 And þere . . . Bedlem] 2C *om.* 27–28 þe ston] C a chappel 28 wiþ] B *om.* whiche] C *adds* chapell

Crist was leyd þerynne, whiche stoon þre Maries sauȝ turned vpward when þei come to þe sepulcre. [þare þey founden an angelle þat seyde vnto hem how þat Cryst was rysen from deþe vnto þe lyfe.] And þer is a litel pece of þe pilere to whiche oure lord was bounde and scourgid. And þer was Anne hous þat was byschop of þe Iewis in þat tyme. [And yn þat same place forsooke seynt Petur þryes byfore þat þe cookke crewe.] And þer is a partye of þe table on whiche God f. 48v made his maunde wiþ his disciplys.| [And yet þer ben alle þe vesselles wyþ water. And þare faste by ys þe place whare þat seynt Stephen was ygrauen. And þere ys þe awtere whare þat oure lady herde þe aungelles synge masse.] And þer apperide Crist to his disciplus after his rising [whanne þat þe yates were ischutte] and seide to hem *Pax uobis*, þat is to say, Pees to ȝow. And on þat mount apperid Crist to seynt Thomas and bade him asaye his woundis, and hym trowyd he first and seide, *Dominus meus et deus meus*, þat is to say, My lord and my God.

In þat same chapel bihynde þe hiȝe autre were alle þe apostlis on whit sonday when þe holi goost descendid on hem in likenes of fuyre, and þer God [mad his] *pas*ke wiþ his disciplis. And þer slepte seynt Ioon þe euangelist in oure lordis kne and sauȝ slepyng many priue þingis of heuen.

þe mount Syon is wiþynne þe cite, and it is a litel heiȝer þan þe oþer side of þe cite. And þe cite is strenger on þat side þan on anoþer side, for at þe foot of mount Syon is a faire castel and strong. On mount Syon was kyng Dauid and Salamon and oþer many yburied. And þer is a place whare seynt Peter grette ful tenderly when he hadde forsaken Crist. [And a stone caste from þat chapelle ys anoþer chapelle whare þat oure lord was iuggyde, for þat tyme was þare Kayphasys hous.] And bytwene temple Salamon and þe mount | f. 49r Syon is þe place whar Crist rerid þe mayde fro deeþ to lyf.

Vndir þe mount Syon toward þe vale of Iosephat is a welle þat

1–40/31 whiche . . . þe day] 2A *out* 1–3 whiche stoon . . . lyfe] 2C *om.* 1 Maries] 2P Iewes 2–3 þare . . . lyfe] G1 *om.* 4 litel] CM *om.* 4–5 bounde and] C 2P *om.* 5 Anne] CDM 2B an was] D *om.* 6–7 And in . . . crewe] G1 *om.* bifore . . . crewe] 2C *om.* 8 wiþ his disciplys] 2C *om.* 8–11 And yet . . . masse] G1 2C *om.* 9 faste] 2P *om.*; G3–G5 nere 10 lady] G3–G5 lord 11–12 And þer . . . disciplus] C *om.* 11 Crist] D *om.* 12 whanne . . . ischutte] G1 *om.* 13 to hem] 2P *om.* 15 hym] CM *om.* he] BD *om.* 19 made his paske] QBD spake slepte] C wrot 20 lordis] D *om.*; C ladiis kne] M brest slepyng] B *om.* 21 priue þingis of heuen] C þingis 24 þe foot of] C *om.* 25 many] B *adds* peple were 27–29 And a stone . . . hous] G1 *om.* 27 chapelle] 2P *om.* 29–30 And bytwene . . . lyf] 2C *om.*

men clepiþ þere *Natatoyr Sylo*. þer was oure lord waische after þat he was baptized. And þer nere is þe tre on whiche Iudas hongid hymself [for despeyre] when he hadde sold Crist. And þanne is þe synagoge whare þe byschop of þe Iewis and *F*arasy*e*s come togidre to holde here counseyls. And þer Iudas kest þe xxxti. pans bifore hem and seide, *Peccaui tradens sanguinem iustum*, þat is to say, I haue ysynned deseyuyng riȝtwys blood.

And on anoþer side of mount Syon toward þe souþ at a stones cast is þe feld þat was bouȝt wiþ xxxti. pans, and it ys yclepid Acheldemak, þat is to say, Feeld of Blood. And þer beþ [many tombes of crysten men, for þere ben many] pilgrimes buried. And also in Ierusalem toward þe west is a faire chirche whare þe tree grew of whiche þe cros was made to oure lord. And þer nere is a faire chirche whare oure lady mette wiþ Elizabeth when þei | were boþe (f. 49v) wiþ childe, and seynt Ion sterid in his moder body and made worschipe to oure lord his makere. [And vnder þe awtere of þat churche ys a place whare þat seynt Iohan was boren] and þer nere is þe castel of Emaux.

And ii. myle fro Ierusalem is þe mount Ioiȝe þat is a faire place and likyng. And þer liþ Samuel þe prophete in a faire toumbe. And it ys yclepid mount Ioiȝe for þere pilgrimes may first se to Ierusalem, of whiche siȝt þei haue grete ioiȝe aftir here traueyl. And in þe myddel of þe vale of Iosephat is a litel ryuer þat is clepid *torrens Cedron*. And ouer þis ryuere lay a tree, of whiche þe crosse was made, þat men ȝeode on ouer þe ryuere. Also in þat vale is a chirch of oure lady, and þere is þe sepulcre of oure lady. And oure lady was of elde when heo deide lxxii. ȝere.

And þer nere is þe place whare oure lord forȝaf seynt Petre alle his synnes. And nere þer is a chapel whare Iudas kissed oure lord þat men clepiþ Gessemayn, and þere was he take of þe Iewis. And þere left Crist his disciplis bifore his passioun whenne he went to | praye (f. 50r) and seide, *Pater si fieri potest transeat a me calix iste*, þat is to say,

2 tre] 2P tere  on whiche] Q þat on whiche; B that  3 for despeyre] G1 2C *om.* 4 Iewis] C Ievis lawe  Farasyes] QBD 2P Sarasyns  8 at] CM well  9 pans] 2P *adds* for when cryst was solde  yclepid] C *adds* þer wiþ þe pepull; D *adds* there 10 þer] 2P in that felde  10–11 many . . . many] G1 *om.*  11 And] C *om.* 13 cros] 2B holy cros  to oure lorde] 2B 2P *om.*  14 mette] B *om.*  16–17 And vnder . . . boren] G1 *om.*; 2C And þer was seynt Iohan ybore  17 nere] B *om.* 21 may] 2P *om.*  22 of whiche . . . traueyl] G2–G5 *om.*  siȝt] C staff þat is to say siȝt here] M *adds* grete  25 þe ryuere] G2–G5 *om.*  28–29 alle his synnes] C his trespas; 2P *adds* and mysdedis that he had done  29–41/15 And nere . . . lord] 2P *out*

Fader if it may be doon, lete þis chaleys go fro me. [And þare fasteby ys a chapelle þere þat oure lord swette blood and watur.]

And þer nere is þe toumbe of kyng Iosephat, of whom þat vale toke his name. And on a side of þat vale is þe mounte Olyuete, and hit is yclepid so for þere growiþ monye olyues þare. And hit is heiȝere þan Ierusalem, and þerfore fro þen men may se into þe stretis of Ierusalem. And bitwene þat hulle and þe cite is not but þe vale of Iosephat, and þat is noȝt ful large. And vpon þat hulle stode oure lord whenne he wente to heuene, and ȝyt semeþ þe stappes of his lyft fote on þe stone.

And þere is an abbey of blake chanouns [þat was somtyme but ryȝt now ys þare but a churche]. And a litel þenne xxviii. paas is a chapel, and þer is þe stoon on whiche oure lord sate and prechid to þe folk seying þus, *Beati pauperes spiritu quoniam ipsorum est regnum celorum*, þat is to say, Blessid be þei þat beþ pore in spiryt [for] hare is þe kyngdome of heuene. And þere he tauȝt his disciplis al þe *pater* | f. 50v *noster*. [And þare bysydes ys a churche of seynt Marye Gypcyane and þare schee lyþe] and [þre bowschetys] is Be*s*fage fro when[s] oure lord sent seynt Petir to fecche an asse on Palme Soneday. And þer toward þe eest is a chapel þat men clepiþ Bethanya. Þer dwellid Symeon þe leprose þat herburwid oure lord and hem þat were baptized of his disciplis, and he was yclepid Iulian. And þat was he þat men clepiþ on for good herburȝ, and he was a byschop.

In þat same place oure lord forȝaf Marie Mawdeleyne here synnes, and þer heo woische his feet wiþ teeris of here iȝen and dried hem wiþ here heer. And þer was Lazar rerid fro deeþ to lyf, þe whiche was deed foure dayes in his graue stynking. And þer is þat place whar oure lady [apperede] to seynt Thomas [and yafe hym] here gurdel aftir hire assumpsioun. [And þare fastby ys þe stoon þare þat oure lord sate on ofte and prechede, and þare vppon schall he sytte at þe day of dome, as hymselfe seyde.] And þer nere is þe mount Galile whare þe apostlis were [gederyde] whenne Marie Mawdeleyn tolde

1–2 And þare . . . watur] G1 2C *om.* 5 so] M *om.* þare] M *om.* þerfore] BM *om.* 6 þen] 2B þat hylle 6–7 and þerfore . . . Ierusalem] G2–G5 *om.* 8 noȝt] D *om.* 9 wente] C stud; M assendyd 10 fote] C *adds* as he stod 11 chanouns] M monkys 11–12 þat was . . . churche] G1 *om.* 13 oure lord] D *om.* 15 for] Q of 17–18 And þare . . . lyþe] G1 2C *om.* 18 þre bowschetys] G1 a litel þenne Besfage] G1 þe Beffage (C balage; D besfage) whens] Q when 19 an asse] 2C *blank* 23 good] C *om.*; 2B goddes loue 28 apperede . . . hym] G1 ȝaf to seynt Thomas (C ȝaf to hir sunis dissipulis seint Thomas) 29–31 And þare . . . seyde] G1 *om.* 32 whare] C *adds* all hem of Cristis risyng fro deeþ. And bitwene mount Olyuet and mount Galile is a chirche whare þe aungel seide to oure lady of her deeþ.

Also fro Bethanye to Ierico ys | f. 51r v. myle. Ierico was somtyme a litel cite, but it is wastid and so is þer now but a litel toun. [Þat towne toke Iosue þorgh myracle of God and byddyng of þe aungele and distroyed it and cursede alle þois þat biggyd it aȝeyne.] Of þis cite was Raab þe comyn womman þat resseyued þe messyngeris of Israel and kepte hem fro many periles and fro deeþ. And þerfore heo was rewardid as holy writ seiþ, *Qui accipit prophetam in nomine meo mercedem prophete accipiet*, þat is to say, He þat takiþ a prophete in my name, he schal take mede of þe prophete.

Also fro Bethanye men goþ to flom Iordan þurȝ wildernesse, and it is nere a daies iourne [bytwene. Towarde þe est vnto a grete hille] whare oure lord fast fourty dayes, and þe fend of helle [bare Cryste and] seyde to hym þus, *Dic ut lapides isti panes fiant*, þat is to say, Seie þat þese stoones be made loofes. And þer is an heremytage whare dwelliþ a manere of cristen men þat beþ yclepid Georgiens, for seynt George conuertide hem. And vpon þat hulle dwellide Abraham a gret while. Also as men goþ to Ierico in þe way sate sike men criyng, *Ihesu fili Dauid miserere mei*, | f. 51v þat is to say, Ihesu Dauid sone haue mercy on me. [Also two myle fro Ierico is flome Iordane.]

And ȝe schal vndirstonde þat þe Deed See departiþ þe lond of Iudee and of Arabye, and þat lastiþ fro Sora to Arabye. And þe water of þe see is ful bitter [and þis watire castis oute a þynge þat men calle *aspaltum* als grete peces als a hors. And Ierusalem is cc. furlongys fro þis see.] And hit is yclepid þe Deede See for yt renneþ nouȝt. And no man noþer beest [þat has lyfe] may deiȝe þerynne, and þat haþ be oft assayed. And þei caste þerynne men þat beþ iuggid to deeþ, and it castiþ hem out aȝen. And no man may dwelle nere it ne drinke of þe water. And if men castiþ yren þerynne it comeþ vp aȝen, and if men caste a feþer þerynne hit synkeþ to þe grounde; and þat is aȝens

1 deeþ] CM *add* to lif   2 lady] M *adds* that tyme was come   5–7 þat towne . . . aȝeyne] G1 *om.*   7 þis] 2A 2B þat   9 and] 2A *om.*   9–10 was rewardid] G2–G5 hade a goode rewarde   11 He] B *om.*   þat²] D *om.*   12 schal] C may and schall   14 bytwene Towarde . . . hille] G1 fro þen   15–16 bare Cryste and] G1 *om.*; 2C temptid and   17 Seie] 2P *om.*   an heremytage] C brennit   18 whare dwelliþ] CM and þare be   19 And] C and also   20 Abraham] C Adam and Abraham also   sike] 2P many sicke   22 me] 2P vs   Also . . . Iordane] G1 *om.*   24 Iudee] 2P Indee   and þat . . . Arabye] G2–G5 *om.*   þat] 2A 2B þat see   25–27 and þis . . . see] G1 *om.*   28 þat has lyfe] G1 *om.*   deiȝe] G2–G5 lyffe   29–30 and it . . . aȝen] G2–G5 *om.*

kynde. [And so werre þe citees þat were þeire loste for synnes aȝeyne kynde.]

And þer sanke þese fyue citez for synne aȝens kynde: Sodom, Gomorre, Aldema, Segor, Solome [for þe synne of sodome þat regned in hem]. But Segor þurȝ preiere of Loth was saued a grete while for it sate on an hul, and ȝit apperiþ myche þerof aboue þe watir [and men may see þe walles] in clere wedir.

And þer growiþ trees þat beriþ fruyt [of] a faire colour and semeþ f. 52r ripe, but when a man brekiþ hem oþer kittiþ | hem, he fyndeþ nouȝt but coles or askes in tokene þat þurȝ veniaunce of God þese citees were brent wiþ firre of helle. And somme clepiþ þat see þe lake of Alsiled [and some calle it þe flome of þe deuyle] and some þe stinkyng flom, for þe watir is stynkyng.

[And there Looth dwellyd a grete while and was made dronkyn of his doghtirs and ley by hem for þei trowed that God schold haue distroyede alle þe werlde als he dide with Noe flode. And þerfore ley þei by here fadire fore men scholde be borne of heme into þe werlde. And if he had noght ben dronken he had noght lyne by heme.] And at þe riȝt side of þis see dwelliþ Lothis wyf a stoon of salt, for heo lookid aȝen when þese citeez sank.

And ȝe schal vndirstonde þat Abraham hadde a sone þat men clepid Isaac, and he was circumcidid when he was of viii. daies old. And he hadde anoþer sone þat me clepid Ismael, and he was circumcidid at xiiii. ȝere old. And þei were boþe circumcidid vpon o day. And þerfore þe Iewys gan circumside hem at viii. dayes and þe Sarasyns [do circumside hem] at xiiii. ȝere.

And into þe *D*eede See renneþ þe flom Iordan and þer endiþ. And þis flom is no riȝt [grete] ryuere, but þer is myche good fysch ynne. And hit comeþ fro mount Lybany fro twey wellis þat men clepiþ Ior f. 52v and Dane, and of hem he takiþ his name. And on þe | o side of þis

1–2 And so . . . kynde] G1 2P *om.* 3–7 And þer . . . wedir] G2–G5 *after* water 13 3 synne aȝens kynde] 2A 2P wreche of god; 2B wreþe of god 4–5 for þe synne . . . in hem] G1 *om.* 6 apperiþ] M *adds* and schewith 7 and men may see þe walles] G1 *om.* 8 of] QBD and 9 nouȝt] CM no þing þere in 11 see] 2A lake 12 Alsided] M alle fylþehed; 2A alle Alphedde; 2B 2P Alphytedde; 2C alle fetida (see Appendix 5) 12 and som . . . deuyle] G1 *om.* some[2]] G1 some clepiþ hit 12–13 þe stinkyng] D þat see *blank* 13 for þe watir is stynkyng] M *om.* 14–18 And there . . . by heme] G1 *om.* 19 Lothis wyf] B Loth on; C Lothe and þer is wyf turnid to 20 þese citeez] 2A 2B 2P þe cite 23–25 And he had . . . o day] G2–G5 *after* dayes l. 8 23 me] 2A 2B 2P he 24 And þei were boþe] 2P whan he was boþe] C not 26 do circumside hem] G1 *om.* ȝere] CM *add* of age 27 Deede] QBCDM reede 28 grete] G1 *om.* good] CM *om.*

ryuere is þe mount Gelboe and þer is a faire playn. And on þat oþer side men goþ by mount Liban to þe desert of Pharao. þis hullis departiþ þe kingdome of Surrie and þe cuntrie of *F*ynes. On þat [hill] growiþ cedris þat beriþ long applis þat beoþ as grete as a mannus hed.

þis flom Iordan departiþ Galile and þe lond of Ydumee and þe lond of Botron, and it renneþ into a playn þat men clepiþ Meldane in Sermoys. And in þat playne is þe temple Ioob. In þis flom Crist was baptized, and þer was herd þe vois of þe fader seiyng, *Hic est filius meus dilectus in quo michi bene complacuit. Ipsum audite*, þat is to say, Here is my sone þat Y loue, in wham I am wel payed. Huryeþ hym. And þe holi goost descendid on hym in likenesse of a dowfe, and so was þer in his baptisyng alle þe trinite.

And þurȝ þat flom Iordan passide þe children of Israel alle drie, and þei sette stones in myddel of þe water in tokne of myracle. And also in þat flom Naa|man of Syre baþed hym þat was a mesel, and he f. 53r was heelid þere. [And a lytylle þeire fro is þe cite of Hay, whiche Iosue asaylede and toke.] Also in þe [entree of] flom Iordan is þe vale of Mambre þat is a faire vale and plenteuouse.

## CHAPTER 8 þE CASTEL OF CARRAS AND OþERE

And ȝe schal vndirstonde þat for to go fro þe Deede See estward out of þe marche of þe lond of promyssioun is a strong castel þat men clepiþ Carras in Sermoys, þat is to say, *Real Mount* [in Frensche]. þis castel lete a kyng of Fraunce make, þat men clepen Bawdewyne, þat hadde wonne al þat londe and put hit into cristen men hondis to kepe. And vndir þat castel is a faire toun þat men clepiþ Gabaoth. þer aboute dwelliþ many cristen men vndir tribute.

And þanne men goþ to Nazareth, of whiche oure lord hadde his

3 Fynes] QBD vynes; G2 Phenys 4 hill] QB cuntre; D *om.* cedris] 2B ful fayre cedres; 2C seedes and beoþ] 2B *adds* y wote ryȝt wel 6 and[2]] C in 8 flom] C forme; G2–G5 *add* Iordan 9 þe vois of] 2B *om.* 11 Y] M *adds* welle 13 trinite] 2B tyme 15 of[1]] 2P of greate And] BCD *om.* 16 þat] 2A *om.* Naaman] CM a man 17–18 And a lytylle . . . toke] G1 *om.* 18 entree of] G1 *om.*; C ouer side of; M oo syde of 19 plenteouse] CM *add* of Carras and oþere castels *and om. rubric* 22 estward] 2P afterwarde 23 marche] M marches and owte 24 in] G2 or (see Appendix 6) *Real*] D *om.* 24–25 in Frensche] QBD *om.* 26 hadde] M *om.* 27 to kepe] C *om.* 29–44/1 of whiche . . . Ierusalem] 2A *om.*

twoname. And fro Nazareth to Ierusalem is iii. iourneys. And men goþ þurȝ þe prouynce of Galile, þurȝ Ramatha, þurȝ Sophym, and by þe hiȝe hulle of Effraym whar Anna Samuelis moder þe prophete was dwellyng, [and þeire was þis prophete borne. And aftre his deþe he was grauen atte mont Ioye, als I haue sayde.]

f. 53v And þanne comeþ men to Sybola whar þe | arke of God was kepid vndir Ely þe prophete. Þere made þe folk of Ebron sacrifise to oure lord, and þer spake oure lord first to Samuel, [and þeire mynystryde Gode þe sacrament]. And þer nere at þe lyft side is Sabon and Rama Beniamyn, of whom holy writ spekiþ.

[And þanne comys men to Sychem, þat some men calles Sichare. Þis is in þe prouynce of Samaritanes, and þeire was sometyme a chirche bot it was casten doune. And it is a faire vale and a plentyouse, and þeire is a goode citee þat men calle Neople. And from þens is on dayes iourne to Ierusalem and þeire is þe welle wheire oure lord spake to þe womman Samaritane.]

And þe cite of Sychym ys x. myle fro Ierusalem, and it is yclepid Neople [þat is to say, Newe Toune]. And þer nere is þe temple Iosophe þat was Iacobis sone þat gouerned Egipt, for fro þenne were his bones brouȝt and leyd in þe temple. [And þiþere come Iewes ofte in pilgrymage wiþ grete deuocion.] And in þat cite was Iacobs douȝter raueisched, for whom hire broþer slowe many men. And þer nere is þe cite of Garrisoun whare Sa[ma]re*t*yns makiþ here sacrifice. [In þis hylle wolde Abraham haue sacrified his sone Isaac.] And þer nere is þe vale of Dotaym, and þer is þe cesterne whare Ioseph was casten of his breþeren bifore þey solde hym. [And it is two myle to Sycar.]

Fro þenne men goþ to Samary þat men clepiþ Sebast, and þat is þe chef cite of þat cuntre. And of þat cite was þe xii. kyn*d*is of Israel, but it is not so grete as it was. Þer was seynt Ioon baptyst graue
f. 54r bitwene þis twey prophetis Heliseus and Abdon, bo|te he was bihedid in þe castel of Makayne biside þe Deede See. And [he was

1 twoname] CM 2P name   3 by] C betwene   þe prophete] 2B he   4–5 and þeire . . . sayde] G1 *om.*   5 I] 2A *om.*   6 arke] 2B whyche or chest or ark   kepid] M *adds* and   8 and] M *om.*   8–9 and þeire . . . sacrament] G1 2C *om.*   9 nere] B *om.*   Rama] G1 Rama and   11–16 And þanne . . . Samarytane] G1 *om.*   14–18 And from . . . Neople] 2A *om.*   15–18 and þeire . . . Newe Toune] 2C *om.*   17 And þe cite of] 2P *om.*   18 þat is . . . Toune] G1 *om.*   20–21 And þiþere . . . deuocion] G1 *om.*   23 Samaretynes] QBD Sarasyns   24 In þis . . . Isaac] G1 *om.*   26–27 And it . . . Sycar] G1 *om.*   29 kyndis] G1 (*ex* M) 2A kyngis; M kynredys; 2P kyndnes   32–45/1 he was . . . grauene ate] G1 his disciples bare hym into

translated of his disiples and grauene at] Samarie but þer lete Iulius Apostata take his boones and brenne hem, for he was in þat tyme emperour. But þe fynger wiþ whiche seint Ioon schewid oure lord seiyng, *Ecce agnus dei*, þat is to say, Bihold þe lombe of God, miȝt not be brend, and seynt Tecle þe virgine lete bere it in þe hullis and þer was do grete worschip þerto.

þer was þe heed of seynt Ioon closed in a wal, but þe emperour Theodosius lete take hit out, and he fond hit lappid in clooþ al blody and so lete he bere hit to Constantynople. And þer is ȝit þe on half of þe heed, and þat oþer half is at Rome in þe chirche of seint Siluestre. And þe vessel in which his hed was leid ynne when it was ysmyte of is at Geene, and men [of Geene] do to it grete worschipe þare. Somme men seiþ þat seynt Ioones hed is at Ameas in Pykardy, and somme seiþ þat hit was | [f. 54v] þe hed of seynt Ioon þe byschop. I wot nouȝt, but God woot.

Fro Sebast to Ierusalem is xii. myle. And bitwene þe hullis of þis cuntre is a welle þat men clepiþ *fons Iacob*, þat is to say, Iacobys welle. Hit chaungiþ his colouris foure tymes in þe ȝere, for somtyme hit is reed, somtyme clere, and somtyme þicke.

And men þat dwelliþ þere beþ yclepid Samaritans, and þei were conuertid þurȝ þe apostlis. And here lawe varieþ fro cristen lawe, Sarasyns lawe, Iewis lawe, and payems lawe. þei trowe wel in a god þat al schal deme, and þei trowe þe bible aftir þe lettre. And þei lappe here heed in reed lynnen clooþ to be knowe fro oþer, for Sarasyns lappiþ here in whyt cloþ, and cristen men [þat] dwelle þere in blewe cloþ, and Iewis in in ȝolewe clooþ, for þere dwelliþ many Iewis paiyng tribute as cristen men dooþ.

And if ȝe wole wite þe lettris, þei beþ siche in þe names of þe lettris as þei clepiþ hem: *alph*, *beth*, *gimel*, *he*, *vau*, *ȝay*, *ex*, *ioth*, *karph*, *lamp*, | [f. 55r] *meu*, *nun*, *samech*, *ey*, *phe*, *lad*, *corth*, *fir*, *soun*, *thau*, *lours*. Now shal ȝe haue þe figures of þe Iewis lettre. . . . . . . . . . .

And fro þis cuntre þat I haue spoke of men goþ þurȝ [þe pleyne

3 seint Ioon] 2P he  schewid] CM *add* to  5–7 it in þe hullis . . . þer was] 2P *om.*  5 hullis] 2A 2B mont  8 out] 2B *adds* and þare ys yet þe on halfe  lappid] M *om.*  11 leid] M *om.*  12 of Geene] G1 *om.*  17 *fons*] 2B *om.*  18 Hit] CM this well  foure] C iii  19 is] 2P was  22 lawe[4]] 2P that  23 þei trowe] M also  24–25 in reed . . . lappiþ] 2B *om.*  24 to be knowe from oþer] C 2B *om.*; G2–G5 (*ex* 2B) for differens of oþer  for] C and  25 whyt] 2A white lynen  þat] QD *om.*  þat dwelle þere] B *om.*  26–28 many Iewis . . . siche] B *om.*  27 paiyng] M panymes  28 ȝe] D 2P thay  siche] 2B *adds* þay ben ful wonderful  in] 2A 2B 2P and  7 of þe Iewis lettre] 2A 2B 2C *om.* (for the characters see frontispiece; for variants see Appendix 7)  32 þurȝ] 2A 2B 2P to  32–46/1 þe pleyne of] G1 *om.*

of] Galile and leueþ þe hullis at þe on syde. And Galile is of þe prouynce of þe lond of promyssioun. And in þat prouynce is þe lond of Nay*me* and Capharnaum and Corosaym and Bethsayda. And of Bethsayda was seynt Petir ybore and seynt Andrew also. And of Corosaym schal Auntecrist be bore, and somme seiþ he schal be bore in Babiloyne. And þerfore seiþ þe prophete þus, *De Babilonia exiet columba que totum mundum deuorabit*, þat is to say, Of Babiloyne schal a dowfe come out þat schal swolewe al þe world. And þis Auntecrist schal be norischid in Bethsayda and he schal regne in Corosaym. And þerfore seiþ holy writ of hem þus, *Ue tibi Corosayme, Ue tibi Bethsayda, Ue tibi Capharnaum*, þat is to say, Woo be to þee f. 55v Corosaym, | Woo be to þee Bethsayda, Woo be to þee Capharnaum. And þe Chane of Galilee is þer also iiii. myle fro Nazareth. [Of þat cite was þe womman of Chananee of whom þe gospelle spekys.] And þere oure lord did þe first myracle at þe weddyng of Archedeclyne when he turnyd water into wyn.

And fro þenne men goþ to Nazareth, þat was somtyme a grete cite but now is þer but a litel toun and it is noȝt wallid. And þere was oure lady bore, but heo was ygete in Ierusalem. Of Nazareth toke oure lord his twoname. And þer Ioseph weddid oure lady when heo was xiiii. ȝere old. And þe aungel Gabriel saluted oure lady Marie seiyng þus to here, *Aue Marie gracia plena dominus tecum*, þat is to say, Hail Marie ful of grace, God is wiþ þee. [And þeire was sommetyme a grete chirche, and now is þeire bot a lytylle closet to resseyue þe offerande of pilgrymes.] And þer *is* þe wel of Gabriel whare oure lord was ywoned to baþe hym when he was litel. At Nazareth was oure lord ynorischid. Nazareth is to say floure of gardyne, and hit may wel be clepid so for þer was norischid þe flour of lyf þat was Crist.

f. 56r At half a myle | fro Nazareth is þe blood of oure lord, for Iewis lad hym vpon an hiȝe roche to cast hym doun to haue slawe hym, but he

1 and leueþ . . . Galile] C *om.* of[1]] CM *om.* 3 Nayme] QBD Naynce And of] B at 11 *Ue tibi Capharnum*] M G2–G5 *om.* 12 Woo[2] . . . Capharnum] M G2–G5 *om.* 13 Chane] CDM 2C caue 13–14 Of þat . . . spekys] G1 *om.* 14 of Chananee] 2A Comanee 15 did þe first myracle] G1 schewid þe first myracle þat he dide 19 but heo . . . Ierusalem] 2A 2P *om.*; 2B *after* twoname 20 twoname] CM name 21 Gabriel] 2A 2B 2P *om.* oure lady Marie] 2A 2B 2P hir 22 to here] 2B *om.* 23–25 And þeire . . . pilgrymes] G1 *om.*; C *adds Latin translation* et quondam ibi exat magna ecclesia set iam non est vna parua capella ad resipiendum obaciones peregrinorum 24 closet] 2B clocher 25 is] G1 was somtyme 29 Crist] C *adds* himsilfe; 2A Ihesu cruste; 2P oure lorde Iesu cryst 31–47/1 he passid] D *om.*; 2A 2P Ihesu cryste passed

passid þurȝ hem and leope on a roche whare his steppis beþ ȝit sene. And þerfore seiþ somme men whanne þei haue drede of þeofis oþer of enemys þes vers þat is here ywrite, *Ihesus autem transiens per medium illorum ibat*, þat is to say, Ihesu forsoþe passyng ȝeode þurȝ þe myddel of hem. And þei seiþ also þes vers of þe sautere [þre tymes], *Irruat super eos formido et pauor in magnitudine brachii tui, domine. Fiant inmobiles quasi lapis donec pertranseat populus tuus domine et populus iste quem redemisti*, þat is to say, Falle on hem drede in þe gretnes of þyn arm, lord. Be þei made not stirand as a stoon vnto þat tyme þat þi folk passe, lord, and þis folk þat þou bouȝtist. And when þis is yseid a man may go wiþoute ony lettyng.

And ȝe schal vndirstonde þat oure lady hadde child when heo was xv. ȝere | old, and heo lyued wiþ hym xxxiii. ȝere and iii. monþis and f. 56v
aftir his passioun heo lyued xxiiii. ȝere.

And fro Nazareth to mount Tabor is iii. myle, and þere oure lord transfigurid hym bifore seynt Peter, seynt Ioon, and seynt Iame, and þere þey sauȝ oure lord gastelich and Moyses and Ely þe prophete biside hem. And þerfore seide seynt Petir, *Bonum hic esse faciamus tria tabernacula*, þat is to say, It is good to be here, make we þre tabernaclis. And Crist bade hem þat þei schulde seye it to no man vnto þat tyme þat he were arise fro deeþ to lyf. And on þat same hulle schal [iiii.] aungels blowe here trumpis and arere alle men þat beþ deede to lyf, and þei schal come in bodi and soule to þe dome. But þe dome schal be on þe vale of Iosephat vpon Ester Day at siche a tyme as oure lord aros fro deeþ.

And a myle fro mounte Tabor is þe mount Ermon, and þer was þe cite of Na*ym*. Bifore þe ȝatis of þat cite oure lord arerid þe widewe sone | þat hadde nama children. And fro þenne men goþ to a cite þat f. 57r
men clepiþ Tibourne, þat sittiþ on þe see of Galile. And if al it be clepid see of Galile, hit is no see ne arm of þe see for it is but a [stange] of freisch water. And hit is nere an hundrid furlongis long

3 enemys] CM þere enimmis þes verse þat is here ywrite] M þis vers; 2A *om.*; 2B 2P þay seyen þus here] B *om.* 4–5 þat is . . . hem] G2–G5 *om.* 5–6 þre tymes] QBD *om.*; C ii timis 8 et] 2B *adds* donec pertrseat 8–11 þat is . . . bouȝtist] G2–G5 *om.* 10 lord] AC *om.* þat tyme þat] CM *om.* 11 wiþoute] Q wiþ oute oute 12 oure] 2P oure blessed 13 xxxiii.] 2A 2P xxii; 2B xxiiii 13–14 and iii . . . ȝere] D *om.* 13 iii.] CM ii 14 his passioun] C þis xxiiii. ȝere] C xiiii ȝere all hole; 2P xxii yere 18 biside hem] AC biside him; 2P *om.* 19 we] M we here 20 Crist] 2P oure lord iesu cryst þat þei schulde] D *om.* 22 iiii.] QABD þre 24 But] C for 26 And] AD also a] 2A ii 27 Naym] QBD 2A 2P Namy; C *adds* and 28 nama] M ix 31 stange] QBD ryuere; 2B lytel ryuere; 2P staumble

and fourty broode, and þer is yn many goode fyschis. And on þat same [see]—but hit chaungiþ þe name after þe citeez þat stondiþ þereupon—ȝeode oure lord drie foote. And þere he seide to seint Petir whenne he come on þe watir and was nere drenchid, and he seide, *Modice fidei quare dubitasti?* þat is to say, þou of litel feiþ why haddest þou doute?

In þis cite of Tybourne is þe table of whiche Crist ete wiþ his disciplis aftir his rising [and þei knewe hym in brekynge of brede als] holy writ seiþ þus, *Et cognouerunt eum in fractione panis*, þat is to say, And þei knewe hym in brekyng of breed.

And ȝe schal vndirstonde þat þe flom Iordan bigynneþ vndir þe f. 57v hulle of Libane, and þere bi|gynneþ þe lond of promyssioun þat lastiþ into Bersabee toward þe norþ and þe souþ. And hit is nere ix. score myle of lengþe, and of brede it lastiþ fro Ierico to Iaffe, and þat is fourty myle. [And ȝe schulle vnderstonde þat þe londe of promyssioun is in þe kyngdome of Surry and hit lastys to the wildernesse of Arabye.]

And ȝe schal vndirstonde þat among Sarasyns in many placis dwelliþ cristene men vndir tribute. And þei beþ of dyuerse maneris [and dyuers maners of monkis, and þei are alle crystenede and haue dyuers lawes], but þei alle trowe welle in God þe fadir and in þe sone and in þe holi goost. But ȝit þei faile in þe articlis of oure treuþe. And þei beþ yclepid Iacobynes for seynt Iame turned hem. And seynt Ioon baptized hem, [and] þei say þat men schal onely to God and noȝt to man schryue hem, for þei say þat God bade noȝt a man schriue hym to anoþer. And þerfore seiþ Dauid in þe sautere, *Confitebor tibi domine in toto corde meo*, þat is to say, I schal schryue me to þee, lord, in al myn herte. And in anoþer place he seiþ þus, *Delictum meum tibi cognitum feci*, þat is to say, My trespace I haue f. 58r made knowe to | þee. And in anoþer place he seiþ þus, *Deus meus es tu et confitebor tibi*, þat is to say, þou art my lord and Y schal ben schryue to þee. And in anoþer place he seiþ þus, *Quoniam cogitacio*

2 see] QABD *om.* 2–3 but hit . . . þereupon] 2C *om.*; A *adds* and on þat same see 2 þat stondiþ] 2B of Scandes 4 and was nere drenchid] C he dowtid and seid mersy nere] B not and he] M owre lord; G1 *add* toke hym by þe hond and 5 seide] A *om.* 8 and þei . . .brede als] G1 of whiche etyng (C wrytyng) 13 Bersabee] M *adds* both; 2A 2B 2P *add* of lengh to go is] C *adds* nyȝe 14 lengþe] 2A 2B 2C brede lastiþ] 2P *om.* and þat] 2P *om.* 15–17 And ȝe . . . Arabye] G1 2C *om.* 20–21 and dyuers . . . lawes] G1 *om.* 21 God] 2A god in 22 ȝit] 2A *om.* 24 Ioon] QABD Ioon baptyst and] G1 for schal] 2B *adds* knele 26–28 And in . . . þee] A *om.* 28, 30 he seiþ þus] 2A 2B 2P *om.* 31 And] M and also

*hominis confitebitur tibi*, þat is to say, For þouȝt of man schal be schryue to þee.

And þei kunne wel þe bible and þe sautere [bot þei alegge hit noght yn Latyne bot in þeire owen langgage, and sas þat Dauid and oþere prophetes says it]. And seynt Austyn and seynt Gregore seiþ, *Qui scelera sua cogitat et conuersus fuerit veniam sibi credat*, þat is to say, Who so knowiþ his synnes and is turned he may trowe to haue forȝeuenes. And seynt Gregore seiþ in þis manere, *Dominus pocius mentem quam verba considerat*, þat is to say, Oure lord takiþ more heede to þouȝt þan to word. And Hillary seiþ þus, *Longorum temporum crimina in ictu oculi perient si corde nata fuerit contempcio*, þat is to say, Synnes þat beþ do of long tyme schal perische in þe twynkelyng of an iȝe if dispising of hem be bore in herte.

And for þese auctoritees þei saye þat men schal | schryue hem al f. 58[v] oonliche to God and not to man. And þis was þe schrift in olde tyme, but seynt Petir and oþer apostlis and popes þat come siþen haue ordeyned it þat man schal schryue hem to prestis, men as þei beoþ. And þis is here skile; for þei seiþ þat men may nouȝt do gode medicyne to a man þat is sike but ȝif þei knowe þe kynde of þe sikenesse, and so say þei þat men may ȝeue no couenable penaunce but if he knowe þe synne; for a maner of synne is more greuous to a man þan to anoþer, and in somme place more þan in anoþer, and in somme tyme more þan in anoþer, and þerfore it is nedeful þat men knowe þe [kynde of þe] synne.

And þer beþ oþer þat men clepiþ Surryens. Þei holde þe lawe of Greces, and þei haueþ longe berdis. And þer beþ oþer þat men clepiþ Georgienz, þe whiche seynt George conuertyd. And þei do more worschipe to þe halewis in heuen þan oþer do, and þei haueþ crownus schaue, þe | clerkis haue rounde crownes and lewid men f. 59[r] haueþ crownus square. And þey holde þe lawe of Grekis. And oþer beþ þere þat beþ yclepide cristen men of girdyng, for þei were

1 For] CM forsowthe 3–5 bot þei . . . it] G1 *om.* 4–5 and sas . . . it] 2C *om.* 5 And] 2P But seiþ] D 2A *add* thus 8 in þis manere] M *adds* also; 2A 2B 2P thus 10 And] 2A *adds* seynt 11 *contempcio*] M intencio; 2P temptatio 12 þat beþ do] M *om.* 13 in] G2–G5 in a mans 14 And] G2–G5 and þus for þese auctoritees] G2–G5 *after* God 15 and not to man] G2–G5 *om.* olde] G2–G5 fyrste 17 it] ABM *om.* prestis] M *adds* þat ben 18 here] CM *add* resuun and gode] CM no 20 þei] 2B and eke þay say couenable] CM resonable 21 knowe] 2P knowethe and vnderstonde 22 and in somme place . . . anoþer] 2P *om.* 23 nedeful] C *adds* and spedfull 24 kynde of þe] G1 *om.* 25 þer] 2P therfore 29 clerkis] 2A Grekes 30 lawe] D holde lawe oþer] M oþer folke 31 for] G2–G5 for als mochel als

gurdles vndirneþe. Somme also beþ yclepid Nesteriens, some Arriens, somme Nubiens, somme Greguroys, somme Yndyns þat beþ of þe lond of Prestre Ioon. And echon of þese haue somme articlis of oure treuþe, but echone varieþ fro oþer. And of here variaunce hit were [to] myche to telle.

## CHAPTER 9 A WAY FRO GALILE TO IERUSALEM ÞURȜ DAMAS

Now siþþe I haue ytolde ȝow of many maner of men þat dwelliþ in cuntrez biforsayd, now wole I turne aȝen to my wey for to turne to þis side. And who so wole turne fro þe lond of Galile þat I spake of to come on þis side, he schal go to Damas þat is a faire cite and ful of [good] merchaundises. And hit is iii. iournees fro þe see and fyue fro
f. 59v Ierusalem. But þey | carie merchaundises vpon camelis, mules, dromundaries, and hors, and oþer beestis. Þis cite foundide Heliseus Damask þat was Abrahams seruant bifore þat Iosiac was bore, and he trowid to haue be [Abraham eyere] and þerfore he clepid [the citee aftre his name] Damas. In þat place slewe Caym his broþer Abel.

And bisid Damas is þe mount Serye. In þat cite beþ many fisicians. And seynt Poul was a fisician to kepe men bodies in heele bifore þat he was conuertid, and siþþe he was a fisician of soulis. And seint Luk was his disciple to lere fisyk and oþer moo.

And fro Damas men comeþ by a place þat is yclepid *nostre dame de Gardemarche* þat is v. myle fro Damas, and it is vpon a roche and it is a faire chirche, and þere dwelliþ monkis and nonnes cristen. In þat chirche bihynde þe hiȝe autre in þe walle is a table of tree in þe whiche an ymage of oure lady is depayntid, and many tymes turneþ
f. 60r into | fleisch and blood. But þat ymage ys [now] seene but litel, but

3 somme] M *om.* 4 but . . . oþer] B and that oþer] G1 *add* (*ex* B) and fro oure feiþ myche 5 to] G1 *om.* 7 IERUSALEM] B *adds* that men go; C *adds* ȝe mott go 8 siþþe] B *om.*; C þat 9 way] C owun way 10 þis] D his And who so] 2A 2B Nowe who so; 2P nowe he that 12 good] G1 (*ex* M) *om.* merchaundises] M merchauntes 2 iii.] A ii 13 vpon] M yn þat contre vpon mules] C *om.* 14 oþer] G2–G5 oþere manere of 16 Abraham eyere] G1 lord aftir Abraham 16–17 the citee aftre his name] G1 *om.* 18 cite] C plas; D cyte of Damas many] CM *om.* 19 seynt] 2P that holy man saynt 19–20 in heele] 2C to hele hem 20 a fisician of] C to 21 And . . . moo] 2P *om.* and] BCDM and mony 22 *de*] 2C de Sarmany þe which is clepid 23 þat is] C is; M þat 24 þere] C *om.* cristen] C *adds* men; M *om.* 25 walle] M 2P vale 26 lady] B *om.* is] 2A 2B 2P was 27 and blood] G2–G5 *om.* now] QAB *om.*

euermore þurȝ grace of God þe table droppiþ oyle as it were of olyue, and þere is a vessel of marbil vndir þe table to resceyue þe oyle. þerof þei ȝeue to pilgrimes for it heliþ of many sikenessis, and he þat kepiþ it clene al þe ȝere þurȝ, at þe ȝere ende it turneþ into fleisch and blood.

And bitwene þe cite of Darke and þe cite of Raphane is a ryuere þat is yclepide Sabatorie, for on þe Satirday it renneþ fast and al þe woke aftir it stondiþ stille and renneþ nouȝt or ellis litel. [And þeire is anoþere ryuere þat on þe nyght freses faste and opon þe day no froste is seen.]

And so goþ men to a cite þat men clepiþ Baruch, and þer men goþ into þe see þat schal into Cypre. And þei londeþ at Port Sure oþer of Tyre and þanne to Cypre; oþer ellis men may go fro þe port of Tyre riȝt and come not at Cipre and alondy at somme hauen of Grece, and þanne þei comeþ to Ierusalem by weyes þat Y spake of bifore.

## CHAPTER 10 þE SCHORTESTE WEYE TO IERUSALEM

| [Nowe] I haue tolde ȝow of weyes now by whiche men goþ f. 60v ferrest and [longest] to Ierusalem, as by Babiloyne and mount Synay and oþer places many þurȝ whiche men turnen aȝen to þe lond of promyssioun. Now wole I telle ȝow þe riȝte wey and þe schorteste to Ierusalem, for somme men wolen not passe it, some for þei haue nouȝt to dispende, somme for þei haue no cumpenye, and oþer causes resonable. [And þerfore I schalle telle ȝow schortely how a man may go with lytylle costage and schort tyme.]

A man þat comeþ fro þe lond of þe west, he goþ þurȝ Fraunse, Burgoyne, Lumbardye, and so to Venys and Geene oþer somme oþer hauen, and he takiþ a schip þer and goþ to þe yle of Griffe, and so he

1–2 as it were of olyue] C *om.* 4 þurȝ at þe ȝere] D *om.* 7–8 renneþ . . . litel] M *om.* 8–10 And þeire . . . seen] G1 *om.* 12 þat schal] C and say Sure] 2A de Sur; 2B de Sureos; 2P of Sur 13–14 oþer ellis . . . Cipre] M *om.* 14 riȝt] QABD euen riȝt 15 Ierusalem] G2–G5 thise countrees 16–17 C *om. rubric*; 2P howe a man may go ferthest and lengest in those countrees as herafter ben rehersed 18 Nowe] G1 *om.* 19 and longest] QD and nerrest; B wey to Ierusalem] G2–G5 *om.* as] C and 20 þurȝ] M *om.* whiche] 2P whiche lond 21 riȝt wey and þe schorteste] G2–G5 wey 22 not] D *om.* it] A by oþer wayes 23 somme] M *om.* oþer] 2A oþere many 24–25 And þerfore . . . tyme] G1 *om.* 27–28 oþer somme oþer hauen] B *om.*; C hem to odyr to hauen; G2–G5 *add* of these marches 28 þer and goþ] B and alondiþ in Greece at Port [Myroch or Valone or] Duras or anoþer, and he restiþ hym þere. And he gooþ aȝen to schip, and þanne he alondiþ in Cypre and comeþ not in þe yle of Roodes and alondiþ at Famagoost, þat is þe beste hauen at Cypre [or elles atte Lamatoun]. And þanne he gooþ to schip [aȝen and passed bysyde the hauen of Tyre] and comeþ no more at lond yf he wol [and so passe by alle þe hauens of þat coste] bifore he come at Port Iaff þat is þe neiȝeste hauen to Ierusalem, for it is but [xxvii.] myle | bitwene.

f. 61r And fro Iaffe men gooþ to þe cite of Rames [and þat is bot lytille thyne and it is a faire citee]. Biside þat cite is a fair chirche [of oure lady wheyre oure lorde schewyde hym to here in thre lyknes þat bytokenyde þe trynyte. And þeire nere is a chirche] of seynt George [wheyre his heed was smytyn of], and so to þe castel of Cheynay, and þanne to mounte Ioiȝe, fro þenne may pilgrimes first se to Ierusalem, and so to mount Modyn [and þanne vnto Ierusalem. Atte monte Modeyn] liþ þe prophetis Machabee. And ouer Ramatha is þe toun [of Douke] of whiche Amos þe prophete was.

## CHAPTER 11 ANOþER WEY TO IERUSALEM

I seyde ȝow last þe way þat is schortest to Ierusalem. But for as myche as many men may not suffre þe sauour of þe see but is leuer to go by londe, yf al hit be þe ferþer wey and þe more peyne, a man schal go to oon of þe hauenes of Lumbardye, as Venys and Geene oþer anoþer. And he schal go by see into Grece to Port Meroch oþer anoþer, and he schal go to Constantynople. And he schal go by þe water þat is yclepid þe brace of seynt George, þat is an arm of þe see. And fro þenne he schal go by londe to Puluerale

1 Myroch or Valone or] G1 *om.* anoþer] G2–G5 some oþere hauen; 2P *adds* of those marches 2 restiþ] CM festis 4 or elles atte Lamatoun] G1 *om.* 5 to] B *om.* 5–6 aȝen and passed . . . Tyre] G1 (C aȝen) 2B *om.* 6 yf he wol] G2–G5 *om.* 6–7 and so . . . coste] G1 *om.* 8 xxvii] Q xv; BCD xvii 9–10 and þat . . . citee] G1 *om.* 10 þat cite] 2A 2B 2P Rames 10–12 of oure . . . chirche] G1 *om.* 11 thre] 2B 2P þys 13 wheyre . . . of] G1 *om.* 14 fro] M and þen fro may pilgrimes first se] 2P pylgrymage pilgrimes] M men 15–16 and þanne . . . Modeyn] G1 whare 16–17 And ouer . . . was] 2C *om.* 17 of Douke] G1 *om.* 20 I seyde . . . But] G2–G5 *om.* last way þat is] M þe laste and þe 21 but] A but hem 22 þe ferþer wey and] G2–G5 *om.* 23 go] A go to Constantantynople 25–26 And he schal go] A *om.* 26 of] A du 27 arm] M grete arm

and siþþe to þe castel of Synople, and fro þenne to Capadoce þat is a grete | cuntre whare beþ many grete hullis. And he schal go þurȝ [f. 61v] Turkye and to þe cite of Nyke, whiche þe Turkys wan fro þe emperour of Constantynople, and hit is a faire cite and wel ywallid, and þere is a ryuere þat men clepiþ þe Lay. And þer men goþ by þe a*lp*es of Mornaunt and by þe valles of Mallebryns and þe vale of Ernay and so to Antioche þe better þat sittiþ on þe Richay. And þere aboute beþ [many goode] hullis and faire and many feire wodis and wilde beestis.

And he þat wol go anoþer way schal go by þe playn of Roman costand þe Roman See. On þat coost is a faire castel þat men clepiþ Florathe. And whan a man is out of þe hullis and roochis, he passiþ þurȝ þe cite of Marioch and Artayse whare is a grete brigge ouer þe ryuere of Ferne, which is yclepid Fassar, and hit is a grete ryuere of berynge schippes, and hit renneþ riȝt fast toward þe cite of Damas.

And byside þe cite of Damas is anoþer ryuere þat comeþ fro þe hullis of Liban | þat men clepiþ Albane. At þe passyng of þis ryuere [f. 62r] seynt Eustace, þat somtyme was clepid Placydas, lost his twey children whe*n* he hadde lost his wyf. And *y*t renneþ þurȝ þe playn of Archades and so to þe Reede See. Fro þenne men comeþ to þe cite of Phenne whare beþ hote welles, and þere beþ hote baþis. And þenne men goþ to þe cite of Ferne, and bitwene Phenne and Ferne beþ many feire wodes.

And þanne men comen to Antyoche þat is a x. myle. Þis cite of Antioche is a faire cite and wel ywallid and many feire touris, for it is ii. myle long and half a myle large, and þe wallis were woned to haue iii. hundrid and fyfty touris. And þurȝ þat cite renneþ þe ryuere of Ferne or Fassar, [and þere is a bryg and] on þat ilke piler of þe brigge was a tour. Þis is þe beste cyte of þe kyngdome of Surrye. And at x. myle fro þis cite is þe port de seynt Symeon, þere goþ þe ryuere of Ferne into þe see.

1 þenne] G2–G5 *add* schall he go 2 grete] M *om.* 3 þe Turkys] G2–G5 þei 4 ywallid] C *adds* and strongly 6 alpes] G1 Aples Mornaunt] 2A aprinant; 2B Aryoprynant valles] 2A walles 8 many goode] QBD grete faire] QBD *add* of Ermony 12 out of] B abought 13 ouer] G2–G5 opon 15 and hit renneþ . . . Damas] G2–G5 *om.* cite] A see 16 And . . . Damas] C *om.* anoþer] G1 *add* grete 18 þat . . . Placydas] G2–G5 *om.* lost] C þat loste 19 children] G2–G5 sonnes when] QBD where yt] QABD þat 21–24 whare beþ . . . x. myle] G2–G5 and so to þe citee of fferne 21 þere beþ] A *om.* 24 cite] A *om.* 25 wel] M ryȝt welle many] M þere aboute be many and many feire touris] G2–G5 *om.* 26–28 and half . . . bryg] G2–G5 *om.* 26 myle] M grete myle 27 fyfty] B *adds* faier 28 and þere is a bryg and] QABD *om.* 30–31 And at . . . see] G2–G5 *om.* 30 myle] CM myle end

f. 62v Fro Antioche men goþ into a cite þat is y|clepid Lacuth, and þanne to Geeble, and þanne to Tortouse. [And þeireby is þe londe of Cambre where is a stronge castelle þat men calle Maubeke.] And þanne to Triple and þanne to Dacres. And þere beþ twey weyes to Ierusalem. On þe lyft wey men goþ to Damas by flom Iordane. On þe riʒt wey þei goþ to [þe londe of Flagame and to þe citee of Kayphas, of whiche Kayphas was lorde, and som calle it] þe castel of Pellerynes. [And fro thyne it is iiii. days iourne to Ierusalem] and so þurʒ Cesare Philippum and so to Iaffe and Rames and þe castel of Emaux and þanne men goþ to Ierusalem.

## CHAPTER 12 A WEY AL BI LONDE TO IERUSALEM

Now haue Y tolde ʒow somme weies by londe and by watir how men may go to Ierusalem. Yf al it be so þat þer be many oþer weyes þat men may go by [after] cuntreez þat þei comeþ fro, neuerþeles þei comeþ al to oon ende. Ʒit is þer a wey by londe to Ierusalem and passe no see fro Fraunce oþer Flaundris, but þat wey is ful long and perilous and of grete trauayl [and þerfore fewe goos þat way]. He þat schal go þat way, he schal go þurʒ Almayn and Pruyse and so to Tartarie.

Þis Tartarie is holde of þe Grete Chan of Catay, of whom Y schal speke aftirward [for thedere lastys his lordschipe and þe lordes of this Tartarye ʒeldith hym trybute]. Þis is a ful yuel lond and sondy
f. 63r and litel fruyt | beryng, for þere growiþ litel corn, no wyn, no benes, no pesyn, but beestis beþ þer yn grete plente. And þerfore þei etiþ but fleisch wiþoute breed, and þei sowpe þe broþ. And þei drinken melk of alle manere of beestis. Þei ete cattis and oþer wilde beestis and ratouns and myss. And þei haueþ litel wode, and þerfore þei

1 þat is yclepid] G2–G5 of yclepid] C *om.* 1–2 and þanne to Geeble] CD *om.* and þanne to Tortouse] BD *om.* 2–3 And þeireby . . . Maubeke] G1 *om.* 3–4 And þanne to Triple] ABD *om.* 6–7 þe londe . . . it] G1 *om.* 8 And fro . . . Ierusalem] G1 *om.* 9 þe castel of] 2P *om.* 11 AL] CM *om.* 13 somme] C iiii 14 to Ierusalem] C thowʒe Yf al it be so] B and 15 after] QBCD oþer 16 ende] CM *add* at þe last and by] CM al be 18 and . . . way] G1 *om.* 22–23 for thedere . . . trybute] G1 *om.* 23 þis] C þis hit; M this Tartary 24 corn] G2–G5 goode of corn no wyn] A wyn; M *om.*; G2–G5 or wyne 25 And þerfore] C *om.* 26 but] BC *om.* 27 of[1]] 2B and oþer] G2–G5 alle manere of 28 wode] CM *add* to brenne

diȝteþ here mete wiþ [hors] mokk of beestis dried at þe sonne. [Prynces and oþere lordes etes bot onys of þe day and ryght lytylle.] þei beþ riȝt foule folk [and of il kynde].

And in somer beþ þere many tempestis and þondris þat sleeþ myche folk and many beestis. And riȝt sodenliche þer is grete cold, and as sodenliche it is þere riȝt hote. þe prince þat gouerneþ þat lond is yclepid Raco, and he dwelliþ in a cite þat men clepiþ Orda. And forsoþe þer wol no good man dwelle in þat lond, for it is good to sowe þerynne hemelokis and netelis and siche oþer weedis, and oþer good noon, as Y haue herd seye, for Y haue noȝt be þere.

But Y haue ybe in oþer londis þat marchiþ þer on, as þe lond of Russye and Nefelond | and þe kyngdome of Crakow and Lettow, and f. 63v in þe kyngdome of Gasten and many oþer placis. But Y went neuer þat wei to Ierusalem, and þerfore Y may not wel telle hit. For as Y haue vndirstonde, man may not wel go þat way but in wyntere for wateris and mareys þat beþ þere, whiche a man may not passe but he haue frost riȝt hard and þat hit be wel snewe aboue, for were noȝt þe snow þere schulde no man go.

And fro Pruysse a man schal go iii. iournees til he come to þe lond of Saresyns þere men dwelliþ. And yf alle hit be so þat cristene men euery [ȝeer] þere passe here way, þei carie here vitailes wiþ hem for þere schal þei noon fynde. And þei make cariage vpon þe yss on slides and chariotis wiþoute wheolis [þat men calle scloys. And als longe als þeere vitailles laste may þei dwelle þeire, bot no langere.] And whenne spies of þe cuntre se cristen men come, þei renneþ to þe townes and crieþ riȝt loude *Kera! Kera! Kera!* and als soone þei kepiþ hem.

And ȝe schal vndirstonde þat þe frost and þe yss ys more hardere

1 diȝteþ] B etith dight hors] G1 *om.*; 2B hors tordes and mokk] ABD 2P mylk beestis] M þere bestys dried at þe sonne] G2–G5 when it is drye 2 Prynces . . . lytylle] G1 *om.* 3 of il kynde] G1 *om.* 6 is] D *om.* 7 is yclepid] 2A þat men calle; 2B 2P þat þay clepen and he] 2A *om.* 9 hemelokis and netelis and siche oþer] G2–G5 þornes and siche] B sede and 10 as] C and haue noȝt be þere] G2–G5 was noght þat wey 11 But] C *om.* 14 as] 2P *om.* 15 haue] C *om.* in] 2B yn harde 16 þay beþ þere] C *om.* 17 þat hit be wel snewe] 2A grete snowe; 2B eke faste snewede; 2P fast snowynge be] B be right 18 go] C pas ne go 19 And] G2–G5 And ȝe schalle vnderstonde þat iournees] G2–G5 *add* to passe þe wey 20 euery ȝeer] QBD euerychon here way] C þere 22 make cariage] M make þer fyre; 2A 2B 2P carry þerefore here vitailles vpon þe yss] C *om.* 23 slides] B gledes wheolis] C scledis or whelis 23–24 þat men . . . langere] G1 *om.* 25 renneþ] C crye and renneþ 27 hem] M þere enemys

f. 64r þere þen here. And þer|fore eueriche man haþ a stewe in hys hous and þere þei etiþ and [doos alle þeire þynggys þat þei may]. For þat is at þe norþ side of þe world whare it is comynliche riȝt cold, for þe sonne schyneþ litel þere [and þat londe is in somme place so colde þat þere may no man dwelle]. And on þe souþ side of þe world hit is in somme place so hote þat no ma*n* may dwelle þere [for þe sone ȝeuys so grete hete in þois contreez].

## CHAPTER 13 TREWþE OF þE SARASYNS

For as myche as I haue told ȝow of Saresyns and of here londis, yf ȝe wole, now schal Y telle ȝow a party of here lawe and of here treuþe aftir here book þat þei clepiþ *Alkaron* seiþ. Somme clepiþ þat book *Mesaþ*, somme clepiþ it *Harme*, aftir langage of dyuerse cuntreez, þe whiche booke Macomet ȝaf to hem; in whiche he wrote among oþer þingis, as Y haue many tymes rad and yseie þerevpon, þat þei þat beþ goode schal go to paradys when þei beþ deede, and þei þat beþ wickid schal go to helle, and þat trowiþ al þe Sarasyns. And yf a man
f. 64v aske of what paradys þei meene, þey | seiþ it is a place of delites whare a man schal fynde alle manere of fruytes in alle tymes and ryuers rennyng wiþ wyn, melk, and hony and freisch water. And þei schal haue faire houses and goode as þei haue deserued, and þat houses beþ ymade of preciouse stones, gold, and siluer; and eueryche man schal haue x. wyfes, alle maydens, and he schal do wiþ hem eche day and þei schal euer more be maydens.

Also þei seiþ and spekiþ many tymes of þe virgyne Marie, and seiþ of þe incarnacioun þat Marie was lerid of aungels and þat Gabriel seide to here þat heo was ychose bifore alle oþere fro bigynnyng of þe world, and þat witnessiþ wel here boke *Alkaron*;

1 þere] C in þat cuntre here] C in þis cuntre and coldar þerfore] 2P *om.* 2 doos . . . may] G1 drinkeþ þat[2]] C þat cuntre 3 riȝt] 2A *om.* 3–5 whare it . . . world] B *om.* 4–5 and þat londe . . . dwelle] G1 *om.* 6 man] Q may 6–7 for þe sone . . . contreez] G1 *om.* 10 and] G1 and of here lawes and and of here londis] M *om.*; C and of relond; 2P *om.* londis] 2P lawes yf ȝe wole] BC *om.* 11 now] G2–G5 *om.* here[2]] C þat lond and 12 þat book] A hit; B þat cuntre 16 when þei beþ deede] G2–G5 *om.* 18 þei meene] B *om.* delites] M alle delytes 20 ryuers] 2P waters and ryuers 20–21 þei schal haue] M *om.* 21 þat] CM þay say þat 24 day] 2P day ones 25 seiþ and spekiþ] 2A 2B 2P spek oft and trowes 26 seiþ] CM *om.* þat] CM and þat and þat] M *om.* 27 fro] B *om.* 28 wel] C *om.* boke] A *om.* *Alkaron*] 2A 2B 2P *om.*

and þat Gabriel tolde here of þe incarnacioun of Ihesu Crist, and þat heo conseyued and bare a child and ȝit was heo mayde; and þat Ihesu Crist spake als soone as he was bore, and þat he was a verrey and an holy prophete in word and dede and meke and riȝtwys to alle and wiþoute vice.

And þei seiþ þat whenne þe aun|gel seide to hure of þe f. 65r incarnacioun heo hadde grete drede for heo was ȝong. A*nd* þer was in þat cuntre a man þat delte with sorsery þat men clepiþ Takyna, þat wiþ enchauntementz couþe make hym like to an aungel, and he lay many tymes by maydens. And þerfore was Marie ferd for þe aungel, and heo wende he hadde be þilke Takyna, and heo coniured hym þat he schulde say here yf he were Takyna. And þe aungel bade here haue no drede for he was certeyn messyngere of God.

Also here boke seiþ þat heo conseyued and hadde a child vndir a palm, and þanne was heo aschamed and grette and seide þat heo wolde be deed. And als soone þe child spake and confortid hure and seide þus to hire, *Ne timeas Maria*, þat is to say, Be no aferd Marie. And in many oþer placis seiþ here book *Alkaron* þat Ihesu Crist spake als soone as he was bore. And þat book seiþ þat Ihesu Crist was sent fro God almiȝty to be ensample to alle men, and þat God schal deeme alle men, þe | goode to heuene, þe wickide to helle; and þat f. 65v Ihesu Crist is þe beste prophete of alle oþere and neiȝest to God, and þat he was verrey prophete þat ȝaf siȝt to þe blynde and heelid mesels and arerid deede men and went al quyke into heuene; and þat þei dooþ grete worschipe to bookis þat þe gospels beþ ywrite ynne, and nameliche to þe gospel *Missus est angelus Gabriel*, whiche gospel þei þat beþ lettrid among hem seiþ often in here preieris wiþ [gret] deuocioun.

Þei faste a monþe al hool in þe ȝere and etiþ noȝt but on þe niȝt.

1 Ihesu] BC *om.* 2 Ihesu] 2P *om.* 3 þat] C say 4 in] CM boþe in 6 seiþ] C *adds* and spek many tymis of þe virgin Mary and of þe incarnacioun and þay say 7 ȝong] 2P right yonge And] G1 Also (CM and allso) 9 lay] 2A 2B 2P ȝode oft and lay by] M by dyuerse 11 Takyna] 2A 2B 2P *add* þat went with þe madyns 13 God] 2A Ihesu cryst 14 conseyued and hadde] A bar; M had conseyued; G2–G5 hadde 16 child] M angel And als . . . hure] 2B *om.* 16–17 and seide] C *om.* 17 þus to hire] AM *om.*; C in þys wise; 2A 2B 2P to mary 18 book] A *om.* *Alkaron*] C *om.* Crist] BD *om.* 20 sent] G2–G5 *om.* 20–21 alle men . . . heuene] B *om.* 23 verrey prophete] C so very prophet þat he was 24 men] 2B *adds* þat þay went alle quyke and he hymselfe al quyke] C aliue; M *adds* alyue heuene] C *adds* body and soule 25 to bookis . . . ynne] G2–G5 if þei may fynde a boke of (2B sakke full of) godspelles 27–28 whiche . . . deuocioun] G2–G5 þei do it grete worschipe 27 gret] Q goode 29 a] 2B seuen al hool] G2–G5 *om.* etiþ] DM *om.*

And þei kepiþ hem fro here wifes al þat monþe. But þei þat beþ sike beþ not constreyned to þis fast.

And þis boke *Alkaron* spekiþ of Iewis and seiþ þat þei beþ wickid, for þei wole not trowe þat Ihesu Crist was sent fro God. And þei seiþ þat Iewis lieþ falslich of Marie and here sone Ihesu when þei seie þat þei dide Ihesu Marie sone vpon þe cros, for Sarasyns seiþ þat was
f. 66r not Ihesu | þat deide vpon þe cros, for Ihesu was Goddis sone and went into heuene al quyke and deide neuer. But þei seiþ þat Ihesu chaungid his likenes into one þat was clepid Iudas Scarioth, and hym dide Iewis on þe cross, but þe Iewis seiþ þat hit was Ihesu. But þei seiþ þat Ihesu went to heuene al quyke, and so schal he come to deeme al þe world. And þerfore þei seiþ þat alle cristen men beþ not of good treuþe when þei trowe þat Ihesu crist was do on þe cross, for þei seiþ yf he hadde be do on þe cross, þan God hadde do þanne aȝens his riȝtwisnesse þat he schulde suffre Ihesu þat was not gilty be do to deeþ wiþoute ony trespas. And in þis article þei seiþ þat cristene men faileþ, for þe grete riȝtwisnesse of God wole suffre no wronge be do.

And þei graunte wel þe workis of Ihesu Crist to be goode and his wordis also and his vn[di]rstondyngis and his gospels and his
f. 66v myraclis to be soþe; and þat þe virgyne Marie is a goode may|de and holy bifore þe beryng of Ihesu Crist and after also; and þat þese þat trowiþ parfytly in God schal be saued.

And for as myche as þei trowe nere oure fey, þei beþ liȝtlich conuertid to oure fey whanne men preche to hem of oure lawe and openeþ to hem þe prophecies. Also þei wote wel, þei say, by here prophecyes þat þe lawe of Macomet schal faile as þe Iewis lawe is yfayled, and þat þe cristen lawe schal laste to ende of þe world.

And yf a man aske hem in whom and how þey trowe, þei seiþ: we trowe in God þat made heuene and erþe and alle oþer þingis

1 al þat monþe] G2–G5 þane  2 fast] C fasting no tyme; 2P *om.*  3 Alkaron] 2A 2B 2P *om.*  beþ] M *adds* yuelle and  5 falslich] G2–G5 *om.*  6 Ihesu Marie sone] B Iesu; G2–G5 hym noght  7–24 for Ihesu . . . be saued] G2–G5 *om.*  8 But þei seiþ þat] B that  12 al þe world] C þe quik and þe dede  alle] AC *om.*  13 treuþe] M *adds* ne of good bylyue  15 his] C *om.*  17 faileþ] C vary  19 goode and] D god in  20 vndirstondyngis] Q unrstondyngis; ACM techynge and his  21 myraclis] C *om.*  is] C was  22 holy] M *adds* was  24 for as myche as þei] G2–G5 Sarȝyns  nere] A ne were; M þus nere on  þei beþ] B but  25 to oure fey] 2P *om.*  whanne] C for whan  25–26 and openeþ to hem þe prophecies] G2–G5 *om.*  26 þe] A alle  openeþ to hem] C of; M reherse to hem  Also] 2A And þei say] C þe saw  29 in whom and how] G2–G5 wheyre in  29–30 seiþ we] 2P say þat they

þat beþ ymade, and wiþoute hym is no þing ydo, and we trowe þe day of dome whare eueryche man schal haue as he haþ deserued, and we trowe þat al is sooþ þat God haþ spoke þurȝ mowþis of his prophetis.

Also Macomet bade yn his *Alkaron* þat eueriche man schulde haue twey wyfes oþer iii. oþer iiii., but now þei takiþ ix. and as many lemmans as þei wole. And if ony of here wifes do amys | aȝens here f. 67r housbande, he may putte here out of his house and take anoþer, but hym bihoueþ [to ȝeue] hure a porcoun of his goodes.

Also when men spekiþ to hem of þe fader and þe sone and þe holi gost, þei seiþ þat þei beþ þre persones but noȝt o god, for here book *Alkaron* spekiþ noȝt of þe trinite. But þei seiþ þat God spake or ellis hadde he be dombe, and þat God haþ a spiryt or ellis hadde he no lyf.

[And þei say þat Abraham and Moyses ware welle with God for þei spake with hym, and Machomet þei say was ryght messanger of God.]

And when men spekiþ of þe incarnacoun, how by þe word of þe aungel God sent wysdome in erþe and liȝted [in] þe virgyne Marie, and þat þurȝ þe word of God þei þat beþ deede schal be rerid vp at þe day of dome, þei seiþ þat ys sooþ and þat þe word of God haþ grete vertu. And so seiþ here *Alkaron* when it seiþ þat þe aungel spake to Marie and seide, Marie, God schal sende to þee word bi his mouþ, and his name schal be clepid Ihesu Crist. And þei seiþ þat Ihesu Crist was þe word and þe goost of God.

And þus þei haue many goode poyntes | of oure fey, and al þese f. 67v þat vndirstondiþ þe prophecies and bookis þat beþ ywrite beþ liȝtliche conuertid, for þei haue alle þe prophecies and gospels and alle þe bible ywrite in here owne langage, and þerfore þei kunneþ myche of holy writ. But þei vndirstondiþ it not but after þe lettre [and so do þe Iewes, for þei vnderstonde noght þe lettre gostely].

1, 3 we trowe] 2P *om.* 1 þat beþ ymade] 2A *om.* 2 whare] G2–G5 whene 7 wifes] C lemans or wyuis 8 house] C cumpany take] 2P *om.* 9 to yeue] Q *om.* 9 a porcoun] G2–G3 *om.*; G4–G5 sum 11 þat þei beþ] C *om.* but noȝt] C and; M *adds* þre persones noȝt] G2–G5 noght þere of ne 12 trinite] BM thre trynyteys seiþ] 2B *adds* þo wordes 13 lyf] G2–G5 *add* and þei say þat goddys worde has a grete strengh and so says þeire Alkaroun 14–16 And þei . . . God] G1 (*ex* C) *om.* 17–24 And when . . . goost of God] G2–G5 *om.* 18 in] Q *om.* 21 here] B *adds* bok seiþ] C payid 24 goost] A spyryt; C holy gost 25 poyntes] G2–G5 articles 26 bookis] G2–G5 scriptures 26–27 beþ liȝtliche conertid] G2–G5 *om.* 27 alle þe prophecies and] G2–G5 hem and þe gospels] ACM alle þe gospels 28 alle] 2A 2P *om.*; 2B eke 29 þe[1]] D here 30 and so . . . gostely] G1 *om.*

And þerfore seiþ seynt Poul, *Littera occidit spiritus autem viuificat*, þat is to say, þe lettre sleeþ and þe goost makiþ quyke.

Also þe Sarasyn seiþ þat Iewis beþ wickid men for þei kepe noȝt þe lawe whiche Moyses toke to hem. And þei seiþ þat cristen men beþ wickid for þei kepiþ noȝt þe maundementis of þe gospels whiche Ihesu Crist toke to ham.

And þerfore I schal telle ȝow what þe sowdan seide to me vpon a day in his chambre. He gart voyde out of þe chambre alle maner of men, lordis and oþer, for he wolde speke wiþ me in counsayl. And he askide me how cristene men gouerned | [f. 68r] hem in oure cuntrez, and Y seide, 'Wel, þankid be God.'

And he seide, 'Sikerly nay, for,' he seide, 'ȝoure prestis make no fors of Goddis seruice, for þey schulde ȝeue good sample to men to do wel and þei ȝeueþ yuel ensample. And þerfore when þe folk schulde gon on þe holi day to chirche to serue God, þei goþ to tauerne to be in glotonye al day and alle niȝt ete and drinke as bestis þat witen not when þei haue ynow. And also alle cristen men aforse hem to fiȝte and eueriche to bigile oþer. And also þei beþ so proude þat þei wote noȝt how þei wole be cloþed, now longe cloþis, now schort, now wide, now streyt, [on alle manere of wyse].

'Ȝe schulde,' he seyde, 'be semple, meke, and soþfast, and do almysdede as Crist dide, in whom þei trowe. Cristen men beþ', he seyde, 'so couetous þat for a litel siluer þei sille here children, here sustren, and here owne wifes to lete men ligge by hem. And oon takiþ anoþeris wyf | [f. 68v] and noon holdiþ his fey to oþer. And so þei dispise and defoule þe lawe, þe which Ihesu ȝaf to ham for here saluacioun. And þerfore,' he seide, 'for ȝoure synnes haue ȝe lost al þis lond þat we holdeþ, for bicause of ȝoure yuel lyuyng and ȝoure

2 goost] CM sprete forsoþe 3 men] G2–G5 *om.* 4 þei seiþ þat] G2–G5 also 6 toke] G2–G5 sent 7 þerfore] C now what . . . to me] 2C a tale I was wiþ þe Sowdan 8 He] C for he voyde] A wyde 10 lordis] 2P *adds* knyghtys 11 Wel] G2–G5 ryght welle 12 for he seide] A for; G2–G5 þo he sayde ȝoure] G2–G5 oure 13 good sample] G2–G5 ensample 14 ȝeueþ] C *adds* þem ensample] 2B *adds* vnto men and þat ys not wel doon 16 alle] B *om.* ete] 2A 2P and ete 17 þei haue] C yhaue ynow] 2A moche alle] C G2–G5 *om.* men] G2–G5 *add* he sayde 18 fiȝte] G2–G5 *add* samen (*va.* togedur) 20 wide] C *adds* now narow on alle manere of wyse] G1 *om.*; 2C cloþes 21 Ȝe] G2–G5 (*ex* 2M) þay soþfast] A stedefasty 22 Crist] 2A 2B Ihesu; 2P iesu cryst þei] CM ȝe Cristen men] G2–G5 And þei 23 siluer] M *om.* 24 owne] G2–G5 *om.* to lete . . . hem] G2–G5 *om.* 25–27 And so . . . saluacioun] G2–G5 *om.* 25 þei] C *adds* say þat we 26 defoule] C fayle 27 ȝoure] 2A 2P þeire ȝe] 2A þe crystyn men 27–28 haue ȝe lost . . . holdeþ] 2P *om.* 28 bicause of ȝowre yuel lyung and] G2–G5 *om.*

synnes ȝoure God haþ ȝeue al þis londis into oure hondis. And we haue hem noȝt þurȝ oure owne strengþe but al for ȝoure synnes, for we woote wel forsoþe þat what tyme so ȝe serue wel ȝoure God, þanne he wole helpe ȝow so þat no man schal do aȝens ȝow. And we wote wel by oure prophecyes þat cristen men schal wynne þis lond aȝen when þei serue wel here God. But while þei lyue so foule as þei do, we haue no drede of hem for here God wole not helpe hem.'

And þanne Y askid hym how he knew and wist þe state of cristen men so. And he seide he knew it wel, boþe of lordis and of comunes, by his messyngeris whiche he sent þurȝ al þe cuntrez as þei were merchauntz wiþ preciouse stoones [and oþere merchaundise] to knowe þe maner of alle cuntrez. And þanne | f. 69[r] he lete clepe aȝen alle þe lordis into þe chambre, and he schewid me foure þat were grete lordis in þat cuntre, whiche deuysed to [me] my cuntre and alle oþere cuntrez of cristendome as þei hadde ybe of þe same cuntre. And þei speken Frensche riȝt wel, and so dide þe sowdan.

And þanne hadde Y grete merueyl of þis grete sclaundre of [oure fayth], for þei þat schulde be yturned þurȝ oure good ensample to þe feiþ of Ihesu Crist, þei beþ ydrawe awey þurȝ oure wickide lyuyng. And þerfore it is no wondre þouȝ þei clepe vs wickid. But þe Sarasyns beþ trewe, for þei kepiþ wel þe comaundementis of here *Alkaron*, whiche God sent to hem by his messyngere Macomet, to whom as þey seiþ seynt Gabriel þe aungel spake many tymes and tolde him þe wille of God.

And ȝe schal vndirstonde þat Macomet was ybore in Arabye, and he was first a pore knaue þat kept hors and ȝeode wiþ merchauntes | f. 69[v] and so he come onys into Egipt wiþ merchauntis, and Egipt was þat tyme cristene. And at þe wildernesse of Arabye he went into a chapel whare was an heremyte, and whan he entrid þe chapel which was riȝt litel, þanne þe entre bycome as grete and hiȝ as it hadde ben ȝatis of

2 owne] C *om.* 4–5 aȝens . . . schal] 2P *om.* 6 wel] 2B *adds* and trewly But] CM but all þe 8 þanne] 2A 2B 2P *om.* þe state of] C *om.*; M *adds* and þe lyuyng 9 men] C meny lyvng it wel] M it fulle welle ynowȝe; 2A 2P well of [1,2] ] M by 10 as] C and 11 and oþere merchaundise] G1 *om.* 13 me] QABD *om.* 17 Y grete] M *om.* 17–18 oure fayth] G1 cristen men 18 for] G2–G5 and so oure] B *om.* 19 ydrawe] M *adds* alle wickide] 2B *adds* and ylle; G2–G5 *add* for þei say sothe 21 wel] A *om.* 22 Macomet] C þat was Machamit 23 as] G2–G5 *om.* spake] B *adds* with him 27 so] QBD so þat merchauntis] 2P marchaundise 28 at þe . . . chapel] G2–G5 þeire was a chapelle biside Araby 30 litel] G2–G5 *add* hous and lawgh (2B lange) and hiȝ] G2–G5 *om.* 30–62/1 and hiȝ . . . paleys] C a ȝate of a cadirt 30 ben] M *adds* grete

a grete paleys. And þis was þe firste myracle þat þe [Sarzyns] say þat he dide when he was ȝong.

Aftir þat bycome Macomet wise and riche, and he was a grete astronomere. And he was made kepere of þe lond of þe prince of Corodan, and he gouerned hit riȝt wisely in siche a manere þat whenne þe prince was deed, he weddid þe lady þat men clepiþ Quadrige.

And Macomet hadde þe fallyng yuel and fel ofte, and þe lady hadde myche sorwe þat heo hadde take hym to here housbande. But he made hire to vndirstonde þat ilke tyme þat he fel so þat þe
f. 70r aungel Gabriel spake to hym | and for þe grete briȝtnesse of þe aungel Gabriel he fel doun. And þerfore seiþ þe Sarasyn þat þe aungel Gabriel spake ofte wiþ hym.

Þis Macomet regned in Arabye þe ȝere of oure lord sixe hundrid and twenty. And he was of þe kynde of Ismael þat was Abrahams sone, þe whiche he gate of Agar his chambrere. And þerfore somme Sarasyns beþ yclepid Ismaelitons, somme Agariens of Agar [and somme ar called Moabites] and somme Ammonytes after ii. sones of Loth, þe whiche he gat of his douȝtris. And somme beþ yclepid propurly Sarasyns of Sara.

Also Macomet louede wel a good man, an heremyte, þat dwellid in þe wildernesse a myle fro mount Synay in þe way as men schal go fro Arabye to Caldee and toward Indee a dayes iourne fro þe see whare merchauntis of Venys comeþ many tymes for to by merchaundises. And Macomet wente so ofte to þis heremyte to hure hym preche þat
f. 70v alle his men were wrooþ þat ȝeode wiþ | hym for he wolde gladliche hure þis heremyte preche and he lete alle hys men wake al þe niȝt. And his men þouȝte þei wolde gladliche þis heremyte were deed. So hit bifel vpon a nyȝt þat Macomet hadde so drunken of good wyn þat he was drunke and fel aslepe. And while he slepte, his men toke out

1 grete] G2–G5 *om.* þe Sarzyns] QABD þei; CM men say] M saw 4 kepere] M ledere 8 hadde . . . ofte] G2–G5 felle ofte into the fallande euelle and fel] C ful 9 myche] M *adds* dole and 12 Gabriel] M *om.* 12–13 And þerfore . . . hym] G2–G5 *om.* 15 kynde] C king Ismael] G2–G5 dysmael 16–19 his chambrere . . . douȝtris] G2–G5 *om.* 17–18 and somme ar called Moabites] G1 *om.* 20 Sara] G2–G5 *add* bot somme are called Moabites and somme amonites aftre tuo soones of Loth 21 a good man] M a goode holy man þat was; 2A a good 24 many . . . merchaundises] G2–G5 *om.* 25 þis] M *adds* holy to hure hym preche] G2–G5 *om.* 26 þat ȝeode wiþ hym] G2–G5 *om.* 27 men] M *adds* ofte tymes too 28 þouȝte þei] A *om.* gladliche] G2–G5 *om.* 29–30 hadde so . . . þat he] A *om.* 29 so] 2A fule of good] C *om.* 29–30 þat he was drunke] G2–G5 *om.*; A *adds* of wyn 30 slepte] 2P lay and slepte

a swerd out of his owne scheþe and wiþ þat swerd þei slowe þis heremyte. And þanne þei put vp his swerd aȝen into þe scheþe al blodye.

And at morwe when he fonde þe heremyte deed, he was fulle wrooþ and he wolde lete do his men to deeþ, for he seide þei hadde slayn þis heremyte. But þei alle wiþ oon acorde and oon assent seide þat hymself hadde yslawe hym in his slepe whan he was drunke. And þei schewid hym his swerd al blody, and þanne trowid he þat þei hadde seide sooþ. And þenne he curside wyn and alle þat it drinkeþ.

And þerfore Sarasyns whiche beþ | deuoute drinkeþ no wyn, but f. 71r
somme Sarasyns drinkeþ wyn gladliche but not openliche but in priuyte. And ȝif þei drinkeþ wyn openliche, þei schal be blamed þerfore. But þei drinkeþ goode beuerage swete and norischaunt, whiche is ymade of calamele, and þerof is sugre made þat is of goode sauour.

Also it falliþ somtyme þat cristene men bicomeþ Sarasyns oþer for pouert oþer for semplesse oþer for wickidnesse of hemself. And he þat [is] Archessleneyn, whan he resceyueþ hem to here lawe, seiþ þus, *La esses ella Macomet rozes alla*, þat is to say, þer is no god but oon and Macomet his messyngere.

And siþþe I haue a party ytolde of here lawe and of here maners and customes, now schal Y telle ȝow of here lettris whiche þei haue, wiþ here names and þe manere of here figuris whiche þei beoþ: *almoy*, *bethath*, *cachi*, *delplox*, *ophoty*, *fothi*, *hechim*, *iocchi*, *kaithi*, *iothim*, *malachi*, *nahaloth*, *orthi*, *choziri*, *zoth*, *rutholat*, *routhi*, | *salathi*, 71v
*thatimus*, *yrchom*, *azazoth*, *aroithi*, *zotipin*, *ichetus*. þis beþ þe names of þe lettres. Now schal Y telle ȝow þe figures. . . . . . . . . . . .

þese foure lettris þei haue ȝit more for [diuersite of] here langage

1 a swerd . . . þat swerd þei] A his owne swerd and þerwiþ  owne] M G2–G5 *om.* 2 þanne þei] A *om.*; M when þey had þus done þey  into þe scheþe] G2–G5 *om.* 4 he] G1 he woke and  5 and] M *om.*  5–6 for he . . . heremyte] G2–G5 *om.*  6 But] M and  oon] M voyce and one  and oon assent] 2A *om.*  7 in his slepe] G2–G5 *om.*  8 swerd] M 2P owne swerd  trowid] D turned  9 hadde] A *om.*  10 drinkeþ] A wil drinke  10–11 but somme . . . wyn] 2P *om.* 11–12 gladliche . . . priuyte] G2–G5 pryuyly  13 goode] G1 riȝt goode  14 þerof is sugre made] A of sugre  14–15 þat is of goode sauour] G2–G5 *om.* 16 somtyme] CM oftyn timis  17 of hemself] G2–G5 *om.*  17–18 he þat is] QAD he þat; G2–G3 (*ex* 2D) þerfore; G4–G5 ther  18 Archessleneyn] 2A Archericlyne; 2B larches leuen; 2C larchesleuen þat is receyuour of cristen men (see Appendix 8)  to here lawe] C *adds* and; G2–G5 *om.*  22–23 whiche þei haue wiþ] M and which þey be  23 and þe manere . . . beoþ] 2P first they haue  27 figures] M *adds* yn þe beste manere þat my hert conceyueth þem; 2P *om. characters* (for the characters see frontispiece)  28 diuersite of] G1 *om.*

for þat þei spekiþ so in here þrotes, as we haue in oure speche in Engelond twey lettres mo þen þei haue in here abc, þat is to say, þ and ȝ which beþ yclepid þorne and ȝoghe.

## CHAPTER 14 DYUERSITEZ OF FOLK AND OF CUNTRES

And siþþe I haue deuysed herebifore of þe holi lond and cuntres þereaboute and many weyes þider and to mount Synay, to Babiloyne, and oþer placis of whiche Y haue spoke, now wole Y telle ȝow and speke of yles and dyuerse folk and beestis, for þer beþ many dyuerse folk and cuntrez whiche beþ departid wiþ þe foure floodis, þe whiche comeþ out of paradys terrestre.

For Mesopotayne and þe kyngdome of Caldee and Arabye beþ
f. 72r bitwene þese two floodes, Tyger and Eufraten. And | þe kyngdome of Medy and Perse beþ bitwene þese twey floodis, Tyger and Nile. And þe kyngdome of Surrye and Palestyn and Fimes beþ bytwene Eufraten and þe see Mediteran, and hit lastiþ of lengþe fro Maroche vpon þe see of Spayne vnto þe Grete See [and so lasteþ hit byyonde Constantynople þre þousaunde and fourty myle of Lumbardye. And toward þe see] þat is yclepid Occyan in Ynde is þe kyngdome of Sichy whiche is al enclosed wiþ hullis.

And ȝe schal vndirstonde þat in þese cuntres beþ many yles and londis of whiche it were to myche to telle al. But of somme schal Y telle more plenerliche aftirward.

For he þat wole go into Tartarie oþer Perse oþer Caldee oþer Ynde, he entriþ þe see [at] Geene or Venys or at anoþer hauen. And he passiþ þe see and aryueþ at Trapazonde, which is a good cite and was woned to be clepid *le Port de Pounce*. [Þeire is the kynge of Persayns and Medoyns and oþere marches.]

In þis cite liþ seint Athanas þat was byschop of Alisaundre and he made þe psalme *Quicumque uult*. Þis man was a grete doctour of

1 oure] G2–G5 oure langage and speche] M *adds* as we haue 4–5 CM *om.* *rubric* 6 deuysed] CM *add* ȝow 7 and to . . . Babiloyne] C *om.* 8 telle ȝow and] M *om.* 8–9 ȝow and speke] A *om.*; C G2–G5 and speke 9–10 for þer beþ many dyuerse folk] C 2A *om.* 10–11 wiþ þe foure . . . paradys] 2B *om.* 12 For] M *adds* a londe that ys clepyd 13–14 Tyger . . . floodis] 2B *om.* 17–19 and so . . . see] Q *om.* 23 more plenerliche] C *om.* 25 at] G1 (*ex* M) *om.* 27–28 Þeire . . . marches] G1 (*ex* C) *om.* oþere] C allso of many odir plasis and 30 doctour] M mayster

dyuynite, and for he | spake so deop in dyuynyte and of þe godheed, he was accusid to þe pope of Rome þat he was an heretyk. And þe pope sent for hym and put hym in prisoun, and þere [while he was in prisone] he made þe salme and sent it to þe pope and seide if he was an heretyk, þan was þat heresye for þat was his treuþe. And whan þe pope sauȝ þat, he seide þerynne was al oure fey and gart delyuere hym out of prisoun. And þe pope comaundid þat salme to be seyd euery day at prime, and he helde Atthanatas for a good [crystene] man. But Atthanatas wolde neuer aftirward go to his byschopriche aȝen for þat þei hadde accusid hym of heresye. f. 72v

Trapazonde was somtyme holde of þe emperour of Constantynople, but a riche man wham he sent to kepe it aȝens þe Turkys helde hit stille vnto hymself and clepide hym emperour of Trapazonde.

And fro þenne men go þurȝ litel Ermonye. In þat cuntre is an old castel þat is vpon a roche whiche men clepiþ | *le castel desperuer*, whiche is bitwene þe cite of Larrays and nere to þe cite of Parcipie, of whom is þe lord of Croke lord and he is a riche man. And in þat castel men fond an hauk sittyng vpon a perche riȝt wel ymade and a faire lady of fayrie þat kepiþ it. And he who wole wake þis hauk vii. daies and vii. niȝtes (and somme seiþ iii. dayes and iii. nyȝtes) aloone wiþoute cumpenye and slepe not, þis faire lady schal come to hym at vii. day (oþer iii. day) ende and heo schal graunte hym [the first þynge] *t*hat he wole aske of þingis þat beþ wordelich. And þat haþ be many tymes asayed. f. 73r

So hit bifel vpon a tyme þat a kyng of Ermonye þat was a douȝty man wakid þis hauk, and at þe ende of þe seuen dayes þe lady come to hym and bade hym aske [what he wolde] for he hadde wel ydo his deuer. And þe kyng seyde þat he was a grete lord ynow and in good pees and þat he was riche, so þat he wolde aske noþing but þe body

1 and for . . . dyuynyte] 2P *om.* and[2] ] C *om.* 2 pope] C *adds* sent to hym 3 and þere] D *om.* 3–4 while he was in prison] G1 *om.* 4 prisone] G1 *om.*; CM in þe mene tym; M *continues* that he lay yn prison salme] A *adds* Quicumque vult; CM þat same eresy 5 heresye] 2B sorserye his] M hys byleue and hys treuþe] 2P *adds* and hys byleue 6 sauȝ þat . . . al] C and all þat was þer saw þat it was; M sawe þat alle þat was þeryn was hooly oure] CM *add* beleve and our 8 crystene] G1 *om.* 9 aftirward] 2P *om.* 10 of heresye] C falsly 12 riche] G2–G5 grete sent] A *adds* þider 17–18 whiche . . . riche man] G2–G5 *om.* 17 nere to] C þat is 18–19 in þat castel] G2–G5 þeyre 20 he] Q heo seide 22 not] DM *om.* 23–24 the first þynge that] G1 what 26 hit bifel] G2–G5 *om.* douȝty] 2P ryght doughty 27 þis hauk] G2–G5 one tyme 28 what he wolde] G1 (*ex* C) *om.* 29 deuer] M *adds* of hys wakyng ynow] 2A *om.*

f. 73v of þe faire lady to | haue to his wille. And heo seide þat [he was a foole for he wiste noght what he askede for here] myȝt he not haue for heo was not wordelich, but bade hym aske of wordeliche þingis. And þe kyng seide he wolde not ellis. And heo seide to hym siþþe þat he wolde not aske, heo schulde graunte him som þing and to alle þat come aftir hym, and seide to hym; 'Sire kyng, ȝe schal [haue were withoute pees alweye vnto þe ix. degree and ȝe schalle] be in subieccioun of ȝoure enemys and ȝe schal haue grete neode of good and catel.' And siþþe þat tyme alle þe kynges of Ermonye haue be in werre and neodeful [and vndyr trybute of Sarzyns].

Anoþer tyme a pore mannus sone woke þe hauk and askid of þe lady þat he myȝte be riche and happy in merchaundises. And þe lady grauntid hym, but heo seide þat he hadde askid [his vndoynge] for grete pruyde þat he schulde haue. But he þat schal wake þis hauk haþ neode to kepe hym fro slepe, for yf he sleepe he schal be lost þat he schal neuer be seye. But þis castel is not [þe ryght wey bot for] þe merueyl.

f. 74r Fro Trapazonde men schal go to grete Ermo|nye to a cite þat men clepiþ Artyron, þat was woned to be a great cite but þe Turkys haue nere destroyed hym [for þeire nere growes no wyne ne fruyt].

Fro þenne men gooþ to an hulle þat men clepiþ [Sabissatolle and þeire is anoþere hille þat men calle] Ararath, but þe Iewis clepiþ it Thano, whare Noe schip restid and ȝit is hit þare. A man may yse it fer in clere wedir, and þe hulle is vii. myle hiȝ. And somme seiþ þei haue be þere and put here fyngris in þe hole whare þe fend ȝeode out when Noe seide *Benedicite*, but þei seyn not sooþ, for no man may vpon þat hulle for snow þat is alwey þere [wynter and somere]. For

1 faire lady . . . wille] C lady heo] 2P this fayre lady answered and 1–2 he was . . . for here] G1 *om.* 2–3 myȝt . . . þingis] 2C she was not worldely 4 ellis] C els but hyt 4–5 seide to hym . . . som þing] C bad aske and he schold have it to him 5 aske] G2–G5 elles som] 2P foure 6 aftir hym] G1 *add* to þe ix degree; C *continues* and he wold not 6–7 haue . . . ȝe schalle] G1 *om.* 10 and] M and pore and and . . . Sarȝyns] G1 *om.* 11 Anoþer tyme] G2–G5 Also þe hauk] 2P the a tyme 13 his vndoynge] Q ondyons 14 haue] G2–G5 haue þare of wake] C have; M kepe þis hauk] G2–G5 *om.* 16 þis castel] G2–G5 þat þe ryght wey bot for] G1 in 17 merueyl] C travell; M trauayle of the hyȝe way 19–20 but . . . fruyt] 2C *om.* 20 for . . . fruyt] G1 *om.* nere] G2–G5 *om.* 21 þenne] G2–G5 þis Artiroun 21–22 Sabissatolle . . . calle] G1 *om.* 23 Noe schip] G2–G5 Archa Noe þare] G2–G5 on þat hille 24 fer] CM fro far vii.] 2P twelue 25 þere] B þere at; CM þere at þe schip in þe hole] 2A *om.* 26 seide] 2P *adds* in this maner of wyse 26–27 for no . . . hulle] CM *om.* 27 þere] G2–G5 on þat hille wynter and somere] G1 *om.*; M so thykke

þer come neuer man at siþþe Noe was but a monk þat þurȝ grace of God ȝeode þedir and brouȝt a planke þat is ȝit at þe abbeye at þe hulle fote, for he hadde grete desire to go vpon þat hulle, and he aforsed hym þerto. And when he was at þe þridde part of þe hulle vpward, he was so wery he miȝt no ferþer, and he restid hym þere and slep[te]. And when he wook he was doun at þe hulle foot. And þenne he preied to God deuoutely þat he wolde suffre him | go vp, f. 74v and an aungel seide to hym þat he schulde go vp, and so he dide. And siþþe come neuer no man þare, and þerfore þei seiþ wrong þat seiþ þat þei haue be þere.

Fro þenne men goþ to a cite þat is yclepid Tauzoro, and þat is a faire cite and a good. Biside þat cite is an hille of salt and þerof may eche man take what he wol. þere dwelliþ many cristen men vndir tribute of Sarasyns. Fro þenne men gooþ by many citez, townes, and castels, and many iourneys toward Ynde, and comeþ to a cite þat men clepiþ Cassake [and þat is a faire cite]. þere mette þe þre kyngis þat went to make offryng to Crist in Bedleem. [Fro þat citee men goos to a citee that men calle Cardabago, and þe panyms say þat crystyn men may noght dwele þeire bot þei deye sone, and þei knowe noght þe cause.]

And fro þen men goþ many iourneys by many citeez and townus [þat were to longe to telle] til þei come to a cite þat is yclepid Carnaa, þat woned to be so grete þat þe wallis aboute was of xxv. myle. [þe walle schwes ȝit, bot it is noght nowe habitide with men.] And þer endiþ þe lond of þe emperour of Perce. On þe oþer side of Carnaa men entriþ into þe lond of Iob þat is | a good lond and grete plente of f. 75r fruyt [and men calle þat londe þe londe of Swere].

[In þis londe is þe cite of Thomare. Iob was a panyme and he was Cosara sone, and he helde þat londe als prynce þereof. And he was so

1 at] G2–G5 vppe and ȝode 2 ȝeode þedir and] G2–G5 *om.* planke] C *adds* þat is to say a bord; M borde of þe shyppe 4 hym] M *adds* gretely of þe hulle] G2–G5 *om.* 6 slepte] QBD sleep 7 vp] G2–G5 vppon þe hille 8 and an . . . go vp] 2B *om.* dide] G1 *add* and he brouȝte þe planke; CM *continue* downe (M downe þe hylle) wiþ hym 9 þei seiþ wrong] D *om.* 9–10 þei seiþ . . . þere] G2–G5 (*ex* 2M) men scholde noght trowe swych wordes 12 and a good] C *om.* 13 what] M when 14 citez] G2–G5 *om.* 15 iourneys] 2P *om.* 16 þat is a faire cite] G1 *om.* mette] G2–G5 *add* togydre 17 offryng to Crist] G2–G5 presente to our lorde 17–20 Fro . . . cause] G1 *om.* 21 many iourneys by] G2–G5 þorgh 22 that were to longe to telle] G1 *om.* til þei com] G2–G5 *om.* þat is yclepid] 2A of 23–25 þat woned . . . Carnaa] 2B *om.* 23–24 þe . . . men] G1 *om.* 25 of] G2–G5 of the citee of 26 and grete] C *om.* plente] A and a plentyous of] G2–G5 of alle 26–27 and . . . Swere] G1 2C *om.* 28–68/6 In . . . body] G1 *om.*

ryche þat he knewe noght þe hundredth party of his good. And aftyr his pouert God made hym rychere þane he was byfore, for aftre he was kynge of Idumea and sithen kynge of Isau. And whane he was kynge he was called Iobab. And in þat kyngdome he leuyde c.lxx. ȝeer, and so he was of elde whene he dyed cc.xlviii. ȝeer. In þat londe of Iob is no defaute of nothynge þat is nedfulle to a mans body.]

And þer is an hulle whare men fyndeþ manna. Manna is yclepid breed of aungelis, þat is a whyt þing riȝt swote and my[che] swetter þan sugre or hony, and þat comeþ of þe dewe of heuene þat falliþ on þe herbis and þere hit coaguleþ and waxiþ white. And men doþ it in medecyns of riche men.

Þis lond of Iob marchiþ to þe lond of Caldee, þat is a grete lond, and þere is riȝt faire folk and wel aparayld. And wymmen beþ riȝt laithe and yuel cloþed, and þei goþ barfote, [and berys an ille cote large, wyde, and schorte vnto the knees and longe scleues doune to þe fote. And þei haue grete heyre and longe hyngand aboute þe scholdres].

And þanne is þe lond of Amasonye, þat is a lond whare is no man but alle wymmen dwellyng, as men seiþ, for þei wole suffre no man among hem noþer to haue lordschipe of hem. For somtyme was þer a kyng in þat lond and men dwellyng as dide in oþer cuntrez [and hade wyffys], and hit bifel þat þe kyng hadde werre wiþ [heme] of Sichy [and he was callede Solapence] and he was sleiȝe in bateil and al þe f. 75v good blood of his lond wiþ hym. And whenne þe | queene and oþer ladies of þe lond herde telle þat þe kyng and þe lordis were þus sleiȝe, þei gedrid hem togedir and armed hem wel and þei slowe al þe men þat were yleft in here lond. And siþþe þat tyme dwellid no man among hem.

And whenne þei wole haue ony man to lye by hem, þei sende for hem into a cuntre þat is nere to here lond, and þe men beþ þere viii.

1 good] 2C *adds* and sithe he was so pore þat he hadde no good but þe grace of god 4 Iobab] 2B Iacob clxxx] 2P lcxx 5–6 In . . . body] 2C *om.* 8 myche] Q my 9–10 on þe herbis] C from þe erbis to þe erbis on erþe 10 coaguleþ] CM *add* þat ys to say (M *om.*) rynis togidur as cruddis of milk; 2B *adds* congyleþ 11 riche men] Q richement 14 laithe and] 2B *om.* 14–17 and . . . scholdres] G1 *om.* 18 þanne] G2–G5 aftre þe londe of Caldee 19 alle] M *om.* dwellyng] 2P *om.* man] G2–G5 *add* lyfe 20 For] M and þys ys þe cause for 21–22 and hade wyffys] G1 *om.* 22 heme] G1 þe kyng 23 and he was callede Solapence] G1 *om.* 24 wiþ hym] G2–G5 *om.* 25 þus] G2–G5 *om.* 26 and armed hem wel] G2–G5 *om.* wel] C *om.* 27 yleft] C *om.* lond] 2P *adds* among theym 27–28 And siþþe . . . hem] G2–G5 *om.* 29 ony] A *adds* among hem sende] D wol sende 30 þe men beþ þere] M when þe men come they be amonges þes wymmen 6 beþ] G2–G5 comes and is

dayes oþer as longe as þe wymmen wole and þenne þei goþ aȝen. And yf þei haue knaue children, þei sende hem to here fadris when þei kunne goo and ete. And yf þei haueþ mayde children, þei kepe hem wel. And yf þei be of gentel blood, þei brenne of þe lyft pap for beryng of a schild; and yf þei be of oþer blood, þei brenne of þe riȝt pap for scheotyng of a bowe. For wymmen þere beþ goode werriouris [and are oft in soude with oþere lordes]. And þe queene gouerneþ þat lond wel.

[This londe is alle enuyrond with watyr. Bysyde Amazone is the londe of Turmagute þat is a good londe and profitable and for goodnesse of þe londe kynge Alisaundre dide make a cite þeire þat he called Alisaundre.]

On þat oþer side of Caldee toward þe souþ is Ethiope þat is a grete lond. In þis lond on þe souþ side is þe folk | ful blak. And in f. 76r
þat side is a welle þat on þe day þe water is cold þat no man may drinke it, and on þe nyȝt hit is so hoot þat no man may suffre [to put his hand þereinne]. In þis lond þe ryueris and alle þe watris beþ trouble and somdel salt for þe grete hete. And men of þat lond beþ liȝtliche drunke and haueþ litel appetyt to mete. And þei haueþ comunliche þe flixe [and þei lyue noght longe].

In Ethiope beþ siche folk þat haueþ but o fote and þei goþ so fast þat hit is merueyl, and þat is a large fote þat makiþ schadewe and coucreþ al þe body fro þe sonne. And in Ethiope is þe cite of Saba, of whiche on of þe þre kyngis þat offrid to oure lord was kyng.

## CHAPTER 15 þE LAND OF YNDE

I haue tolde to ȝow of Ethiope, fro when men goþ to Ynde þurȝ many dyuerse cuntrez. Hit is yclepid Ynde þe more and hit is partid in þre partyes, þat is to say, Ynde þe more þat is a ful hote lond,

1 goþ] CM wende hom 3 and ete] 2B *om.* 4 wel] 2P *om.* gentel] M grete blode or of gentylle 5 oþer] G2–G5 lytylle riȝt] Q riȝt riȝt 6 of a bowe] G2–G5 *om.* 7 and are . . . lordes] G1 *om.* in soude] 2B yn sewde; 2C ysouded queene] G2–G5 *add* of þat londe 9–12 This . . . called Alisaundre] G1 *om.* 9 enuyrond] 2B enmyrede; 2C closed 10 of] 2P that 13 Ethiope] CM 2B Egypt þat is] 2A *om.* 15 is[2]] G2–G5 is so 16 it] C þe water 16–17 to put his hand þereinne] G1 hit 17 and alle þe watris] C *om.* 18–20 And men . . . longe] 2C *om.* 20 flixe] G2–G5 *add* of body and þei . . . longe] G1 *om.* 21, 23, 26 Ethiope] 2B Egypte 21 siche] A *om.* 22 is[1]] 2P is a greate 23 al] 2P *om.* cite] CM lond 24 offrid to] G2–G5 sought 25 QBCDM *om.* *rubric* 26 I haue . . . fro when] G2–G5 from Ethiope 28 to say] D *om.*

f. 76v Ynde þe lasse þat is a tempre lond, and þe þridde part | which is toward þe norþ. þare it is riȝt cold so þat for grete cold and frost and grete yss þe water bicomeþ crestal, and on þat growiþ þe goode dyamaund whiche is yliche to a troublid colour. And þat dyamaund is so hard þat no man may breke it. Oþer dyamaundis men fynde in Arabye þat beþ nouȝt so goode, whyche beþ more naysche. And somme beþ in Cypre and somme men fynde in Macydoyne, but þe beste beþ yn Ynde. And somme beþ yfounde many tymes yn a masse þat comeþ oute whare men fyneþ gold fro þe myne [when men breke þe masse in peces. And sommetyme men fyndez somme of gretnesse of a pees and somme lesse] and þese beþ as harde as þese of Ynde.

And yf al it be þat men fynde goode dyamaundes in Ynde vpon þe roche of crestal, also men fynde dyamaundis goode and harde vpon þe roche of þe adamaunde in þe see and vpon hillis as it were notes of hasel. And þei beþ alle square and poynted of here owne kynde and þei growe togedir, male and femal. And þei beþ ynorischid wiþ | f. 77r dewe of heuene, and þei engendre comynliche and bringeþ forþ smale children þat multeplieþ and growiþ al þe ȝeris. I haue many tymes assayed þat if a man kepe hem wiþ a litel of þe rochis and wete hem wiþ Mayes dewe ofte si*þ*es, þei schal growe eche ȝere and þe smale schal wexe grete.

And a man schal bere þe dyamaund at his left side and þan it is of more vertu þan on þe riȝt side, for þe strengþe of his growyng is toward þe norþ whiche is at þe lyft side of þe world and at þe lyft side of a man when he turneþ his face toward þe eest.

And if ȝe wole knowe þe vertu of þe dyamaund, Y schal telle ȝow as þei þat beþ ouer þe see seiþ. þe dyamaund ȝeueþ to hym þat beriþ it hardynesse and kepiþ þe lymes of a man hoole. Hit ȝeueþ hym grace to ouercome his enemys, if his cause be riȝtwise, boþe in werre and in pledyng. [It kepys hym þat berys it in god wyte], hit kepiþ

1 tempre] 2A fulle tempre  1–2 which is . . . it is] C toward þe norþe is; M þere it is  2–3 so þat . . . yss] C and of þe gret frost and ise þat is þere in  3 grete[2]] 2P *om.* þat] M þat crystalle  5 men fynde] C þere ben fownd many  7 Cypre] 2B Egypt  8 yn[1]] 2B yn þys northe  9 fyneþ] Q fyndeþ  9–11 when . . . lesse] G1 2C *om.*  12–13 in Ynde . . . harde] 2B *om.*  13 also] M ȝet  and harde] A and fyne; 2P *om.*  17 comynliche] G2–G5 samene (*va.* togedur)  20 Mayes] 2P many  siþes] Q sides  23 þan on þe riȝt side] G2–G5 *om.*  riȝt] C todur  24 at] G2–G5 *om.*  24–25 of þe world . . . side] D *om.*  24–26 of þe world . . . ȝow] 2P *om.*  27 þei þat beþ ouer þe see] G2–G5 men of þois countreez  28 of a man hoole] G2–G5 of his body  29 grace to ouercome] G2–G5 victorie of  cause] M *adds* þat he vndyrtakyth  29–30 boþe . . . pledyng] G2–G5 *om.*  30 pledyng] A metynge  It kepys . . . wyte] Q *om.*  wyte] 2P wyll

hym fro stryues, debatis, and riotis, and fro yuel dremynges and fantasies and fro wickide spirites. And yf ony man | þat deliþ wiþ f. 77[v] sorserie oþer enchauntemenz wolde greue hym þat beriþ þe dyamande, he schal not dere hym. Also no [wilde] beest schal asayle hym þat beriþ hit.

Also þe dyamaunde schulde be ȝeue, not ycoueited, and not bouȝt but freliche, and þanne it is of more vertu and makiþ a man more staleworþ aȝens his enemys. Hit heeliþ hym þat is l*un*atyk [and that is traueylede with a deuylle]. And yf venym oþer poysoun be brouȝt in place whare þe dyamaund is, als soone hit wexiþ moyst and bygynneþ to swete. And men may wel police hit [bot many werkmen for malice wille noght polyce heme] for þat men schulde trowe þat þei miȝte [not] be polyschid.

And men may wel assaye þe dyamaunde in þis manere. First men schere wiþ hem in safires oþer in somme oþer precious stoones vpon crestal or siche oþer, and þanne men take þe adamaund, þat is þe schipman stoon þat drawiþ þe nedle to hym, and þei leye þe dyamaund vpon þe adamaund and leyþ a nedle byfore þe adamaund, and yf þe dyamaund be goode and vertuous þe adamaunde drawiþ not þe nedle to hym | while þe dyamaund is þare. And þis is þe assay f. 78[r] whiche þei makiþ biȝonde þe see. But hit falliþ somtyme þat þe goode diamaund leosiþ his vertu defaut of hym þat beriþ it, and þerfore it is nedeful to make hit to haue his vertue aȝen oþer ellis it is of litel prys. And þer beþ many oþer maners of preciouse stoones.

And hit is yclepid Ynde for a water þat renneþ þurȝ þat lond þat men clepiþ Ynde. In þat water men fyndeþ eelys of xxx. feete long. And men þat dwelliþ nere þat water beþ of yuel colour, ȝolewe and

1 debatis] G2–G5 *om.* and[3]] CM of 2 fantasies . . . deliþ wiþ] G2–G5 *om.* wickide] C all 3–4 wolde . . . dere hym] G2–G5 *om.* 4 Also] 2B *adds* anoþur þyng wilde] QA wickide 5 þat beriþ hit] G2–G5 *om.* 6–7 not ycoueited . . . but] G2–G5 *om.*; 2C 2P *add* wiþoute couetyng oþer beggyng; 2B *adds* withouten couetyse and elles hyt scholde ben trewly bouȝt wiþ trewe byyeten catelle and yet hyt haþ nouȝt halfe þe vertues to ben trewly bouȝt as hit haþ to ben trewly yeue wiþouten grete coueytyse as men seyen þare 7–8 makiþ a man . . . enemys] G2–G5 *om.* 8 lunatyk] Q lymatyk 8–9 and that . . . deuylle] G1 *om.* 10 place whare] G2–G5 presence of 11–13 police hit . . . polyschid] 2B parseyue hit and þenne hyt may make hem wel leuen and sicour to be þat he be not poysenyd 11–12 bot . . . heme] QD 2P *om.* 13 not] QD *om.* polyschid] C no craft don to hem 14 And men] M and þus ye men[2]] G2–G5 *om.* 15 safires] A glases; C glas; DM G2 gasirs 16–19 þat is . . . dyamaund] 2P *om.* 20 þare] C *om.* 22 vertu] CM *add* by 23 haue] G2–G5 couer 24 oþer maners of] D oþer of; M of oþer stoones] M *adds* yn the contres of Ynde 25–26 for a water . . .Ynde] 2P *om.* 25 renneþ] C riȝt þere lond] M *om.*

greene. In Ynde beþ mo þan fyue þowsand yles þat men dwelliþ ynne, goode and grete, wiþoute oþer þat men dwelliþ noȝt ynne. And in eueryche of þese beþ many citez and townes and myche folk, for men of Ynde beþ of o condicoun þat þei passiþ not out of here lond comunliche. For þei dwelliþ vndir a planete þat me clepiþ Saturne, and þat plantet makiþ his torn by þe xii. signes in xx. ȝere, f. 78v and þe moone passiþ þurȝ þe xii. | signes in a monþe. And for Saturne is of so late steryng, þerfor men þat dwellen vndir hym and þat clymate haueþ no goode wille to be myche steryng aboute. And in oure cuntre is al þe contrarie, for we beþ in a clymate þat is of þe moone and of liȝt steryng, and þat is þe planete of way. And þerfore it ȝeueþ vs wille to be myche stering and to go in dyuerse cuntrez of þe world, for hit passiþ aboute þe world more liȝtlich þan anoþer planet.

Also men gooþ þurȝ Ynde by many cuntrez vnto þe grete [see of] Occian and þanne þei fynde þe yle of Hermes, whider merchauntz of Venys and Geene and oþer parties of cristendome comeþ to bigge merchaundises. But it is so hote þare in þat yle þat men [ballokez] hongiþ doun to here schankis for þe grete dissolucioun of þe body. And men of þat cuntre þat knowiþ þe maner lete bynde hem vp ful strayte and oynteþ hem wiþ oynementis ymade þerfore to holde hem vp, oþer ellis myȝt þei not lyue.

f. 79r In þis lond and many oþer men and wym|men leiþ hem al naked in ryueris and watris fro vndren of þe day til hit be passid noon. And þei lieþ alle in þe water but þe visage for grete hete þat is þare. In þis yle beþ þe schippis wiþoute nayles oþer bondes of yrun for rochis of adamaundis þat beþ in þe see þat wolde drawe schippis to hem.

Fro þis yle men goþ to þe yle of Canaa by see whare is grete plente of wyn and of corn. [And þe kynge of þis ile was sommetyme so myghty þat he helde werre with þe kyng Alisandre.] And men of þis yle haue dyuerse lawis, for somme worschepiþ þe sonne and somme

1 fyue] D fyfty þowsand] AD *om.* 3 And in eueryche of þese] M *om.* and townes] G2–G5 *om.* 5 For] M and by þys encheson for 6 torn] 2P cours xii.] C *adds* palyne in xx. ȝere . . . signes] D *om.* 8 Saturne] 2A þat and] G2–G5 and in 9 myche] D *om.*; G2–G5 *add* meuynge or 10 þat is] C *om.* 11 liȝt] 2A moch 12 ȝeueþ] BD ryueth myche] G2–G5 *add* mouande and styrande 15 see of] G1 *om.* 18 ballokez] G1 *om.* (B *corrected by later hand*) 19 doun . . . dissolucioun] C so lusioun doun] M and stowpe alle downe 21 oynteþ] D vnte 25 in þe water] C þerein 26 beþ] C þere ar mad oþer bondes] A *om.* for] CM for dred of 27 to hem] C *adds* ar bownd wiþ iroun; 2B doun to hem 28 þis yle] M *adds* of Hermes 29–30 And . . . Alisandre] G1 *om.* 30 helde] 2B *adds* strange 31 þe sonne and somme] C *om.*

þe fuyr, somme naddris, somme treez, somme þe firste þing þat þei meten [in] þe morwenyng, somme worschipe symylacris, somme ydols. But bitwene symylacris and ydols is a grete difference, for symylacris beþ ymagis made to what likenesse of a þing þat a man wole þat is not kyndelich, for somme ymage haþ þre hedis, on of a man, anoþer of an hors, and anoþer of an oxe oþer anoþer beest þat no man haþ seye.

And ȝe schal vndirstonde þat þei þat worschipe symylacris, þei worschipe hem for | [f. 79v] some worþi men þat were somtyme as Hercules oþer siche ooþer, whiche dide many merueyles in here tymes. For þei say þei wote wel þei beþ not God of kynde þat made alle þing, but þei beþ riȝt wel wiþ God for merueiles þat þei dooþ [and þerfor þei worschip hem]. And so þei seiþ of þe sonne, for it chaungiþ ofte tymes of þe ȝere and ȝeueþ hete to norische alle þingis of þe erþe. And for it is of so grete profyt, þei say þei wote wel þat hit is [noght Gode bot it is] w*e*lle wiþ God and þat God loueþ hit wel more þan ony oþer, and þerfore þei worschipe hit. And þus say þei of fuyre for hit is profitable. And þus make þei skiles why þei worschipe oþer planetis and þinges.

And of ydolis þei say þe oxe is þe moost holiest beest þat is in erþe and most profitable, for he doþ many goode þinges and noon yuel. And þei wote wel þat þat may not be wiþoute special grace of God. And þerfor þei make here god half man and half oxe, for man is þe fairest and best creature þat God made and þe oxe | [f. 80r] þe holiest.

And þei dooþ worschip to naddris and oþer beestis whiche þei meete first in þe morwenyng, and namelych to þeese bestis whiche haue good metyng, aftir wham þey spede wel al day, which þei haue

1 firste] D *om.* 2 in] Q *om.* somme] 2P and 3 But . . . ydols] C *om.* symylacris] 2P som sacres a grete] 2A a; 2B a wele grete; 2P no 7 seye] C *adds* idolfis ben alle of quyck bestis 10 oþer siche] G2–G5 and 11–12 þei beþ . . . but] 2B *om.* 11 God] BCD good 12 riȝt] 2A 2P *om.* 12–13 and . . . hem] G1 *om.* 13 seiþ of] 2B sal also þulke þat leuen vppon ofte] CM in 14 of þe ȝere and] G2–G5 somme tyme hete] G2–G5 grete hete 15–16 noght . . . is] G1 *om.* 16 welle] QD wille; 2B hys wille and þat hyt is 17–19 worschipe . . . þinges] G2–G5 say it is good skylle to worschipe it And so þei make skyllys of oþere planetis And of fyre also for it is so profitable and nedfulle (*After* planetis 2B *continues* And þanne oþer seyen þat to worschepen þe fyre hyt ys moost worthy ffor ne myȝt noon man lyue wiþ outen fyre why ffor hit ys helpynge to dyȝtten oure lyflode and many oþere necessarytees þat vs be houeþ And by þys skyle þey worschepen hyt) 18 þus] A *om.* skiles] CM *add* and resunys 19 and þinges] C *om.* 20 moost holiest] CM *om.* is] 2P they may fynd 21 profitable] G2–G5 *add* of alle oþere 23 god] CM idolf 24 creature þat God made . . . holiest] C þyng in þe worlde and þe oxe þe holiest best in þe worlde; G2–G5 creature of þe worlde 26 first] B *om.* 26–74/7 and namelych . . . say] 2C *om.* 27 haue good metyng] CM þay have in þere dremis

proued of long tyme. And þerfore þei seiþ, þis goode metyng comeþ fro God. And þerfore haue þei lete make ymages liche to þese in here houses þat þey may worschipe hem bifore þey meete wiþ ony oþer þingis.

[And yit are somme cristen men þat say þat somme beste are better to mete þan somme, for hares swyne and oþere bestes ar il to mete first als þei say.]

In þis yle of Canaa beþ many wilde beestis, and ratouns of þat cuntre beþ as grete as houndis here, and þei take hem þere wiþ grete mastyfs for cattis beþ to smale. [Fro þyne men come to a cite þat men calle Sarchie, and it is a faire and a good citee and þeire dwellys many crystyn men of good faythe, and þeire is men of religioun.]

Fro þenne men goþ to þe lond of Lombe whare is þe cite of Polome, and vndir þat cite is an hulle þat men clepiþ Polome, of whiche þe cite takiþ his name. And at þe fot of þe hulle is a faire welle þat haþ swete sauour and smel of alle manere of spices, and at eueryche oure of þe day hi*t* chaungiþ his sauour. And who so | f. 80v drinkeþ þries on þe day of þat welle, he is ymade hool of alle sikenesse þat he haþ. [I haue sommetyme dronkyn of þat welle and me þynke ȝit Y fare þe bettyre.] Somme clepiþ hit þe welle of ȝowþe, for þei þat drinkeþ þerof semeþ alwey to be ȝong [and lyuys withoute grete seknes]. Þei seiþ þis welle comeþ fro paradys terrestre for it is so vertuous. [In þat contree growys gyngyuer, and þedyr comys many good marchauntes for spices.]

In þis cuntre men worschipe þe oxe for his grete semplesse and his mekenesse and þe profyt þat is in hym. Þei make þe oxe to traueile vi. oþer vii. ȝere and siþþe men ete hym. And þe kyng of þis lond haþ alway an oxe wiþ hym. And he þat kepiþ hym takiþ eche day [his fees for þe kepynge and also iche day he gedyrs] his vryn and his

1 of long] C many 2 God] 2P Goddes grace þese] C hir bestes þat þey mete of and kepe hem 2–3 in here houses] G2–G5 þyngys 5–7 And yet . . . say] G1 *om.* 5 yit] 2A it 9 grete] 2P *om.* 10 beþ to smale] G2–G5 may not take heme 10–12 Fro . . . religioun] G1 *om.* 11–12 and þeire . . . religioun] 2C *om.* 13 þenne] M þys yle of Cana þe[2]] 2B þre 14 and vndir . . . Polome] M *om.* 15 his] 2B *adds* manly hulle] 2P same hyll faire] 2P righte fayre and a clere 16 haþ] M *adds* soote and smel] A G2–G5 smelleth 17 hit] Q his sauour] G2–G5 *add* dyuersely 19 þat he haþ] 2B of alle þat yere; 2C *adds* and þis telle I forsothe 19–20 I haue . . . bettyre] G1 *om.*; 2B *adds* and euermore Y trowe Y schal 19 sommetyme] 2B myselue welle] C *adds* of grase and 21 þat] C *om.* 21–22 and lyuys . . . seknes] G1 *om.* 23–24 In þat . . . spices] G1 *om.* 25 grete] C *om.* his] M his goode 27 and] Q and and men] 2B men sleen hem and lond] M lond Cana 28 alway] C *om.* he] 2A *om.* 29 his fees . . . gedyrs] G1 *om.*

dunge in a vessel of gold and beriþ it to here prelate þat ys yclepid Archiprotapapaton. And þis prelate beriþ it to þe kyng and makiþ þervpon a grete blessyng. And þanne þe kyng puttiþ his hond þerynne, and þei clepiþ hit *gaule*, and he anoynteþ his [front and his] breest þerwiþ. And þei don hit grete worschip and seiþ he schal be fulfilde wiþ vertues of þe oxe [byforsayde] and þat he schal be halewid þurȝ vertu of þat holy | þing, as þei seiþ. And whanne þe f. 81r kyng haþ do, þanne takiþ oþer lordys and þanne oþer men as þei beþ in degre when þei may gete a remenaunt.

In þis cuntre here ydoles, þat is to say, false goddis, beþ half man and half oxe in schap, and in þes false goddis spekiþ to hem þe deuel and ȝeueþ ansuere of what þei aske. Bifore þese false goddis þei slee here children many tymes and springe þe blood of hem vpon þe false goddis, and þus þei make sacrifice to hem.

And yf ony man deiȝe in þat lond, þei brenneþ hym [in tokenynge of penaunce] for þat he schulde suffre no penaunce yf he were leid in þe erþe of etyng of wormes. And yf [his wyf] haue no children, þei brenne his wyf al quyke wiþ him and seiþ it is good skile þat heo make hym cumpeny in þe oþer world as heo dide in þis. And yf heo haue ony children, heo may lyue wiþ hem yf heo wole. And yf þe wyf deiȝe first, men brenne hure and here housbande yf he wile. In þis lond growiþ good wyn, and wymmen | drinkiþ wyn and men f. 81v nouȝt, and wymmen schaueþ here berdis and men nouȝt.

Fro þis lond men goþ to anoþer lond þat is x. iourneys long, whiche men clepiþ Mabaron. And þis is a grete kyngdome whare beþ many feire citez and townes. In þis lond liþ seynt Thomas in fleisch and fel in a [fayr] toumbe in a cite þat is yclepid Calamy. And þe arm wiþ þe hond whiche he putte in oure lordis body when he was arise and oure lord seyde to hym, *Noli esse incredulus sed fidelis*, þat is to

1 beriþ] M kepyth 3 hond] 2B ryȝt hande þereyn and sythen hys lefte hande 4 þei] G1–G5 þenne þei front and his] QBD *om.* 6 byforsayde] G1 *om.* schal be] 2A is 7 þat holy . . . seiþ] C þe wordis þat þay say ouir þat þing þei] 2B *adds* yn þat countree 8 haþ] G2–G5 has thus takiþ oþer lordys] M do oþer lordys anoynte þem as þe kyng dude 10 þat is . . . goddis] G2–G5 *om.* 11 in schap . . . goddis] G2–G5 and in thise idoles deuel] G2–G5 wykyde gast 12, 13–14 false goddis] G2–G5 idoles 14 to hem] G2–G5 *om.* 15–16 in . . . penaunce] G1 *om.* 16 suffre] B *om.* yf he were leid] M *om.* 17 his wyf] G1 he 18 his wyf al quyke] G2–G5 here good] C *om.* 19 as heo dide] B for he made her cumpeny 20 wiþ hem] B *om.* yf] A G2–G5 also yf 21 wile] C *adds* and els not 22, 24 lond] M lond of Cana 24 x.] G2–G5 many long] C þens; G2–G5 *om.* 25 grete] M *adds* londe and a grete 26 Thomas] M *adds* of Ynde 27 and fel] ADM G2–G5 *om.*; C and blood fayr] QB *om.* 28 he putte] C was arise] CM *add* from deþe to lif

say, Be nouȝt of wanhope but trewe, þat same hond liþ ȝit wiþoute þe toumbe bare, and wiþ þis hond þei ȝeueþ iugementz and domes in þat cuntre to wite who haþ riȝt. For ȝif ony stryf be bitwene twey parties, þei lete write here riȝt in tweye bullis, and þese bullis beþ yput in þe hond of seynt Thomas. And als soone þe hond castiþ awey þe bulle of hym þat haþ wrong and holdiþ stille þat bulle whiche haþ riȝt. And þerfore men comeþ fro ferre to haue doome of f. 82r here cau|sis þat beoþ in doute.

In þe chirche of seynt Thomas is a grete ymage of a fals god wel diȝt and richelyche wiþ preciouse stones and perlys, and to þat ymage men comeþ fro fer in pilgrimage wiþ grete deuocioun as cristen men goþ to seynt Iame. And þer comeþ somme in pilgrimage þat beriþ scharpe knyues in here hondis, wiþ whiche as þei gooþ by þe way þe[i] scheren here shankis and here þies þat þei bleede for loue of þat god. [And þei say þat he is holy þat wolle dye for þat god sake.] And somme beþ þere þat fro þat tyme þat þei go out of here hous til þei come þere, at eueryche þridde stap þei kneliþ on þe erþe. [And whan þei come þeire þei haue encense or soch oþere swete þyng to encense þeire idole, als we wold do to Goddys body.]

And bifore þat chirche is a veuer ful of water in whiche pilgrimes castiþ gold and siluer, precious stones and perlis wiþouten noumbre in stede of offryng. And þerfore whenne þe chirche hadde neode of helpyng, þei take of þat veuere what þei mystre and sille hit and do aparayle þe chirche.

And ȝe schal vndirstonde whenne grete feestis come of þat false god, as þe dedicacioun of þe chirche oþer þe tro|nyng of þat god, al

2 bare] C all bare iugementz and] G2–G5 *om.* 3 riȝt] B *adds* for þereby þey wollen knowe þe ryȝt; G2–G5 *add* and who noght be] B be in that land 3 riȝt] M *adds* and þare cause 6 þat bulle] C G2–G5 þe todur 7 whiche] A of hym þat 7 doome] M *adds* þere 9 of a fals god] G2–G5 þat is a similacre 10 richelyche] CM *add* araid; G2–G5 ryche 12 And þer comeþ] C so cum; M and þerfore 14 þei] Q þe and here þies] D *om.*; M *adds* and þemselfe þei bleede] G2–G5 (*ex* 2B) þe blode may come oute; 2B þe bloode so wylfully and scharpely renneþ out also blyue as hyt may and alle togedur þat ys 15 god] G2–G5 idole 15–16 And þei . . . sake] G1 *om.* 15 he] 2B he or schee wheþere þat hyt be 17 on þe erþe] 2P *om.* 18–19 And when . . . body] G1 *om.*; 2B *adds* and wel mochel more þanne eny crysten man dooþ 18 haue] 2B *adds* redy wiþ hem 19 do] 2B doon amonges vs 20 chirche] G2–G5 mynstyre of þis idole veuer] 2A *adds* or a stonge; 2B 2P ryuere; 2C stocke 21 perlis] 2B *adds* and somme drowen yn of holyest þyngges and mooste precyouste þat þey han so þat ylke ryuere ys golde seluere precyous stones and perlees 23 helpyng] M þat offryng 23–24 and sille . . . chirche] 2A 2B to apperelynge of þe mynstre; 2P *om.*; 2B *adds* somme seyen þat hyt scholde ben a ryuere but hyt ys nouȝt so for hyt ys a pool or else a veyuere 25–26 false god] G2–G5 idole 26 tronyng] B trowyng god] G2–G5 idole

þe cuntre is assemblid þedir and men settiþ þis false god oþer ellis a mawmet wiþ grete worschip in a chariot wel ydi3t wiþ riche cloþis of gold and oþer and lede hym wiþ grete solempnite about þe citee. And bifore þe chariot goþ first in processioun al þe maydouns of þe cuntre, twey and twey togedre, and þanne al þe pilgrimes, of whiche somme falliþ doun bifore þe chariot and letiþ hit go ouer hem and so beþ þei slei3e, and somme here armus and schankis tobroke [and þis do þei for loue of þe idole]. And þei trowe þe more peyne þat þei suffre here for here mowmet sake, þe more ioi3e schal þei haue in anoþer world. [And a man schalle fynde fewe crysten men þat wolle suffre so mochel penance for oure lorde sake als þei do for þeire idole.]

And next bifore þe chariot goþ alle þe mynstrels of þat lond [as it were withouten nombre, with many dyuers melodyes]. And whenne þei beþ ycome a3en to þe chirche, þei sette vp þis mawmet in his trone, and for worschipe of þe mawmet twey men oþer þre doþ slee hem [with scharpe knyvys] wiþ here good wille. And [als a man þynke in oure countree þat he has a grete worschip and he haue a holy man in hys kynne, so] whenne þei beþ deed þei seiþ þat þese beþ seyntes and þei beþ ywrite in here | bookis and here letonyes. f. 83r And here frendes letiþ brenne he*r* [bodyes] and þei take þe askis and kepiþ hem as relikes [and þei say þat þat is holy þynge], and þey haue no doute while þei haue of þese askis on hem.

Fro þis cuntre men goþ þur3 many cuntreez and yles, of whiche were to long to telle, by two and fyfty iurnees to a cuntre þat is clepid Lamory. In þat lond is a grete hete and is þe custome þare þat

1 settiþ] C fet . . . and settis   false god] G2–G5   idole god oþer ellis a] M *om.*   oþer ellis a mawmet] G2–G5 *om.*   2–3 of golde] 2P and gode   3 oþer] M *adds* precous iewellys; 2B *adds* precious stones   4–5 of þe cuntre] C of al þe cuntre abowt; M *om.*   5 þanne] M þes be þe maydons of alle þe contre and þer aftur þes maydons   pilgrimes] 2P *adds* that are come from ferre countrees   5–6 of whiche somme] B *om.*   7 and somme] QABD somme and (D and so) and somme; C dede and sum; M and so sum   7–8 and þis . . . idole] G1 *om.*   9 sake] A *om.*   10 world] C *adds* whan þay ar dede   10–12 And a man . . . idole] G1 2C *om.*   13 next bifore þe chariot] C betwene þe charyet and þe maydin   13–14 as it were . . . melodyes] G1 *om.*; 2B *adds* so many skynnes melodyes þat hyt weere to longe to telle   15 mawmet] C and wiþ ii or iii men; 2P idol ageyne   17 with scharpe knyvys] G1 *om.*   178–19 als a man . . . so] G1 *om.*   19 whenne . . . þese] G2–G5 say þey þeire that þois þat ar þus sclayne   20 letonyes] M *adds* and þey haue no dowte but þat þey be seynttys; 2B *adds* and ben prayed to yn heere synagogiis as we doon enye seynt of heuen and yet more worschyppe doon þey to hem   21 And] G2–G5 and when þei ar þus dede   her bodyes] G1 hem   21–22 take . . . kepiþ] A *om.*   22 and þei . . . þynge] G1 *om.*   23 doute] G2–G5 *add* of perile   24 cuntre] M *adds* of Mabaron   24–25 of whiche . . . telle] G2–G5 *om.*   26 In] C þat is in   þare] 2A 2B soche; 2P sith

men and wymmen alle go nakid and þei scorne hem þat beþ ycloþid, for þei seiþ God made Adam and Eue nakid and þat men schulde haue no schame of þat þat God made, for noȝt is foule þat God made. And þei trowe in God þat made Adam and Eue and alle þe world.

And þer beþ no wymmen yweddid, but wommen beþ alle in comune and þei forsake no man. And þei seiþ þat God comaundid to Adam and Eue and alle þat come of hem, seiyng *Crescite et multiplicamini et replete terram*, þat is to say, Wexeþ and beþ multeplied and fulle þe erþe. And no man þere | [f. 83v] may say 'þis is my wyf', no womman 'þis is myn housbande'. And whenne þei haue children, þei ȝeue hem whom þei wole of men þat haþ leye by hem.

[Also] þe lond is comune, for þat a man haþ o ȝere anoþer man haþ anoþer ȝere. Also al þe goodes and cornes beþ in comune for þere is noþing vndir loke, and as ryche is o man as anoþer. But þei haueþ oon yuel custome; þei etiþ gladloker mannus fleisch þan oþer. And þedir bringeþ merchauntis here children to sille, and þese þat beþ fatte þei etiþ hem, and oþer þei kepe and fede til þei be fatte and þanne beþ þey yȝete, for þei seiþ it is þe best and swettist fleisch of þe world.

In þis londe neþer in many oþer þeraboute men may not se þe sterre þat is yclepid Transmountayne which stondiþ euen norþ and steriþ neuer, by whiche schipmen beþ ylad, for it is not seye toward þe souþ. But þer is anoþer sterre which is yclepid Antertyk and þat is euen aȝenst þat oþer sterre, and by þat sterre schipmen beþ ylad; þerfore | [f. 84r] þat is nouȝt seye toward þe norþ. And þerfore men may wel se þat þe lond and þe see is al round, for parties of þe firmament

1 hem] C all þem  3–4 for noȝt . . . made] 2B 2P *om.*  4 made] C *om.*  6 þer] B þerfor  7 comune] 2B *adds* þare yn euery place of þat lande þere ne ys noon oþere and also þe moost merueyle of alle  man] 2B *adds* þat wolle hem aske þe pley of loue but wel fayn graunteþ hem heere lykynge and a skyle whyfor  comaundid] D made  8 seiyng] AB *add* þing  9 say] 2P *adds* in englysshe  10 þere] G2–G5 *om.*  may say] C *adds* sir; D *om.*  12 hem] 2A 2P *om.*; 2B þe chylde  wole] 2B *adds* and þat þey beest louen  men] C seche men  13 Also] Q and; CM and also  is] G2–G5 is alle  14 cornes] G2–G5 *add* of þe countre  15–16 þei . . . custome] 2B yf hyt be so þat eny of hem haþe an hylle of custome by wytte þat he hathe byfore anoþere and þat he haþe yette by assente of hem alle for hys goude techynge and rulynge of þe people (see Appendix 9)  16 oþer] C ony odur mete; M oþer flessche  18–19 til þei . . . yȝete] C whyll þay wyll  19 for] C tyl  19–20 for þei . . . world] G2–G5 *om.*  21–82/13 In þis lond . . . world] G2–G5 (*ex* 2C) *om.*  22–23 and steriþ neuer] B *om.*  23 ylad] CM *add* into þe see  not] A north  24 þer] M *adds* in toward þat contre  sterre] M *adds* þat sytteth euyn y þe sowth  26 þerefore] 2C toward the souþ for it noȝt  nouȝt] A south  27 parties] Q *adds* and planetis  of þe firmament] B *om.*

whiche schewiþ in o place apperiþ nouȝt in anoþer. And þat may men proue þus, for ȝif a man myȝt fynde schippyng and men wolde go to see þe worlde, þei miȝte go al aboute aboue and byneþe. And þat proue Y þus after þat Y haue seye. For Y haue be in Braban and seye þe astrolobre of þe sterre Transmountayne, and hit is fyfty and foure degreez hiȝe in Almayne, and toward Beeme hit haþ fifty and viii. degreez, and more norþ hit haþ sixty and twey degreez in heiȝþe and somme mynutes.

And ȝe schal vndirstonde þat aȝens þat sterre in þe norþ is þe sterre Antertyke. Þese twey sterris steriþ neuer more, and by hem turneþ þe firmament as a wheol doþ on an axeltree so þat þese twey sterris departiþ al þe firmament in twey parties.

And þanne went Y toward þe souþ and Y fond þat in Lybye seeþ men first þe sterre Anter|tyke. And as Y went ferþer, Y fond þat in f. 84v hiȝe Libye hit haþ in heiȝþe xviii. degreez and somme mynutes, of whiche mynutes sixty makiþ a degre. And so passyng by londe and by see toward cuntreez þat Y haue spoke of bifore and oþer londis and yles aȝens hem, Y fonde þis Antertyke of xxxiii. [degrees] in heiȝþe and many mynutes.

And yf Y hadde cumpenye and schippyng þat wolde haue go ferrer, I trowe forsoþe þat we wolde haue seye al þe roundenesse of þe firmament. For, as Y seide ȝow, half þe firmament is bitwene þese twey sterris, whiche half Y haue seye, for half þe firmament haþ no more [but] ix. score degreez, of whiche Y haue seye sixty and twey degreez and ten mynutes of þe sterre Transmountayne, and of þe Antertyke toward þe souþ Y haue seye xxx. and þre degreez and xvi. mynutes. Þis beþ foure score and fiftene degreez and nere half a [degre]. And so hit lackiþ but iiii. score and foure degreez and nere half a degre þan Y haue seen alle þe firma|ment. f. 85r

And þerfore Y say sikerliche þat a man miȝte go al þe world aboute, aboue and byneþe, and come aȝen to his owne cuntre, he þat hadde schippyng. And alwey he schulde fynde men, londis, and yles

1 apperiþ] A and; 2C and appereþ 3 þe worlde] B *om.*; C *adds* all abowt; 2C *after* aboute aboue] C *om.* 6 hiȝe] A heghere; C *om.* 6–7 fifty and viii.] C lxxii; 2C lix 7 norþ] M nouȝt 10 Anteryke] CM *add* in þe sowþe 11 doþ on an axeltree] 2C in a ex tre 13 and Y fond] A *om.* 13–15 seeþ . . . Libye] 2C *om.* 15 Hiȝe Libye hit haþ in] A *om.*; B Libye of 17 of] 2C on 18 Y] 2C þey degrees] QAD *om.* 20–26 And yf . . . degreez] 2C *om.* 23 half] AM al 24 but] QD by 28 degre] QD mynute; C *adds* saf iiii. minutis; 2C minyte 28–9 nere half a degre] A an half and iiii. minutes 29 þan Y] CM þat I ne 31 byneþe and come] C bene þen and 32 men] 2C many

as beþ in þis cuntreez, for ȝe wote wel þat þese men þat dwelliþ riȝt vnder Antertyke beþ fote aȝens fote of þese þat dwelliþ riȝt vndir þe Transmountayne as wel as we. And þese men þat dwelliþ aȝens vs beþ fote aȝens fote, for alle partyes of þe erþe and see haue here contraries of þinges whiche beþ euen aȝens hem.

And ȝe schal vndirstonde þat þe lond of Prestre Ioon emperour of Ynde is vnder vs, for ȝif a man schal go fro Scotlond oþer Engelond toward Ierusalem, he schal go euer vpwarde, for oure lond is in þe lowist partye of þe west and þe lond of Prestre Ioon is in þe lowist partyre of þe eest, and þei haue day when we haue niȝt and niȝt when we haue day. And as myche as a man riseþ vpward out of oure cuntrez to Ierusalem he schal go dounward toward þe lond of f. 85v Prestre | Ioon fro Ierusalem, and þat is for al þe erþe is round.

Now ȝe haue herde telle þat Ierusalem is in þe myddel of þe world, and þat may wel be proued þus. For and a man þare take a spere and sette hit euen in þe erþe at mydday when niȝt and day is like long, hit makiþ no schadewe. And Dauid beriþ witnes when he seiþ þus, *Deus operatus est salutem in medio terre*, þat is to say, God haþ wroȝt heele in þe myddel of þe erþe.

And þerfore þei þat goþ out of oure cuntrez of þe west toward Ierusalem, as many iourneys as þei make to go þider vpward, as many iourneys schal þei make to go into þe lond of Prestre Ioon dounward fro Ierusalem. And so he may go into þese yles [enuyronyng] al þe roundnesse of þe erþe and of þe see til he come euen vndir vs.

And þerfor I haue many tymes þouȝt of a tale þat Y herde when þat Y was ȝong, how a worþy man of oure cuntre went a tyme for to see þe world. And he passide Ynde and þe yles biȝonde Ynde where f. 86r beþ mo þen. v. m[l]., and he went so long by lond and | by see goyng aboute þe world þat he fond an yle where he herde men speke his owne speche and dryue beestis, seying siche wordis as men doþ in his cuntre, of whiche he hadde grete merueyl for he wist not how þat miȝt be. But Y seye he hadde so longe went on londe and see goyng

1 cuntreez] M *adds* byforesayde wote wel] CM may welle wyt and know riȝt] C *om.* 3–4 as wel . . . aȝens fote] A *om.* 4 and see] 2C *om.* 6 þat] D *adds* in 7 is] M is ryȝt for] D fra 10–11 when we haue . . . day] B *om.* 11 a man] CM we vpward] C *adds* going 12 he] CM so moche he 13 round] C *adds* as a balle 15 world] M erthe or of þe worlde 16 euen] M *adds* vppe ryȝt 17 hit] 2C þe sper 21 to go] M *om.* 23–24 enuyronyng] QBD 2C euene round 24 erþe] C world erþe euen] C *om.* 29 v.[m]] CM *add* ilis goyng] 2C seynge 30 þat] 2C and he] D *om.* men speke] 2C *om.* 31 seying] CM and seid to hem men] B we 32 his] B this; D *adds* owen

aboute þe world þat he was ycome into his owne marchis. But for he mi3t haue no passage ferþer, he turned a3en as he come and so he hadde a grete trauayl. And hit bifel aftirward þat he went into Norwaye, and a tempest of wynd in þe see droof him so þat he aryued in an yle. And whan þat he was þare, hym þou3te þat hit was þe yle in whiche he hadde ybe bifore where he herde speke his owne speche as þe men droof beestis.

And þat mi3t ri3t wel be, if al hit be þat symple men of kunnyng trowe not þat men may go vndir þe erþe, for as vs þink þat þese men beþ vndir vs, so þink hem þat we beþ vndir hem. For yf a man | [f. 86v] mi3t falle fro þe erþe vnto þe firmament, by more skile þe erþe and þe see þat beoþ so heuy schulde falle vnto þe firmament. But þat may not be, and þerfore seide God, *Non timeas me suspendi terram ex nichilo*, þat is to say, Haue no drede þat Y haue hongid þe erþe of nou3t.

And if alle hit be possible þat a man may go al aboute þe erþe, neuerþeles of a þowsand men on schulde not take þe nexte wey to his cuntre, for it beþ so many weies and cuntrez þat a man mi3t faile but if it were special grace of God. For þe erþe is gret and long, and hit holdiþ in roundenesse aboute, aboue, and byneþe, an xx. m[l]. CCCC. and xxv. myle after opynyoun of olde wise men þat sayn hit; whiche Y wole not reproue, but aftir my litel wit me þinkeþ, saue here grace, þat it is more aboute.

And for to vndirstonde better þat Y wole say, Y ymage a figure whare ys a grete cumpas, and aboute þe poynt of þat compas, þat is yclepid þe centre, b*e* anoþer litel compas departid by lynes in | [f. 87r] many parties, and þat alle þese lynes meete togidre on þe centre; so þat as many parties oþer lynes al*s* þe grete compas haþ be on þe litel cumpas, of alle þe space b*e* lasse. Now b*e* þe grete cumpas sette for þe firmament, þe whiche by astronomeris is departid in xii. signes, and eche signe is departid in xxx. degrez; þis is ccc. and sixti degreez þat is aboute. Now be þe erþe departid in als many parties as þe firmament, and eueriche of þese ansuere to a degre of þe firmament; þis beþ in alle seuen hundrid and twenty. Now be þis alle

1 for] D *om.* 4 and] C wiþ; M and wiþ; 2C in see] 2C see and so] M so abowte 5 whan þat] BD *om.* 5–6 And whan . . . yle] A *om.* 8 kunnyng] CM *add* and of discressioun 9 men] A men þat dwellen in Ynde; 2C *om.* 11 firmament] A *adds* but þat may not ben 14 þat] A of me 15 aboute] M *om.* 16 on] B *om.* his] CDM 2C his owen 17 and cuntreez] 2C *om.* 18 long] A large 19 in roundenesse] B *om.* 19–20 ccc. and xxv.] B ccc. and xxvi. 20 þat sayn hit] A *om.*; CM þat is to say þus 24 grete] C *adds* clerkes 25, 28 be] Q 2C by 25, 27 lynes] 2C lymes 26 alle] D *om.* lynes] 2C lemes 27 als] QBD alle 28 for] A by; D forth; 2C forþ 33 seuen] B viii

ymulteplied iii. hundrid tymes and sixti, and hit schal amounte in al to xxxi. m[l]. myle and fyue, eche myle viii. furlong as myles beþ in oure cuntreez. And so myche haþ þe erþe in compas and in roundenesse al aboute after myn opynyoun and myn vndirstondyng.

And ȝe schal vndirstonde after þe opynyoun of [olde] wise philosofris and astronomeris þat Engelond, Scotlond, Walis, ne f. 87v Irlond beþ nouȝt rekened in þe heiȝþe of þe er|þe, as hit semeþ wel by alle þe bookis of astronomye, for þe heiȝþe of þe erþe is departid in vii. planetis whiche beþ yclepid clymates. And þese cuntreez þat Y spake of beþ not in þese clymates, for þei beoþ dounward so toward þe west. And also þe yles of Ynde whiche beoþ euen aȝens vs beþ not rekened in þe clymates, for þei beþ toward þe eest so lowe. And þese clymates goþ aboute al þe world.

And nere þis yle of Lamori whiche Y spake of is anoþer yle þat men clepiþ Somober þat is a good yle. Men of þat yle lete marke hem in þe visage wiþ an hote yren [men and þe wommen] for grete noblesse to be knowe fro oþere, for þei holde hemself moost worþi of þe world. And þei haueþ werre euermore wiþ þese men þat beþ nakid, which I spake of bifore.

And þer beþ many oþere cuntrez and yles and dyuerse maner of men, of whiche it were to myche to speke. But to passe a litel þen by see, men schal fynde a grete yle þat is yclepid Iaua. And þe kyng of f. 88r þat cuntre haþ vii. kynges vn|dir hym [for he is full myghty]. In þat yle growiþ alle manere of spices yn more plente þan in anoþer place, as gynger, clowis, canel, notemygge, maces, and oþer. And ȝe schal vndirstonde þat þe notemygge beriþ þe maces. Alle þing is þer yn grete plente but wyn.

Þe kyng of þis lond haþ a faire paleys and a riche, for alle þe grecis into his halle and chambris is oon of gold, anoþer of siluer, and alle

2 xxxi.] B xxx; 2C xxi   3 oure] 2C oþer   in compas and] A *om.*   3–4 and in roundenesse] C *om.*   4 after myn] M *adds* dome and myne   5 olde] QD alle; BC *om.*   7 beþ] D bote   8 by alle] B *om.*   9–10 And þese . . . clymates] 2C *om.*   11 so] M so lowe   also] C all   13 so] B to   al] C *om.*   14 nere þis] B ther is an; G2–G5 Bysyde þis   of . . . of] G2–G5 *om.* (see Appendix 9)   15 þat is a good yle] 2C *om.*   Men] C *om.*   yle] 2C *adds* and wymmen   16 men and wommen] G1 *om.*   17 to] G2–G5 and to   20–21 And þer . . . speke] 2B *om. and adds account of* ile of Hogge (see Appendix sub 2B)   20 cuntreez and] G2–G5 *om.*   21 myche] C *adds* to tell or; M *adds* alle   21–22 to passe . . . fynde] G2–G5 þeire is   21 þen] M fro Lamosy   23 for he is full myghty] G1 *om.*   24 place] B cuntrees   25 maces] 2P *om.*   oþer] M meny oþer dyuerse spyces   27 but wyn] CM *om.*   28 þe kyng] CM *add* and ȝe schall wyt þe kyng   faire] G2–G5 ryche   and a riche] CM *om.* G2–G5 *om. and add* and þe beste þat is in þe werlde   29 is] Q euer is   gold and] C *om.*

þe wallys beþ keuered and platid wiþ gold and siluer, and in þese plates beþ [wrytyn] stories of kniȝtes and batailes. And þe pauement of þe halle and chambris is of gold and siluer, and no man wolde trowe þe richesse þat is þare but yf he hadde seye hit. And þe kyng of þis yle [is so myghty þat he] haþ many tymes ouercome þe Grete Chan of Catay in bateil, whiche is þe miȝtiest emperour of al þe world [for þere is ofte werre among hem for þe Grete Chane wolde do hyme holde his lande of hym].

And for to go forþ by see, men fynde anoþer yle þat is yclepid Salamasse, and somme clepiþ hit Paten, þat is a grete kyngdome wiþ many faire citez. In þis lond growiþ trees þat beriþ mele of whiche men ma|kiþ breed faire and white and of good sauour, and hit semeþ f. 88v
as it were of whete. And þer beþ oþer treez þat beriþ venym aȝen whiche is no medicyne but oone, þat is to take leeuys of þe same tree and stampe hem and tempre wiþ water and drinke hit, oþer ellis a man schulde deiȝe sodenliche for triacle may not helpe.

And if ȝe wole knowe how treez beriþ meele [I schale say ȝowe]. Men hewe wiþ an hachet aboute þe fote of þe treez nere þe erþe so þat þe rynde be perischid in many placis, and þanne comeþ out a licoure þicke whiche þei takiþ in a vessel and settiþ hit to þe sonne to drie. And when hit is drie þei do hit to þe mylle to grynde, and þanne hit is faire mele and white. And wyne, hony, and venym beþ ydrowid in þe same manere of oþer trees and do in vessels to kepe.

In þat yle is a deed see þat is a watir þat haþ no ground, [and if any þynge falle þereinne it schalle neuere be founden]. Biside þat see growiþ grete cannes, and vndir here rootis men fynde preciouse stones of grete vertu, for he þat beriþ [on of] þese stones vpon hym, no maner of iren | may dere hym noþer drawe blood of hym. And f. 89r
þerfore men of þat cuntre fiȝteþ riȝt hardeliche [for þeire may no qwarelle no such þynge dere heme]. But þei þat knowiþ þe maner lete make querels wiþoute yrun, and wiþ þese men sle ham.

1 gold and] C *om.* 2 wrytyn] G1 *om.* kniȝtes] M kyngges 4 hit] C *adds* as I did 5 of þis yle] C *om.* is so myghty þat he] G1 *om.* 6 in bateil] G2–G5 *om.* 7–8 for þeire . . . hym] G1 *om.*; 2C *adds* and to be his soget vnder hym and he wolde nouȝt 11 mele] M a maner of mele 12 and of good sauour] C *om.* semeþ] C se man 13 beriþ] C *adds* wyne and hony sum and sum 15 hit] 2B *adds* yn haste 15–16 a man] 2A he 17 meele] C *adds* how þay do þerwiþ I schale say ȝowe] G1 *om.* 19 þe rynde] 2P no berke perischid] M *adds* and þe tre ben departyd in many places] G1 *after* erþe comeþ] CM *add* rynyng 24–25 and if . . . founden] G1 *om.* 26 cannes] C cave redis 27 on of] G1 *om.* 29 men of þat cuntre] G2–G5 þei þat haue þis stones riȝt] CM *om.* 29–30 for þeire . . . heme] G1 *om.* 30 But] G2–G5 þerfore maner] G2–G5 *add* of heme 31 lete make] CM ordeyn schot and

And þanne is anoþer yle þat men clepiþ Calonach, þat is a grete lond and a plenteuous of goodis. And þe kyng of þat lond haþ as many wifes as he wole [for he has a m[l]. or mo] and he liþ neuer by on of hem but o tyme, and þerfore he haþ many children. And he haþ iiii. hundrid of tame olyfauntis, þe whiche he doþ kepe, for if he hadde werre wiþ ony oþer lord he schuld make his men go aboue into þe castel aboue þe olyfauntz to fiȝte aȝens his enemys, for þat is þe maner of fiȝtyng among lordis in batayles in þilke londis.

And in þat lond is anoþer merueyl þat is in noon oþer lond, for al maner of fyschis of þe see comeþ a certeyn tyme of þe ȝere, eche maner of fysch aftir oþer, and leiþ hem nere to þe lond and vpon þe lond. Somme þer lieþ iii. dayes. And men of þe cuntre comeþ þedir
f. 89v and takiþ of hem what þei wole, and þanne | wendiþ þese fyschis away. [And comes anoþere manere and lyes þere oþere þre days and men takes of heme.] And þus dooþ al maner of fysch til alle haue be þere and men takiþ of hem what þei wile. And men woot noȝt þe cause but þei of þat lond seiþ þis fyschis comeþ þedir to do worschip to here kyng as for moost worþi of þe world for he haþ so many wifes and getiþ so many children of hem. And þis þinkiþ me þe grettist merueyl þat I haue seye, þat fyschis þat haueþ al þe see at wille to be yn schal wiþ here owne good wille come þedir to profre hemself to deeþ.

Also þer beþ snayles so grete þat in somme of here schellis men may be herburwid as in a litel house. And yf a man deiȝe in þat cuntre, þei graue his wyf wiþ hym al quike and seiþ it is good skil þat heo make hym cumpeny in þe oþer world as heo dide in þis.

Fro þis lond men gooþ by þe see Occyan to anoþer yle þat men clepiþ Gaffolos. Men of þis yle when here frendis beþ [seeke þat þei
f. 90r trowe þei schalle dye], þey | hongiþ hem vpon treez [alle qwyke] and

3 for he . . . mo] G1 2C *om.* 4 of hem] C lady 4–8 and þerfore . . . londis] G2–G5 *om.* 7 aboue] CM *om.* aboue þe olyfauntz] B *om.*; C *adds* bake 8 among . . . londis] C go in þat londis and contreis in batayles] B *om.* 10 maner of fysch] A *om.* 11–12 vpon þe lond] C *om.* 12 Somme] C *om.*; M *after* and Somme þer] 2A somme and þei; 2P somtyme they Somme . . . dayes] 2B and þare ys heere kynde to lyggen þere þree dayes or more and þat ys but lytel [*blank half-line*] þedir] 2A *om.* 13–16 and þanne . . . what þei wile] A *om.* 14–15 And . . . heme] Q *om.*; C *adds* what þat wyll; M *adds* as they dude of þat oþer byfore 16 wile] CM *add* and þe remenawnt þat þay leve swym in þe se aȝen 17 cause] G2–G5 *add* why it is 19 hem] C *adds* þat he most nediis be grasius 19–26 And þis . . . in þis] G2–G5 *om.* 20–21 to be yn] A to be þerynne; B to be in thral; C *om.* 26 þis] C *adds* same world here; M *adds* worlde 27 men gooþ to] G2–G5 is 28–29 seeke . . . dye] G1 dede 29 alle qwyke] G1 *om.*

seiþ it is better þat briddes whiche beþ aungels of God ete hem þen wormes in þe erþe.

Fro þen men gooþ to anoþer yle whare men beþ of ful yuel kynde; þei norische houndis to [worry] men. And whenne here frendis beþ sike þat þei trowe þei schal deiȝe, þei lete here houndis strangely hem, for þei wole noȝt þat þei deiȝe kyndeliche, for þanne schulde þese men suffre to grete penaunce as þei seiþ. And when þei beþ þus straungelid, þei etiþ here fleisch in stede of venesoun.

And fro þenne men goþ þurȝ many yles to anoþer yle þat is yclepid Melke. Þere beþ ful yuel folk, for þei haueþ noon oþer likyng but to fiȝte and sle men, for þei drinkiþ gladliche mannus blood, whiche blood þei clepiþ god. And he þat may slee moost men is of moost name among hem. And yf twey men be alle at bate and þei be made at oon, hem bihoueþ boþe drinke of oþer blood or ellis þe accord is noȝt.

Fro þis yle men goþ to | anoþer yle þat men clepiþ Tracota, whare f. 90v
þe men beþ a*s* beestis and noȝt resonable, and þei dwelle in caues for þei haue no wit to make houses. And þei eteþ naddris and þei spekiþ noȝt but makiþ siche noyse as addris doþ when þei yssche to anoþer. And þei make no fors of richesse but of a stoon þat haþ xl. colouris which is yclepide traconyte after þe yle. But þei knowe not þe vertu þerof, but þei coueyt hit for þe grete fairenesse.

Fro þat yle men goþ to anoþer yle þat men clepiþ Natumeran, þat ys a grete yle and a fair. And men and wymmen of þat yle haueþ houndis hedis and þei beþ resonable. And þei worschipe þe oxe for here god. And þei goþ al nakid but a litel clooþ bifore here pryue membris. Þei beþ goode men to fiȝte, and þei beriþ a grete targe wiþ whiche þei couereþ al here body, and þei haueþ a sper in here hond.

And yf þei take ony man in batail þei sende hym to here kyng, which is a grete lord and deuout in his feiȝ, for he haþ aboute his

1 of God] 2B of heuene and of god scholde han seyde fyrst 3 ful] G2–G5 *om.* 4 worry] QBCDM swolewe 5 trowe] 2P hope 6 kyndeliche] G2–G5 *add* dethe 7 þese] M þe syke penaunce as þei seiþ] C payne 8 straungelid] CM *add* to deþe; 2P ded 9 þenne] ABD þat yle many yles] C oþer ilis and by many be se and so; M *adds* be see and come 11 but] 2B *adds* alle þe day and þe nyȝt 12 god] M goode 13 name] A mayn alle at bate] G2–G5 atte stryffe 16–22 Fro . . . fairenesse] 2A *om.* 16 yle] M *adds* of Melke 17 as] QBD al; C *om.* 18 make] 2P make theym 19 when þei yssche] G2–G5 *om.*; 2P *adds* one to another 22 grete] B *om.* fairenesse] B faier colores; C *adds* þerof 23 þat yle] M *adds* of Tracote 25 houndis hedis] B wifes and husbondes 25–26 þe oxe] 2B c. x 27 pruye] C *om.* fiȝte] C þe feyþe 31 in] 2B yn hys prayer yn

f. 91r necke a corde on whiche | is CCC. perles grete and orient in maner of *pater noster* of lambre. And as we seiþ oure *pater noster* and *aue*, riȝt so þe kyng seiþ eche day CCC. preieris [to] his god bifore he ete. And he beriþ also aboute his necke a rubye orient, fyne and good, whiche is nere a foot long and fyue fyngris; for when þei chese hym to kyng, þei ȝeue hym þat rubie [to bere] in his hond and so he rideþ aboute þe cite. And þerfore he beriþ þat rubye alway aboute his necke, for yf he bere hit noȝt he schuld no lenger be yholde kynge. And þe Grete Chan of Catay haþ myche coueitid þat rubye, but ȝit miȝt he neuer haue it for werre noþer for catel. And þis kyng is a ful riȝtwise man and trewe, for men may go ful sikerliche and saueliche þurȝ his lond [and bere alle þat he wille] and no man so hardy to lette hym.

Fro þis yle men goþ to anoþer yle þat is yclepid Dodym þat is a grete yle. In þis lond beþ many dyuerse maner of men and haueþ f. 91v yuel maneris, for þe fader etiþ þe sone and þe so|ne þe fadir, þe housbande his wyf and þe wyf hire housbande. And if a mannus fader be seke [or þe moder or any frende] þe sone goþ [als tyde] to a prest of þe lawe and preieþ hym þat he wole aske of here god, whiche is a mawmet, if his fader schal deiȝe of þat sikenes [or noght]. And þan þe prest and þe sone kneliþ bifore þe mawmet and askiþ hym, and he ansueriþ to hem. And yf he seie þat he schal lyue þei kepiþ him wel. And if he sey þat he schal deiȝe þe prest comeþ wiþ his sone to his fader [or with þe wyfe or whate frende it be to hyme þat is seke] and þei leiþ here hondis vpon his mouþ and stoppiþ his breeþ and so þei sleeþ hym. And þanne þei hewe al þe body in pecis and lete preye alle his frendis to come and ete of hym þat is deed, and þei makiþ a grete feest [and haue many mynstrals þeire]. And

1 CCC.] 2C þre  2 as] D *om.*; CY ryȝt as  3 to] QBD bifore  god] 2B *adds* þe whyche god þat þe contre worschepen and clepen for heere god and þat doþ þe kyng euery day  5–6 hym to] G2–G5 þeire  6 to bere] QABD *om.*  he rideþ] G2–G5 þei led hym rydande  10 catel] G2–G5 oþere cattelle  ful] C *om.*  11 sikerliche and] 2B *om.*  12 and bere alle þat he wille] G1 *om.*  14 þis yle] M *adds* of Natumerane  goþ] 2B *adds* a lytel furþer  15 dyuerse] A *om.*  16 maneris] CM condissyoun  17 a mannus] G2–G5 it be so þat þe  18 or þe moder or any frende] G1 *om.*  als tyde] G1 *om.*  19–20 here god whiche is a mawmet] G2–G5 þe idole  20–21 if his fader . . . askiþ hym] C *om.*  20 or noght] G1 *om.*  21 mawmet] G2–G5 idole deuoutely  hym] 2B *adds* yf þat hyt be hys wille to certefye hem wheþer þat he schal lyue or dye of þat sykenesse or nouȝt  22 hem] 2B *adds* and also he telleþ hem þe trewþe  þei] D þe sone  23 he sey þat] B *om.*  24–25 or with . . . seke] G1 *om.*  26 þei hewe] D thewe  27 lete] A *om.*  þat is deed] C þat is þus dede; M *om.*  28 grete] C *om.*  and haue . . . þeire] G1 2C *om.*

when þei haue yȝete þe fleisch þei burieþ þe bones. [And alle þois þat are his frendys þat was noght þeire *to* ete of hym, has a grete schame and vilanye so þat þei schalle neuere more be haldyn als frendes.] And þus doþ eueriche frend to oþer.

And þe kyng of þis lond is a grete lord and he haþ vndir hym [four] and fyfty yles, and in eueriche is a kyng. And in one of hem beþ haueþ but on iȝe, and þat is in þe myddel of here frount. And þei etiþ | noȝt but fleisch and fysch rawȝ. f. 92r

And in anoþer yle dwelliþ men þat haueþ noon heedis and here iȝen beþ in here schuldris and here mowþis vpon here breestis.

And in anoþer yle beþ men þat haueþ noon hedis noþer iȝen and here mowþis beþ bihynde in here schuldris.

And in anoþer yle beþ men þat haueþ a plat face wiþoute nose and iȝen, but þei haue tweye smale holes in stede of iȝen and þei haueþ a plat mouþ lip*l*es.

In anoþer yle beþ foule men þat haueþ þe lippe aboue þe mouþ so grete þat when þey slepe in þe sonne þei couere al þe face wiþ þat grete lippe.

In anoþer yle beþ folk þat beþ boþe men and wymmen and haueþ þe menbre of boþe. And whanne þei wole þei vse boþe, on o tyme and anoþer anoþer tyme. And whenne þei vse þe menbre of man þei getiþ children, and when þei vse þe menbre of womman þei beriþ children.

Many oþer [manere of folk] beþ þere in þese yles, of whiche hit were to long to telle al. And for to passe forþ, men comeþ to an | yle f. 92v
whar men beþ riȝt smale. And þei haue a litel hole in stede of þe mouþ, and þei may nouȝt ete, but al þat þei schal lyue lyf wiþal þei takiþ it þurȝ a pipe of a feþer oþer siche anoþer þing.

Þan men comeþ to an yle þat men clepiþ Sylha, whiche is nere viii. c. myle aboute. In þis lond is myche waast, for þer beþ so many naddris and dragouns and cocadrilles þat men dar not wel dwelle þer. Þese cocadrilles beþ naddris ȝolewe and rayed aboue, and þei

1 burieþ] 2P bery and graue 1–4 And alle . . . frendes] G1 *om.* 4 to] 2A at And þus . . . oþer] G2–G5 *om.* 5 lord] G2–G5 *add* and myghty 6 four] G1 fyue; 2P iii 8 rawȝ] CM alle rawe 9 men] G2–G5 foul mene 13 in anoþer yle beþ men] 2A oþere men is þeire 14 haue] 2A *om.* in stede of iȝen] CM *om.* 15 liples] G1 and lippes 16 foule men] A folk 18 grete] G2–G5 *om.* 20 boþe] G2–G5 *add* for to engendire with 22 children] CM men children and when . . . children] M *om.* 23 oþer] M *adds* marvelous manere of folk] G1 *om.* 26 lyue lyf wiþal] A lyue by; B lyue with; G2–G5 ete or drynke 27 it þurȝ] C *om.* siche anoþer þing] B a rede; M *adds* ordayned þerfore 28–88/23 Þan men . . . þe see] G2–G5 *om.* 30–31 þat men . . . cocadrilles] C *om.* 30–31 dar not wel dwelle þer] B *om.*

haue iii[i]. feet and schorte schankis and grete nailes and meruelous. And whenne þei goþ by þe way whiche is sondy it semeþ as a man hadde drawe buske þurȝ þe sond. And þer beþ many oþer wilde beestis, and namelich olyfauntz.

In þis lond is an hille and in þe myddel of þat hulle is a grete pond in a playn wharynne is myche water. And men of þat cuntre seiþ þat Adam and Eue wepe vpon þat hulle an hundrid ȝere aftir þat þei were put out of paradys, and þei seiþ þat watir is here teeris. And in f. 93r þis water beþ | many cocadrilles and oþer naddris.

And þe kyng of þat lond euery ȝere o tyme ȝeueþ leeue to pore men for þe loue of Adam to go in þat water and gedre hem precious stones, for þer beþ many. And for þe vermyn þat is wiþynne þe water men anoynte here armes and schankys of an oynement made þerfore, and þan haueþ þei no drede of cocadrilles neþer of oþer naddris. And men seiþ þere þat naddris and wilde beestis of þat cuntre don neuer harm to straunge men þat comeþ þedir but onlich to men of þat same cuntre.

In þis lond and many oþer aboute hit beþ wilde gees wiþ ii. hedis, and þer beþ lyouns al white as grete as oxen and many oþer beestis and briddis. And ȝe schal vndirstonde þat þe see is so hiȝe þer þat it semeþ vp to þe clowdis and þat hit schuld falle ouer al þe lond. And þerfore seiþ Dauid, *Mirabiles elaciones maris*, þat is to say, Wonderful beþ risynges of þe see.

## CHAPTER 16 ÞE LOND OF MANCY

f. 93v He þat goþ fro þis lond toward þe see þat is | yclepid Occian toward þe eest, he schal go many iourneis til he come to þe kyngdome of Mancy, and þis is in Ynde þe best lond and most likyng and most plenteuouse of alle goodis þat is in power of man. In

1 iiii.] QBD iii; B short *before* feet meruelous] A ryȝt hidous; M hidows tose 2 whenne] CM *om.* 3 buske] B *adds* of thornes; C *adds* of thornis aftur him wilde] B wikked 4 namelich] A many 8 teeris] M *adds* þat þey wepte 11 hem] AB *om.* 12 wiþynne] D wiþoute 14 oþer] BD *om.* 15–16 of þat cuntre] B *om.* 16 þat comeþ þedir] C *om.* onlich] B *om.* 20 briddis] A *adds* ben þere 22 Dauid] C *adds* in þis wise; D *adds* thus 24 CM *om. rubric* 25 He . . . lond] C there is a lond; M *adds* of Sylha; G2–G5 for to go fro þis ile þat is yclepid] A *om.* 26 go . . . come to] G2–G5 fynde; 2A *adds* and 27 þe best lond] G2–G5 the moste and þe beste (2P lest) 27–28 and most likyng] CM *om.*

þis lond dwelliþ cristene men and Sarasyns [for it is a grete londe. þeire is inne ii$^{ml}$. citez grete and many oþere townes. In þis lande no man goos on beggynge for þeire is no pouere man inne. And þe men haue berdes thynne of heyre als it were cattes.]

In þis lond beþ feire wymmen, and þerfore somme clepiþ hit Albanye [for þe white folke. And þeire is a citee þat men calle Latorym and it is mochel more þane Parys. In þat cite is a faire watyre berande schippes. And in þat londe are birdes twys als mochelle als in any oþere place of þe werlde.] And þer is grete plente of vitailes and also of grete naddris, of whiche þei make grete feestys [and ete heme atte grete solempnitees]. For if a man lete make a feste and he hadde ȝeue al þe beste metis þat he miȝt gete and he ȝaf hem noon naddris, he haþ no þank of alle his feste.

In þis cuntre beþ [white] hennus þat beriþ no feþeris but white wolle as scheep doþ in oure cuntre. Wymmen þat beþ weddid þere beriþ crownes vpon here heed þat þei may be knowe by. In þis lond þei take a beest þat is yclepid *loyrys* and þei teche hit to go into watris and *v*yueris and als soone he bringiþ vp good fysch and grete. And þus þei take fyschis til þei haue as many as þei wile.

Fro | þen men goþ [by many iournes] to a cite þat is yclepide f. 94$^{r}$
Cassay, þat is þe moste citee of al þe world. And þat cite is fifty myle aboute. And þer is in þat cite moo þan xii. m$^{l}$. [ȝates], and at euery [ȝate] a goode tour whare men dwelliþ to kepe þe toun aȝen þe Grete Chan, for hit marchiþ vpon his lond. And vpon o side of þe cite renneþ a grete ryuer, and þer growiþ good wyn whiche þei clepiþ *bygoun*. And þer dwelliþ cristen men and oþer also, for it is a goode [contree and plentyuous. þis is a noble] cite, and þer was þe kyng of Mancy wond to dwelle. [þeire dwelles religious men, crysten freres.]

1–4 for it . . . cattes] G1 *om.* 5 wymmen] 2B syȝt of wymmen for þey ben wonder wymmen of fayrenesse hit] C þem falke of; G2–G5 þat londe 6–9 for . . . werlde] G1 *om.* 9 þe] 2B alle þe wyde 9–10 grete plente] G2–G5 good chepe (2B wonder grete) 10 þei] C *adds* made and 11 and ete . . . solempnitees] G1 *om.* 12 feste] B mete; C *adds* þat he makis beste] G2–G5 *om.* 13 his feste] G2–G5 þat he doos 14 beþ] C *om.* white$^{1}$] G1 *om.* white$^{2}$] G2–G5 *om.* 15 þere] G2–G5 of þat contre *after* Wymmen 17 þei teche hit to go] B he goþ 18 vyueris] G1 ryueris 18–19 als soone . . . wile] B he taketh his keper moche good as mony as his keper will haue 18 good] G2–G5 grete and grete] A G2–G5 *om.* 19 til . . . wile] A þere as many as þei wile] G2–G5 fyssches þat heme nedys 20 þen] G2–G5 þis citee by many iournes] G1 *om.* yclepide] M *adds* in þat contre 21 al] G2–G5 *om.* 22 ȝates, ȝate] G1 brigges, brigge 23 whare . . . toun] B and ther beth euermore to kepe þat brigge men] G2–G5 þe kepers aȝen] M for 25–26 and þer . . . *bygoun*] G2–G5 *after* plentyuous 26 *bygoun*] G1 rygoun 27 contree . . . noble] G1 *om.* 28 þeire . . . freres] G1 *om.*

And men goþ vpon þat ryuer til þei come to an abbey of monkis a litel fro þat cite. And [in] þat abbey is [a gardyn] grete and faire, and þer beþ many treez of dyuerse fruytes. And in þat gardyn beþ many dyuerse bestis, as [baboyne], marmesetis, apes, and oþere. And whenne þe couent haþ yȝete, a monk takiþ þe relyf and *d*oþ bere hit into þe gardyn wiþ hym, and he smyteþ oo tyme vpon a cliket of siluer whiche he holdeþ on his hond. And þanne comeþ out alle þe f. 94$^{v}$ beestis out of here claperes | as it were iii. m$^{l}$. oþer [iiii. m$^{l}$.] and beþ set yn a rewe. And he ȝeueþ hem þis relyf in faire siluer, vessel, and þei etiþ hit. And whenne þei haue yȝete he smyteþ þe cliket aȝen and þei go þider þat þei come fro. And þe monk seide þat þese beestis [are soules of men þat are dede and þois bestes] whiche beþ faire and gentel beoþ soulis of lordis and gentel men [and þois þat are foule are soules of oþer commyners]. And Y askid hym if it were not bettre to ȝeue þat relif to pore men þan to þese beestis. And he seide þat in þat cuntre beoþ no poore men, and if it were ȝit were hit more almes to ȝeue hit to þese soulis þat suffre þere here penaunce and may go no ferþer to gete here mete þan to men þat haue wit and may trauayle for here mete.

Fro þenne men goþ nere sixe iournees and þei fynde a grete cite which is yclepid Chibence. Þis ys nere xx. myle aboute þe wallis. In þis cite beþ sixty brigges faire and goode. And in þis cite was first þe sege of þe kyng of Mancy, whiche is a grete lord, as Y haue seid bifore.

2 in] QABD *om.* a gardyn] QABD *om.* 4 dyuerse] G2–G5 *add* maner of baboyne] G1 *om.* 5 doþ] QD goþ 6 wiþ hym] G2–G5 *om.* tyme] C *om.* 7 whiche . . . hond] B *om.* 7–8 alle þe beestis . . . claperes] G2–G5 thise bestes þat I spake of 8 as it were iii.] B more than a; M ynto þe noumbre of iii iiii. m.] G1 moo 8–9 and beþ . . . rewe] G2–G5 *om.* 9 vessel] B *om.* 9–10 and þei etiþ hit] G2–G5 *om.*; B *adds* fast 10 etiþ] CM take and ete aȝen] 2A *after* go 11 þider . . . fro] B to her clapers ayene 12 are . . . bestes] G1 *om.* whiche beþ] CM *om.* 13 gentel] G2–G5 oþere ryche; 2C *om. phrase* 13–14 and þois . . . commyners] G1 *om.* 15 þanne to þese beestis] G2–G5 15–93/9 seide . . . vnder] B *out* 16 ȝit] CM so þat þere were ȝit 17 here] C *adds* payne and; D harde 18 wit] D wharewith 19 mete] C leving 20 Fro . . . grete] G2–G5 þane comes men to a citee 21 þis is . . . wallis] G2–G5 *om. and put next sentence after* Mancy 22 faire and goode] G2–G5 als faire als it (2B eny yn þe world) may be 23–24 whiche . . . bifore] G2–G5 *om.* 23 lord] CDM *add* and a rych

# CHAPTER 17 þE LOND OF þE GRETE CHANE OF CATAY

Fro þe cite of Chibence men passiþ ouer a grete ryuer of freisch watir which | is nere iiii. myle broode, and þat comeþ into þe lond of f. 95r þe Grete Chane. þis ryuere goþ þurȝ þe lond of Pegmans, whiche beþ men of litel stature for þei beþ bote iii. spanne long, and þei beþ riȝt faire of here mychel. And þei beþ yweddid when þei beþ half ȝere old, and þei lyueþ but viii. ȝere, and he þat lyueþ viii. ȝere is yholde riȝt old. þese smale men traueileþ noȝt but þei haue among hem grete men as we beþ to trauayle for hem and þei haue as grete scorn of þese men as we wolde haue of geauntez among vs.

Fro þis lond men goþ [þorgh many contres citees and tounes] til þei come to a cite whiche is yclepid Menke. In þat cite beþ [a grete nauy of] schippis, and þei beþ as white as snow of kynde [of] þe wode þat þei beþ ymade of, and þei beþ ymade as hit were grete houses wiþ [halles] chambris and oþer esementis.

Fro þenne men goþ vpon a ryuere þat men clepiþ Caromosan. þis ryuere goþ þurȝ Catay and doþ many tymes harm when it wexiþ grete. Catay is a grete cuntre, faire and good and riche and ful of goode merchaun|*diz*. To þis comeþ merchauntis eche ȝere to f. 95v fecche spicery and oþer merchaundiz more comunly þan to oþer cuntreez. And ȝe schal vndirstonde þat merchauntez þat comeþ fro Venys oþer Gene or oþer placis of Lumbardye oþer Romain, *þ*ay trauayle bi see oþer by lond xi. moneþis and more or þei come to Catay.

And toward þe eest is an old cite [in þe prouynce of Chathay] and nere to þe cite þere þe Tartaryns haueþ ymade anoþer cite þat is yclepid Cadom. And þat haþ xii. ȝatis and euer fro o ȝate to anoþer is

2 OF CATAY] A *om.*; CM *om. rubric* 3 grete] C *om.* 4 nere] A *om.* 5 lond of] Q *adds* pees of whiche] A in whiche land 7 of here mychel] M of þare vysage and of þare shappe; G2–G5 men of alle þei be lytille 8 and þei lyueþ but viii.] C *om.* but viii.] B but seuen 11 among vs] 2A *om.*; 2B 2P þat weere amonge vs 12–16 Fro . . . esementis] 2C *om.* 12 lond] CM lond of Pugmans þorgh . . . tounes] G1 *om.* 13–14 a grete nauy of] G1 many 14 of] QD and 16 halles] G1 *om.* 19 grete] C *adds* and huge and good] C *om.* 20 goode] G2–G5 goodes and merchaundiz] QD merchauntez To þis] A *adds* land; G2–G5 theder 21 and oþer merchaundiz] A *om.*; C *adds* and þider þay go þan] G2–G5 þane þei do 23 þay] QD may 26 in þe prouynce of Chathay] G1 *om.* 27 nere to] G2–G5 bysyde 28 q xii.] C *adds* hy; 2P seuen

a [grete] myle [so þat thyse two citeez þe olde and þe newe is more aboute þan xx. myle].

In þis cite is þe sege of þe Grete Chan in a riȝt faire paleys, of whiche þe wallis aboute beþ nere ii. myle, and wiþynne þat beþ many oþer paleys faire. And in þe gardyn of þat paleys is a faire hulle, vpon whiche hulle is anoþer paleys [and it is þe fayreste þat may be founde yn any place]. And al aboute þe hulle beþ many treez beryng dyuerse fruytes. And aboute þat hulle is a greete diche and oþere *v*yueris whare beþ many dyuerse briddes þat he may take when he goþ ryueryng and comeþ [not] out of his paleys.

f. 96r And þe halle of his paleys is richeliche diȝt for | wiþynne þe halle beþ xxiiii. pilers of gold. And alle þe wallis beþ keuered wiþ reede skynnes of beestis þat beþ yclepid panters. Þese beþ faire beestys and wel smellyng, and for þe smelling of þe skynnes no wickid sauour may come þeryn. Þilke skynnes beoþ as reed as blood, and þei schyne so aȝen þe sonne þat men may noȝt wel biholden hem. And men preyseþ þese skynnes as myche as þei were fyne gold.

[Inne myddys of þat palays is a place made þat þei calle þe mountour for þe Grete Chane, þat is made wele with precious stones and grete perles hyngand alle aboute. And at foure corners of þat montour are iiii. neddyrs of golde. And vndyre þat montour and abouen are conduytz of beuerage þat þei drynke in þe emperours court. And þe halle of þa[t] palas is rychely dyght and welle.]

At þe vppermore ends of þe halle is þe troone for þe emperour riȝt hiȝ whare he sittiþ at þe mete. And þe table which he etiþ of is wel bordured wiþ gold, whiche bordure is ful of precious stonus and grete perlys. And þe greces vpon whiche he gooþ vp beþ of dyuerse preciouse stoones bordurid wiþ gold.

At þe lyft side of his trone is þe sege of his wyf at a degree lower þan his, and þat is of iasper bordurid wiþ gold. And þe sege of his

1 grete] G1 *om.* 1–2 so þat . . . myle] G1 *om.* 3 paleys] G2–G5 *add* and grete 4 nere] A 2P *om.* 5 oþer] G2–G5 *om.* faire] C *om.* faire[2] ] G2–G5 grete 6–7 and it . . . place] G1 *om.* 7 may be] 2B *adds* yn alle þe worlde þe hulle] 2A þat ilke 9 vyueris] QD ryueris; G2–G5 many ryuers and vyueres (2C vyne) dyuerse] C *om.*; G2–G5 wylde briddes] A brigges 10 when he goþ ryueryng] M *adds* in hys pleyng; G2–G5 *om.* not] QAD *om.* 11 And . . . wiþynne] G2–G5 wiþoute 12 reede] 2P riche 15 þeryn] G2–G5 in to þe palas 17 fyne gold] A gold; C *adds* and as moche cherischid 18–23 Inne . . . welle] G1 2C *om.* 22 conduytz] 2B pypes grete of gold and seluer lastyng vppe abouen yn to þe montour yn to a fayre condyȝt of fyn gold and precyous stones comyng vppe and rennyng fulle 23 þat] 2A þa 24 At] G2–G5 and first at 25 hiȝ] D *om.* wel] A *om.* 27 vp] CM vp to þe bord (M hys sete) 30 his] G2–G5 he sittes

secounde wyf is a degre lowere þan his first. þat is of iasper also and | f. 96v bordurid wiþ gold. And þe sege of þe þridde wyf is a degre lower þan þe secunde, for he haþ euermore iii. wifes [with hym where so he is]. Bisides þe wyfes vpon þe same side sitteþ oþer ladies of þe emperouris kyn [echon lawere þane oþere] as þei beþ of degree.

And al þese þat beþ weddid haueþ counterfetis of a mannus foot aboue here hedis a schaftmount long, made wiþ precious stones and pecok feþeris þat beþ schynyng ri3t wel di3t, in tokne þat þei beþ vnder man and in his subieccioun. And þei þat beþ no3t weddid haue no siche.

And on þe ri3t side of his trone sittiþ his eldest sone which schal be emperour after hym [and he sittes also a degre lawere þane þe emperour] in siche maner segis as þe emperice haueþ. And þenne oþer lordis of his kyn [echon lawere þane oþere] as þei beþ of degre.

And þe emperouris table is of fyne gold and precious stones [or of white cristille or 3alowe] bordured wiþ gold, at whiche he sittiþ himself. And euerich one of his wyfes haueþ a table by hemself. And vndir þe emperouris table sittiþ iiii. clerkis at his foot to write al þat he seiþ at his mete, good and yuel.

And at grete festis aboue þe emper|ouris table and al aboute þe f. 97r halle ys ymade a grete vyne of fyne gold, and it haþ many braunchis of grapis [lyke to grapes] of vynes, of whiche somme beþ white, some 3olewe, somme rede, somme blake, somme grene. And þese þat beþ rede beþ ymade of rubies oþer cremaus oþer alabance; þe white beþ of crestal oþer beryl; þe 3olewe beþ of topacez; þe grene beþ of emeraudes oþer of [crystolites]; and þe blake beþ of *on*ices oþer

1 of] 2P of gode 2 gold] 2B *adds* ry3t fyne 3 secunde] CM sete of his ii wyf 3–4 with him where so he is] G1 *om.* 5 echon lawere þane oþere] G1 *om.* 8 ri3t wel] M *adds* curyously; G2–G5 *om.* di3t] G2–G5 *add* or soche oþere 9 man] B mannes; G2–G5 man foote and in his] AD and his; B *om.* 11 his trone] G2–G5 þe emperour 12 hym] 2B *adds* yf þat he lyue 11–12 and he . . . emperour] G1 *om.* 13 in] AD *om.* maner] B a emperice] B 2P emperour 14 oþer] 2B *adds* ladyes lower by degrees þe whyche ben of hures kynne ry3t so þe echon lawere þane oþere] G1 *om.* 15–17 is of . . . himself] B that he sitteth at is bordred wiþ golde and ful of precious stones 15 precious stones] A bordured wiþ precious stones 15–16 or of . . . 3alowe] G1 *om.* 17 table] C *adds* of love; M *adds* alone 18 table] C fett þat is to say vndir his tabyl iiii.] B iii at his foot] C *om.* 19 at his mete] B G2–G5 *om.* 20 al aboute] G2–G5 alle oþere tables in 21 ys made . . . gold] G2–G5 *ex* 2B *add* þat goos alle aboute þe halle; 2B comeþ spryngynge sodeynly a vyuere fulle of vynes vn to euery lord hangynge ful of grapes clostre by clostre also þykke as þey mowen honge 22 lyke to grapes] QBD *om.* 23 somme grene] G2–G5 *om.* 24 ymade] B *om.* 24–25 alabance . . . topacez] B paces 26 crysolites] Q mastyk onices] G1–G5 (*ex* 2C) quices

gerandys. And þis vyne is þus ymade of preciouse stones as propurliche þat hit semeþ as hit were a vyne growyng.

And bifore þe table of þe emperour stondiþ grete lordis and non so hardy to speke wiþ hym but he speke first to hem, but hit be mynstrels [for to solace þe emperour]. And alle þe vessel of whiche he ys yserued in his halle and chambris beþ of precious stoones and nameliche at tablis whare grete lordis sittiþ, þat is to saye, of iasper, crestal, amatyst, oþer of fyne gold. And þe coppes beþ of emeraudes, saffres, topacez, f. 97v p[er]ydes | and oþer many maner of stones. Siluer vessel makiþ þei noone, for þei preiseþ siluer but litel to make vessel of hit; but þei makiþ of hit greces, pyleris, and pauementis to hallis and chambres.

And ȝe schal vndirstonde þat my felawis and Y were in sowde wiþ þe Grete Chan xvi. moneþis aȝens þe kyng of Mancy [to whome he made were]. And þe cause was for we herd myche speke of hym and we desired to se þe nobilte of his court, yf it were siche as men seyde. And sikerly we fond hit more riche and noble þan euer herde we say. And we schulde neuer haue trowe hit yf we hadde noȝt ysey hit.

But ȝe schal vnderstonde þat mete and drinke is more honest in oure cuntre þan þere, for alle þe comunes ete no fleisch as we do but of alle manere of beestis. And whenne þei haue yȝete þei wipe here hondis on here skirtes [and þei ete but ones on þe day]. And þei drynken melk of alle [maner] beestis.

## CHAPTER 18 WHY HE IS YCLEPID ÞE GREETE CHAN

f. 98r And why he is yclepid þe Grete Chan, somme seiþ | þus. [Ȝe wote wele þat alle þe werlde was distroyed with Noe flode but Noe and hys wyfe and þeire childre, and] þat Noe hadde iii. sones, Sem,

1 gerandys] BCDM *add* and the grene (B yelowe; M grete) of mastik  of] CM *add* gold and  2 þat hit semeþ] A *om.*  as hit were] B it is  4 but he . . . hem] G2–G5 *om.*  5 for . . . emperour] G1 *om.*  alle] A also  yserued] Q *adds* and  7 sitteþ] G2–G5 ete (2A site *expuncted*)  amatyst] B mastik  9 perydes] Q pydes; G2–G5 pidos  11 grecis] A grete  12 in sowde] 2B *adds* and toke wages; 2C soudeours; 2P in fauoure  13 þe Grete Chan] G2–G5 hym  13–14 to whome he made were] G1 2C *om.*  14 for] CM þat we put to hym for  16 noble] G2–G5 more solempne  17 noȝt] B *om.*  19 no] Q no clene; G2–G5 noght but  as we do but] D G2–G5 *om.*  20 yȝete] 2B *adds* ful cherlesly  21 hondis] B knyfes; 2B bawdy handes  skirtes] A awen lappes; D schertis; M cloþes þat þey were  and þei . . . day] G1 *om.*  21–22 And þei . . . beestis] G2–G5 *om.*  22 maner] QA *om.* 23–24 CM *om.* *rubric*  25 somme seiþ þus] G2–G5 Ȝe schalle wite þe cause  25–27 Ȝe wote . . . childre and] G1 *om.*

Cham, and Iaphet. Cam was he þat sauȝ his fader bak naked when he slepe and scorned it, and þerfore was he cursid; and Iaphet couerid [it] aȝen. Þese þre breþeren hadde al þe lond of þe worlde. Cam toke þe beste partye estward whiche is yclepid Assye. Sem toke Affryke. Iaphet toke Europe. Cam was þe miȝtiest and þe richest of þese breþeren, and of hym beþ ycome þe payen folk and dyuerse maner of men of þe yles, somme [hedles] and oþer disfigurid and myschape men. And for þis Cham þe emperour clepiþ hym Chan for he holdeþ þat lond, and so he clepiþ hym lord of alle.

But ȝe schal vndirstonde þat þe emperour of Catay is nouȝt clepid Cham but Chan, and for þis skile. Hit is nouȝt viii. ȝere ago þat al Tartarie was in subieccioiun and þraldome to [oþer] nacions aboute, and þei were made herdmen to kepe beestis. And among hem was vii. lynages oþer kynnes, of whom þe | firste was yclepid Tartarie, þe f. 98v
secunde was clepid Tanghet, þe þridde was clepid Eurace, þe ferþe Valayr, þe fifþe Semeth, þe sixte Menchy, þe seuenþe Sobeth. Þese beþ yholde of þe Grete Chan.

Now hit bifel so þat in þe firste kyn was an old man and he was not riche and men clepid hym Chaungwise. Þis man lay in his bedde vpon a niȝt and þer come to hym a kniȝt al white sittyng vpon an hors al white and seide to hym, 'Chan, slepist þou? God þat is almiȝty sent me to þee, and hit is his wille þat þou sey to þe seuen kynnes þu schalt be here emperour, for þou schalt wynne alle þe londis þat beþ aboute ȝow and þei schal be in ȝoure subieccioun as ȝe haue be in heris.'

And vpon þe morwe he seide þus to þe seuen kynnes, and þei scorned hym and held hym a foole. And þat niȝt folewynge come þe same kniȝt to þe seuen kynnes and bade hem [of Goddys byhalfe] maken Chaunwise here emperour, and þei schulde be out of subieccioun and þei schulde haue oþer londis vndir hem [in subieccioun]. And vpon | þe morwe þei made Chaungwise here f. 99r

1 bak] A priuete; 2P balockes 2–3 couerid it] Q conuertid 3 of þe worlde] G2–G5 *om.* 5 Europe] B Ethiopie 7 hedles] QBD meruelous 7–8 and myschape men] G2–G5 *om.* 8 clepiþ hym Cham] D *om.* 8–9 for he . . . hym] G2–G5 *om.* 10 nouȝt] A now 11 viii] Q *adds* c.; C long; D *has blank*; 2A vii 12 oþer] QBD here 13 beestis] 2B *adds* yn þe feeldes 14 lynages] Q langages oþer kynnes] B *om.*; CM of kinred was yclepid] A *om.* 16 þese] 2B *adds* here alle as I haue tolde þey 17 Chan] 2P *adds* of chatay 19 lay] G2–G5 ley and sclepe 26 he] G2–G5 he ros vppe and (2B *adds* yeode and) kynnes] C *repeats* 23–25 þu schalt . . . heris 27 þat] M þat same 28 seuen] 2P same of Goddys byhalfe] G1 *om.*; 2B yn goddes name 29 maken Chaunwise] B chaunge 29–30 and þei . . . subieccioun] 2B 2P *om.* 30–31 in subieccioun] QABD 2B 2P *om.*

emperour and dide to hym alle worschipe þat þei miȝt and clepid hym Chan as þe white kniȝt hadde yclepid [him] bifore. And þei seide þei wolde do al þing þat he bade hem.

And he made hem many statutes and lawis, whiche beþ clepid *Isakan*. And þe firste statute was þat þei schulde be obedient to God almiȝty and trowe þat he schulde delyuere out hem of here þraldome, and þat þei schulde clepe on hym in al nere neode. Anoþer statute was þat alle men whiche miȝt bere armes schulde be nombrid, and to eueriche x. schulde be a mayster, and euerich c. a mayster, and eueriche m$^{l}$. a maister.

And þan he comaundid to alle þe grettist and richest of þe vii. kynnes þat þei schulde forsake al þat þei hadde in heritage and lordschipe, and þat þei schulde [holde hem] payed of þat he wolde ȝeue hem of his grace, and þei dide so. [Also] he bade þat euerich
f. 99v man schulde bringe his eldest sone by|fore hym and sle his owne sone wiþ his owne hondis and smyte of here hedis, and [alsone] þei dide so. And when he sauȝ þat þei made no lettyng of þat he bade hem do, þanne he bade hem folewe his baner. And þanne he wan al þe londis aboute hym.

And hit bifel vpon a day þe Chan rode wiþ litel cumpenye to se þe londe þat he hadde wonne, and he mette wiþ a grete multitude of his enemys and þer was he cast of his hors and his hors ysleye. And whenne his men sauȝ hym at þe erþe þei wende þat he hadde be deed and fliȝ, and here enemys folewid hem.

And when he sauȝ his enemys were fer, he creepe into a boisch [for þe wodde was þyke þeire]. And when þei were come aȝen fro þe chace, þey went to seke in þe wode yf ony were hud þere and þei fond many. And þei come to þe place þer he was, and þei sauȝ a brid sitte on a tree whiche men clepid an owle. And þanne seide þei þer was no man [for þat birde sate þeire] and so went þei awey, and þus

1 alle] M *adds* þei grete 2 him] QD *om.* bifore] G2–G5 *om.* 3 al þing] B as; D *om.* 4 hem] 2P than 7 neode] C *adds* and nesesyte 8 be] G1 be armed and be 9 x.] C *om.* mayster] G1 *add* and eueriche xx. a maister 11 richest] G2 principals 12 þat þei hadde in heritage] C ken of women and goodis and crytage 13 holde hem] QABCD be 14 dide] 2B assentede Also] Q And; G2–G5 and also 16 alsone] G1 *om.* 17 so] G2–G5 his bidding; 2B *adds* þere ne was noon þat oones darste ne wolde seyen nay no] M *adds* taryng ne 18 do] C *adds* faste and 19 hym] C *adds* anon 21 wonne] 2B *adds* and wel faryngly gete and wyþinne a lytel whyle 22 cast] G2 casten doune 24 hem] C *adds* and so sclow many of þem in þe chace; M *adds* and lefte þe Cane lyyng stylle 25 he sauȝ] B *om.* fer] M*adds* fro hym 26 for . . . þeire] G1 *om.* 27–28 þey went . . . many] 2B *om.* 27 wode] A feld 28 sauȝ] D *om.* 30 for . . . þeire] G1 *om.*

was he saued fro deeþ. And he | f. 100r went away a niȝt and come to his owne men [whiche were fayne of hyme.] And siþþe þat tyme men of þat cuntre haue ydo grete worschipe to þat brid [and þerfore byfore alle birdes of þe werlde þei worschip þat manere of bryde.] And þanne he assemblid alle his men and rode vpon his enemys and destroied hem. [And whene he hade wone alle þe londes þat were aboute hym he helde hem in subieccion.]

And whanne he hadde wonne alle þe londis aboute hym vnto þe mounte Belyan, þanne þe white kniȝt come to h*y*m in a visioun and seide, 'Chan, þe wille of God is þat þou passe þe mount Belyan and þan schalt wynne many londis. And for þou schalt fynde no passage, go þou to mount Belyan þat is vpon þe see side and knele þere ix. tymes aȝens þe eest in þe worschipe of God, and he schal schewe þee a wey how þou schalt pase.'

And þe Chan dide so, and als soone þe see whiche touchid to þe hulle side wiþdrowe hym and schewid hym a feire wey of ix. feete brode bitwene þe hulle and þe see. And so passid he wiþ alle his men. And so he w*a*n al þe lond of Catay, which ys þe moste lond of þe world. And for þese ix. knelyngis and ix. foote of way þe Can | f. 100v and men of Tartary holdiþ þe noumbre of ix. [in] gret worschipe.

And whenne he hadde wonne þe lond of Catay he deide, and þan regned after hym Chito Chan, his eldest sone. And his br*e*þer went to wynne hem londis in oþer place, and þei wan þe lond of Pruys and Rossy. And þei clepid h*e*m Chan, but he of Catay is þe Grete Chane. [The kyngdome of Chatay is þe most of þe werlde and þe grettest Chane for he is þe gretest lord of þe werlde.] And he clepiþ hymself lord of al þe worlde in his lettres þat he sendiþ, in whiche he seiþ

1 he[1]] G2–G5 þe Chane   away a niȝt and come] B *om.*   2 which . . . hym] G1 *om.*   fayne] 2B wondur gladde   2–3 of þat cuntre] C *om.*   3–4 and þerfore . . . bryde] G1 *om.*   5 þanne] 2B whanne þat he was comen vnto alle his men   6 hem] 2B *adds* doune rriȝt   6–7 And whene . . . subieccion] G1 *om.*   6 he] G2–G5 þe Chane   8 hadde] D *om.*   hym] Q hem   9 and] G2–G5 aȝeyn and   11 go þou] C *om.*   15 Chan] D *om.*   16 wiþdrowe hym and schewid hym] D *om.*   schewid] B saw   17 he] 2P *adds* righte wel   18 wan] QD went; B yode   lond] 2P *adds* and grettest   19 And for . . . way] B *om.*; C *adds* playne and smothe   knelyngis] C *adds* þat he made   20 in] Q *om.*   22 hym] 2A *om.*   breþer] QBD broþer; G2–G5 oþer breþer   23 hem] Q hym   25–26 The kyngdome . . . werlde] G1 *om.*; 2B of alle þe þree and þerefor hys name ys loos is suche þat he ys cleped þe grete chan of chatay for he ys þe chefe lord of alle þe world; 2P *om.* The kyngdome . . . for he is   27 worlde] 2B *adds* saue godde aloone   þat he sendiþ] G2–G5 *om.*; 2B *adds* grettest of þe world ffor he recomendeþ hym more worþyer þanne he ys or eny erþely man wolde leue ffor hys entensyoun ys suche þat hyt ys grete wonder þat eny erþely man derste for þe eye of godde seyen as he dooþ

þus, *Chan filius excelsi vniuersam terram colencium summus imperator et dominus dominancium*, þat is to say, Chan Goddus sone [emperour] til alle þese þat tilieþ þe lond and lord of lordis. And þe writyng aboute hys grete seel þat he sendiþ seiþ þus, *Deus in celo Chan super terram. Eius fortitudo omnium hominum imperatoris sigillum*, þat is to say, God in heuen, Chan vpon erþe. His strengþe þe seele of þe emperour of alle men. [And þe wrytyng aboute his pryue seal is þus] *Dei fortitudo omnium hominum imperatoris sigillum*, þat is to say, Strengþe of God, seele of þe emperour of alle men. [And ȝife alle it be so þat þei be noght crystenede ȝit þe emperour and the Tartaryns trowes in God allemyghty.]

## CHAPTER 19 ARAYE OF þE COURT OF þE GRETE CHAN OF CATAY

f. 101r | I haue yseide now why he is yclepid þe Grete Chan. Now schal Y telle ȝow þe araye and þe gouernyng of his court when þei make grete festis, and þat is in foure tymes of þe ȝere principaliche. þe first is at siche a tyme as he was bore; þe secunde at siche a tyme as he was circumcided; þe þridde at siche a tyme as here mawmet bigan first to speke; and þe ferþe at siche a tyme as here mawmet bigan first to do myraclis.

And þese tymes he haþ men wel arayed by þousandis and by hundredis, and echon woot wel what he schal do; for first beþ yordeind iiii. m[l]. of barones [ryche] and myȝty to ordeyne þe feest and to serue þe emperour. And alle þese barouns haueþ crownes of gold vpon here hedis wel ydiȝt wiþ preciouse stones and perles. And þei beþ alle ycloped in cloþis of gold and camocas and siche oþer also

1 *Chan*] A Oshan 2 emperour] QBD *om.* 2–3 til alle þese] A of alle men; CM of tilliarris 3 þe lond] G2–G5 alle þe londe lordis] G2–G5 alle lordes 4 þat he sendiþ] G2–G5 *om.* *Chan*] 2A god 7 And . . . þus] G1 (*ex* F) *om.* 7–9 *Dei* . . . men] AM *om.* 9–11 And . . . myghty] G1 *om.* 13 GRETE . . . CATAY] A Chane; CM *om. rubric* 15 þe araye and] G2–G5 *om.* 17 at . . . bore] G2–G5 of his berynge 17–18 at . . . was] G2–G5 when he is borne to þe temple to ben 18, 19 here mawmet] G2–G5 þe idoles 19 first[1] ] ABC 2P *om.* first[2] ] BD *om.* 20 myraclis] C *adds* no miracullis Y say but mavmetry 21 arayed] 2B *adds* and freschly 21–22 and by hundredis] B *om.* 22 for] A *om.*; B and 23 ryche] QABD *om.* and myȝty] B *om.* 24 þe emperour] 2B tendauntly þe emperour þe grete chan to alle hys plesaunse and nouȝt so hardy þe grettest of hem to fayle for ho so fayleþ þat he ne be nat attendaunte to serue hym vnto hys lykynge he worþe deede 25 vpon here hedis] G2–G5 *om.* and perles] C *om.* 26 in] 2B wondurly welle and gayly and alle yn and siche oþer] G2–G5 *om.*

richeliche as þey may be maad. And þei may wel haue siche cloþis for þei beþ of lasse pris þare þan wollen cloþis beþ here.

And þese iiii. ml. barouns beþ departyd in iiii. cumpeny|es and euery cumpenye is cloþed in a sute of dyuerse colour. And whanne þe firste ml. is apassid and haþ serued hym, þei holdeþ hem biside and þanne comeþ þe secunde, and þanne þe þridde, and so þe ferþe. And noon of hem spekiþ a word, and þus þei goþ aboute þe halle. f. 101v

And at þe side of þe emperouris table sittiþ many philosofris of many sciencez, somme of astronomye, somme of nygromancye, and somme of geometrie, and somme of pyroma[n]cie, and siche oþer many sciencez. And þei haueþ biforen hem astroloberis of gold oþer of precious stones ful of sond oþer of coles brennyng. Somme haueþ orlagis wel ydiȝt and richely and oþer many instrumentis of here sciences.

And at certeyn houris when þei se tyme þei seiþ to men þat stondiþ bifore ham, 'Now make pees.' And þanne seiþ þe men to alle þe halle wiþ a lowd voys, 'Now make pees, stille a while.' And þenne seiþ on of þe philosofris, 'Now euery man do reuerence and bowe hym to þe emperour whiche is Goddis sone and lord of alle [þe world] for now is | tyme.' And þanne euery man lowtiþ his heed toward þe erþe and þanne seiþ þe philosofir to ham, 'Rise vp aȝen.' And anoþer houre seiþ anoþer philosofir, 'Euery man put here litel fyngris in here eeris,' and þei doþ so. And at anoþer houre seiþ anoþer philosofir, 'Euery man ley his hond bifore his mouþ,' and þei doþ so. And þanne he biddeþ hem leye here hondis vpon here hedis, and þei doþ so, and he biddeþ hem take awey, and þei doþ so. And þus euery houre þei biddeþ dyuerse þingis, and þei seiþ þese þingis haueþ grete tokenyng. f. 102r

1 haue siche cloþis] 2B *om.*; C *adds* þere 2 beþ here] Q here beþ 3 iiii.] D iii 4 a sute of] G2–G5 *om.* colour] ACM *add* fro oþer G2–G5 *add* riȝt richely 5 is apasid and] C *om.* serued] G2–G5 schewed þei holdeþ hem biside] G2–G5 *om.* 6 þe ferþe] B forth 7 noon] D *om.* and þus . . . halle] G2–G5 *om.* halle] C *adds* and spek no worde 9–10 and somme of geometrie] M *om.* pyromancie] Q 2A pyromacie; A cyromancye 12 coles brennyng] C presius stonis þat is to say cokyll schellis 13 many] C maner 16 seiþ þe men to] B sitteth al the men in 17 make pees] A beth; M lordelynges bethe; G2–G5 be; 2B *adds* and yet þay cryen pees and þanne þay seyen at þe þrydde tyme 18 on] Q on on bowe] G2–G5 bowe and loute 19–20 þe world] QBD *om.* 20 tyme] G2–G5 *add* and oure lowtiþ] C bowis to þe emperour and lowtis; M lowteth and boweth wyth; G2–G5 *add* to him and kneles 20–21 his head toward] C to; G2–G5 on 21 erþe] C cane 22 litel] C G2–G5 *om.* 24–25 bifore . . . hondis] 2P *om.* 25 And þanne . . . hedis] 2B *om.* 26 so] QBD *add* and he biddeþ hem take awey 27–28 and þei . . . tokenyng] G2–G5 *om.*

And Y askid priueliche what þese þingis schulde meene, and on of þe philosofris seide þat þe bowing of þe hed at þat tyme bitokeneþ þat al þese þat bowiþ þen schal euermore be obedient to þe emperour and trewe, þat for no ȝift noþer for no bihoting þei schal neuer be fals noþer traytoures to hym. And puttyng of þe fyngris in þe eere haþ þis tokenyng, þat none of þese schal hure no f. 102v man speke yuel | of þe emperour, fader noþer broþer ne sone, but yf he seye hit to þe emperour or somme of his counseyl.

And ȝe schal vndirstonde þat men diȝt ne make no þing to þe emperour, þat is to say cloþis, breed, and drink, ne none oþer siche þingis, but at certeyn tymes whiche þe philosofris telliþ. And yf ony bigynne werre aȝens þe emperour in ony cuntre, als soone þe philosofris wote hit and telliþ þe emperour oþer his counseyl, and he sendiþ men þider.

And whanne mynstrels hadde made here melodyes a grete while in þe halle, þanne one of þe offyceris of þe emperouris goþ vpon a stoone wel ymade and richeliche and crieþ lowde, 'Make pees' and þenne beþ alle men stille. And in þat mene tyme alle þese þat beþ of þe emperouris kyn goþ and arayeþ hem wel and richely in cloþis of gold and oþer. And þanne seiþ þe stiward of þe court, 'N and N, come alle men and do reuerence to þe emperour whiche is lord of alle.' And þanne comeþ men of þe emperouris kyn and eueriche f. 103r bringeþ a white steede oþer a whi|te hors and makiþ presaunt to þe emperour, eueriche aftir oþer. And þanne alle [oþer] barouns and lordis presentiþ hym wiþ somme ȝift oþer somme iewel. And whenne þei haueþ al þus yoffrid to þe emperour þanne þe grettest prelatis þat beþ þere ȝeueþ a grete benesoun, seiyng an orisoun of here lay. And þanne makiþ þe mynstrels melodyes aȝen.

And whenne þei haueþ ymade mynstrelcy a while men biddeþ

2 philosofris] 2A mastirs   of þe hed] G2–G5 and knelyng (2B *adds* and þulke lowerynge) on þe erth   3 bowiþ þen] 2B kneled so and dyde vn to hym alle þys reuerence   euermore] C *om.*   obedient] G2–G5 trew   4 and trewe] D and trowe; G2–G5 *om.*   5 neuer] A *om.*   noþer traytoures] B *om.*   7 yuel] C yll worde   7 þe emperour] 2B heere lyge lord þe emperour of no namere of man of alle þe wyde world   7–8 fader . . . somme of] 2P *om.*   8 somme of] B 2A *om.*; 2B *adds* þe grettest lordes þe whyche ben of   9 ne make] G2–G5 *om.*   10 breed] 2B mete   and drink] B ale   11–13 And yf . . . telliþ] CM *om.*   14 þider] 2B *adds* for he haþ ynowe to destroye alle þe world ne weere goddes wylle allone; 2C *adds* to make an eynde   15–101/12 And whanne . . . arise from mete] G2–G5 *om.*   17 Make] B *om.*   19 goþ and] B *om.*   wel and] A wel; C *om.*   20 and oþer] BC *om.*; B *adds rubric* Honour of the Cane   N and N] M *om.*   21 þe] Q þe þe   23 bringeþ] B *adds* ether   24 oþer] QD here; BM the   26 whenne] B *om.*   þei haueþ al þus] C all þes lordis have hyly

hem be stille. And þanne men bringe bifore þe emperour lyouns, lybardis, and oþer maner of beestis and briddis and fyschis and naddres, for þei seiþ al þing þat haþ lyf schal do worschipe to þe emperour and be obedient to hym. And þenne comeþ iogelouris and doþ many merueiles, for þei makiþ to come in þe eyr as hyt semeþ þe sonne and þe mone to do hym reuerence, which schyneþ so bri3t þat a man may no3t biholde hem. And þanne þei make damesels to come bringyng cowpes of gold ful of mere melk and 3eueþ lordis and ladies to drinke of. And þanne makiþ þei kni3tes to iouste in þe ayr wel | yarmed, and þei smyteþ so togedre wiþ here speris þat þe f. 103v strokis fleeþ al aboute þe tablis in þe halle, and þese ioustez lastiþ to þei arise fro mete.

þis emperour whiche is yclepid þe Grete Chan haþ many men to kepe briddis, as gerfaucouns, sperhaukys, faucouns, gentiles, laueris, sacres, papyniayes spekyng, and oþer many briddis syngyng. And he haþ of wilde beestis ten þowsand, as olyfauntez, baboynez, marmesetez, and oþere.

And he haþ many phisicyans, of whom ii. hundrid beþ cristen men and xx.[ti] Sarasyns, but he tristiþ moost in cristene men. And þer beþ in his [court] many barouns and oþer þat beþ cristene and yconuertyd to cristene fey þur3 preching of cristen men þat dwelliþ þere. But þer beþ many þat woleþ not lete men wite þat þei beþ cristened. And yf alle hit be so þat þe emperour and his men be not cristened, 3it trowe þei wel in God almy3ty.

[And he is a ful grete lorde for he may spende what he wylle.] And he haþ in his chambre a faire pylour of gold, vpon whiche is a rubye and a charbugle of a foot | long, whiche li3teþ al þe chambre vpon þe f. 104r

1 þanne men bringe bifore] C so men go forþe 2 lybardis] B *om.* 5 many merueiles] M meruelous many and grete 8 ful] D *om.* 3eueþ] QD leueþ 9 to] C *adds* dryull and ayr] B halle 11 strokis] C pesis lastiþ] M *adds* fro þay bygyne 13 þis . . . Chan] G2–G5 for he has 14 kepe] M *adds* dyuers 15 many] 2C maner of 15–16 briddis . . . beestis] G2–G5 *om.*; 2B stares or sterlynggiis þat ben of þe same condyciouns and egles and grypes and ernes and many oþer dyuersytees of foules and also he haþ many men to kepen dyuers beestes boþe of þe kynde of tame and of þe kynde of wylde as lyounes lybardes and passyng 16 baboynez] B raboyns 17 oþere] 2B *adds* bestes and foules of þe whyche alle þe names to telle hyt wolde aske wonder long tyme but forsothe my wytte ne my3t nou3t comprehende þe dyuersytees of hem alle ne heere names 19 moost] M *om.*; G2–G5 more . . . þane of sar3yns 20 court] G1 (*ex* C) 2P cuntre oþer] G2–G5 *add* seruauntz 21 cristene[2]] G2–G5 þe gode of] G2–G5 of gode 22 many þat] 2B many but þay ne lete] A *om.* men] 2B *adds* of heere owyn nacyouns 23–24 And yf . . . almy3ty] G2–G5 *om.* 24 wel] M *om.* almy3ty] BC *om.* 25 And he . . . wylle] G1 2C *om.* 26 faire] G2–G5 *om.*

niȝt. And he haþ many oþer precious stoones and rubies, but þis is þe moste and þe grettyst and most preciouse of alle oþer.

[This emperour dwelleþ in þe somere towarde þe north in a cite þat men calle Saduz, and þeire is colde inogh. And in þe wynter he dwelles in a cite þat men calles Camalac þeire is right hote londe, and þeire dwelles he for þe moste party.]

And whenne þis Grete Chaan rideþ fro o cuntre to anoþer þei schal ordeyne iiii. hostes grete of folk; of which oon oost wendiþ a dayes iourne bifore hym [for þe ost lyes at euen wheire þe emperour schale ly on þe morwe, and þeire is plente of vitails]. And anoþer oost is at þe riȝt side of hym, and anoþer at þe lyft side [and in ech ost is moch folke], and þe ferþe comeþ bihynde a bowis drauȝt. And in þat oost beþ mo men þan ony of þe oþer þre.

And ȝe schal vndirstonde þat þis emperour rideþ vpon noon hors but yf he ride to ony place wiþ priue maigne. But he rideþ in a chariot wiþ foure wheolys, and þervpon is a chambre made of tree þat men clepiþ *lignum aloes* þat comeþ out of paradys terrestre. And þat chambre is al keuered wiþynne wiþ platis of [fyne] gold and preciouse stones and grete perles. And iiii. olyfauntis and iiii. steedis goþ þerynne. And v. oþer sixe grete lordis rideþ aboute þe chariot so
f. 104v þat noon oþer man schal come | to hym but yf he clepe hym.

And in þe same manere of chariotis [and soche ostes] rideþ þe emperessse by anoþer wey, and his eldest sone of þe same aray, and þei haueþ so myche folk þat it is merueil to telle.

And þis lond of þe Grete Chan is departid in xii. prouyncez and yn eueriche prouynce is a kyng, and in eueriche kyngdome mo þan ii. m[l]. citez and many oþer grete townes. Also when þe emperour rideþ [þus þorȝh þe contree and he passes þorgh citez and tounes ich man

1 niȝt] 2B *adds* þat hyt ys also lyȝt þere ynne as þe brennynge of þree torches of goude wexe and fyn newe and wel brennynge vp euery torche vi. wekes and vppon euery weeke xx. þreeses of coten and also moche lyȝtteþ þees stones as wylle suche þree torches þus ymade  2 and þe grettyst . . . oþer] G2–G5 *om.*  preciouse of alle oþer] B of price  3–6 This . . . party] G1 *om.*  4–6 Saduz . . . calles] 2C *om.*  4 he] 2B tyme he ne wol noon lengur soiourne but dresseþ towarde þe souþ and  8 grete of folk] C *om.*; G2–G5 of folke  9–10 for . . . vitails] G1 *om.*  10 is] 2A *om.*  11 oost] 2A *om.*  11–12 and in . . . folke] G1 *om.*  13 þe oþer þre] B a nother hoste; G2–G5 þe oþer  14 noon] C an  17 terrestre] CM *om.*  18 al] B *om.*  wiþynne wiþ] C wiþ whyt  fyne] G1 *om.*  19 grete] 2P *om.*  20 v. oþer] B *om.*  21 to] G2–G5 nere  22 of chariotis] A *om.*  and soche ostes] G1 *om.*  23 emperesse] BD emperour  24 is] G2–G5 is a grete  telle] G2–G5 se  26–27 is . . . townes] 2P hathe more than two thousande kynges  28–103/1 þus . . . hous] Q by a grete cite þe prelate þerof comeþ aȝen hym wiþ solempne aray beryng a sensure of gold ful of brennyng colis; A in placis þer he schal come; B *om.*; CM in hys char; D he schal come

makes a fyr byfore his hous], and þei cast þerynne encense or oþer þingis þat may ȝeue good smel to þe emperour.

And yf cristene men of religioun dwelle nere whare þe emperour schal passe, þei comeþ aȝens hym wiþ processioun wiþ a croice and holy water and þei syngeþ lowde, *Veni creator spiritus*. And whenne he seeþ hem come he comaundiþ to lordis whiche rideþ nere hym to make wey þat þese men of religioun may come to hym. And als soone as he seeþ þe croys he doþ of hys hat whiche ys ymade ful richeliche wiþ | perles and preciouse stones, þat is a merueyl to telle. f. 105r And þanne he louteþ to þe croys and þe prelate of þese religiouse men seiþ orisouns bifore hym and ȝeueþ hym benesoun [with þe crose and he loutes to þe benysoun] ful deuouteliche. And þanne þat same prelate ȝeueþ hym som maner of fruyt of þe noumbre of ix. and a plate of gold, for þe maner is siche þere þat no straunge man schal come bifore þe emperour but yf he ȝeue hym som þing, aftir þe olde lawe þat seiþ, *Nemo accedat in conspectu meo uacuus*, þat is to say, No man come in my siȝt toome. And þen goþ þei home aȝen to here place [so þat men of his ost defoule hem noght].

And in þis same maner doþ men of religioun þat dwelliþ whare þe emperice and þe emperours sone comeþ, for þys Grete Chan is þe grettyst lord of þe worlde, for Prestre Ioon noþer þe sowdan of Babiloyn noþer þe emperour of Perse beoþ not so grete as he.

In his lond a man haþ an hundrid wifes, somme fourty, somme mo, somme lasse. And þei takiþ to wifes of here kyn al but modris and douȝtris. And al [men and] wymmen ha|ueþ a maner of cloþing f. 105v so þat þei may nouȝt be knowe, but þat wymmen whiche beoþ weddid bere here tokenes vpon here hedis, of whiche Y haue yspoke.

1 and þei] A þey; B peple of the cuntre; CM men þerynne] B in the fire 5 lowde] C *adds* þus 6 whiche rideþ nere hym] B *om.* 7 men] 2B crysten men may come] C make speke 8–9 ymade . . . wiþ] B *om.* ful richeliche] G2–G5 *om.* 9 perles] G2–G5 grete perles þat is] G2–G5 þat hat is so riche þat is . . . telle] B *om.* 10 and þe] CM and þe most (M *om.*) grettest 11 seiþ] M *adds* goode 11–12 with . . . benysoun] Q *om.* 13 som maner of fruyt] B yiftes; G2–G5 some fruyt ix.] ABCDM xi 17 toome] AB voyde; D to me voyde; 2A to me tome; 2P to me; 2B ydel þat is to say þat he come nouȝt to me but yf he brynge sumwhat þat he may yeue me 17–18 goþ . . . place] G2–G5 þe emperour biddys thyse religiouse men þat þei schale 18 place] C abbey so þat . . . nouȝt] G1 *om.* 19 þat dwelliþ] C *om.* 20 emperice and] A *om.*; BEF emperour and 21 worlde] C *adds* brod and rounde 23–104/3 In his lond . . . none] 2C *om.* 24 to] A two; CM to þer 24–25 al but . . . haueþ] 2B *om.* 25 and[1]] 2A and þe sones; 2P sonnes and men and] G1 maner of 26 nouȝt] B *om.* knowe] C *adds* from odur 27 of whiche Y haue yspoke] G2–G5 *om.*

[And þei dwele noght in houses with þeire housbandes bot þe housbande may ly with whiche þat he wylle. þei haue plente of alle maner of bestes bot swyne, for þois wille þei none.]

And þis emperour þe Grete Chan haþ iii. wyfes, and þe principal wyf was Prestre Ioon his douȝter. And his men trowiþ wel in God þat made al þing, but ȝit haue þei mawmetis made of gold and siluer to whom þei offre þe firste melk of here beestis. þe men of þis cuntre bigynneþ to do al here þinges in þe newe moone and þei doþ grete worschip to þe sonne and þe moone. And þese men rideþ comynliche wiþoute spores.

And þe emperour what name so he haþ, þei puttiþ þerto Chan. And when Y was þere þe emperouris name was Tyak and þei clepid hym Tyak Chan. And of wyfes þe first was yclepid Seroch Chan, and þat oþer Baruch Chan, aned þe þridde Charauk Chan.

And men of þat cuntre holdiþ it grete synne to breke a boon wiþ
f. 106r anoþer and cast melk oþer ony oþer licour on þe erþe | þat men may drinke. And þe moste synne þat þei may do is to pisse in here howses whare þei dwelliþ, and he þat pisseþ þere schal be slawe. And þat place whare a man haþ pissed bihoueþ to be halewid or ellis no man may dwelle þere.

And of alle synnes þat þei beþ schryue of to here prestis þei ȝeueþ siluer for here penaunce. And whenne þei haueþ do here penaunce þei schal passe þurȝ a fuyr to make hem clene of here synnes. And when a messynger bringeþ a presaunt to þe emperour he schal passe þurȝ a fuyre for to make þe þing clene, so þat he bringe no venym noþer no þing to greue þe emperour.

þei etiþ gladlich houndis, lyouns, ratouns and al oþer beestis smale and grete [saue] swyn and bestis whiche were forbode in þe olde lawe. And þei etiþ litel breed but hit be grete lordis. [When þei haue etyne þei wyppe þeire hondes on þeire lappes, for þei haue no borde clothes bot it be of grete lordes.] And when þei haue ete þei

1–3 And þei . . . none] G1 *om.* 2–106/8 bot þe housbande . . . frendis] 2P *two pages misplaced in facsimile after sig. gvii recto* 4–5 And þis . . . douȝter] G2–G5 *after* beestis l. 20 11–14 And . . . Chan] G2–G5 *om.* 15 men of þat cuntre] G2–G5 þei 16 anoþer] CM *add* bone 18 þere] G2–G5 in his house 18–20 And þat place . . . þere] G2–G5 *after* penaunce l. 9 20 may dwelle] A dar entren; G2–G5 may come 23 fuyr] G2–G5 *add* or two (2B tweyne); 2P fayre fyre 23–29 And when . . . lordis] G2–G5 *om.* 25 venym] B *adds* with him 27 ratouns] C cattys rattys 28 saue] QABD boþe 29–31 when . . . lordes] G1 *om.*; 2B *adds* yf þey han and yet hyt mote ben ryȝt grete lordes þat eny han for symple men han noon 30 lappes] 2B hemmes byfore of garnementes; 2P skyrtes puttiþ þe vessel noȝt waische, wiþ fleisch þat þei leueþ, aȝen into þe pot oþer caudroun vnto þei wole ete anoþer tyme. And riche | f. 106v men drinkeþ melk of meris oþer assis oþer siche oþer beestis. And þei haueþ anoþer maner of drinke þat ys ymade of melk and water for in þat cuntre is no wyn [ne ale].

And when þei goþ to werre þei werriþ ful wiselich, and euerich one of ham beriþ twey bowis oþer þre and many arwis and a grete hachet. And gentel men haueþ schorte swerdes scharp on þat o side and haue platis ymade of coerboyle aboue here helmus and trapping to hors. And he þat fleþ in bateyl þei sleeþ hym. And þei beþ euer in purpos to bringe alle londis yn here subieccioun, for þei seiþ here prophecys seiþ þei schal be ouercome wiþ schote of archeris and þat þese men schal turne hem to here lawe, but þei woot not what men þese schul be. And hit is grete peryl to pursue þe Tartaryns when þei fleeþ, for þei wole scheote bihynde hem fleyng and sle men as wel as bifore hem.

[And þei holde oyle of olyf for a good medycyne.] And þei haue smale iȝen and litel beerdis. And þei beþ comynliche fals for þei holdeþ noȝt þat þei hiȝt. And whan | f. 107r a man schal deyȝe among hem þei stykeþ a spere in þe erþe by hym. And whanne he drawiþ to þe deeþ eueriche goþ out of þe house vnto þat he be deed. And when þat he is deed þei beriþ hym vnto þe feld and þei puttiþ hym into þe erþe.

And when þe emperour, which is yclepyd þe Grete Chan, is deed þei settiþ hym in a chayre in myddel of a tent, and þei settiþ bifore hym a table and a clooþ and fleisch and oþer mete and a cowpe ful of melk of a mere. And þei settiþ a mere wiþ here fool bifore hym and an hors ysadelid and ybridelid and þei leiþ vpon þe hors gold and siluer. And al aboute þe tent þei make a grete graue, and hym

1 þe vessel] G2–G5 þeire dissches and þeire doublers  noȝt waische] C vpon a wasschyn  2 wole] AB *om.*  tyme] C *adds* of þe day  3 siche] G2–G5 *om.* beestis] Q siche beestis  4 melk] 2B mylette  water] G2–G5 *add* togydre  5 ne ale] G1 *om.*  8–10 scharp . . . hors] G2–G5 *om.*  9 helmus] A hauberioynes 10 fleþ] 2P fighteth  euer] B *om.*  11 bringe] M brenne  seiþ] D *om.* 11–12 here prophecys seiþ] *om.*  12 be] 2A *om.*  13 þese men] G2–G5 þei 14 be] 2B *adds* þat schullen turne hem but þey woten welle þat þey schullen comen 15 fleyng] 2P *om.*  17 And þei . . . medycyne] G1 2C *om.*; 2B *adds* and most pryncypalle of alle þat euere ben yn þys world  18 beerdis] 2P byrdes  20 spere] C *adds* at his hed  20–23 And whanne . . . erþe] B *om.*  21–22 when . . . feld and] G2–G5 þanne  23 erþe] G2–G5 *add* in þe felde (2B fer oute in þe felde) 24 which is . . . Chan] G2–G5 *om.*  25 settiþ] B geteth  26 fleisch and] 2B *adds* fysche and dyuersytees of  27 wiþ] D whit  29 þe tent] G2–G5 hym

and þe tent [and alle þise oþere þyngys] þei puttiþ togedir in þe erþe. And þei seiþ whan he comeþ to anoþer world he schal not be wiþoute an hous, hors, [gold] ne siluer, and þe mere schal ȝeue hym drinke and bringe forþ mo hors til þat he be wel storid in þat oþer worlde. For þei trowiþ when þei beþ deede þat þei schal in anoþer
f. 107v world ete and drinke [and haue solace with þeire wyffys] as | þei doþ here. And fro þat tyme þat he be leyd in þe erþe no man schal be so hardy to speke of hym bifore his frendis.

And when þis emperour is deed, þe seuen kyn*d*es gederiþ hem togedre and þei chese his sone oþer þe nexte of his blood to þe emperour.

[And þei [seiþ] þus, 'We wile and we praye and we ordeyne þat þou schale be oure lorde and oure emperour.' And he answers, 'If ȝe wile þat I regne opon ȝowe echon of ȝowe do þat I bide ȝowe.' And if he bide þat any be sclayne he schale be sone sclayne. And þei answere alle with o voice, 'Alle þat ȝe bide schale be done.' Thanne says þe emperour, 'Fro nowe forth my worde schale be keruande als my swerde.'

[And þane þei sete hym in a chayer and corownes hym. And þane alle þe good tounes senddys hym presantez so þat he schalle haue þat same day more þane a cartfulle of golde and siluere and oþere many iewels þat he schale of lordes, of precious stanes and gold withouten nombre and hors and riche cloþes of chamachas and tartaryns and soche oþere.]

þis lond of Catay is yn Assye þe deope, and hit marchiþ toward þe west vpon þe kyngdome of Trachie, whiche was somtyme [to] one of þe þree kynges þat went to seche oure lord in Bethleem. [Thyse men of Tartary drynke no wyne.] *I*n þe lond of Corasyne þat is at þe norþ side of Catay is grete plente of alle goodis but no wyne. And at þe eest side beþ grete wildernessis which lastiþ more þan an hundrid iourneys. And þe beste cite of þat lond is yclepid

1 and þe tent] B *om.* and alle þise oþere þyngys] QBD *om.* 3 gold] QBD 2A *om.* 4 drinke] G2–G5 mylk 6 world] C *om.* and haue . . . wyffys] G1 *om.* 8 of hym . . . frendis] B a worde of him 9 kyndes] G1 (*ex* C) kynges; G2–G5 lynages 10 chese] 2P touche oþer] 2B *adds* and yf he haþ noon þanne þey taken 10–11 to þe emperour] G2–G5 *om.* 12–24 And þei . . . suche oþer] G1 *om.* 12 seiþ] 2A *om.* 13 lorde] 2B *adds* and eke þat þow be oure alle myȝtty chan answers] 2P enquyreth 17 keruande] 2B kyttynge 20–21 þat same day] 2P *om.* 25 and hit] G2–G5 The londe of Chatay 26 somtyme] M *adds* dwellyng to] QB *om.* 27 one of þe þree] C of þe 28 Thyse . . . wyn] G1 *om.* In] Q And 28–30 In þe lond . . . wyne] 2P *om.* 29 Catay] Q *adds* in þat lond grete] 2P ryghte greate

Corasyne, and after þat cite is þe lond yclepid. [Men of þis londe are good werriours and hardy.]

And þere nere is þe kyngdom of Comayn which is a grete kyngdome, but hit is not al inhabite, for in o place þat lond is so
cold þat no man may dwelle þere and in anoþer | place so hote þat no f. 108r
man may dwelle þer. [And þeire are so many flees þat a man wote noght on what syde he may torne hym.] In þis lond beþ *but* fewe treez beryng fruyt. þere men liggeþ in tentis. þer þei brenneþ mokk of beestis for defaute of wode. þis lond comeþ toward Pruysse and Russy. And þurȝ þis lond renneþ þe ryuere of Ethel, which is on of þe grete ryueris of þe world. And hit is somtyme so hard yfrore þat men fiȝteþ þervpon in grete bateyles on hors and on foote, mo men þan an hundrid m.[1] at oonus.

And a litel fro þat ryuer is þe [grete] see Occyan þat þei clepiþ Maure. And bitwene þis Maure and þe Caspie is a ful strayt passage to go toward Ynde. And þerfore kyng Alisaundre lete make þere a cite whiche was yclepid Alisaundre to kepe [þat passage] þat no man schulde passe þer but yf he hadde leeue, and now is þat cite yclepid Port de Feare. And þe principal cite of Comayn is yclepid Sarachie.

þis is oon of þe [þre] weyes to go vnto Ynde, but in þis way may
not many man go but yf it be in wynter. And | þis passage is yclepid f. 108v
Berbent. And anoþer wey is þer to go fro þe lond of Turkestoun to Perse [and in þis wey are many iournes in wildernes]. And þe þridde wey ys [þat comys fro Cosmany] to go þurȝ þe grete see and þurȝ þe kyngdome of Abchare. And ȝe schal vndirstonde þat alle þese kyngdomes and londes vnto Perse beþ yholde of þe Grete Chan of Catay and many oþer, and þerfore he is a grete lord of men and of many londys.

1 after þat cite] G2–G5 þeire aftre cite] ACM *om.* lond] B cites 1–2 Men . . . hardy] G1 *om.* 3 a grete] G2–G5 þe most 4 kyngdome] G2–G5 *add* of þe worlde 5 cold] G2–G5 grete colde þere] 2P there for cold 5–6 and in . . . þer] A 2B *om.* 5 hote] G2–G5 grete hete 6–7 And þeire . . . hym] G1 *om.* 7 but] Q ful 8 þer] C in þys lond ar but few men and mokk] ACD mylk; B musk; 2A muske 9 wode] C *adds* or colys comeþ] G2–G5 descendes 11 grete] G2–G5 greteste somtyme] G2–G5 eche ȝere 12 men] A *om.* 14 ryuer] QAD grete ryuer; C Ethell; M grete Ethel grete] G1 *om.* 15 þe] Q þe cite of 17 þat passage] G1 *om.* 20 þre] G1 *om.* 21 passage is] C *adds* now 22–24 fro þe lond . . . to go] B *om.* 23 and in . . . wildernes] G1 *om.* 24 þat comeþ fro Cosmany] G1 *om.* to go] G2–G5 and þat goos see] 2B see of occyane; 2P cyte 27 grete] G2–G5 fulle grete 28 many] G2–G5 *om.*

# CHAPTER 20 þE LONDE OF PERSE

Now haue I tolde ȝow of londes and kyngdomes toward þe norþ to come doun fro þe lond of Catay vnto þe lond of Pruyse and Russy whare cristen men dwelliþ. Now schal Y say ȝow of oþer londes and oþer kingdomes in comyng doun fro Catay to þe see of Grece whare cristen men dwelliþ. And for as myche as next þe Grete Chan of Catay þe emperour of Perse is þe grettist lord, þerfore Y schal first speke of hym.

And ȝe schal vndirstonde þat he haþ ii. kyngdomes, of whiche on bigynneþ estward at þe kyngdome of Turkestoun and hit lastiþ
f. 109[r] westward to þe [see] of Cas|pye and souþward to þe lond of Ynde. And þis lond is good and playn and [welle manned] and many citeez but ii. þe mooste citeez of þat kyngdome beþ yclepide Baccria and Sormagraunt. þe oþer kyngdome [of Percy] lastiþ fro þe ryuer of Physon vnto þe grete Ermonye and norþwarde to þe [see] of Caspye and souþward to þe lond of Ynde. And þis is a ful plenteuouse lond and good, and in þis kyngdome beþ þre principal citeez, Nessabor, Saphan, Sarmasse.

And þan is þe lond of Ermonye in whiche was somtyme foure kyngdomes. þis is a grete lond and a plenteuouse and good. And hit bygynneþ at Perse and lastiþ westward to Turky in lengþe, and in brede hit lastiþ fro þe cite of Alisaundre, þat now is yclepid Port de Feare, vnto þe lond of Meddy. In þis lond of Ermonye beþ many feire citez but Taurissy is moost of name.

þan is þe londe of Meddy þat is ful long and litel brode, þat
f. 109[v] bygynneþ estward at þe lond | of Perse and Ynde þe lasse and lastiþ westward to þe kyngdome of Caldee and northward to litel Ermonye. In þis lond of Meddy beoþ many grete hullys and litel playn, and þere dwelliþ Sarasyns and anoþer maner of men þat men clepiþ Cordynz. þe beste citez of þat lond beþ yclepid Saray and Carmen.

1 CM *om. rubric* 2 and kyngdomes] 2P *om.* 3 doun] 2P *om.* þe lond[1]] C *om.* lond[2]] 2A londe londe 6 dwelliþ] M *adds* also next] 2A was 7 first] D *om.* 11 westward] ACD estward 11, 15 see] G1 cite 12 welle manned] G1 (*ex* A) many men; A townes þere many] G2–G5 many good citeez] 2B *adds* ben þare 13 mooste] G2–G5 most principal of þat kyngdome] G2–G5 *om.* 14 of Percy] QABD *om.*; CM 2B of þe emperour of Perce 19 foure] 2P thre 20 kyngdomes] 2B fayre kyngdomes and grete grete] B G2–G5 *om.* and a plenteuouse] C *om.* 21 westward] Q west toward 23 þis lond of] BC G2–G5 *om.*; M þis 25 ful] B *om.* litel] 2A noght 27 westward] A estward 28 hullys] CM *add* and gret mowtaynys 29 dwelliþ] A *adds* many 24–25 þe beste . . . Saray] 2P *om.*

þen is next þe kyngdome of George, þat bygynneþ eestward at a grete hulle þat men clepiþ Abyor. þis lond lastiþ fro Turkye to þe grete see and þe lond of Meddy and of grete Ermonye. In þis lond beþ ii. kynges, on of Abcaz, anoþer of George, but he of George is vndir þe Grete Chan. But he of Abcaz haþ a strong cuntre and he defendiþ hym [wel] aȝens alle men.

In þis lond of Abcaz is a grete merueyl, for þer is a cuntre þat is nere iii. iournez long and hit is yclepid Hampson. And þat cuntre is [al] ykeuered wiþ derknes so þat hit haþ no liȝt þat no man may se þer, and no man dar go vnto þat cuntre for þe derkenes. And neuerþeles men of þat cuntre þer | nere seiþ þat þei may somtyme hure þeryn þe voys of men and hors neiȝe and cokkys crowe, and þei wote wel þat men beþ dwellyng þare but þei wote noȝt what maner of men. f. 110r

And þei seiþ þis derknes comeþ þurȝ þe myracle of God whiche he schewid for cristen men þere, and þat þei fyndeþ in olde stories write in bookis among oþer wordis and merueiles. For þer was somtyme a wickid emperour of þe lond of Perse and he was yclepid Saures. þis emperour pursued alle cristene men a tyme þat were in his lond, and he wolde haue destroyed hem or ellis to lete hem make sacrifice to his mawmetis, for þer dwellid many cristen men, þe whiche forsoke alle here richesse and goodis and [catels] and wolde haue go ynto Greece.

And whenne þei were alle gederid togedir in a grete playn þat ys yclepid Megoun, þe emperour [and his] men come for to sle cristen men. And þe cristen men sette hem alle vpon here knees and | prayed God of help. And als soone come a þicke cloude and ouerlappid þe emperour and alle his men þat he myȝte not go awey. And so dwelliþ f. 110v

2, 3 lond] CM *add* of George 2 lastiþ] D *om.* 3 see] 2B *adds* of occyane 4 he of] 2P the 6 wel] QBD *om.* alle men] G2–G5 his enemys 7 grete] M *adds* wondre and a grete cuntre] G2–G5 *add* in þat londe 8 long] G2–G5 *add* and aboute 9 al] QBD *om.* 10 þer] M or knowe 11 cuntre] AM *add* þat ben þere þer nere] B *om.* 13–14 but þei . . . men] A *om.* 16–17 and þat . . . merueiles] G2–G5 *om.* 16 olde] A *om.* 17 among . . . merueiles] B *om.* wordis and] CM *om.* 18 somtyme] G2–G5 *om.* wickid] G1 *add* man whiche was 19–20 þat were in his lond] G2–G5 *om.* 21 mawmetis] G2–G5 fals goddys men] QAD *add* þat tyme 22 and goodes and catels] B *om.* catels] G1 fliȝ 24 gederid togedir] G2–G5 *om.* 25 emperour and his] QBD emperours 27 of help] 2A 2P *om.*; 2B ynwardely to almyȝtty godde yn trynyte as wyssely as þey vppon hym leuede and eueremore wolden for welle or for woo þey þat þey scholde be deeþe taken for hys loue þat he wolde sende somme myracle vnto hem þat þey myȝtten holden forþe heere purpos to come to þe countreez þare crysten men dwelled inne; 2C þat he wolde help hem 28 men] Q men and; D men and so; G2–G5 ost þei ȝit in þat derkenes and euermore schal. And þe cristen men went whar þei wolde. And þerfore þei may say wiþ Dauyd þus, *A domino factum est istud et est mirabile in oculis nostris*, þat is to say, Of oure lord is þis ydo and hit ys wonderful in oure iȝen. Also out of þis derke londis comeþ a ryuer þat men may se by [good] tokenyng þat men dwelliþ þere [bot no man dar go þeder ine].

þenne next is þe lond of Turkye þat marchiþ to grete Ermonye and þerynne beþ many cuntreez as Capadoce, Saure, Bryke, Quesion, Pytan, and Seneth. In eueriche of þese beþ many goode citeez. And hit is a playn lond and fewe hullis and fewe ryueris.

And þer is þe kyngdom of Mesopotayne, and þat bygynneþ estward at þe ryuere of Tygre at a cite þat men clepiþ Meselle and hit lastiþ westward to þe ryuere of Eufraten to a cyte þat men
f. 111[r] clepiþ Rochayz and fro hiȝe | Ermonye vnto þe wildernesse of Ynde þe lasse. And hit is a good lond and a playn, and þer beoþ [fewe] ryueris in þat lond and but ii. hullis, of whiche on is yclepid Symar and þat oþer Lyson, and hit marchiþ to þe lond of Caldee.

And ȝe schal vndirstonde þat þe lond of Ethiope marchiþ eestward to þe grete wildernesse, westward to þe lond of Nubye, souþward vnto þe kyngdome of Moritane [and northewarde vnto þe Reede See. And þanne ys Marytane] which lastiþ fro þe hulles of Ethiope to Libye þe hiȝe [and hit marcheþ vnto Nubye, whare ben crysten men, and þanne Lybye þe heye] and þe lowe, and hit lastiþ into [þe] grete [see of] Spayne.

## CHAPTER 21 þE LOND OF CALDILHE

Now Y haue yseid and yspoke of many cuntreys on þis side of þe grete kyngdome of Catay, of whom many beþ obedient to þe Grete Chan. Now schal Y speke of londis and cuntrez and yles whiche beþ

1 euermore schal] M *adds* at þe wylle of god; G2–G5 þei come neuer oute sethen 2 wiþ Dauyd] G2–G5 *om.* 5 men . . . tokenyng] B bitokeneth good] QAD *om.* 6 bot . . . ine] G1 2C 2P *om.* 10 is a] M is a ryȝt 11 kyngdom] B *om.* 12–13 of Tygre . . . ryuere] 2A *om.* 13 westward] A estward; M alle westward 14 fro] 2A 2P westwarde fro; 2B estwardes from 15 fewe] G1 *om.*; M *adds* fayre 19 grete] C *om.* 20 kyngdome] 2P londe 20–21 and . . . Marytane] G1 2A *om.* 22–23 and hit . . . heye] G1 2A 2P *om.* 23 þe[2]] QAD *om.* 24 see of] Q *om.*; DM of Spayne] 2B *adds* and þere ben no mo landes þat weye 25–26 CM *om. rubric* 27 Now] C now schall Y spek of oþer cuntreys for yseid and] CM *om.* cuntreys] 2P *om.* 28 of] G2–G5 of some

biȝonde [þe lond] of Catay. And þerfore he þat wol go fro Catay to Ynde þe [heygh and þe lawe], he schal go þurȝ a kyngdom þat is yclepid Caldilhe þat is a grete lond, whare growiþ a maner of fruyt [als it were gurdes]. And | when it is ripe men scheriþ [asonder] and f. 111v þei fyndeþ þeryn a beest as it were of fleisch and blood and boon, and hit is liche to a lytel lombe wiþoute wolle. And men etiþ þe beest and þe fruyt also, and þat ys a grete merueyl.

Neuerþeles Y seide Y helde þat for no grete merueyl, for Y sayde þat in my cuntre beþ treez þat beriþ a fruyt þat bicomeþ briddis fleyng þat men clepiþ bernaclis, and þei beþ goode to ete, and þat þat in þe watir falliþ lyueþ and [þois þat falles on þe erthe dyes. And þei hade grete merveile of this. In þis londe and in many oþere þeire aboute are treez þat bere clowes, nutemuges, and canelle and many oþere spices. And þeire are vynes þat bere so grete grapes þat a strong man schale haue inewght to do to bere a clustre of þe grapes.]

In þis same lond beþ þe hullis of Caspe whiche men clepiþ Vber. And among þese hullis beþ þe Iewis of þe ten kyndes encloosid, whiche men clepiþ Gog and Magog, and þei may come out at no side. [þeire was enclosede xxii. kynges with þe folke þat dwellede byfore bytwene þe hylles of Siche.] And þe kyng Alisaundre chased hem þedir for he trowid to haue enclosid hem þer þurȝ werching of man. And when he sauȝ þat he miȝt not, he preied to God he wolde fulfille þat he hadde bigonne. And God herde his preiere and encloosid þe hulle[s] togedre, whiche beþ so grete | and hiȝ þat no f. 112r man may passe hem [so þat þe Iewes dwele þeire als þei were lokkide or sperrede ine. And þeire is hille alle aboute heme bot at o syde, and þeire is þe see of Caspy. And somme man myght aske, seþen þeire is a see on o syde why go þei noght oute þeire. Bot þeireto I answere þat of alle it be called a see, it is no see bot a stonge standand among hilles, and it is þe greteste stonge of the werlde. And if þei wente

1 þe lond] Q *om.* 2 heygh and þe lawe] G1 lasse and þe more 4 als it were gurdes] G1 þat is riȝt grete asonder] G1 þeryn; M *adds* wiþ knyues 5 as it were] B *om.* 8 Neuerþeles . . . merueyl] 2P *om.* Y helde] 2A *om.* 9–10 þat beriþ . . . fleyng] M *om.* 10 þat men clepiþ bernaclis] G2–G5 *om.* 11–16 þois . . . grapes] G1 noon ellis 16 grapes] 2B *adds* to passe wyþoute fallynge of þat grapes in þat lande 17 þe] G1 (*ex* M) þre 19 may] CM neuere may 2—21 And þeire . . . Siche] G1 *om.* 20 xxii] 2B xii 22 þedir] G2–G5 *add* among þois hilles 22–23 werching of man] M strengthe of mannys hondys; 2P *adds* but he myght not 23 when he sauȝ þat] G2–G5 *om.* God] M *adds* as he was myȝty 24 bigonne] C be god 25 hulles] QABD hulle 25–26 whiche . . . hem] G2–G5 *om.* 26–112/2 so þat . . . owen] G1 *om.*

ouer þat see þei wote noght wheire for to aryue for þe[i] cane no spech bot þeire owen.]

And ȝe schal vndirstonde þat þe Iewis haueþ no lond of here owne to dwelle ynne but among þe[se] hullis, and ȝit þerfore þei paieþ tribute to þe queene of Ermonye. [And somme tyme it is so þat somme of þe Iewes goon ouere þe hilles, bot many men may noght pase þeire samen for þe hilles are so grete and so hey.]

And men seiþ in þe cuntre þer nere þat in þe tyme of Auntecrist þei schal do myche harm to cristen men. And þerfore alle þe Iewis þat dwelliþ in dyuerse parties of þe worlde lere for to speke Ebrew, for þei trowiþ þat þe Iewis þat dwelliþ among þe hullis schal come out and þei spekiþ noþing but Ebrew. And þanne schal oþer Iewis speke Ebrew to hem and lede hem to cristendome for to destruye cristen men, for þese Iewis seiþ þat þei wote by here prophecys þat þe Iewis whiche beþ among þese hullis [of Caspe] schal come out and cristen men schal be vndir hem as þei haue be vndir cristen [men].

And yf ȝe wole wite how þat þey schal fynde þe passage out, as Y f. 112v haue vndirstonde I schal telle ȝow. In þe | tyme of Auntecrist a fox schal make his den in þe same place whare kyng Alisaundre lete make þe ȝatis to þese hullis. And he schal so werche in þe erþe vnto þat þe come among þese Iewis. And when þei seeþ þis fox þei schal haue grete merueyl of hym, for þei sauȝ neuer no siche beest, but þei haueþ oþer beestis among hem many. And þei schal chace hym and pursue hym vnto þat he be flowe aȝen to his hole þat he come fro. And þenne shal þei graue aftir hym so longe vnto þei come to ȝatis whiche [Alisandre dide make] wiþ grete stones and morter wel ydiȝt, and þey schal breke þese ȝatis and so schal þei fynde þe passage.

Fro þis lond men schul go to þe lond of Bakarie whar beþ many wickid men and felle. In þis lond beþ treez þat beriþ wolle as it were of scheep, of whiche þei makiþ cloþis. In þis lond beþ many ipotaynes þat dwelliþ somtyme on lond, somtyme on water, and

3 lond] 2P lawe   owne] G2–G5 *add* in alle þe werlde   4 þese] G1 þe   5 tribute] G2–G5 *add* for þeire londe   queene] A kyng   5–7 And somme . . . hey] G1 *om.*   8 And] G2–G5 Neuereþeles   þer nere] B *om.*   9 þerfore] C *adds* þe iewys say in þat þey wot by þer prophesy   11 trowiþ] 2P *om.*   hullis] G2–G5 *add* byforesayde   12 out] G2–G5 *add* of þe hilles   oþer] G2–G5 thise   13 hem to] M þem alle abowte yn   14 wote] M *adds* welle   15 of Caspe] G1 *om.*   17 men] Q *om.*   18 out] C onto hem   21 to þese hullis] G2–G5 *om.*   erþe] G2–G5 *add* and peerse it þorgh   25 flowe] B go   26 so longe] G2–G5 als he wente   27 Alisandre dide make] G1 beþ ymade   29 lond[1]] CM *add* of Caldee   31 cloþis] C good cloþe; 2B *adds* as wee doon here   32 somtyme on lond] C *om.*

þei beþ half | men and half hors, and þei etiþ no3t but men when þei f. 113r may gete ony.

In þys londe beþ many griffouns mo þan in oþer placis. And somme seiþ þat þei haueþ þe body bifore as an egle and byhynde as a lyoun, and þei sey sooþ. But þe griffoun haþ a body gretter þan viii. lyouns and gretter and staleworþer þen an hundrid eglys, for certenliche he wole bere to his nest fleyng a grete hors and a man vpon hym or twey oxen 3okid as þei goþ togedir at þe plow, for he haþ longe nayles vpon his feet and grete as þei were hornes of oxen, and þei beþ ri3t scharpe. And of þese nayles men makiþ coppes to drinke of, as we doþ of horn of buglis, and of his ribbes þey make bowis to scheotyng.

## CHAPTER 22 þE LOND OF PRESTRE IOON

In þe lond of Prestre Ioon beþ many kyngdomes, to whiche lond fro þe lond of Bakarie beþ many iourneys. þys Prestre Ioon is emperour of Ynde and men clepiþ his lond þe yle of Pentoxore. þis Prestre Ioon þe emperour holdiþ grete | londis and many goode f. 113v citeez and goode townes and [in his kyngdome] many grete yles and large, for þis lond of Ynde is departid in yles bycause of grete flodys þat comeþ out of paradys. And also in þe see beþ many grete yles. þe beste cite þat is in þe yle of Pentoxore ys yclepid Nyse, for þat is a noble cite and a riche.

Prestre Ioon haþ vndir hym many kynges and many dyuerse folk. And his lond is good and riche but not so riche as þe lond of þe Grete Chan of Catay, for merchauntis comeþ no3t so myche to þat lond as to þe lond of [þe Grete Chan], for it were to long way and also þei fyndeþ in þe yle of Catay al þat þei haue nede of, as spicery,

1 etiþ no3t] A etiþ; M no3t   5 sooþ] G2–G5 *add* for þei are made so   viii.] C eny   6 gretter and staleworþer] B a grette; C strengar   7 fleyng] C *om.*   grete] 2P *om.*   8 vpon hym] 2B armed vppon hym and þat ys a wonderful þyng   togedir at þe plow] B to plow; G2–G5 samen als þei go at ploghe   9 vpon . . . were] B as grete as any; C *adds* gret   10 and þei beþ ri3t scharpe] G2–G5 *om.*   11 as we . . . buglis] G2–G5 *om.*   12 bowis] 2B *adds* yn þat countre and yn oþer   13–14 CM *om. rubric*   15 In . . . whiche lond] G2–G5 *om.*   16 beþ] G2–G5 men go   þys] G2–G5 to þe londe of   is] G2–G5 þat is   18 þe emperour] B *om.*   19 in his kyngdome] G1 *om.*   23 riche] C *adds* and a good   24 hym] QBD *add* many kyngdomes and   25 good . . . not so] B ful   26 of Catay] G2–G5 *om.*   26–27 þat lond as to] B *om.*   27 þe Grete Chan] G1 (*ex* C) Catay; C þe Cane

cloþis of gold, and oþer riche þingis. Also [if alle þei myght haue better chepe in þe londe of Prestre Ion neuereþelese] þei lette for to go þider for long way and grete periles in þe see, for þer beþ in many placis of þe see grete rochis of stoon þat is yclepid adamaunde, þe whiche of his owne kynde drawiþ to hym yrun, for þer schulde passe f. 114[r] no schip þat hadde nayles of yrun for þe | stoon adamaund [scholde drawe it to hym þeirfore þei dare noght wende into þat contre with schippes for drede of adamandes] and schippis in þat cuntre beþ ymade alle of wode and non yrun.

I was somtyme in þat see and Y sauȝ as long as hit hadde ybe a grete yle of treez and braunchis [and stokkes] growing. And þe schipmen seide þat al þat was of grete schippis þat adamaundis hadde ymade dwelle þere, and of þingis þat were in þe schippis were þese þinges yspronge. And for þese perels and oþer and þe longe way þei wendiþ to Catay [þat is nere þeyme]. And ȝit Catay is noȝt so nere þat hem bihoueþ fro Venys *or* *G*e[n]e or oþer place of Lumbardye be in see toward þe lond of Catay xi. oþer xii. monþis.

Þe lond of Prestre Ioon ys long. And merchauntis passiþ þider þurȝ þe lond of Perse and comeþ to a cyte þat men clepiþ Hermes, for a philosofir þat men clepiþ Hermes foundid it. And þey passiþ an arm of þe see and comeþ to anoþer cite þat is yclepide Soboth, and f. 114[v] þere þei fyndeþ alle merchaundises and papyniayes as gret | plente as beþ in oure cuntree of larkis. In þis cuntre is litel whete and barliche, and þerfore þei etiþ milet and rys and cheese and oþer fruytes.

Þis emperour haþ in his lond papynyaies many, whiche þei clepiþ in here langage *pystake*. And þei spekiþ of here owen kynde as propurliche as a man, and þese þat spekiþ wol haue longe tunges and

1 of] B *om.* oþer riche þingis] B al richesse; CM oþer riche marchaundyse; 2P other rychesse 1–2 if alle . . . neuereþelese] G1 *om.* 3 for long . . . grete] M as long way and] B *om.* 3–4 in many placis of þe see] B *om.* 6 no schip . . . of] B þat hath; C þer 6–8 scholde . . . adamandes] G1 *om.* 8–9 and schippis . . . yrun] G2–G5 *om.* 10 somtyme] C on o syde 11 and braunchis] B *om.*; CM and wode and stokkes] G1 *om.* 12–14 al þat . . . yspronge] 2C þilke trees were of shippes mastes; G2 (*ex* 2C) þat were dwelland þeire þorgh vertu of þe adamande and waxen and swich roches are in many places in þat se (2P *om. all after* waxen) 14 for . . . oþer and] G2 (*ex* 2C) þeirfore dare noght schipman pase þeire and also þei drede 14–16 And for . . . xii. monþis] 2C *om.* 14 way] G2–G5 *add* þerfore 15 þat is nere þeyme] G1 *om.* 16 þat hem bihoueþ] B *om.* or Gene] QBD ouer see 16–17 or oþer place of Lumbardye] B or Lombardye; G2–G5 *om.* 17 be in see] B bi the seyling of; D be in by; 2P *om.* 22 alle] CM *add* maner of 24 milet] 2P mylke oþer] QABCD *add* maner of 25–115/2 þis . . . litel] G2–G5 *after* 116/12 (as in Insular Version) 25 many] B *om.* 26 owen] B *om.* 27–115/2 and þese . . . litel] 2C *om.* 27 wol] B *om.*

large and vpon eche foot v. toos, and somme papyniaies haueþ but iii. toos and þei spekiþ noȝt or ellis litel.

þis emperour Prestre Ioon weddiþ comynliche þe douȝter of þe Grete Chan, and þe Grete Chan his douȝter. In þe lond of Prestre Ioon beþ many dyuerse þingis and many preciouse stoonys so grete [and] so large þat men makiþ of hem vessels, [platers] and coppis and many oþer þingis [of whiche it were to longe to telle]. But somme þing of his treuþe and of his feiþ schal Y telle [ȝowe].

þe emperour Prestre Ioon is cristene and a greet partye of his lond [also] but þei haueþ not alle þe articlis of oure fey. But þei trowiþ wel in þe fader and þe sone and þe holi goost and þei beþ riȝt deuoute and trewe euerichon to oþer | and þei makiþ no fors of f. 115r
catel. And he haþ vndir hym sixty and twelue [prouynces or] cuntrez and in eueriche is a kyng, and þese kynges haueþ oþer kynges vndir hem.

And in his lond beþ many merueyls, for in þat lond is þe grete grauely see whiche is of sond and grauel and no drope of water. And hit ebbeþ and flowiþ wiþ grete wawes as doþ anoþer see, and hit is neuer stille noþer in rest. And no man many passe þat see by schip noþer noon oþer wise and þerfore men wote noȝt what lond is biȝonde hit. And yf alle hit be so þat þer be no watir in þat see, ȝit men fyndeþ þere good fysch of oþer schap þan beþ in oþer seez, and þei beþ of good sauour and swete and good to ete.

And at iii. iourneys fro þat see beþ grete hullis þurȝ whiche comeþ a grete flood þat comeþ fro paradys, and hit is ful of precious stones and no drope of watir. And hit renneþ wiþ grete wawis vnto þat grauelly see. And þys flood renneþ iii. dayes eueriche woke | so fast f. 115v
þat [and stirres þe grete stones of þe roches with hym þat makez mykylle noyse, and als son als þei come into þe grauely see þei are no more seen. And in þois þre days when it rynnes þus] no man dar

5 and] C þat ys ryȝt fele  6 and] QB *om.*  platers] G1 *om.*  and coppis] M *om.* 7 of whiche . . . telle] G1 2C *om.*  8 þing] B *om.*  feiþ] C *adds* and how  ȝowe] G1 *om.*  10 also] G1 *om.*  þe] C owre  13 prouynces or] G1 *om.*  14 þese kynges] A þey  16 merueyls] C *adds* wondyrrys  18 grete] C *om.*; 2P right greate 19–20 see . . . wise] 2P londe beyonde it  20–21 and þerfore . . . see] 2C *om.* 21 hit] CM þat see  22 fyndeþ] 2A *om.*  schap] G2–G5 fasoun and schappe  þan] C *adds* ony odur fyscheys  23 þei beþ of good sauour] B right good fisch  and good] B *om.*  24–116/2 And . . . stoones] 2C *om.*  25 þat comeþ] BCM *om.* 27 see] G1 *add* and þan beþ þei no more yseye  iii. dayes eueriche] C euery daye þat is to say iii in þe  28–30 and stirres . . . þus] G1 *om.*  30–116/2 dar . . . stoones] C ne dare cum þere nye at þer wyll to take of þe stonys þat ys þereyn

come þerynne, but alle þe oþer dayes men may go þerynne when þei woleþ and take of þe stoones.

And also biȝonde þat flood toward þe wildernesse is a grete playn al sondy and grauely among hullis, in whiche playn beþ treez vpon whiche euery day at þe sonne arisyng bigynneþ a fruyt to springe out. And þat growiþ so til hit be mydday and þanne turneþ hit ynne aȝen, so þat whenne þe sonne goþ adoun þer is nouȝt yseye. And of þis fruyt no man dar ete for it is a maner of yrun. [And so doos it ich day.]

And in þat wilderenesse beþ many wilde men wiþ hornes vpon here heedis as beestis and þei beþ riȝt hidous. And þei spekiþ noȝt but grunt as swyn dooþ.

þis emperour Prestre Ioon, when he wendiþ to bateyl, he haþ no baner ybore bifore hym but [he has byfore hyme] ybore iii. crossis of fyne gold which beþ grete and long, wel ydiȝt wiþ precious stoonus. And to kepyng of eueriche cross beþ ordeynd a m$^{l}$. men of armes and f. 116$^{r}$ moo þan an hundrid m$^{l}$. a foote yn | maner as kepyng of a standard in bataile in oþer placis. And he haþ men wiþoute noumbre when he goþ to bateil aȝens oþer lordis.

And when he rideþ not in bateile but wiþ priue maigne, þan is ybore bifore hym a cross of tre noȝt ypaynted and wiþoute gold and precious stonus but al playn in tokne þat oure lord suffrid deeþ vpon a crois of tree. And [also] he haþ ybore byfore hym a plate of gold ful of erþe in tokne þat his nobley and his lordschip [schalle torne to noght] and his fleisch schal turne vnto erþe. And þey beriþ bifore hym also anoþer vessel, ful of gold and iewels, precious stones as rubiez, dyamandis, saphires, emeraudis, topaces, geraundes, crissolites, and oþer moo precious stones, in tokne of his lordschipe and his miȝt.

1 but alle] B and alle; G2–G5 bot 2 and take of þe stoones] G2–G5 *om.* 3 þat] C *adds* se and 3 treez] C *adds* growyng 5–6 a fruyt to springe out] G2–G5 to growe 6 And þat growiþ so] M *om.* mydday] G2–G5 *add* and beres fruyt 6–7 and þanne . . . yseye] G2–G5 *after* yrun 7 aȝen] G2–G5 *add* to the erthe yseye] M *adds* of þe frute 8 yrun] A yre; 2C ire 8–9 And . . . day] G1 2C *om.* 10 wilde] A wikkede 11 as beestis and þei beþ] G2–G5 *om.* 12 dooþ] G2–G5 *have here* 114/25–115/2 14 he haþ byfore hyme] QA *om.* 16 a] A two; 2B more þan vii 17 m$^{l}$. a foote] 2B knyȝttes 19 lordis] C kingys 22 lord] G2–G5 *add* Ihesu crist 23 also] Q *om.* 24 lordschip] A worschipe 24–25 schal . . . nought] G1 *om.* 25 and his fleisch . . . erþe] 2B *om.* 26 vessel] G1 *add* of gold 26–27 as rubiez] C and ryche; D rubies; M as of ryche 26–28 as rubiez . . . stones] G2–G5 *om.* 28 moo] B *om.*; C maner of his] G1 his grete 29 his] G1 his grete

# CHAPTER 23 ARAY OF þE COURT OF PRESTRE IOON

Now schal Y telle of aray of Prestre Ioon in his p[a]lace, which is in þe cite of Suse whare he dwelliþ comunliche. And þat p[a]lace is so riche þat merueyl is to tel|le, for aboue þe principal tour beþ ii. f. 116v pomels of gold al round, and eueriche of þese haueþ ii. charbuclis grete and large þat schyneþ riȝt clere vpon þe nyȝt. And þe principale ȝatis of his p[a]lace beþ of preciouse stones þat men clepiþ sardyn, and þe boordys of þe barres beþ of [iuorye]. And þe wyndowis of þe halle and chambres beþ of crestal and þe tablis of whiche he etiþ, somme beþ of mastyk and somme of emeraudis, somme of gold and somme of preciouse stones. And þe pilers þat beriþ þe tablis beþ of siche stonus also.

And þe greces of whiche þe emperour goþ to his sege whare he sittiþ at mete, on is of mastyk, anoþer of crestal, anoþer of grene iasper, anoþer of dyasper, anoþer of sardyn, anoþer of cornilyn, anoþer of septoun. And þe grece of whiche he settiþ his feet beþ of crissolites. And þe grecis beþ ybordured wiþ fyne gold wel ydiȝt wiþ grete perles and precious stones [and þe sydes of his see are of emeraudes bordurede with golde and with precious stones].

Þe pilours in hys chambre beþ of fyne gold wiþ ma|ny charbuclis f. 117r and oþer riche stones þat ȝeueþ grete liȝt vpon þe niȝt. And if al hit be þat þe charbuclis ȝeueþ grete liȝt vpon þe niȝt, neuerþeles þer brenneþ in his chambre xii. grete vessels of crestal ful of bawme to ȝeue good smel and swote and to drawe awey wickid air.

And þe fourme of his bed is al of saphires wel ybounde wiþ gold to make hym to slepe wel and for to destroye leccherie, for he wol noȝt

1–2 CM *om. rubric* 3–4 Now . . . whare] G2–G5 at þe cite of Suse 3 of[2]] A of þe court of in his palace] A *om.*; QBD in his place 4 þat palace] QABD þat place; G2–G5 þeire is his pryncipalle paleys þat 5 aboue] A abouten tour] G2–G5 *add* of þe paleys ii.] M *adds* grete 6 þese] CM the pomellys 7 riȝt clere] CM *om.* 8 palace] QABD place 9 barres] B yates; C ȝat iuorye] G1 yrun 11 somme beþ] C are of dyverys þingys sum 12 preciouse] CM odur presius 13 also] CM as þe tabyllys ben 14 sege] C tabyllis 15–18 grene . . . crissolites] 2C iasper and oþer precious stones 17 þe grece] G2–G5 þat settiþ] 2B *om.* feet] C *adds* on whan he syttys at met; M *adds* at hys met 18 þe grecis] C all þes; M all þes stayres; 2P all these greses 18–20 wiþ grete . . . stones] C *om.* 19–20 and . . . stones] G1 *om.* 21 beþ] D *om.* many] 2B blysful 22 riche] 2P such vpon þe niȝt] 2A *om.* 22–23 And if . . . niȝt] AM *om.* 23 vpon þe niȝt] G2–G5 *om.* 24 in his chambre] M 2P *add* euery nyȝt; 2A *om.* ful] C *om.* 25 and swote] CM *add* to þe emperour; G2–G5 *om.* air] M *adds* and yuelle vmoures

lye by his wyf but [þrys] at iii. sesouns in þe ȝere, and þat is al oonliche for getyng of children.

And he haþ euery day in his court moo þan xxx. m$^l$. of folk wiþoute comers and goers [but] xxx. m$^l$. þere and in þe court of þe Grete Chan spendiþ noȝt so myche as xii. m$^l$. in oure cuntre. Þis emperour haþ euermore vii. kynges in his court to serue hym, and eche of þese serueþ a monþe aboute. And wiþ þese kynges serueþ alwey lx. and xii. dukis and ccc. erlis and oþer many lordis and
f. 117$^r$ kniȝtes. And eueriche day etiþ yn | his court xii. erchebyschops and xx$^{ti}$. byschopis.

Þe patriark of seynt Thomas is as it were a pope. Erchebyschopis and byschopis and abbotis beþ alle kinges in þat cuntre. And somme of þese lordes beþ maistres of þe halle, somme of þe chambre, somme stiward, somme marchal, and somme oþer office, and þerfore he is ful richeliche serued.

And his lond lasteþ iiii. monþis iournay in brede, and hit is of lengþe wiþoute mesure. In þis yle of Prestre Ioon is plente of good and myche richesse and many perlis and oþer preciouse stones. And he haþ a faire paleys at þe cite of Nise whare he dwelliþ when he wole, but þe aire is is not so atempre as it is at þe cite of Suse.

In þat lond was a riche man [noght long sethyn] whiche was yclepid Catolonabes. He was ful riche and he hadde a fayre castel vpon an hille and a strong. And he hadde let make a wal aboute it riȝt
f. 118$^r$ strong, and withynne þe castel he hadde a fayre gar|dyn whare were many trees bering dyuerse fruytes [þat he myght fynde]. And he lete plaunte þerynne al maner of herbes of good smel and hit bare feire flouris. And þer were many feire wellis [and by þeyme was made many faire halles and chambres] arayed wiþ gold and azure, and he

1 þrys] G1 *om.* iii.] G1 *add* certeyn 2 al oonliche] B *om.* children] G2–G5 *have here* 118/18–20 (as in Insular Version) 3 his] C *adds* hows and in hys 4 comers and goers] C *adds* of strange folk; M strangers but] Q *om.* court] CM *add* and in þe cuntre 5 myche] G1 *add* vpon o day of mete xii.] A xiii 6 vii.] A viii 8 alwey] 2A ech day xii.] A iiii; B viii; M xx dukes] 2B knyȝttes dukes ben heere names erlis] 2B knyȝttes erles ben þare names but neuere a knyȝt bachylere serueþ þare 8–9 and oþer . . . kniȝtes] G2–G5 *om.* 9 etiþ] C he haþe 10 xx$^{ti}$. byschopis] 2B *om.* 11 seynt Thomas] C makyn; 2B *adds* and he 13 maistres] CM stewardys 14 oþer office] CM 2P odur offycerys; 2A in oþer offices 15 richeliche] G2–G5 *add* and wel 16 monþis iournay] C iurnayis þat is to say ȝe may ryde iiii monþys togedur 17 wiþoute] Q *adds* noumbre and wiþoute 18 perlis and oþer] G2–G5 *om.* 20 at] M yn the contre abowte 21 riche] C *adds* and worthy noght longe sethyn] G1 somtyme 23 riȝt] CM *om.* 24 strong] G2–G5 *add* and fayre þe castel] 2A in þat 25 þat he myght fynde] G1 *om.* 26 smel] M smellyng and of odure 27–28 and by . . . chambres] Q *om.*

hadde ymade þere dyuerse stories and beestis and briddes þat songe and turnede by engyn as orlagis as þei hadde be [alle] quyke. And he hadde in þat gardyn alle maner of briddis and bestys as þat he miȝt fynde to make a man solace and disport.

And he hadde in his gardyn also maydouns wiþynne elde of xv. ȝere, þe fairest þat he miȝt fynde, and knaue children of þe same elde. And þei were alle cloþed in cloþis of gold, and he seide þat þese were aungels. And he hadde ymade iii. wellis faire and goode, al enclosed aboute wiþ precious stoones of iasper and crestal and wel ybounde wiþ gold and perlys and oþer maner of stones. And he hadde made a condyt vndir þe erþe so þat whan he wolde one of þese wellis ronne | of wyne, anoþer melk, anoþer hony. And þis place he f. 118v clepid paradys.

And when ony ȝonge bachelere of þe cuntre come to him, [knygh or sqwyere], he ladde hym into his paradys and schewid hym alle þis dyuers þingis and dyuerse song of briddis and his damysels and his wellis. And he hadde dyuerse [instrumentz of musyke] in anoþer hiȝe tour þat þei miȝte not be seiȝe and he seide þese were aungels, and hadde dyuerse manere of musyk. And he seide þat was paradys þat God grauntide to þese þat he loued seiyng, *Dabo vobis terram fluentem lac et mel*, þat is to say, I schal ȝeue to ȝow lond flowyng melk and hony.

And þanne þis riche man ȝaf to þese men a maner of drinke of whiche þei were dronke. And he seide to hem if þei wolde deiȝe as for his sake, whenne þei were deede þey schulde come into his paradys and þei schulde be of elde of þese maydouns, and þei schulde dwelle euermore wyþ hem and haue likyng of hem, and þei schulde euermore be maydens, and he schul|de putte hem in a faire[r] paradys f. 119r whare þei schulde se God in his ioiȝe and his maieste.

2 alle] CM alyve; QABD *om.* 2–4 And he . . . disport] D *om.* 2–3 alle . . . as þat] 2P *om.* 3 briddis] M herdys to kepe þem and many oþer dysportes 4 and disport] B *om.* 2A and comfort 8 aungels] 2B *adds* of heuen wellis] G2–G5 hilles and goode al] B *om.* 9 aboute] Q aboute aboute 10 maner of] A *om.*; BC precious; M ryche 11 whan he wolde] B *om.* D he wolde one of þese] G2–G5 the 12 ronne] G2–G5 *add* sommetyme 14 him] G2–G5 *add* for solace or disporte 14–15 knygh or sqwyere] G1 *om.* 16 dyuers] QAD dyuersite of 17 instrumentz of musyke] G1 mynstrals anoþer] CDM an 18 tour] 2A *om.* aungels] M *adds* þat myȝt nouȝt be knowe; G2–G5 *add* of god 18–19 and hadde . . . musyk] G2–G5 *om.* 19 þat[1]] C þat place; M þat sayde place 20 he loued] 2A louede; 2P beloued 21 lond] C *om.* 23–120/12 And þanne . . . distroyed] 2C *om.* 23 men] C *adds* þat come onto hym 25 sake] C *adds* and for hys love 26 of þese maydouns] B his 27–28 and haue . . . putte hem] A *om.* and haue . . . maydens] G2–G5 *om.* 28 fairer] G1 faire; 2B fayrest place of 29 ioȝe] 2A face

And þanne þei grauntid to do al þat he wolde. And þanne he bade hym go and slee siche a lord oþer a man of þe cuntre whiche was his enemy, and þat þei schulde haue no drede for yf þei were deede þei schulde be in þat paradys. And þus let he sle many lordis of þat cuntre, and þese men were ysleiȝe as yn hope to haue þis paradys. And þus he was yvengid of his enemys þurȝ þis deceyt.

And whenne lordis of þe cuntre and riche men perceyued þis malice and þe [cautele] of hym þis Catolonabes, þei gedrid hem togedir and asayled þis castel and slow hym and destruyd al his richesse and faire [places] þat were in his paradys. Þe place of þe wellis is ȝit þare and somme oþer þingis but no richesse [and it is noght longe sethen he was distroyed].

A litel fro þat place [on the left syde] nere toward þe ryuer of Physon is a grete merueyl. Þer is a valey bitwene ii. hullis þat is iiii.
f. 119v myle long. Somme men clepiþ hit þe valey | enchaunted, somme þe valey of deuelis, somme þe valey perilous. In þis valey beþ many tempestis and many noyses and hydous euery day [and euery nyȝt] somme tyme as it were a noyse of tabres and nakers and trumpis as it were at a grete feste. Þis valey beþ ful of deuelis and alway haþ ybe, and men seiþ þere is an entre to helle.

In þis valeye is myche gold and siluer, wherfore [many] cristen men and oþer þat goþ þider for coueytyse of þat gold [and siluer] beþ ystranglid wiþ deuelis þat fewe comeþ aȝen. And in þe myddel of þat valey vpon a roche is a visage and þe hed of a deuel bodeliche riȝt hidous and dredful to se, and þer is noþing yseye but þe hed fro þe schuldris. And þer is no man in þe world, cristen ne oþer, [so hardy] but he schulde haue grete drede to byholde hit. For he biholdeþ euery man so scharplych and so fellich, and his iȝen beþ so fast stiring and sprenglyng as fire, and he chaungiþ [so] ofte his

1 þei] M suche men as come vnto hym 2 oþer a man] B *om.* 3–4 for yf . . . paradys] G2–G5 of no man and if þey were scleyne þeyme self fore his sake he scholde put þeyme in his paradys whene þei were dede 4 lete he sle many] G2 (*ex* 2B) wente thise bachilers to scle grete; 2B *om.* 6 was] M *adds* ofte tyme deceyt] C fals deceit; 2P desert 7 lordis . . . men] G2–G5 riche men of þe contre 8 cautele] G1 wile hym] CDM *om.* 10 faire places þat were in] A *adds* his castel and in; C all hys gardayne and places] G1 (*ex* C) þingis 11 wellis] 2P walles 11–12 and it . . . distroyed] Q *om.* 12 noght longe] B *om.*; D noȝt 13 on the left syde] G1 *om.* 14 iiii.] B iii 15 þe valey enchaunted somme] B *om.* 16 somme þe valey] B *om.* perilous] QD of perilous; A of periles many] G2–G5 grete 17 and hydous] B wonderful and euery nyȝt] QBD *om.* 21 many] G1 *om.* 22 þat] D thay and siluer] G1 *om.* 24 bodeliche] C þat ys; M *om.* 25 riȝt] 2A riche yseye] M *om.* fro] G2–G5 to 26 schuldris] CM *add* vpward 26–27 so hardy] G1 *om.* 29 fast] G2–G5 *om.* so] G1 *om.*

cuntenaunce [þat no man dare come nere for alle þe worlde] and out of his mouþ and nose comeþ grete plente of fuyr of dyuerse colours and | some [tyme] þe fuyre is so stynkyng þat no man may suffre hit. f. 120r But alwey goode cristen men þat beþ stable in þe fey may go in þat valey wiþoute grete harm and þei be clene yschryue and blesse hem wiþ tokenyng of þe cross, for þan schal not deuelis dere hem.

And ȝe schal vndirstonde when my felawis and Y wente þurȝ þat valey we hadde grete drede [if we scholde put oure bodyes in auenture to go þorgh it. And somme of my felawes acordede þeireto and somme noght.] And þer was in oure cumpenye ii. frere menours of Lumbardye, and þei seide yf ony of vs wolde go yn þei wolde go also. And [when þei hade sayde so] vpon trist of hem we seide we wolde go, and we lete hem synge a masse and we were yschryue and yhouselyd. And we wente yn xiiii. and when we come out þer were but x. And we wist not whider oure felawis were ylost [þeire] or þei were turned aȝen, but we sauȝ hem no more. Oþere of oure felawis whiche wolde not go yn [with vs] went aboute by anoþer way to be bifore vs, and so þei were.

And we went þurȝ þe valey and we sauȝ many meruelous þingis, gold | siluer and precious stoonus, iewels grete plente on euery side f. 120v as vs þouȝt. And whider it were as it semyd I wote nouȝt for Y touchid hem not, for deuelis beþ so [sotel and] queynte þat many tymes þei makiþ þingis to seme þat þei beþ noȝt for to bigile men. And þerfore Y wolde touche noone for drede of deuels whiche Y sauȝ in many likenes, what of deede bodyes þat Y sauȝ in þat valey; but Y dar not seie þat þei were alle deede bodies, but þei semyd bodies, and many of hem semyd in cloþing of cristen men, and þei semyd so many as ii. [grete] kynges hadde fouȝte þer and þer men hadde be slawe.

And ȝe schal vndirstonde þat we were many tymes cast doun into

1 þat . . .worlde] G1 *om.* 2 fuyr] QBD *add* and 3 tyme] QB 2A *om.* 4 goode] B *om.* 4–5 in þat valey] DM *add* welle; G2–G5 þeire 5 grete] G2–G5 *om.* clene] C *om.* 7 wente þurȝ] G2–G5 were in 8 grete] C *om.* drede] 2A 2B 2P þoght 8–10 if we . . . noght] G1 *om.* 8–9 if we . . . it] 2C *om.* 10 in oure cumpenye] 2B *om.* menours] M *om.* 12 when . . . so] G1 *om.* of] M of god and 15 not] C *adds* where owre feloschyp were becum þeire] G1 *om.* 17 with vs] G1 *om.* 19 þingis] M grete 20 iewels] B *om.* euery] G2–G5 many 22 sotel and] G1 *om.* 23 seme] C *adds* good 24 deuels] G2–G5 enemys Y] B we 25 sauȝ] 2A *adds* lye likenes] C syckenys 26 dar not seie] B wote not whether 27–30 and many . . . vndirstonde þat] G2–G5 þorgh makyng of deueles and (2C *om. last five words of* G1) 28 grete] QBD cristen 30 many tymes] C *om.* 30–122/1 into þe erþe] C *om.*

þe erþe wiþ wynd and þonder and tempestes, but God halp vs alwey and so we passid þurȝ þat valey [withoute perelle and harme, þankede by God allemyghty þat vs kepyde wele].

And biȝonde þat valey is a grete yle whare þe folk beþ [als grete als] geauntez of xxviii. oþer ellis xxx. fete long. And þei haue no f. 121r cloþing but skynnes of beestis þat hongiþ on hem, and þey | etiþ no breed but fleisch rawȝ and drinkiþ melk. [And þey haue no houses] and þei etiþ gladloker fleisch of man þan oþer.

And men seiþ þer biȝonde þat yle is anoþer yle whare geauntz beþ of lxv. oþer fyfty foot long and somme of fifty schaftmount long, but Y sauȝ neuer hem. And among þese geauntz beþ grete scheep as it were ȝonge oxen and þei beriþ grete wolle. Of þese scheep Y haue oft yseye.

Anoþer yle is in þe see Occiane whare beþ [many il and felle] wymmen þe which haue preciouse stonus in here iȝen. And þey haueþ siche a maner yf þei biholde eny man wiþ wreþþe, þei sleeþ hym of þe siȝt as þe basilisk doþ.

And anoþer yle ys þere of faire folk and goode whar þe maner is siche þat þe firste niȝt þat þei beþ yweddid, þei takiþ a certeyn man þat is yordeyned þerto and lete hem lye by here wyfes to haue here maydenhood. And þei ȝeueþ hym grete reward for here trauayl, and þese men beþ yclepid *gadlibiriens*, for men of þat f. 121v cuntre holdiþ hit a gre|te *þynge* and a perilous to make a womman no mayde. And yf it be so þat þe housbande fynde here mayde þe nexte niȝt, for perauenture he þat was wiþ hire was dronke or for ony oþer skil, þe housbande schal playne on hym to þe lawe þat he haþ not do his deuer, and he schal greuously be punischid. But after þe firste niȝt þei kepiþ here wifes wel þat þei speke no more wiþ þese men.

And Y askyd what was here cause whi þei dide so, and þei seide somme housbandis lay by here wyfes [first] and non oþer but þei,

1 þonder and] B many other 2–3 withoute . . . wele] G1 *om.* 2 perelle or] 2C *om.* 4–5 als grete als] G1 *om.* 5 oþer ellis xxx.] C *om.* 7 breed] C mete And þey haue no houses] G1 2C *om.* 9 And men . . . whare] B other; G2–G5 *add* grettere þer] G2–G5 vs 10 fifty] B lx schaftmont] G2–G5 cubitez 14 many il and felle] G1 *om.*; 2B many wykkede 15 wymmen] M men 17 basilisk] CM *add* þat ys callyd þe cocatrys doþ] 2B *adds* cokyntryces 21 And þei . . . trauayl] D *om.* here] C *adds* labur and for þer 23 þynge] G1 synne and a perilous] CM and a grete perell; G2–G5 *om.* 25 or for ony oþer skil] B then 26 lawe] A keperes of þe lawe 27 punischid] Q punschid; G2–G5 *add* and chastisede 29 dide so] G2–G5 hade þat custume 30 somme housbandis] G2–G5 somme tyme men first] G1 *om.*

and somme of here wyfes hadde naddris in here bodyes þat twengid here housbandis vpon here ȝerdys in þe bodyes of þe wymmen, and so was many a man yslawe. And þat was þerfore here custome to make oþer men to asaye þe passage bifore þat þei were put in auenture.

Anoþer yle ys þer whar wymmen makiþ myche sorwe when here childen beþ ybore and myche ioiȝe when þei beþ dede [and kast þeyme in a grete fyre and birne þeyme. And þei þat loue wele þeire housbondes when þei are dede þei kast þeyme in a fyre to byrne also, for þei say þat fyre schalle make þeyme clene of alle fylth and alle vices and þei schalle be clene in anoþere worlde. And þe cause why þei wepen and make sorowe whene þeire childre are borne and at þei make ioy of þeire deth] þei seiþ | a child when he is ybore f. 122r comeþ into þis world to traueyl and sorwe and heuynes, and when þei beþ deede þei goþ to paradys, whare ryueris beþ of melk and hony and þer is lyf and ioiȝe and plente of goodis wiþoute traueyl and sorwe.

In þis yle þei makiþ here kyng þurȝ chesyng, and þey chese hym noȝt for his richesse oþer nobley but þei chesiþ hym þat is best of condicions and most riȝtwise and trewe to eueriche man, as wel pore as riche, and iuggiþ euery man after his trespas. And þe kyng may do no man to deeþ wiþout assent and counseil of barouns. And if it be so þat þe kyng do a [grete] trespas, as sle a man or siche anoþer þing, he schal be deed but he schal noȝt be sleiȝe. But þei schal forbede þat no man schal be hardy to make hym cumpeny neþer speke to him neþer come to hym noþer ȝeue hym mete neþer drinke, and þus schal he deiȝe. [They spare no man þat has don trespace for loue ne for lordschipe ne rechese nore nobley þat men do so hym right aftre þat he has done.]

And þer is anoþer yle in þe see whare is grete plente of folk, and þei etiþ neuermore fleisch | of haris noþer of hennus neþer of gees f. 122v

1–2 in here . . . ȝerdys] D *om.* þat twengid . . . wymmen] 2A *om.* 2 in þe bodyes of þe wymmen] AB *om.*; 2P and their bodyes 3–4 custome to make] G2–G5 to lete oþere men haue þeire madenhodes for drede of deeþe and þus þei suffre asaye] say þem and were] CM be not 6–17 Anoþer . . . sorwe] 2C *om.* 7–13 and kast . . . deth] G1 ffor 16 lyf] C *adds* and neuyr deþe goodis] M *adds* and ryches 18 chesyng] M goode electyon 19 best of] G2–G5 of good 20 condicions] CM consyens trewe] G1 *add* þei makiþ (A to ben) here kyng and he doþ resoun and trewþe 22 and counseil] B *om.* 23 grete] G1 *om.* 24 noȝt] 2P *om.* forbede] G2–G5 defende (2A þe fende) and forbede 25 cumpeny] CM no (M no manere of) comfort nor to do hym no counsayle (M company) 27–29 They . . . done] G1 *om.* 27–124/9 They . . . heris] 2C *om.* 30 in þe see] G2–G5 *om.*

but ȝit þer beþ þer many of ham. But þei etiþ gladliche fleisch of alle oþer beestis and þei drinkiþ melk.

[In þis contre þei wede þeire sonnes and doughtres and oþer of þeire kyne als þeyme lykes.] And ȝif x. oþer xii. dwelle in an hous þere, echon of here wifes schal be comyn to oþer [and o nyght schalle on haue on of þe wyuys and anoþere nyght anoþere]. And yf ony of þe wifes haue children, heo may ȝeue hit to whom heo wole of þese men, so þat no man woot whoos þe child [is]. And yf a man saye þat so may þei fader oþer mennus children, þei say þat so dooþ oþer men heris. [In þis londe and many oþere places of Ynde are many cokadrilles, þat is a manere of a longe neddyre. And on nyghtes þei dwelle in watyre and on dayes þei dwelle on londe and roches, and þei ete noght in wyntere. This nedire scloos men and etes þeyme gretand, and has no tonge.]

In þis lond and many oþer beþ trees beryng cotoun, for men sowe þe seed euerich ȝere and þanne growiþ smale treez whiche beriþ cotoun.

In Arabye beþ grete beestis whiche men clepiþ *girsant*. He is a fair beest, heiȝer þan a grete steede, and his necke is nere of lengþe of xx. schaftmountz. And his tayl and his croppen is like to an hert, and he may loke ouer an hiȝe hous.

And þer beþ many camelyouns, which is a litel beest, and he noþer etiþ ne drinkiþ neuer. And he chaungiþ ofte his colour, for
f. 123r somtyme he is of o | colour, somtyme of anoþer, and he may chaunge hym into alle colouris but white and reede.

And þer beþ many wilde swyn of many colouris and as grete as oxen, and þei beþ alle spottyd as it were smale fownes. And þer beþ lyouns al white. And þer beþ oþer beestis as grete as steedis þat men clepiþ *lonhorans* and somme clepiþ hem *toutes*, and here hed is blak and iii. longe hornes in hys frount scheryng as scharpe as a swerd, and he chasiþ and sleeþ þe olyfauntz. And þer beþ many oþer maner of beestis, of whom it were to long to telle.

1 But þei] 2B þat  2 oþer beestis] C maner of oþyr  3–4 In þis . . . lykes] G1 *om.*  3 sonnes] 2P *om.*  5 to oþer] D *om.*  5–6 and o nyght . . . anoþere] G1 *om.*  7 of þese men] 2A þeyme; 2B of þe men; 2P *om.*  8 woot] C *adds* ne know is] QBD *om.*  8–9 And yf . . . heris] G2–G5 *om.*  10–14 In þis . . . tonge] G1 *om.*  15 beþ . . . cotoun] G2–G5 men castes sede of cotoun  16 þanne . . . treez] C þerof cumys many odur small treys  growiþ] G2–G5 *add* als it were  17 cotoun] G1 *add* good and fayre (ACM fyn)  18 grete beestis] G2–G5 many birdes  whiche] 2B and som of hem  19 steede] G2–G5 coursere or a stede  20 schaftmountz] G2–G5 cubites  23–24 for . . . anoþer] 2B *om.*  28 oþer] C many odur  31 chasiþ] B taketh  31–32 maner of] C *om.*

And þanne is anoþer yle goode and grete and plenteuouse, and þer beþ goode men and trewe and of good feye and lyf. And yf al þei be not cristen, ȝit by lawe of kynde þei beþ ful of good vertues. And þei fleeþ alle synne, alle vices, and alle malice, for þei beþ not enuyouse noþer proude noþer couetous noþer lechours noþer glotouns, and þei doþ noȝt to anoþer man but as þei wolde þei dide to hem. And þei fufille þe ten | comaundementis, and þei makiþ no forse of richesse f. 123v noþer of hauyng, and þei sweriþ noȝt but seyþ ȝhe and nay for þei seiþ he þat wol swere he wol bygyle his neiȝebore. And somme men clepiþ þis yle þe yle of Bragmen and som clepiþ hit þe lond of feiþ. And þurȝ hit renneþ a grete ryuere þat men clepiþ Thebe. And generaliche al men in þat yle and oþer þerby beþ trewer and riȝtwiser þan beþ in oþer cuntrez.

In þis yle beþ no þefis noþer mordereris ne comyn wymmen [ne beggare]. And for as myche as þei beþ so trewe and so good men þer is no tempest, no þondre, no werre, no hungre, noon oþer tribulacions, and þus semeþ hit þat God loueþ hem wel and is wel apayd of here lyuyng and of here fey. And þei trowiþ in God þat made alle þing and hym worschipe þei. And þei lyue so ordynetly in mete and drinke þat þei lyueþ riȝt longe [and many of þeyme dye withoute sekenes þat kynde fayles þeyme for elde].

And kyng Alisaunder sent his men somme [tyme] þedir to wynne þat lond. And þei sente lettris to hym þat seyde: 'What miȝte | be f. 124r ynowȝ til a man to whom al þe world may not suffice? Þou schalt fynde noþing in vs why þou schuldist werre vpon vs, for we haue no riches and alle þe goodis and þe catels of oure lond beþ in comune. Oure mete þat we etiþ is oure richesse, and in stede of tresure of gold and siluer we makiþ tresure pees and acord and loue. And we haueþ noȝt but a clooþ vpon oure bodies. Oure wifes beþ not arayd richely to plesyng of men, for we holde hit a grete folye a man to diȝte his body to make hit seme fairere þan God made hit. We haue be

1 And þanne] B ther  2 trewe] C *adds* and of good savyr  feye and lyf] G2–G5 lyfe aftre þeire fayth  3 by lawe] 2P *om.*  3 ful of] Q of ful; D of ful of  4 alle[1]] Q alle alle  synne alle vices] BCM vices of synne  6 anoþer man] B her neygbour  8 hauyng] C *adds* of goodys  seyþ] ABCM *om.*  12 oþer] C *adds* ile; M *adds* yles  12–13 and riȝtwiser] C rychar and wysar; G2–G5 *om.*  14–15 ne beggare] Q *om.*  16 oþer] M *adds* charge of  18 lyuyng] G2–G5 dedes  19 so] CM *add* avsydly and so  20–21 and many . . . elde] G1 *om.*  22 tyme þedir] G1 þedir; G2–G5 tyme  23 seyde:] see Appendix 10  24 not] D *om.*  26 riches] G2–G5 *add* nor tresore  and þe catels] 2B *om.*  28 acord] C rest  29 clooþ] 2A cote  oure bodies] A vs  30 of men] 2P *om.*  grete] CM grete (C sely) syn and a grete

euermore in pees vnto now, of whiche þou wolt disherite vs. And we haue a kyng among vs not for to iugge no man, for þer is no trespassour among vs, but al only to lere vs to be obedient to hym. And so may þou no3t take fro vs but oure goode pees.'

And whan kyng Alisaundre sau3 þis lettre, hym þou3te he schulde f. 124v do miche harm [to] trouble hem. And he sent to hem þat | þei schulde kepe wel here goode maneres and haue no drede of hym for he schulde not dere hem.

[Anoþer ile is þeire þat is callede Synophe wheyre also are good folke and trewe and full of good fayth. And þei are moche lyke in lyuyng to men byforesayde, and þei go alle nakyde. And into þat ile come kynge Alysandre. When he sawe þeire good fayth and treuth, he sayde he scholde do þeyme no harme and bade þeyme aske of hyme rychese or oughte elles and þei scholde haue. And þei answerde þat þei hade rychese enough whene þei hade mete and drynke to susteyne þeire bodyes. And þei sayde ryches of þis werlde is noght worth, bot 3ife it were so þate he myght graunt þeyme þat þei scholde ne*ue*r dye þat wolde þei pray hym. And Alysaundre sayde þat myght he noght do fore he was dedly and scholde dye as þei scholde. Þane sayde þei: 'Why art þou so proude and wolde wyne al þe werlde and haue it into þi subieccioun als it were a god? And þou has no terme of þi lyue and þou wile haue alle rychese of þe werlde, þe which schalle forsake þe or þou forsake it. And þou schalt bere no þyng with þe bot it shalle dwele to vþere, bot als þou was borne nakyde rith so schalle *þ*o be done in erth.' And Alysaundre was gretly stoniede of þis answere.]

And yf al it be so þat þei haueþ not þe artyclis of oure feiþ, neuerþeles Y trowe þat God [loues þeyme [well] fore þeire good entencioun and at he takes þeire seruyce to gree] as he was of Iob, whiche was a peynym whom he held for his trewe seruaunt, and many oþer also. I trowe þat God loueþ wel al þese þat loueþ hym and serueþ hym mekeliche and trewliche and þat dispiseþ veynglorye of þe world as þese men doþ and as Iob dide. And þerfore seiþ oure

2 iugge] G2–G5 saue (2P law) nor deme man] M *adds* ne for to mysdo no man 3–131/17 trespassour . . . to say trowble] B *out* 5 sau3] C hard 6 to] QD and hem[1]] C *adds* of þere good levyng; M *adds* of thare lyuyng that was so goode and so parfy3te 7–8 kepe wel . . . for he] D *om.* for he . . . hem] G2–G5 *om.* 9–26 Anoþer . . . answere] G1 *om.* (see Appendix 11) 14 oughte] 2P nought 17 noght worth] 2B ry3t nou3t 18 neuer] 2A ner' 21 al] 2A als 25 þo] 2A do 27 feiþ] 2B *adds* þat wee vse 28–29 loues . . . gree] G1 holdiþ hym wel apayd of here lyuyng 28 wel] 2A *om.* 31 þese] A *om.* 32 hym[2]] M *adds* wiþ goode herte 33 doþ and] C dyd ry3t Iob] Q Iacob

lord þurȝ þe mouþ of his prophete Ysaye: *Ponam eis multiplices leges meas*, þat is to say, I schal putte to hem my lawis manyfold. And þe gospel seiþ: *Alias oues habeo que non sunt ex hoc ouili*, þat is to say, I haue oþer scheep whiche beþ not of þis foold. And þerto acordiþ a visioun of seynt Petir þat he sauȝ at Iaffe, how þe aungel come fro heuene and brouȝt wiþ hym alle manere of beestis and naddris and fowlis and seide to seynt | Petir, Take and ete. And seynt petir f. 125r ansueride, I ete neuer of beestis vnclene. And þe aungel seide to hym þanne: *Non dicas immunda que deus mundauit*, þat is to say, Clepe þou nouȝt þese þingis vnclene whiche God haþ yclensid. þis was ydo in tokenyng þat men schulde noȝt haue many men in dispyt for [þeire] dyuerse lawis, for we wote not whom God loueþ ne whom he hatiþ.

And þanne ys anoþer yle whare þe folk beþ alle feþeris but þe visage and þe pawmes of here hondis. þese men goþ as wel vpon water as vpon lond, and þei etiþ fleisch and fysch [alle] rawȝ. In þis yle is a grete ryuere [þat is tuo myle brode and a halfe] þat men clepiþ Renemare. And biȝonde þat ryuere is a grete wildernesse as men seiþ, in whiche wildernesse as men say [þat hauen ben þeire] beþ treez of þe sonne and þe moone which spake to kyng Alisaundre and told hym of his deeþ. And men seiþ þat folk þat kepiþ þese treez and etiþ of þe fruyt of ham lyueþ iiii. hundrid ȝere [or $v^{c.}$] þur[ȝ] vertu of þe fruyt.

And we | wolde gladliche haue go þider but [I trowe] an hundrid f. 125v $m^{l}$. men of armes schulde not passe þat wildernesse for grete plente of wilde beestis þat beþ þere, as dragouns and naddris [þat sclee men when þei may haue ony]. In þis lond beþ many olyfauntz al white and blewe wiþoute noumbre and vnycornes and lyouns of many maneres.

Anoþer yle is þer þat men clepiþ Pytan. [Men of þis ile tilles no

1 Ysaye] G2–G5 *add* þus  2 manyfold] G2–G5 in many maners  3 seiþ] G2–G5 *add* þus  7 fowlis] G2–G5 *add* in alle maner  7–9 Take . . . þanne] 2B *om.*  7–8 And seynt . . . ete] C *om.*  9 þanne] 2P *om.*  11 many] AD *om.*  12 þeire] G1 *om.*  not] G2–G5 neuer  13 hatiþ] G2–G5 *have here* 127/30–128/4 (as in Insular Version)  15 hondis] C *adds* and þe solys of þe fete  16 water] G2–G5 þe see  alle] G1 *om.*  17 þat is . . . halfe] G1 *om.*  19 men] C *adds* tell and  þat hauen ben þeire] G1 *om.*  21 deeþ] 2C dedes  men seiþ] D many syes  22 of ham] M *om.*  iiii.] 2B iii  or $v^{c.}$] G1 and more  þurȝ] Q þur  24 I trowe] G1 as men seyd; C *adds* þere þat  25 þat] C þat way and  25–26 þat wildernesse for grete plente of] 2A for  26 þat beþ þere] G2–G5 *om.*  26–27 þat sclee . . . ony] G1 and many oþer; CM *add* maner of wyld (M *om.*) wormys; 2C *om.*  29 maneres] M *adds* colours; 2C coloures  30–128/5 Anoþer . . . bestes] G2–G5 *place at* 127/13  30–128/1 Men . . . litel] G1 whare þe folk beþ litel and etiþ nouȝt

londe fore] þei etiþ nouȝt. Þe folk beþ litel [bot noght soo smale as Pegmans]. But þei lyueþ by smel of wilde applis and [when þei go fere oute of þe contree þei bere apils with þeyme], and als soone as þei forgooþ þe smel of þese applis þei deiȝeþ. [Þei are noght fulle resonable bot als it were bestes.]

Many oþer yles beþ þere in þe lond of Prestre Ioon and myche richesse and precious stonus, which were to long to telle of.

## CHAPTER 24 WHY HE IS YCLEPID PRESTRE IOON

I trowe ȝe haue herde say why þis emperour is yclepid Prestre Ioon, but for þese men þat woot noȝt Y schal saye þe cause. Þer was somtyme an emperour of Ynde whiche was a noble [prynce] and a douȝty, and he hadde many cristen kniȝtes wiþ hym as he þat is now f. 126r emperour haþ. And þis emperour | þouȝt þat he wolde se þe maner of seruyse of cristen chirchis, and þanne was cristendome in Turkye, Surrye, Tartarie, Ierusalem, Palastyne, Arabye, and Harap, and al þe lond of Egipt. And þis emperour come wiþ a cristen kniȝt into a chirche in Egipt, and it was vpon a satirday after whyt sonday whenne þe byschop made ordris. And he biheld þe seruise and he askyd of a kniȝt what maner of folk schul*de* þese be þat stoode bifore þe byschop. And þe kniȝt seyde þey schulde be prestis. And þanne seyde he þat he wolde no more be clepid kyng noþer emperour but prest, and also he wolde haue þe name of þe firste prest þat come out of þe chirche. And þe prest þat come first was yclepid Iohan, and þerfore þat emperour and oþer siþþe haue be yclepid Prestre Ioon, þat is to say, Prest Ioon.

In þat lond beþ many cristen men of good fey and good lawe, and þei haueþ prestis to synge massis. And þei makiþ þe sacrament as

1 litel] CM *add* and smal 1–2 bot . . . Pegmans] G1 *om.* 2–3 when . . . þeyme] G1 *om.* 4 þe smel of þese applis] C þat appyll and þe saver þerof 4–5 þei . . . bestes] G1 *om.* 6 lond] M lordeschyppe 7 richesse] G2–G5 *add* and nobley stonus] G2–G5 *add* in grete plente 8–9 CM *om. rubric* 11 þat] C *adds* knowys yt now now ys no nede to tell but I will tel to þem þat þe cause] G2–G5 *om.* 12 of Ynde] G2–G5 *om.* prynce] QD kniȝt 13 kniȝtes] 2A kyngys 13–14 as he . . . haþ] G2–G5 *om.* 15 of seruyse] M *om.* chirchis] C men was] G2–G5 was (2A *om.*) chirches of 16 and Harap] C 2C *om.* 17 kniȝt] M kynge 20 schulde] Q schulle 21 þanne] 2P *om.* 23–24 wolde . . . come first] 2B *om.* 23 name] Q first name firste] C *om.* 26 þat . . . Ioon] 2B 2P *om.*

men of Grece dooþ but | þey sey nouȝt so many þinges as oure prestis doþ, for þei seiþ nouȝt but þat þe apostlys seide, as seynt Petir and seynt Thomas and oþer [apostels], when þei songe masse [and seyde] *pater noster* and þe wordis of whiche þe sacrament is ymade. We haue many newe addiciouns whiche popes þat haue ybe siþþe haþ ordeyned, of whiche men of þese cuntrez knowiþ nouȝt. f. 126v

Toward þe eest side of þe lond of Prestre Ioon is a good yle þat men clepiþ Tabrobane, and þat is riȝt plenteuouse. And þer is a greet kyng and a riche, and he holdeþ his lond of Prestre Ioon, [and þat kynge is alwey made by chesynge]. In þis yle beþ ii. wynteris and ii. someris and þei ripeþ corn twies in þe ȝere, and eueriche tyme of þe ȝere beþ þere gardynes floryst. Þere dwelliþ good folk and resonable and many cristen men among hem þat beþ ful riche. [And þe water bytuyx þe londe of Prestre Iohn and þis ile is noght fulle depe, for men may see þe grounde in many places.]

And more eestward beþ ii. [oþere] yles, of whom on is yclepid Orelle and þat oþer Argete, in which al þe lond is myn of gold and siluer. In þese yles may men se no sterris schynyng but a sterre þat me clepiþ Canapos. And þere men may not se þe | moone but in þe laste quarter. f. 127r

And in þat yle is a grete hulle of gold þat pysmyres kepiþ, and þei puriþ þe fyne gold fro þat is not fyne. And þese pysmyres beþ as grete as houndes, so þat no man dar come þer for drede of þese pysmyres which schulde assayle hem, so þat no man may gete þat gold but by queyntise. And þerfore whan it is riȝte warme þese pysmyres hideþ hem in þe erþe fro vndren to noon of þe day; and þanne men of þe cuntre takiþ camelys, dromedaries, and oþer beestis and gooþ þider and charge hem wiþ gold and goþ awey fast bifore þat þe pysmyres comeþ out of þe erþe for drede þat þei schulde be slawe of hem.

1 so] 2A half so   3 Petir] C *adds* and Poule   apostels] G1 *om.*   4 and seyde] Q *om.*   4–5 þe sacrament is ymade] G2–G5 goddis body is sacrede   5 many newe] C now; 2B many   popes] A *erased*   þat] 2B *adds* ben and   7–15 Toward . . . places] 2C *om.*   7 good] G2–G5 *om.*   8 plenteuouse] G2–G5 good and fructuouse   9–10 and þat . . . chesynge] G1 *om.*   13 many] G1 *add* goode   13–15 And þe water . . . places] G1 *om.*   16 oþere] G1 *om.*   17 al þe lond] C all þe angell all þe lond   myn of ] CM *om.*   18 may] QD many   sterris] G2–G5 *add* clere   21 gold] C *adds* þat sum men call fyr myn mowntt   22 pysmyres] CM *add* or emptys (M emotes)   22 puriþ] AD putten; CM departe; G2–G5 do   pysmyres] C *adds* þat ys to say emptys   24 which . . . hem] C *om.*   gete] G2–G5 noght wirche in þat golde ne gete   25 is] C *adds* clere and   26 erþe] C *om.*   of þe day] A *om.*   26–133/8 men . . . hewiþ] 2C *out*   27 and[1]] M and olyfantes and   29 comeþ] M *adds* fro þer restyng place   29 for drede . . . hem] G2–G5 *om.*   hem] C þe wormys; M þese forsayde beestys

And oþer tymes of þe ȝere when it is noȝt so hoot þat þe pysmyres hide hem not, þei takiþ meeris þat haueþ ȝonge fooles and þei leiþ vpon þese meeres twey vessels [als barels] voyde and þe mouþ vpward, and þei dryueþ hem þider and holdeþ þe voles at home. f. 127v And whenne þese pysmyres seeþ þese vessels, for | þei haueþ of kynde to suffre noþing voyde, þei fulliþ þese vessels wiþ gold. And whenne men trowiþ þat þese vessels beþ ful, þei takiþ þese voles and bringiþ hem as nere as þei dar. And þey neye and þe meres huriþ hem and comeþ als soone to here voles, and so men takiþ þe gold þanne, for þese pysmyres wole suffre beestys come among hem but no men.

Biȝonde þe yles and þe lond of Prestre Ioon [and his lordesshippe of wildernese] to go riȝt eest, men schal not fynde but hilles and grete rochis and þe derk lond whare no man may se þe day noþer þe niȝt, as men of þe cuntre seiþ. And [þis wildernese and] þat derk lond lastiþ to paradys terrestre whare Adam and Eue were yput, but þei were þere but a litel while, and þat is toward þe eest [at þe begynnynge] of þe erþe. But þat is not oure eest þat we clepiþ whar þe sonne aryseþ to vs, for whanne þe sonne ariseþ in þilke cuntreez [toward paradys] þan it is mydnyȝt in oure cuntre for þe roundenesse of þe erþe, for oure lord made þe erþe al round in myddel of þe f. 128r firmament, as Y ha|ue yseid more openliche bifore.

Of paradys can Y not speke propurly for Y haue noȝt ybe þare, and þat angriþ me. But as Y haue herd of wise men, Y schal seye ȝow of hit. Men seiþ þat paradys terrestre hit is þe hiȝest lond of þe world, and hit is so hiȝe þat hit touchiþ nere to þe cercle of þe moone, for hit ys so hiȝe þat Noes flood miȝt come not þerto, whiche keuered al þe erþe aboute hit. And paradyse is enclosed al aboute hit wiþ a wal. Men woot not wharof þe wal is. And þe wal is al keuered wiþ moss [as hyt semeþ] þat men may yse noon stoon noþer not ellis wharof hit is.

1 of þe ȝere] G2–G5 *om.* 1–2 when . . . not] 2B *om.* 2 ȝonge] G2–G5 *om.* 3 als barels] G1 *om.* 5 whenne] 2B *adds* þe vesselles ben þare and vessels] AM *add* voyde 6 suffre] CM se 7 takiþ þese voles and] 2B *om.* 9 comeþ] M *adds* rennyng 11 and] 2P of 11–12 and his lordesshippe of wildernese] G1 *om.* 13 rochis] M ryches þe derk] 2P other myrke noþer] 2B but euere 14 as men . . . seiþ] 2B *om.* þis wildernese and] G1 *om.* 15 yput] CM 2B *om.* 16–17 at þe begynnynge] QA *om.* 17 clepiþ] CM calle eeste 18 þe sonne . . . whanne] 2P *om.* 19 toward paradys] G1 *om.* 21 as Y . . . bifore] G2–G5 *om.* more] C *om.* 22 Of] C but of 23 of wise men] C wys wytty men tell; G2–G5 *om.* 25 nere] C *om.* 27 paradyse] 2P *adds* terrestre 28 Men . . . wal is] 2P *om.* 29 moss] A myst as hyt semeþ] Q *om.* 29–30 noon . . . hit is] C *adds* made; 2B *om.*

And in þe hiȝest place of paradys, in þe myddel of hit, is a welle þat castiþ out iiii. flodis and renneþ þurȝ dyuerse londys. Þe firste flood ys yclepid Physon oþer Ganges, and þat renneþ þurȝ Ynde. In þat ryuere beþ many precious stonus and gret plente of a tree þat is yclepid *lignum aloes* and grauel of gold myche. Anoþer is clepid Nilus oþer Gyoun, and | þat renneþ þurȝ Ethiope and Egipt. Þe þridde is f. 128v
yclepid Tygris, and hit renneþ þurȝ Assye and Ermonye þe grete. And þe ferþe is yclepid Eufrates, þat renneþ þurȝ Medy, [Ermonye] and Perse. And men seiþ þere þat alle þe [swete and] freisch watris of þe world takiþ here springyng of hem.

Þe firste ryuer is [cleped] Physon, þat is to say gederyng, for many ryueris gederiþ and falliþ into þat [ryuere]. And somme clepiþ hit Ganges for a [kyng] þat was in Ynde þat me clepid Gangeras, for it renneþ þurȝ his lond. Þis ryuer is in somme place clere, in somme place trowble, in somme place hoot, in somme place cold.

Þe secunde ryuere is yclepid Nilus oþer Gyon for it ys euer trowble, for Gyoun is to say trowble. Þe þridde ryuer ys yclepid Tigris, þat is to say fast rennyng [for hit is euere faste rennynge] and þer is a beest þat renneþ fast þat men clepiþ tygris. Þe ferþe is yclepid Eufrates, þat is to say wel beryng, for þer growiþ many goode þinges vpon þat ryuere.

And ȝe schal wel vndirston|de þat no man lyuynge may go to þat f. 129r
paradys, for by londe may no man go for wilde beestis whiche beþ in þe wildernesse and for hullis and roches whiche no man may pase. And by þese ryueris may no man passe for þei comeþ wiþ so grete cours and so grete wawis þat no schip may go noþer saile aȝens hem. Many grete lordys haueþ assayed many tymes to go by þese ryueris to paradys but þei mowe not spede in here way, for somme deied forwery of rowyng, somme wexed blynde, somme deef for noyse of þe watris, so þat no man may passe þare but þurȝ special grace of God.

And [for] Y can telle ȝow no more of þat place, I schal seye of þat Y haue yseye in yles and lond of Prestre Ioon, which beþ vndir þe

1 hiȝest . . . hit] 2B myddes of paradys  4–5 gret . . . yclepid] G2–G5 moche  5 myche] G2–G5 *om.*  Anoþer] CM *add* ryuer  7 þe grete] CM and Grese  8 Medy] G2–G5 *om.*  Ermonye] QD *om.*  9 swete and] G1 *om.*  11 cleped] QD *om.*  12 ryuere] G1 *om.*  13 kyng] QD man  14 þis] C þys same  in somme place clere] 2B *om.*  18 for hit is euere rennynge] QBD *om.*  19 fast] C allway fast; M smertely  20 wel] CM *om.*  beryng] 2P brennynge  23 in] C in þe forest and  24 and] CM and allso  25 grete[1]] C vyolent  26 go noþer] C *om.*  31 God] C *adds* abovyn  32 for] QBD *om.*  no more] C þe maner  33 beþ] C *om.*

erþe as to vs. And oþer yles þer beþ, who so wolde pursue hem to go aboute þe erþe. Who so hadde grace of God to holde way, he miȝt come to þe same cuntrez þat he were of and come fro, and so go al aboute þe erþe as Y haue seide bifore. And for hit were to | f. 129v long tyme and also many periles to passe þat way, fewe men assaye to go so, and ȝit miȝt it riȝt wel be do.

And þerfore men turneþ fro þese yles to oþer coosting of þe lordschipe of Prestre Ioon, and þei comeþ to an yle þat men clepiþ Cassoun. And þat lond is nere lx. iourneis long and more þen l. in brede, þat is [þe beste londe þat is] in þe cuntre but Catay. And yf merchauntis come þider as comunlich as þei doþ to Catay, hit schulde be beter þen Catay, for citez and townes beþ þere so þicke þat whan a man goþ out o cite he seeþ als soone anoþer in euery side. Þer is grete plente of alle spices and oþer goodes, and þer beþ grete woodes as of chasteyneris. Þe kyng of þis yle is ful riche and miȝty and he holdeþ his lond of þe Grete Chan of Catay, for þat is one of þe xii. prouynce þat þe Grete Chan holdiþ vndir hym [withoute his owen londe].

Fro þis yle men schal go to anoþer grete kyngdome þat men clepiþ Ryboth, þat ys | f. 130r also vndir þe Grete Chan. Þis is a [good] cuntre and a plenteuouse of wyn [corn] and of al oþer þingis. Men of þis lond haueþ no houses but þei dwelliþ in tentis ymade of tree. And þe principal cite of þat lond is al blak ymade of blake stonus and [white], and al þe stretis beþ ypaued wiþ siche maner of stones. In þat cite is no man so hardy to spille blood of a man noþer of beest for loue of a mawmet þat is worschepid þere. In þis cite dwelliþ þe pope of here lawe, whiche þei clepiþ *lobassy*, and ȝeueþ alle dignites and benefices þat falliþ to þe mawmet. And men of religioun and men þat haueþ chirches in þat cuntre beþ alle obedient to hym as we beþ to oure pope.

1–2 go aboute] G2–G5 enuyroun  3 to] G2–G5 right to  were of and come fro] M come fyrst oute of  4 as Y haue seide bifore] G2–G5 *om.*  5 many] CM to many  þat way] C *adds* þerefore; G2–G5 *om.*  6 so] A þat way; CM abowt þe erþe  ȝit miȝt it] C yt myȝt lyȝt  riȝt wel] G2–G5 *om.*  7 oþer] G2–G5 *add* iles  coosting] B costes  8 lordschipe] C land and hys lordschypys; M yles  comeþ] G2–G5 *add* in þe turnynge (2P comynge)  10 þe beste lande þat is] Q *om.*  12 and] G1 and gode  12–13 so þicke þat] D to thicke þanne  14 and] Q and alle  14–15 and . . . chasteyneris] G2–G5 *om.*  15 as] AM al  16 of Catay] CM *om.*  17 xii.] C *om.*  prouynce] B prince  18 withoute his owen londe] G1 *om.*  19 grete] C *adds* ile and a; G2–G5 *om.*  kyngdome] 2B ile  20 good] Q faire; AB *om.*; C presius  21 corn] QAB *om.*  þingis] 2B *adds* þat needeþ  23 and white] QD and swete; B 2B *om.*  24 wiþ siche maner of] B of the same; G2–G5 with soche  26 is] M is honowred and  pope] A *erased*  28 and men[2] M *om.*  chirches] C crokys  29 oure] 2A 2P þe  pope] AB *erased*

In þis yle þei haueþ a custome þurȝ alle þe cuntre þat when a mannus fader is deed and þei wol do hym grete worschip, þei sendiþ after alle his frendis, prestis, men of religioun, and oþer many. And þei beriþ þe body to an hulle wiþ grete ioiȝe and | merþe. And when f. 130v hit is þere, þe grettyst prelate smyteþ of his heed and leiþ hit vpon a grete plate of siluer oþer of gold, and he ȝeueþ hit to his sone. And his sone takiþ hit to his oþer frendis singyng and seiyng many orisouns. And þanne þe prest and religiouse men hewiþ þe fleisch of þe body in pecis and seiþ orisouns. And briddis of þe cuntre comeþ þedir for þei knowiþ þe custome, and þei fleeþ aboute hem, as eglis and oþer briddis [þat] etiþ þe fleisch. And þe prestis castiþ þe fleisch to hem, and þei beriþ hit a litel þenne and etiþ hit. And as prestis in oure cuntre syngeþ for soulis *Subuenite sancti dei*, þat is to say, Helpiþ seyntes of God, so þese prestis syngeþ þer wiþ hiȝe voys in here langage, Byholdeþ how good a man þis was þat þe aungels of God comeþ to fecche hym and bere hym to paradys. And þanne þenkiþ þe sone þat he is gretelich worschipid when briddes haue þus yȝete his fader. And whar beþ most plente of þese briddis, he haþ most worschip. And | þanne comeþ þe sone home wiþ alle his frendis f. 131r and makiþ hem a grete feste. And þe sone lete make clene his fadris hed, and þe fleisch of þe heed he scheriþ hit and ȝeueþ hit to his moost special frendis, eueriche man a litel for a deynte [and in remembrance of þis holy man þat þe birdes haue eten]. And of þe scolle of þe heed þe sone lete make a cuppe and þerof drinkiþ he al his lyf in remenbraunce of his fader.

And fro þenne to go ten iourneys þurȝ þe lond of þe Grete Chan is a wel good yle and a grete kyngdome. And þe kyng is ful miȝty [and he has eche a ȝeere ccc. hors chargede with ryes and oþere rentes]. And he haþ a ful noble lyf and riche after þe maner of þe cuntre, for he haþ fyfty damesels þat serueþ euery day at his mete

2–3 þei sendiþ after] B to  3 alle] C *om.*  4 wiþ] B where is  5 þere] B *om.*  prelate] B *adds* men  6 grete] G2–G5 *om.*  8 men] B with other men  9 and seiþ] C syngyng and sayyng; M sayng  10 hem] C þys man; M alle þys pepylle  11 þat] QABD and  12 þenne] C and lyȝt downe  13 *sancti*] QBD sancte  13–14 þat is . . . God] G2–G5 *om.*; 2P and so forth  14 þer] B *om.*  15 langage] 2P *adds* in this maner of wyse se and  good] 2P *adds* and gracyous  18 þese] G2–G5 *om.*  19 alle] C *om.*  21 hed] G2–G5 *add* and ȝeues his frendys to drinke þeireof  scheriþ hit and] 2B *om.*  22 eueriche man] G2–G5 somme a lytylle and somme  litel] C lyȝt aftur of þe same for a litel  22–23 and in . . . eten] G1 2C *om.*  24 scolle] G2–G5 scalpe  27 yle] CM *adds* and a gret lond  28–29 and he . . . rentes] G1 2C *om.*  29 rentes] 2P tentes  ful] G2–G5 *om.*  noble] C *om.*  and riche] 2B *om.*

and bed and doþ what he wol. And when he sittiþ at þe table, þei bringeþ hym his mete and euery tyme v. messe togedre and syngiþ in þe bringyng a good song. And þei kittiþ his mete and put [hit] in his mouþ, for he kittiþ none but holdiþ his hondis bifore hym vpon þe table for he haþ so long nayles þat he may noȝt hol|de.

f. 131v And hit is a grete noblay in þat cuntre to haue long nayles, and þerfore þei letiþ here nailes growe als long as þei woleþ. And somme letiþ hem growe so longe til þat þei wole come al aboute here hond, and þat þinkiþ hem it is a grete noblay and a grete gentry. And þe gentri of wymmen þere is to haue smale feet, and þerfore als soone as þei beþ ybore þei byndeþ here feet so strayt þat þei may not wexe so grete as þei schulde.

And þis kyng haþ a wel fair paleys and a riche whare he dwelliþ, of whiche þe wal is ii. myle aboute. And þer beþ yn many feire gardynes, and alle þe pauement of þe halle and þe chambres is of gold and siluer. And in þe myddel of oone of þe gardyns is a litel hille wharevpon is a litel p[a]lace ymade wiþ touris and pynaclis al of gold. And þer he wole sitte ofte to take þe eir and disport for hit is ymade for nouȝt ellis.

Fro þis lond may men go þurȝ þe lond of þe Grete Chan. And ȝe
f. 132r schal | vndirstonde þat alle þese men and folk of whom Y haue spoke þat beþ resonable haueþ somme articlis of oure treuþe. If al þei be of dyuerse lawis and dyuerse trowynges, þei haueþ somme gode poyntes of oure treuþe. And þei trowiþ in God of kynde whiche made al þe world, and hym clepe þei God of kynde as here prophecys seiþ, *Et metuent eum omnes fines terre*, þat is to say, And alle endis of erþe schal drede hym; and in anoþer place þus, *Omnes gentes seruient ei*, þat is to say, Alle folk schal serue to him.

But þei kan not propurly speke of God but as here kyndelich wit techiþ hem, for þey spekiþ noȝt of þe sone noþer of þe holi goost

2 his mete] 2A *om.* 3 bringyng] M *adds* þere seruyse good] G2–G5 *om.* hit] QD *om.* 4 he kittiþe . . . noȝt holde] G2–G5 þei haue ryght longe nayles on þeire hende 6 noblay] 2A *adds* and gentry 7 woleþ] A may; C wyll or may 8 til þat þei] B that theis nayles 9 þat þinkiþ hem] G2–G5 *om.* 9 grete] B G2–G5 *om.* 11 strayt] CM *add* and so fast 11–12 so grete] 2A 2P halfe; 2B *om.* 12 as þei schulde] 2B *om.*; CM *add* do by kynde 13 wel] B *om.* 14 feire] B *om.* 16 siluer] C *adds* and syluyr platys litel] 2P *om.* 17 palace] QBD G2–G5 place 19 ellis] C also but for dysport; M but onely for hys delyte 20 lond] M *adds* of Rybeth 21 vndirstonde] C *adds* and know 22 oure] C *adds* fayþe or 23 gode] 2A *om.* 24–25 whiche . . . kynde] G2–G5 *om.* 25 world] C word 26 *metuent*] QC metuant 27 þus] C he seiþ aftur; 2P *om.* 29 þei kan] B the Cane of God] G2–G5 parfitely kyndelich] B *om.*

as þei schulde do. But þei can wel speke of þe bible and specialiche of Genesis and of þe book of Moyses. And þei seiþ þese þinges whiche þei worschipiþ beþ noone goddis, but þey worschipe hem for þe grete vertues whi|che [f. 132$^{v}$] beþ in hem, which þei say may not be wiþoute special grace of God.

And of symylacris and mawmetis þei seiþ þat alle men haueþ mawmetis and symylacris, for þei seiþ þat cristen men haueþ ymages of oure lady and oþere. But þei woot nouȝt þat we worschipe not þese ymages of stoon noþer of tree for hemself but þe seyntes for wham þei beþ ymade. For as þe letter techiþ þe clerkis how þei schal trowe, so ymages and payntures techiþ lewide men to worschipe þe seyntes for whom þei beþ ymade.

þei seiþ also þat þe aungel of God spekiþ to hem in here mawmetis and þat þei doþ myraclis. þei seie sooþ; þei haueþ an aungel wiþynne hem. But þer beþ two manere of aungels, goode and wikkid, as men of Grece seiþ, Chaco and Calo. Chato is yuel and Calo ys good. But þis is no good aungel but yuel þat is in þe mawmetis to bigile hem and for to meyntene hem in here mawmetrie.

þer beþ many oþer cuntreez and merueyles whiche Y haue noȝt yseye, and þerfore Y can not speke propurliche | [f. 133$^{r}$] of ham. And also in cuntrez whare I haue ybe beþ many merueyles of whiche Y speke nouȝt for hit were to longe tale [and þeirfore holde ȝow payede as þis tyme of þat I haue sayde]. And also Y wole seye no more of merueyles þat beþ þer, so þat oþer men þat wendiþ þider may fynde many newe þingis to say of whiche I haue nouȝt told noþer yspoke, for many man haþ grete likyng and desire to hure newe þinges.

And I Ioon Maundeuyle kniȝt, þat went out of my cuntre and passid þe see þe ȝere of oure lord a m$^{l}$.ccc.xxx.$^{ti}$ and tweye, and haue ypassid þurȝ many londis, cuntrez, and yles, and now am ycome to rest; I haue compiled þis booke and lete write hit þe ȝere of oure lord

1 as þei schulde do] G2–G5 *om.* 2 book of] C *adds* holy þinges] M kynges; G2–G5 creatures 3 beþ] D bote noone goddis] B in god 6 And . . . mawmetis] C for 7 mawmetis and] G2–G5 *om.* þat] G2–G5 þat we 9 for hemself] G2–G5 *om.* 11–12 to worschipe . . . ymade] G2–G5 *om.* 14–15 þei seie . . . hem] A *om.* 14–18 þei haueþ . . . bigile hem and] G2–G5 bot þat is an il aungele þat dos myracles 16–17 and Calo . . . yuel] C *om.* 18 here] M *adds* fals 19 noȝt] 2P nat ben nor 20 yseye and þerfore . . . speke] B *om.* 22–23 and þeirfore . . . sayde] G1 2C *om.* 24 þer–136/25 Amen] 2B *out* 25 þingis] CM *add* and tydyngys; G2–G5 inowgh 25–26 noþer yspoke] M *adds* and maruelous fro ferre contres 25–27 noþer . . . þinges] G2–G5 *om.* 28 kniȝt] M *adds* þouȝe Y were vnworþy; G2–G5 *om.* 29–31 lord . . . oure] 2A *om.* 31 I haue . . . hit] C *om.*

a m[l].ccc.lx. and sixe at xxxiiii. ȝere aftir my departyng fro my cuntre, for Y was in trauelyng xxxiiii. ȝere.

And for as myche as many men trowe not but þat þei se wiþ here owne iȝen or þat þei may conseyue wiþ here owne kyndely wit, f. 133v þerfore Y made my wey in my comyng hamwarde to Rome | to schewe my book to þe holy fader þe pope and telle to hym merueyles whiche Y hadde seye in dyuerse cuntreez, so þat he wiþ his wise counseyl wolde examyne hit wiþ dyuerse folk þat beþ in Rome, for þer beþ euermore men dwellyng of alle manere naciouns of þe world. And a litel tyme after, when he and his wise counseyl hadde examyned hit alle þurȝ, he seyde me for certeyn þat alle was sooþ þat was þerynne. For he seide þat he hadde a book vpon Latyn þat conteyned þat and myche more, after whiche boke þe *mappa mundi* ys ymade, whiche book he schewid to me. And þerfore þe holy fader þe pope haþ ratefyed and confermed my book in alle poyntes.

And Y preye to alle þese þat rediþ þis book or huriþ hit be radde þat þey wole preie for me, and Y schal preye for hem. And alle þese þat seiþ for me a *pater noster* and *aue* þat God forȝeue my synnes, Y make hem partyneris and graunte hem part of alle my gode | f. 134r pilgrimages and oþer goode dedis whiche Y euer dude oþer schal do to my lyues ende. And Y preye to God, of whom al grace comeþ, þat he wole fulfille of his grace alle þe rederis and hureris of þis book and saue ham in bodies and soules and bringe hem to his ioiȝe þat euer schal yleste, he þat is in trinite fader and sone and holi gost, þat lyueþ and regneþ God wiþoute ende. Amen.

## EXPLICIT IOHANNES MAUNDEUYLE

1 xxxiiii.] 2A xxiiii; 2P xxiii 2 for Y was . . . ȝere] G2–G5 (*ex* 2C) *om.* (3R *conflated*) 4 owne[1]] M *om.* owne kyndely] M *om.* 6, 14 þe holy] 2A oure holy 6 pope] AB *erased* 7 cuntreez] M *adds* þere Y haue been 8 hit . . . beþ] B my boke 9 men] B in Rome manere] D *om.* 10 wise] G2–G5 *om.* 12 þat was þerynne] G2–G5 *om.* þat he hadde] B certeyn he had made 14 he schewid to me] G2–G5 I sawe 15 ratefyed and] B *om.* 16 or huriþ hit be radde] G2–G5 *om.* 17 and Y . . . hem] M *om.* 21 grace] C *om.* 22 alle] 2A *adds* þe wryters of þis book] G2–G5 þat are cristen men 23 saue] D *adds* haue 26 A explicit liber domini Iohannis Maundeuyle militis exuuii cuius anime propitietur deus Amen Nomen Iesu collandemus; B explicit Maundeuyle; 2A 2P Her endys the boke of Iohn Maundevile knyght Of wayes to Ierusalem and of merveyles of ynde and othere contrees

# COMMENTARY

These editions of works used in the making of *Mandeville's Travels* are cited in the commentary:

Albert of Aix, *Historia Hierosolomitanae Expeditionis*, 1125: *Recueil des Histoires des Croisades, Historiens Occidentaux* (Paris, 1879) IV, part 3.

Brunetto Latini, *Li Livres dou Tresor*, *c.*1264: ed. P. Chabaille (Paris, 1863).

Burchard of Sion, *De terra sancta*, *c.*1330; ed. J. C. M. Laurent, *Peregrinatores Medii Aevi Quatuor* (Leipzig, 1864).

Giovanni del Pian Carpini, *Historia Mongolorum*, 1247: ed. A. Van den Wyngaert, *Sinica Franciscana* (Firenze, 1929) I, and included in Vincent of Beauvais, *Speculum Historiale* XXXI. 2–52.

Haiton, *Fleurs des Histors d'Orient*, before 1308: *Recueil des Historiens des Croisades, Documents Arméniens* (Paris, 1906) II.

Jacques de Vitry, *Historia Hierosolomitana*, before 1240; ed. Bongars, *Gesti Dei per Francos* (Hanover, 1611); S. de Sandoli, *Itinera Hierosolymitana*, Studium Biblicum Franciscanum (Jerusalem, 1978–83) III. 300–90..

*Letter of Prester John*: ed. F. Zarncke in *Abhandlungen der philologisch-historischen Classe der koniglich sächsischen Gesellschaft der Wissenschaften* VII (1879), VIII (1883).

Odoric of Pordenone, *Relatio*, 1330: ed. Wyngaert, op. cit., and in the French translation used by 'Mandeville' ed. H. Cordier, *Voyages en Asie . . ., Recueil de voyages* X (Paris, 1891).

Pseudo-Odoric, *De terra sancta*, *c.*1250: ed. Laurent, op. cit.

Peter Comestor, *Historia Scholastica*, before 1179; printed in J. P. Migne, *Patrologia Latina* 198.

Vincent of Beauvais, *Speculum Naturale* and *Speculum Historiale*, *c.*1250: *Bibliotheca Mundi* (Douai, 1624) II and IV.

William of Boldensele, *Itinerarius*, 1336: ed. C. L. Grotefend, 'Des Edelherrn Wilhelm von Boldensele' in *Zeitschrift des historischen Vereins für Niedersachsen* (1855), and in French translation by Jean le Long, ed. C. Deluz, *Guillaume de Boldensele*, Exemplaires ronoéotypés (La Sorbonne, 1972), being vol. 2 of her thesis (Bibl. de la Sorbonne, pressmark I.1907.4).

William of Tripoli, *De statu Saracenorum*, 1270: ed. H. Prutz, *Kulturgeschichte der Kreuzzüge* (Berlin, 1883).

Two other accounts by travellers, Marco Polo *c.*1298 and Friar William of Rubruck 1255, and their learned commentators are indispensable to an understanding of *Mandeville's Travels*. 'Mandeville' used neither, but Odoric based much of his account on Marco Polo, possibly in Fra Pipino's

Latin version. Rubruck, whose work was incorporated by Roger Bacon in his *Opus Maius*, enlarges Carpini's report. These works are cited in the commentary:

Marco Polo, *Le Divisament dou Monde*, 1298: ed. L. F. Benedetto, *Marco Polo. Il Milione* (Firenze, 1928) in 234 chapters, and in Fra Pipino's Latin translation ed. J. V. Prášek, *Marka Pavlova z Benátek 'Milion'* (Prague, 1902). Pipino's text has three books and numbered chapters, an order followed by the Everyman edition of Marco Polo (ed. W. Marsden, rev. T. Wright 1865).

William of Rubruck, *Itinerarium*, 1255: ed. and trans. P. Jackson, *The Mission of Friar William of Rubruck*, Hakluyt Society 2nd ser. 173 (London, 1990).

P. Pelliot, *Notes on Marco Polo*, 3 vols. (Paris, 1959–73).

P. Pelliot, *Recherches sur les Chrétiens d'Asie centrale et d'extrême-orient* (Paris, 1973).

A. C. Moule, *Quinsai, with other notes on Marco Polo* (Cambridge, 1957).

These atlases and reference works are useful for locating places mentioned in the text and commentary:

L. H. Grollenberg, *Atlas of the Bible* (London, 1957).

K. M. Setton (ed.), *A History of the Crusades* vols. I–VI (Madison, 1969–89).

J. Riley-Smith, *The Atlas of the Crusades* (London, 1991).

*Philip's Atlas of Exploration* (London, 1996).

The quotations of the Vulgate bible in the text are identified by reference to that Latin version which agrees in chapter and verse with the Authorized Version except in Psalms where the numbering of the latter differs by one from the Vulgate.

6/15 *ile towun*: i.e. Maleville, near Belgrade. The translator perhaps wrote *evyle toun*, as in 2H.

6/23 *Pynceras*: i.e. the Petchenegs, the Turkish conquerors of the Magyars, who were crushed by Alexius I at Lebunion in 1091. They are reported by Albert of Aix I. 8 (p. 278).

6/29 *seynt Sophie*: the church was dedicated by Justinian in 538 to *Αγία Σοφία* 'Holy Wisdom'.

6/31 *round appul*: i.e. the orb in the left hand of the statue of Justinian which stood in the Forum Augusteum until 1492. Nicephoras Gregoras, the Byzantine historian (d. 1359), reports that the orb, blown down in 1317, was restored in 1325.

9/8 *seynt Elyn*: the fiction of the Invention of the Cross is first reported by St Ambrose in 495, almost 150 years after her death. Her mythical father, the British King Coel, is first reported by Geoffrey of Monmouth III. 6 *c.*1136. Bede I. 8 reports that Constantine was the son of Helena, a concubine of Constantius.

9/17 *chapel of þe kyng*: i.e. Sainte-Chapelle, founded by St Louis in 1246 as a reliquary for the holy relics redeemed by him from the Venetian merchants (not the Jews) to whom Baldwin II had pawned them. The holy lance of the crucifixion was reportedly found during the siege of Antioch in 1098.

9/21 *ionqes of þe see*: i.e. *iuncis marinis . . . quorum acies non minus spinis dure sunt et acute*, reported by Durand, *Rationale* VI. 77, before 1330. The plant was the evergreen bog-rush *juncus glaucus*, grey-blue in colour and with needle-like leaves, which fades when cut. Like all such relics, the exhibits at Sainte-Chapelle were medieval forgeries. The Crown of Thorns reported in the gospels is now believed to have been made of the spines of the date palm (*phoenix dactylifera*), with pinnate mid-green leaves up to six inches long and so weavable, as the only suitable flora then available in Jerusalem.

11/1 *idriouns*: i.e. the *enhydros* reported by Pliny and Isidore as an agate containing water vapour.

11/5 *Hellespounte*: this confusion of the historical Hellespont and the Bosphorus is a commonplace of crusading histories.

11/12 *þe mount Athos*: the false location of Mt Athos, which dominates its promontory in Macedonia, is due to a misreading of Pliny who, after Plutarch, reports that in the summer solstice its shadow fell on the market-place of Myrina in Lemnos.

11/14 *Turcople*: i.e. Turcopoli 'sons of Turks', a name given to the sons of Christian fathers and native mothers in Syria and later applied to native cavalry armed with bows. Cf. note to 68/17 below. *Princynard* are the Petchenegs noted at 6/23. *Comange* is Cumania 'land of the Cumans' which stretched from the northern shore of the lower Danube to the northern shore of the Caspian Sea.

11/16 *Strages*: i.e. Stageirus, a Greek colony on the Macedonian peninsular Chalcidice, where a yearly festival was held in honour of Aristotle in ancient times. But he died at Chalcis in 322 BC.

12/3 *emperouris paleys*: i.e. the Imperial Palace next to the Hippodrome.

12/17 *Ermogynes*: properly the mythical sage Hermes Trismegistos, who is confused here by a scribe with Hermogenes of Tarsus (*fl.* 2nd century AD). William Wheatley, *De disciplina scholarium*, 1309, reports that a golden tablet was found in Plato's tomb, and John Ridevall, *Lectura in Apocalypsim c.*1332 converts this to a medal in a context which considers Hermes Trismagistos; see B. Smalley, *English Friars and Antiquity* (Oxford, 1960), pp. 119–20.

12/23 *Ioon*: Pope John XXII's proposals to re-unite the Church were rebuffed by Andronicus III, emperor 1328–1341, but this letter is a forgery. During his papacy at Avignon 1316–34 he undertook wide-ranging administrative reforms, including a more efficient fiscal organization and the imposition of new taxes. This policy was resented by many, including the Benedictines, and gave rise to an unjust reputation for avarice.

13/5 *schere þorsday*: so named from the ceremonial shaving of the tonsure before Good Friday and now Maundy Thursday.

14/13 *ȝate of Chiuitot*: i.e. port of Civetot, a fortified camp prepared by Alexius I (d. 1118) for his English mercenaries on the south coast of the Gulf of Nicomedia, near Helenopolis, reported by Orderic Vitalis, and the terminus of the ferry from Aegiali; see S. Runciman, *A History of the Crusades*, 3 vols (Cambridge, 1951–4) I. 128–9, 152.

14/16 *seynt Nicolas*: translated by Italian merchants from Myra to Bari in 1087. At San Nicola, Bari an oily substance *manna di San Nicola* is still reverenced. The mastic of Chios is reported by Boldensele (p. 240).

14/28 *alle Assye þe lasse*: 'Mandeville' follows Boldensele (p. 240), who wrote in 1336. But Smyrna was retaken by the Knights of St John from the Turks in 1344 and held until its capture by Timur and his Mongols in 1402. See N. Housley, *The Later Crusades* (Oxford, 1992).

15/7 *wyn of Marca*: 'Mandeville' or his source has confused the city of *Marrea* (ed. Warner 12/12), properly Myra in Lycia, with Malmasia (now Monemvasia) a small island off the SE Peloponnese from where malmsey (otherwise malvoisie) was exported. Malmsey from Cyprus is praised by Ludolph von Sudheim, *De itinere terre sancte*, ed. F. Deycks (1851), p. 34 who here, as elsewhere, closely follows Boldensele p. 211. D'Anglure, *Le saint voyage* who visited Cyprus in 1395 reports *tres bon vin de Marboa*.

15/7 *Grece*: properly Crete, given to Boniface of Montferrat after the fall of Constantinople in 1204 by the emperor Alexius V, and then sold to the Venetians who held it until 1669. *Ionas* is a corruption of *Ianeweys* 'Genoese', itself an error.

15/9 *Cophos and Lango*: the island of Cos, traditionally the home of Hippocrates and Aesculapius the god of medicine, was known as Lango in the Middle Ages. The source of these legends is unknown. There is some echo of the myth of *le fier baiser*; Hippocrates' son was called Draco, presumably the dragon here; the name of the goddess *Deane* is merely the Latin *dea* 'goddess', perhaps confounded with Diana of the Ephesians. The knight of Rhodes is a Hospitaller, which suggests that 'Mandeville' found the fable in a crusading history.

16/28 *Colles*: Colos was the Byzantine Greek name for Rhodes, captured by the Hospitallers in 1309 and held until 1523. It is about 500, not 800 miles from Constantinople. The confusion with Colossae in Phrygia where St Paul addressed an epistle was common.

17/5 *Sathalay*: i.e. Attalia (now Antalya but removed from the ancient site, founded by Attalus II king of Pergamum *c.*150 BC) stands on its Gulf notorious for its storms. Thence St Paul sailed to Antioch (Acts 14: 25). The legend told here is a version of the myth of the Gorgon's head, and the necrophily repeats the story of Callimachus and Drusiana of Ephesus, but its immediate source is unknown. Cf. Walter Map, *De nugis curalium*, 1190 vv.

17/23 *hulle of þe holi croys*: the monastery of this name, cited at 7/16 above, at Stavrovouni 'the mountain of the cross' was reportedly founded *c.*327 by St Helena to house a relic of the True Cross. It was destroyed by the Arabs in 1426 and is now a modern refoundation, about 10 miles south-west of Larnaca.

17/27 *Genenoun*: i.e. Zozonius reported by Boldensele (p. 242) and identified with Sozomenos bishop of Potamia, about 10 miles north-west of Larnaca, and Church historian of the fifth century.

17/28 *castel of Amours*: known to the crusaders as *Deudamor* and *Dieu d'amour*, from *didymos* 'twins' specifying two small crags above the cave of St Hilarion the hermit. The monastery, founded before 1100, was fortified in 1191 and 1220 and stands on the mountains about 5 miles south-west of Kyrenia.

17/30 *Bernard*: properly Barnabas, as in Boldensele (p. 242), styled the apostle (Acts 14: 14 and 4: 36) and traditionally the founder of the Cypriot church.

17/30 *paupiouns*: Thietmar VIII. 27 (ed. Laurent p. 22), followed by De Vitry (p. 1101), describes *papiones* as *canes silvestras* and Boldensele (p. 242) reports unnamed *domesticis leopardiis*. The animal is the trained hunting lynx, imported into Europe in the early 13th century. See A. C. Moule, *Quinsai* pp. 65–6, and Rubruck p. 86.

18/20 *Fons ortorum*: a collection of springs which supplied ancient Tyre, mentioned in the Song of Solomon 4: 15. The following quotation of Luke 11: 27 is also quoted by Boldensele.

18/28 *Sarepte oþer Sydonis*: i.e. Sarepta Sydoniorum, now Sûrafend, about 12 miles north-east of Tyre (1 Kings 17: 9). *Ionas* is named by Jerome, *Comm. in Jonam* (Migne PL 25. 1118) as the widow's son raised from death by Elijah (1 Kings 17: 22), and here by scribal misplacement is called the prophet. The whole passage is taken verbatim from Vincent, *Spec. Hist.* (p. 36) who follows Eugesippus.

19/3 *Dido fader*: here identified as the Tyrian king Matgenos, of which *Agenor* is not certainly the form used by the translator. His description of

Dido as the daughter of Matgenos (properly of Belus) and the wife of Aeneas suggests that he did not know the story in the *Aeneid*.

19/15 *bones of a geauntis side*: i.e. supposedly a relic of the monster which attacked Andromeda in the legend reported by 'Mandeville' in the Insular Version, and properly the rib of a whale or elephant.

19/21 *myle of Lumbardy*: continental leagues, approximately the same as English miles and half the great leagues. The terms are often confused, and with the susceptibility of roman numerals to scribal corruption this confusion makes all distances reported in the text subject to caution. The translator omits the explanation given in the Insular Version, *miles de Lumbardye ou de nostre pais qi sont auxi petites* (ed. Warner 58/33).

19/22 *Grece*: properly Crete. The error recurs at 15/7.

19/25 *hulle of Carme*. reputedly the site of Elijah's meeting with the priests of Baal (1 Kings 18: 19).

20/7 *Scale de Tyreys*: i.e. the 'ladder of Tyre', the mountain road (not the mountain itself) between Acre and Tyre (1 Maccabees 11: 59).

20/9 *fosse of Mynoun*: an area of vitreous sand at the mouth of the Belus near Acre, named from the nearby statue of Memnon, son of Tithonus and Eos, killed by Achilles. The source is Vincent, *Spec. Nat.* VII. 77, who follows Pliny and Josephus.

20/18 *see grauely*: a huge area of shifting sand which 'Mandeville' describes at 115/6 below in its proper geographical location.

20/26 *castel of Pillerynes*: i.e. Château Pèlerin, the Templar fortress at 'Atlit, 13 miles north of Caesarea, which was built in 1217/18 and fell to the Arabs in 1291.

21/3 *Babiloyne*: i.e. Arabic *Bāb-al-yūn* 'the city of On', mistakenly derived from the earlier *Pi-Hapi-n-On* of the Pharaohs. Its proximity to Cairo and its familiar name meant that it often stood for Cairo in Western sources, distinguished from the historical Babylon in Chaldea. See K. Setton, *A History of the Crusades* II (Madison, 2nd edn. 1969), maps 14 and 15 op. p. 487. Its common Arabic name was al-Fusṭāṭ.

21/6 *castel Dayre*: i.e. Castle Darum, 9 miles south of Gaza, fortified by Amaury in 1170 and recaptured by Richard I in 1192. The name derives from Arabic *deir er Rum* 'house of Greeks', referring to the nearby monastery.

21/11 *Canopater*: a form of Canopus, the ancient city 15 miles east of Alexandria famous for its temple of Serapis, at the mouth of the most westerly branch of the Nile delta. *Mersyne* is Arabic *Mesryn*, from Hebrew *Mizraim* 'land of Egypt'.

21/13 *Beleth*: properly Belbeis, visited by Boldensele (p. 245), about 30 miles north-east of Cairo, and nowhere near the kingdom of Aleppo. 'Mandeville' perhaps confused the town with Ba'albek, the site of a crusader castle, 35 miles north of Damascus within the march of Aleppo.

21/19 *iii. children*: there were traditionally four 'children of God', Jews with a Chaldean education who opposed Nebuchadnezzar (Daniel 1: 7). Daniel, otherwise Belteshazzar, is omitted here. The interpretation of the Chaldean or Arkkadian names given here is fanciful, but the source is unknown.

21/25 *faire castel*: i.e. *al-kalah* 'the citadel', built by Saladin in 1166. It is named in the Insular and Cotton Versions but not by Boldensele (p. 245) on whom the passage otherwise depends.

22/11 *Calaphes*: i.e. caliph. After the extinction of the 'Ayyubid sultanate in 1260 the rulers of Egypt were caliphs for the Mameluk dynasty, and Egypt denoted all the lands under their authority including Palestine and much of Syria. The title is the dignity of succession from Mahomet.

22/12 *Roys Yles*: the phrase is a relic of the Insular reading *roi il y soleit* (ed. Warner 18/42) which immediately precedes the lacuna of the 'Egypt Gap'. The Defective text resumes in the valley of the monastery of the Forty Martyrs (ed. Warner 32/36), having lost the bulk of the description of Egypt and the beginning of a new itinerary from the ports of northern Italy to Babylon where the sultan dwells, Sinai, and so to the monastery of St Catherine of Sinai.

22/19 *þe colect*: the Collect for St Catherine of Sinai on 27 November reports one site, and Boldensele (p. 256) and other travellers report two. The reference indicates that 'Mandeville' was able to cite the breviary, presumably as a religious, and that he had no knowledge of the locations which he describes.

23/1 *Ascopardes*: i.e. the Azopart of 'Ethiopia' reported by Albert of Aix (p. 490) as *gens nigerrime cutis*, presumably the Sudanese.

23/20 *Bersabe*: i.e. Beersheba 'well of the oath' (Genesis 21: 31). The alleged foundation by Bathsheba is fanciful.

23/29 *geauntis*: perhaps a reference to Goliath (1 Samuel 17: 4) but cf. Numbers 13: 33. Hebron was one of the cities of refuge (Joshua 20: 7).

24/10 *spelunk*: i.e. *spelunca agri duplici* reported by Boldensele (p. 258), otherwise the cave of Machpelah 'division in half' (Genesis 23: 19). *Cariatharba* is Kirjath-arba, another name for Hebron. *Arbothe* is Hebrew *Me'arat* 'cave'. The Latin is an echo, not a quotation, of Genesis 18: 2; 'Mandeville' misinterprets Boldensele here.

24/31 *chambille*: apparently the kamala spice. Burchard, *De terra sancta* (ed. Laurent p. 81) reports *Ager iste in rei veritate valde rubeam habet terram que omnino flexibilis sicut cera . . . Saraceni insuper terram istam portant camelis*, where 'Mandeville' read the better *vocant* for *portant* (caused by confusion of an abbreviated *por-* for *v-*). The term *cambil* occurs in Matthaeus Silvaticus, *Pendecte medicine c.*1317 (ed. 1641, fol. xiii) where it is explained as *terra rubea minuta que affertur Mecha*, cf. John of Garland's term καμβήλ. This medical substance reported by Burchard is probably the same as the kamala spice (Arabic *kinbīl*) imported from Arabia and India.

25/3 *dirpe*: the name is taken from Pseudo-Odoric (p. 154) where it is perhaps Arabic *dulb* 'plane tree'. See Pelliot, *Notes on Marco Polo* II. 633–4. Its identification here with the legendary Dry Tree of Alexander's story (see G. V. Smithers, *Kyng Alisaundir*, EETS os 237, note to 6755) and with the oak of Mamre by which Abraham pitched his tent (Genesis 13: 18 and 18: 1) and which Jerome calls *drys* is fanciful. The prince of the West in the prophecy here was sometimes identified with Frederic II (d. 1230) during the latter part of his life.

25/16 *þe fallyng yuel*: both Vincent, *Spec. Hist.* XXXI. 59 and Burchard say that the virtue of the dry wood prevents a fall from a horse, which 'Mandeville' inflates to a cure for epilepsy.

25/27 *feld floridous*: a name given variously to the site of Elijah's ascent into heaven, the garden of Gethsemane, the site of the divine salvation of Abraham's daughter by Keturah his second wife. 'Mandeville' follows Pseudo-Oderic who, however, places the *champ flori* between Jerusalem and Bethlehem (p. 153) as the site of Elijah's ascent. The source of the legend of the fair maid is unknown, but there are close parallels in a French *Vita beate Marie* concerning Abraham's daughter (FitzWilliam Museum MS 20 ff. 1–3, dated 1323) and the Apocryphal legend of Susanna. The punishment of adultery by burning, rather than by stoning, suggests a Western origin of the story.

26/17 *Cassake*: the source is Odoric (p. 419), who locates the meeting-place of the Magi at *Cassan* identified as Qashan in Persia, 50 days' travel from Jerusalem, a distance covered *virtute miraculosa*. 'Mandeville's claim that the journey took 13 days is due to scribal confusion.

26/31–27/1 *Massap . . . Harme*: i.e. Arabic *maṣḥaf* 'book' and *horme* 'holy'. 'Mandeville' follows William of Tripoli (p. 590). The quotation is Psalm 7: 16.

27/27–30 *Ierusalem*: this false derivation is variously reported by Pseudo-Odoric (p. 148) and De Vitry (p. 93) among many others. The name derives from *Urasalem* 'city of peace', the Canaanite name in pre-Israelite times.

28/13 *Mercaritot*: i.e. St Chariton, abbot of a monastery south of Bethlehem, whose death supposedly excited the lamentations recorded in a painting which is, however, a literary creation. Comestor ch. 178 reports that the *compaginati* 'skeletons of the monks' are still to be seen, and the word has been misread as *compincti*. But the monastery was a ruin when seen by Ludolph of Sudheim (p. 93) before 1350.

28/22 *xl. ȝere*: Saladin recaptured Jerusalem in 1187, and the Hospitallers surrendered Acre in 1291; 'Mandeville' wrote '*140 ans*', which suggests a source (if not scribally corrupt) dated 1327.

29/21 *Grew lettris*: the first quotation is the Septuagint Psalm 74: 12, reported by Comestor ch. 179 'For God is my king of old, working salvation in the midst of the earth', and the second is based on the Septuagint Psalm 95: 10 'The stone which thou seest is the foundation of the world's faith.'

30/2 *Boþe beþ soþe*: the argument depends on the absurdity that in a year of ten months the days of each month equal the number of days in a calendar month.

30/21 *of Constantynople*: properly Constantine. The phrase *wel lowe in Ethiope* 30/26 translates *bien parfonde en Ethiope* (ed. Warner 40/29) 'into the depth of Ethiopia'.

30/29 *bokis of þe fader lyf*: i.e. the *Vitas Patrum*, the standard authority on the Patriarchs based on the 6th-century *Apophthegmata patrum* (Migne PG 65. 71).

31/7 *þe myddel of þe world*: the belief was widely held, and is traceable to Jerome, *Comm. in Ezechiel* 2. 5. 'Mandeville' follows Pseudo-Odoric (p. 149). The maker of the Latin Vulgate Version ch. 14 interpolates a lengthy argument to refute a literal interpretation of Ezechiel 2: 5.

31/22 *prestis*: properly *prestres Yndiens* (ed. Warner 40/40) whom Boldensele (p. 265) describes as *Indici Presbyteris Johannis fidem tenentes*, perhaps Malabar Christians whose faith was traditionally founded by St Thomas of India but who, more probably, were Nestorians.

32/11 *nostre dame le graunt*: so named to distinguish it from the adjacent *Notre Dame de latinis*, the centre of the Latin institutions founded by Charlemagne. The larger church was built on a site granted by the Fatimid caliph Abu 'Ali al-Mansur 1014–23 to merchants from Amalfi.

32/31 *Charlemayn*: his visit to the Holy Land and the miraculous arrival of the prepuce of Jesus are legend. But such a relic was deposited at Aix-la-Chapelle and thence transferred by Charles the Bald (d. 877) to Charroux in Poitou where Charlemagne had founded a Benedictine monastery. The story occurs in Vincent, *Spec. Hist.* XXV. 5, William of Tripoli (p. 426), and Comestor (col. 1541). *Parys* is a scribal error.

34/10 *holy writ*: an echo, not a quotation, of Ezechiel 47: 1. Moriah 'the pitted rock' was deemed to have survived the destruction of the Temple in AD 70 and in 637 the caliph Omar decreed that it was the rock whence

Mahomet ascended into heaven. Its identification with Beleth, the site of Jacob's dream, is reported by Boldensele (p. 262) and disputed by Burchard (p. 60). The supporting quotation is Genesis 37: 16.

35/27 *seynt Iame*: the legend of St James the Less, thrown down from the Temple by Scribes and Pharisees, is examined by P.-A. Bernheim, *James brother of Jesus*, trans. J. Bowden (London, 1989).

36/2 *Templeris*: the Order was suppressed in 1312. *dwelliþ* reflects a scribal error.

36/15 *probatica pissina*: i.e. the pool of Bethseda where Jesus healed the paralytic (John 5: 2).

36/23 *Herode*: 'Mandeville' takes the story of Herod from Comestor (cols. 1535, 1544). His dying request to his sister Salome is fanciful; similar legends are told of Alexander the Great and Nero.

37/15 *chirche of þe sauyour*: perhaps the chapel, near the Tower of David in the west of the city, where the relics of St John Chrysostom were kept. Pseudo-Odoric mentions (p. 150) *ecclesia sancti salvatoris que fuit domus Cayphas* but not the relics, cf. 38/29.

39/1 *Natatoyr Sylo*: i.e. the pool of Siloam where Jesus healed the blind man (John 9: 7). The following quotation is Matthew 27: 4.

39/18 *castel of Emaux*: the biblical Emmaus is about 7 miles west of Jerusalem. The small fortress Toron des Chevaliers, sometimes called *castel du bon larron*, was dismantled by Saladin in 1131.

40/9 *lyft fote*: a complementary stone with the imprint of the right foot was venerated at Westminster Abbey from 1249 until the Reformation. 'Mandeville' customarily mentions such associations, and his failure to do so here undermines his claim to English nationality. The source is Boldensele (p. 273).

40/17 *seynt Marye Gypcyane*: perhaps St Pelagia the virgin martyr whose church on Mount Olivet is reported by Pseudo-Odoric (p. 151). St Mary of Egypt, converted by Zosimus in 383, is not known to have had a church in Jerusalem.

41/10 *holy writ*: the quotation is Matthew 10: 47, followed by Luke 4: 3 and Matthew 9: 27.

41/18 *Georgiens*: i.e. priests and monks from the kingdom of Georgia, reported by De Vitry (p. 1095).

42/11 *lake of Alsiled*: properly *lacum asphaltitem* 'lake of asphalt', first reported by Josephus, *De bello Judico* IV. 8. 4 and known to the crusaders as *mare diaboli*. The fancies of floating iron and sinking feathers are inflated from Comestor's report (col. 1101) *etiam gravissima in eum jacta referuntur in altum*.

43/7 *Meldane in Sermoys*: i.e. *maydān* 'square, market-place' in Arabic. A tributary of the Jordan, the Yarmuk, which joins the river from the east south of the Sea of Galilee, flows through an open plain which was traditionally the site of a ten-day fair held for pilgrims to Mecca. The quotation is Matthew 3: 17. *Sermoys* is corrupted from *sarasinoiz* (ed. Warner 52/35).

43/24 *Carras in Sermoys*: 'Mandeville' confuses the smaller crusader castle *Krak* (the ruins lie south of the Dead Sea by the village of Shobek) with the more famous *Krak de Moab*, built by Pagan the Bulter in 1142 as the capital of his lordship of Oultre-Jourdain. The smaller *Krak*, built by Baldwin I king of the Franks (not of France), was known as *Montréal*.

44/2 *Ramatha . . . Sophym*: properly one town, Ramatha Sophim, otherwise Rama in Ephraim, which Boldensele (p. 276) reports.

44/11–14 *Sychem . . . Neople*: the biblical Shechem was destroyed by John Hyrcanus in 128 BC and rebuilt by the Romans farther west as Flavia Neapolis, called Nablus by the Arabs. Six miles north-west lies Sebastiyeh (originally Sebastos, the Greek name given to Samaria by Herod the Great in honour of Augustus) reputedly the burial place of John the Baptist, executed in the Herodian fortress of Machaerus on the Dead Sea. The prophets Elisha and Abdias (otherwise Obadiah, of whom only the name is known) are reported by Eugesippus *c.*1155 (Migne PG 133. 997) whose account was absorbed into an unidentified tract used by 'Mandeville' here.

45/5 *Tecle*: St Thecla, invited by Boniface to Germany where she became abbess of Kitzingen near Wurzburg, allegedly carried the relic to Maurienne in the Savoy alps. Faced with differing sources, 'Mandeville' reconciles different claims with tolerance. Where he found the reference to the glass bowl, captured by the Genoese at Caesarea, in which the Baptist's head was reportedly placed is unknown. The *Golden Legend* states that the head was wrapped in cloth of purple and taken to Rome, and that the ashes only are at Genoa.

45/17 *fons Iacob*: i.e. the bath of Job reported by Isidore XIII. 13. 8 and De Vitry (p. 1098) *in partibus Samarie*, and now called *hummām Ayyūb* 'bath of Job', a spring at Sheikk Sa'ad.

45/20 *Samaritans*: 'Mandeville' follows Boldensele (p. 277) who states that the Christians wear yellow and the Jews blue.

46/7 *columba*: properly *coluber* 'serpent'. The prophecy (not the prophet) of Antichrist is perhaps based on Genesis 49: 17 and Comestor's gloss (col. 1454) on Daniel 6.

46/13 *Chane of Galilee*: i.e. Chana in Galilee, the scene of the wedding feast where the *architriclinus* 'ruler of the feast' presided (John 2: 8). 'Mandeville' confuses the place with Canaan, the home of Simon and the woman with the sick daughter (Matthew 15: 4 and 22).

46/30 *blood*: properly leap, i.e. the rock from which Jesus leaped to escape the Jews (Luke 4: 30), reported by Boldensele (p. 280). The quotations are Luke 4: 30 and Exodus 15: 16 (not the Psalter as stated), which was when recited three times a charm against robbers, cf. R. H. Robbins, ed., *Secular Lyrics of the XIVth and XVth Centuries* (Oxford, 1952), pp. 58–9.

48/23 *Iacobynes*: i.e. Jacobites, followers of Jacob Baradeus the Syrian Monophysite who believed that Christ had only one divine nature. Their disuse of auricular confession is here supported by quotations based on AV (Vulgate) Psalms 111 (110): 1, 32 (31): 5, 118 (117): 28, 94 (93): 11. The Monophysites became the largest Christian community in Syria.

49/25 *Surryens*: i.e. the Syrian Maronites, who separated from the Monophysites and after the arrival of the Crusaders in 1181 entered into formal communion with Rome while retaining a form of the Greek liturgy, reported by De Vitry (p. 1089). The Georgians are reported above at 41/18.

49/31–50/3 *cristen men of girdyng*: in 856 the caliph al-Mutawakkil imposed restrictions on Jews and Christians, compelling them among other things to wear distinctive leather girdles, as reported by Burchard (p. 89). The latter were sometimes identified as Copts. The remaining Christian sects are Nestorians, the Nubians (otherwise Copts), the Arians (properly Armenians), the Gregorians (properly Greeks), and the Indians (properly Malabar Christians reported above at 31/22). All are described in F. L. Cross, *Oxford Dictionary of the Christian Church* (Oxford, 1957).

50/14 *Heliseus Damask*: 'Mandeville' follows De Vitry (p. 1073) in falsely making Eliezer of Damascus (Genesis 15: 2) the founder of the city. Both Burchard (p. 81) and Pseudo-Odoric (p. 154) record the site of Abel's murder at the *ager Damascenus* at Hebron, reported at 24/23 above.

50/22 *nostre dame de Gardemarche*: the church of Our Lady of Sardenak (Saidenaya, 12 miles north of Damascus), was renowned for its miraculous portrait of the Virgin Mary, supposedly painted by St Luke and bringing instant death to the beholder. It is reported by Boldensele (p. 285). A description of the portrait by the Franciscan John Lathbury (d. 1362) who spoke to a witness of the miraculous tears is quoted by B. Smalley, *English Friars and Antiquity* (Oxford, 1960), p. 340. The exudation of oil may have been adopted from the Hebrew practice of anointing stone pillars.

51/7 *Sabatorie*: an intermittent spring north-east of 'Arka, the *riuus Sabbaticus* of Pliny XXXI.2 which *ceases* on the Sabbath. 'Mandeville' follows De Vitry (p. 1098) who reports the freezing river in Persia.

51/28 *Griffe*: properly Corfu, which lies south of Dyrrachium (where the First Crusade began its march to Constantinople in 1096) and Avalona (where Bohemond disembarked to join the main route of that crusade at Vodena). Between 1147 and 1386 Corfu was attached to the kingdom of Sicily (not Genoa).

52/13 *castel of Cheynay*: i.e. Toron des Chevaliers at Emmaus, noted at 39/18 above.

52/27–53/23 *Puluerale*: i.e. the *castellum imperatoris Pulveral nomine* and Sinope are both on the southern coast of the Black Sea. Albert of Aix (pp. 570–1), from whom 'Mandeville' took the whole of this itinerary, mentions them as refuges of the routed survivors of Count Raymond's troops, and their inclusion here as stations on the way to Jerusalem is nonsense. *Mornaunt* is *Nigri montes*, *Mallebryns* is *Malabrunias*, and the *vale of Ernay* is *valles Orellis* (i.e. Dorylaeum) in Albert. *Richay* is properly the town *Recleum* (otherwise Heraclea and Eregli). The river *Lay* is properly the lake of Nicaea. *Florathe* is the *Foloraca arx que est iuxta mare et confinia regni Russie*. The bridge over the river *Ferne* (the ancient Orontes, later Fer) was known to the crusaders as *pons ferreus* 'iron bridge'. The river *Albane*, the Abana which flows from the Anti-Lebanon mountains east through Damascus, and the plain Archades through which it flows to the Mediterranean (i.e. the Great Sea, not the Red Sea as here) are reported by Eugesippus (p. 994). *Phenne* and *Ferne* are Philomelium and Ferna (later Ilgun) in Asia Minor which Albert mentions in a digression as the site of the destruction of reinforcements advancing towards Antioch. The confusion of the itinerary is characteristic of 'Mandeville' even if due allowance is made for scribal error.

54/3–8 *Maubeke*: i.e. the Muslim fortress of Ba'albek. The route from Antioch given here is *via* Laodicaea, Gibellum, Tortosa, and Emessa which in De Vitry (p. 1073) is *hodie Camela seu Chamele*. The Templar fortress Château Pèlerin is noted above at 20/26. The *londe of Flagame* is a scribal invention from the palmary reading *tor de Flagram* in De Vitry, properly *le tor Destroit* on the coastal road between Château Pèlerin and Haifa.

54/20 *Tartarie*: the account of Tartary which begins here, excluding the long account of Saracen beliefs, is derived from Giovanni del Pian Carpini O.F.M., *Historia Mongolorum* which records his embassy sent by Innocent IV to the Tartars in 1245–7. 'Mandeville' follows the version incorporated into Vincent of Beauvais, *Spec. Hist.* XXXI. 2–52 (pp. 1286–303); on which see G. G. Guzman in *Speculum* 49 (1974), 287–397.

55/7 *Raco*: properly Batu khan of the Golden Horde, whom Carpini visited on his way to Guyuk Khan. The Mongol *orda* 'camp' was established on the Volga about 1241.

55/13 *Gasten*: perhaps a corrupt form of Durostorum (later Silistria) in northern Bulgaria, which is then the southernmost of the regions named here (Russia, Livonia, Crakow, Lithuania). The source of this itinerary is not known.

55/27 *Kera! Kera! Kera!*: the origin is unclear. Neither Arabic *karrah* 'attack' or the war-cry *Allahu akbar* 'God is great' reported by Ralph of Caen (PL 155. 521) and others, suits the context which requires 'look out, beware, hide'. Probably, Persian *khār* 'trouble'.

56/10 *Saresyns*: this chapter, apart from the imaginary colloquy with the sultan, is closely based on William of Tripoli. *Mesap* and *Harme* are explained at their earlier occurrence at 26/31.

57/8 *Takyna*: this misunderstanding of Arabic *taki* 'God-fearing' is already present in William of Tripoli (p. 592) who glosses *Taquius* as *quidam incantator qui subito intrabat super virgines et supprimebat eas*. The Latin translation of the Koran made for Peter abbot of Cluny in 1143 avoids the error, reading *si deum timeat* instead of William's *si tu es Taquius*, in its account of the Annunciation.

57/29 *faste*: i.e. the fast of Ramadan.

60/1 *Poul*: the quotation is 2 Corinthians 3: 6.

60/7 *what þe sowdan seide*: the source of this imaginary colloquy is perhaps Caesar of Heisterbach, *Dialogus miraculorum* IV. 15 (ed. J. Strange (Cologne, 1851) I. 187–8), who reported such a discussion between William of Utrecht and an emir after the fall of Acre in 1187. It is a common literary device, full of contemporary complaints about Christian behaviour; see J. D. Peter, *Complaint and satire in early English literature* (Oxford, 1956). A metrical version of the colloquy is printed in *Journal of the Australasian Universities Language and Literature Association* 21 (1964), 39–52.

61/29 *an heremyte*: called Bahira (otherwise the Nestorian monk Sergius, traditionally the mentor of the Prophet) by William of Tripoli (p. 576).

62/7 *Quadrige*: i.e. Khadija, the wealthy widow of a merchant (not a prince of Khorasan, otherwise Persia) whom the Prophet married in 595. 'Mandeville' takes these details from Vincent, *Spec. Hist.* XXIII. 39 and De Vitry (p. 1053), and reports all the disputed etymologies of *Saraceni* including the incongruous derivation from Sarah wife of Abraham which De Vitry denies. See R. W. Southern, *Western Views of Islam in the Middle Ages* (Harvard, 1962), pp. 17–18, and William of Rubruck p. 67 note 4.

63/18 *Archessleneyn*: properly *archiflamen*, a Latin designate for heathen hierarchs. The *shāhada* quoted by William of Tripoli (p. 579) is properly *lā ilāh illa allah Muhammed rasul allah*. The Saracen alphabet which follows has fanciful names, no doubt much corrupted, derived from Hrabanus Maurus, *De inventione linguarum* (PL 112. 1579); Warner p. 194 suggests a Slavonic origin, and M. Letts, *Sir John Mandeville* (London, 1949) p. 157 claims the forms are Runic. Only 24 names and forms are given here, not 28 as implied by the following *foure lettris* and then contradicted by *twey lettres mo*; since there was only graphic distinction between *i* and *j* and between *i* and *y*, the alphabet in England which retained *þ* and *ȝ* had 26 letters.

64/17 *Grete See*: i.e. the Black Sea. Cf. Rubruck p. 1, note 1. The Great Ocean Sea is the term for the seas which surround the known landmasses of Europe, Africa, and Asia. See note to 107/14 below.

64/27 *Pounce*: i.e. the classical *Pontus Euxinus*, now the Black Sea. 'Mandeville' here begins to follow the itinerary of Odoric, supplemented by Vincent and Haiton.

64/29 *Athanas*: the Athanasian Creed is (*pace* Odoric p. 415) the work of St Ambrose, but otherwise this account of Athanasius (d. 373) reflects his involvement in the Arian schism, his banishment by Constantine to Trier, and his acquittal at Rome under Julius in 340 of the charge of heresy. However, it is another saint of the same name but of the tenth century who lies at Trebizond. The mistake is inherited from Odoric.

65/12 *a riche man*: i.e. Alexius Comenus, reported by Haiton, who established himself as emperor of Trebizond in 1204. The ancient Armenia lay thereabouts, but its occupation by the Seljuk Turks after the battle of Manzikert in 1071 led the Armenians to migrate to Cicilia. This Lesser Armenia is the country of the legend of the sparrowhawk.

65/16 *castel desperuer*: the castle of the *épervier* 'sparrow-hawk' is 'the Maiden's Castle' Kizkalesi (properly two castles once connected by a causeway) built to protect Korikos in 1151. The two major ports of Lesser Armenia were *Larrays* (now Ayas) and *Croke*, otherwise Korikos (the ancient Corycus). The lords (not princes) of Korikos were Oshin (d. 1264), his son Gregorius, his son Haiton after 1280 who wrote the history used by 'Mandeville', and his son Oshin. The *ladye of fayrie* is Melior, sister of Mélusine whose legend includes her interview with the king of Armenia and a waking period of three days and nights (as stated here). The watching of a hawk until it falls asleep is part of the falconer's lore in taming wild birds. The king is Leon II, after whose death in 1289 began the gradual erosion of Lesser Armenia which surrendered its last towns to the Saracens in 1385. Jean d'Arras, secretary to Jean duc de Berri, compiled the romance *Mélusine* after 1387 from various *croniques*. 'Mandeville' inserted this fable where Oderic (p. 414) refers to a castle near Trebizond.

66/13 *heo seide*: because of a scribal omission here two separate anecdotes of a poor man's son and a Knight Templar are merged. This last clause refers to the Templar whose order was suppressed in 1312.

66/19 *Artyron*: i.e. Erzerum, sacked by the Seljuk Turks in 1048 and the Mongols in 1241. Mount Ararat is about 200 miles east. Odoric (p. 416) does not report the legend of the monk, traditionally St James later archbishop of Nisibis, which is briefly noted by Vincent, *Spec. Nat.* VI. 21, and William of Rubruck (pp. 267–8); the latter notes the various resting places assigned to the Ark in other sources. The relic is still venerated in the cathedral of Etchmiadzin. The monastery below Mount Ararat was destroyed by earthquake in 1840.

67/16 *Cassake*: i.e. the *Cassam* of Odoric (p. 419), midway between Sultanieh and Yezd. Odoric does not mention *Cardabago*, properly the Persian *chau bagh* 'four gardens', the designation of the royal palace of Isphahan, and reports Yezd, 170 miles south-east of Isphahan, as the city where Christians die. See W. Barthold, *An Historical Geography of Iran* (Princeton, 1984).

67/22 *Carnaa*: i.e. the ancient Persepolis. Odoric (p. 420) mistakenly identifies the land of Job with the rich cattle-bearing country in the mountains of Kurdistan. The identification of Job with Jobab, son of Zerak of Bozrah (Genesis 36: 33) derives from Isidore, *De ortu et obitu patrum* (PL 83. 136), but is not in Odoric.

68/7 *manna*: reported by Odoric (p. 420). The description comes from Vincent, *Spec. Nat.* IV. 84–5 and properly refers to an exudation obtained by excisions in plants and used in the medieval pharmacy.

68/12 *Caldee*: i.e. Baghdad in the kingdom of the biblical Chaldaea. Odoric reports the foul women, presumably beggars.

68/17 *lond of Amasonye*: the classical tribe of Amazons was traditionally sited on the borders of Scythia on the Black Sea. Their story is told by Vincent, *Spec. Hist.* I. 96 (p. 36) who names Scolopitus as the king whose death in battle caused the women to establish their state. One element in this myth told here is perhaps that young Mongol women used to ride and fight with their menfolk using short, light, and deeply curved Turkish bows made from layers of springy wood and horn; on their construction see T. Severin, *Crusader* (London, 1989), p. 192. The myth occurs widely in the medieval legends of Alexander where the right breast is commonly seared off for the better drawing of the bow. Only 'Mandeville' has the imaginative variation due to status.

69/10 *Turmagute*: i.e. Termegite on the site of Alexandria Margiana (later Merv) mentioned by Brunetto Latini (p. 158) and a corruption of the classical *terra Margine*. As with the land of the Amazons, 'Mandeville' departs far from Odoric's route.

69/13 *Ethiope*: an ill-defined area south of Chaldea and west of India, themselves both vague designations. Cf. note to 110/12 below and Pelliot II. 653. Since the people here are *ful blak* 'Mandeville' presumably intends Africa. The well is reported by Vincent, *Spec. Nat.* XXXII. 15, who also lists the classical *sciapodae* among his monsters. Their appearance here may have been triggered by Odoric's reference (p. 423) to *unam pedem faxiolorum*, apparently an aromatic basil venerated by Hindus, which was corrupted in the French translation used by 'Mandeville'. As with other monsters, the legend may have a basis of fact in the presence of a single mutated gene among African tribes, like the 'lobster-claw' tribe with feet of huge deformity which lives in the Zambesi valley.

69/23 *Saba*: properly Saveh, about 50 miles south-west of Teheran, which contained the tombs of the Magi reported by Marco Polo (pp. 24–5). It is here confused with the south Arabian biblical kingdom of Sheba and so sited in 'Ethiopia'.

69/26–70/1 *Ynde*: like 'Ethiopia' an ill-defined land. Its three parts as designated here are *Ynde þe more* the sub-continent proper; *Ynde the lasse*, Odoric's *India infra terram*, the land between the mouth of the Euphrates and the Persian Gulf; and *þe þridde part* the vast area of the Hindu Kush and the Himalayas. Cf. the different explanation at 110/18–20 above.

70/4 *dyamaund*: this account is based on Vincent, *Spec. Nat.* VIII. 39. All other medieval lapidaries, like Isidore and Bartholomaeus Anglicus cited by the Egerton Version (ed. Warner 79/20), give similar descriptions.

71/17 *þe schipman stoon*: i.e. the mariner's compass, taken from De Vitry (p. 1107), who is also the source for the huge eels in the Ganges (p. 1106), not the Indus as here. The greenness of the Indians is reported by Brunetto Latini (p. 159), who mentions 5000 *villes*, not *iles*, as does Vincent, *Spec. Hist.* IV. 47.

72/16 *Hermes*: i.e. Hormuz in the Persian Gulf, the chief medieval entrepôt of the Indian trade. See Pelliot I. 576–82. Having completed his overland journey from Trebizond on the Black Sea, Odoric followed by 'Mandeville' now embarks on his voyage along the western coast of India to the southern seas.

72/26 *schippes wiþoute nayles*: reported by Odoric (p. 422) and Marco Polo (p. 30), the planks (aini-wood from Calicut) were fastened with cord made from coconut coir. A modern reconstruction of such a ship is described by T. Severin, *The Sindbad Voyage* (London, 1982), p. 20. The fanciful explanation of the magnetic rocks, not found in Odoric, is taken from Vincent, *Spec. Nat.* VIII. 21.

72/28 *Canaa*: Thana on the isle of Salsette near Bombay, which Odoric reached from Hormuz after 28 days at sea, was a major trading centre and port where all south-bound ships called.

72/30 *Alysandre*: Odoric (p. 423) reports that the king who opposed Alexander the Great was *Porus*, a powerful Punjabi rajah, but his empire never extended to Thana. *Porus* is also the name of the king in the *Epistola Alexandri* (p. 22), which is included by Vincent, *Spec. Hist.* The southernmost thrust of Alexander's advance across the Hydaspes did involve a battle with Porus; see R. L. Fox, *Alexander the Great* (London 1973), pp. 353–61. 'Mandeville' has confused *Canaa* with *Caldee* at 68/12 above. The account of simulacra and idols is not in Odoric, but he does report the veneration of the ox. The creatures as big as dogs are *mures* (p. 423), here *ratouns*.

74/11 *Sarchie*: perhaps Calicut, the major port on the coast before the spice city of *Polome*, medieval Kaulam (now Kollam or Quilon) on the Malabar Coast. But the only city with a Christian community which Odoric mentions here is *Caitum* (p. 438), the destination of the ship on which he embarked at Quilon and which he describes later (p. 460). It is identified by Pelliot as Ch'uan-chou, the major city of the Amoy harbour region.

74/20 *welle of ȝowþe*: reported by the *Letter of Prester John* (p. 912). There is nothing in Odoric to explain its presence here except perhaps the description of the anointing by ox-dung which 'Mandeville' inflates by introducing a prelate *Archiprotapapaton*, a title sometimes used of the chief priest of the Nestorian Church. The title also occurs in the *Letter* (p. 920).

75/4 *gaule*: Odoric reports the practice but does not name the substance, which is presumably ox-gall, the secretion of the liver used from ancient times as a cleansing agent and in painting and pharmacy. Cf. Bartholomaeus Anglicus XVIII. 15. Odoric was apparently misinformed about its nature.

75/23 *wymmen schaueþ*: this detail, copied from Jean le Long's French version of Odoric (ed. Cordier p. 102), distorts Odoric's Latin (p. 441).

75/25 *Mabaron*: i.e. the medieval Ma'bar, the name given by Arab traders to the Coromandel Coast. Odoric (p. 442) merely reports the body of St Thomas in the region. Its location at *Calamy*, i.e. Mailapur near Madras, where it was seen by Marco Polo who attests the veneration shown to the saint by the Arabs, is reported by Brunetto Latini (p. 74). The source of the story of the judgements of St Thomas is unknown, but in a different form it is reported by Odo abbot of Rheims in 1122 (see *Letter of Prester John*, introduction) and Gervase of Tilbury III. 26. Odoric says these Malabar Christians were Nestorians.

76/9–12 *a fals god*: probably one of the Trimurti (Brahma, Vishnu, or Siva) honoured by Hindus. Most of the details, including the description of the Juggernaut car, are reported by Odoric. His reference *ad sanctum Petrum* in Rome is, however, changed to *seynt Iame*, the shrine of St James at Compostella which attracted many English and French pilgrims. Le Long's French translation of Odoric, which 'Mandeville' follows, mentions both shrines.

77/2 *a chariot*: a tall ceremonial chariot (*ratha* in Sanskrit) is still used in Hindu processions in southern India.

77/26 *Lamory*: properly Komari (the land about Cape Comorin, the southernmost point of India) which Odoric here confuses with Lambri, a kingdom in north-west Sumatra, on which see Pelliot II. 761. Odoric (p. 445) follows Marco Polo's account of Komari (p. 198) very closely, including his celestial observation, and adds only the length of his voyage to Lambri, 50 days' sailing. Such a voyage would have been directly from Quilon to Sumatra and strongly suggests what the confusions in the text point to, that Odoric had no personal knowledge of the intermediary islands, including Ceylon, which he describes.

Where Odoric after Marco Polo says that he began to lose sight of the North Star (which at 8° N is only distinguishable in very clear atmosphere at a small height above the horizon) owing to the curvature of the earth, 'Mandeville' introduces this discussion of the rotundity of the world. The sources are various. The *polum antarcticum* is taken from the *Directorium ad faciendum passagium transmarinum* c.1330 (ed. *American Historical Review* 12. 821) where it is probably Canopus, after Sirius the brightest star in the sky and visible only below latitude 37° N. The calculations of sightings of the Pole Star in Brabant, Alemania, and Bohemia by the astrolabe are genuine, though of unknown origin. The sighting of the Antarctic Star (if Canopus) in High Libya is also genuine. It sets briefly over parts of Australia and South Africa but below the latitude of 33° 16′ S (roughly Sydney and Cape Town), the most southerly latitude 'Mandeville' claims to have visited (after Odoric who follows Marco Polo), it is circumpolar. The main source of the ideas of the earth expressed here is Sacrobosco, *De sphera mundi* c.1220, a comprehensive explanation of the Ptolemaic concept of a symmetrical globe, with additions from Macrobius and Alfreganus, within a traditional Christian framework. According to this system, the world had seven 'climates', i.e. zones distinguished by the varying lengths of their longest day. Lands like England and Ceylon, not included in these zones (roughly between 16° 30′ S and 50° 30′ N) by the early geographers, were added in the Middle Ages to most northerly and southerly zones without further distinction. Each of the seven climates was supposedly governed by one of the seven planets (e.g. England by the restless Moon, Ceylon by sluggish Saturn), and from such influences came the dispositions of the inhabitants.

80/8 *toward Jerusalem*: the idea that one travelled upwards to the 'bulge' of the earth to Jerusalem at its centre is expressed in the *Mappa mundi*. In 1120 Lambert, *Liber floridus*, writes of the earth as a sphere, apparently basing his belief on such a map. This idea of the 'bulge' is not, of course, part of the Ptolemaic system.

80/16 *a spere*: the fancy that a spear casts no shadow at the equinox at Jerusalem was a common medieval delusion. Its origin is Eratosthenes' report that on the summer solstice in Syrene, Upper Egypt, when the sun was directly overhead, a vertical pointer cast no shadow and the sun's rays reached the bottom of a well dug for that purpose.

80/26 *a tale*: for a suggestion that this tale is an echo of Norse voyages to North America see M. C. Seymour in *An English Miscellany . . . W. S. Mackie*, ed. B. S. Lee (Cape Town, 1977). One element in the story may derive from the legend of the land of darkness; see Pelliot II. 616–24.

81/20 *olde wise men*: 'Mandeville' here cites Brunetto Latini (p. 126) who calculated the circumference as 20,247 miles before offering his own calculation *aftir my litel wit*. This properly is the work of Eratosthenes which he found in Vincent, *Spec. Nat.* VI. 13 (col. 377). There, taking one degree as 700 *stadia*, generally equated with furlongs, the multiple of 700 × 360 is 252,000 *stadia* or 31,500 miles. The Ptolemaic calculation of the circumference of the equator (after adjustment for his confusion of Olympic Philetarian *stadia*) is 24,545 statute miles; unadjusted, it is 20,684 miles and the source of Latini's calculation. The modern figure is 24,901.8 statute miles. Vincent's immediate source is Pliny II. 247; Eratosthenes' work now survives in fragments.

82/15 *Somober*: Odoric's *Sumoltra* (p. 446), a kingdom in Sumatra and not the whole island. Likewise, Java is properly a kingdom, albeit the most powerful, of the island. Odoric's report of Kublai Khan's attempt to conquer this kingdom in 1293 is more fully described by Marco Polo (p. 169), his source here.

83/10–26 *Salamasse*: Odoric's *Malamasini* or *Paten* (p. 447) is perhaps the same as Marco Polo's *Fansur*, i.e. Barus on the west coast of Sumatra. The trees that bear meal are sago-palms, and those that bear poison are upas-trees; Odoric exaggerates their venom. His description of making palm-wine resembles that of Marco Polo, who reports that the wood of these trees sinks like iron. This observation (part of the traditional description of the Dead Sea, cf. 41/31) may be the origin of Odoric's *deed see* here, which is unknown to modern geography. The *grete cannes* are bamboo, reported by Vincent, *Spec. Nat.* XII. 57 and Brunetto Latini (p. 158, who calls them *tabi*) as well as Odoric. Pelliot II. 802 tentatively identifies *Paten* with Bintan island off Sumatra.

84/1 *Calonach*: Odoric's *Zampa* (p. 450) and Marco Polo's *Chamba*, i.e. Tchampa, a major kingdom in southern Indo-China. The marvel of the fish is the annual running of spawning fish which Odoric appears not to have heard of before. The snails are tortoises. Odoric reports one huge shell as big as the dome of St Antony's at Padua (at least 40 feet in diameter), presumably a carving or sculpture. De Vitry (p. 1106) says that they are used for houses.

84/28 *Gaffolos*: this land and the following three lands are not described by Odoric, Marco Polo, or Ibn Battuta whose records of voyages to the southern sea were the only reports then available. 'Mandeville' inserts them here where Odoric (p. 452) says that he will not describe other marvels beyond belief, as in note to 86/14 below. The source of all four is possibly Vincent, *Spec. Hist.* I. 87, but only some details are found there. The earliest dated French manuscript calls the first island *Boffo*.

85/12 *god*: 'Mandeville' wrote *dieu*, if not his invention perhaps the result of successive corruptions of a native word. Marco Polo reports this practice in Kon-cha province. Vincent, *Spec. Hist.* I. 88 reports that the Scythians drank blood, following Solinus and his source in Pliny, to sanctify their treaties.

85/16 *Tracota*: properly the land of the Troglodytae in Libya, reported by Vincent, *Spec. Hist.* I. 87, who follows Isidore XVI. 12. 5, Solinus 31, and ultimately Pliny 37. 10. They all call the gem *hexecontalithos* 'sixty-coloured stone', which is unknown outside this literary tradition. There are troglodytes in North Africa (Tunisia) and Ethiopia, but neither is associated with precious stones. The explanation of the name *traconyte* (perhaps confused with the *draconitis* 'the dragon-stone', also fabulous) is apparently an echo of Vincent, *unde et hoc sibi nomen adoptavit*, who explains the proper Greek name as a description of sixty colours.

85/23–86/10 *Natumeran*: Odoric's *Nicuneram* (p. 452), identified with the Nicobar Islands, north-west of Sumatra and the most southerly of the Andaman chain in the Bay of Bengal. Its position here in Odoric's itinerary towards China, like that of the Andaman Islands and Ceylon which follow, is out of geographical coherence; after the Malabar Coast Odoric, though sailing east from India, mistakenly follows Marco Polo's itinerary (p. 176) as he sails homewards towards India. The men with the heads of dogs are the classical *cynocephali* reported by Vincent, *Spec. Hist.* I. 92 and by Marco Polo in the Andaman Islands; the myth is perhaps linked to the larger lemur indris of Madagascar but the common baboon in southern Africa also have dog-like heads. Marco Polo places the king and the coveting of his huge ruby by Kublai Khan in Ceylon in the chapter which follows his record of the dog-headed men.

86/14–87/27 *Dodym*: Odoric's account (p. 455) closely follows Marco Polo's description of Dagroian (p. 173) in Sumatra, but the kingdom has not been certainly identified. Odoric attests that he is here following others' reports; *de hac insula diligenter inquisivi multos qui hoc sciunt*. He does, however, say that 64 crowned kings are found in India and not, as here, vassals of the king of *Dodym*. Where he says *multe alie novitates illic habentur quas non scribo nam si homo eas non videret credere non posset*, 'Mandeville' peoples these kingdoms with monsters of antiquity. His source is Vincent, *Spec. Hist.* I. 92–3, perhaps supplemented by De Vitry (p. 1111), which ultimately depends on Pliny VI and VII. The men with *plat face* are lepers, and the men who use oat-straws to take nourishment are reported by Pliny VI. 35 immediately afterwards. In the Insular Version and Odoric the account of *Dodym* follows that of *Sylha*, known to the Indians as *Sinhala* and the Chinese as *Si-Lan*.

87/20–88/17 *Sylha*: 'Mandeville' follows Odoric's account (p. 454) which gives the circuit of Ceylon as *2000 milliariorum*, cf. 2400 in Marco Polo. The measurement given here, 800 miles, is much closer to the real circumference of about 700 miles but this reading is due to a mistranslation of *dccc lieus*. The *hille* is Adam's Peak, a site of many legends. The vermin are leeches and the local remedy against their bites is lemon-juice. Only 'Mandeville' claims its efficacy against the crocodile, though Pliny XXIII. 67 says that lees of vinegar with melanthium is a powerful antidote to the infection from such bites.

88/18 *wilde gees*: i.e. hornbill which have a large growth above their heads, thus appearing two-headed at a distance. The optical illusion of a towering sea, here supported by Psalm 92: 4, is the second report of its phenomenon; its first report is a sentence omitted in this Defective Version at 64/18. The white lions, not found in Odoric, are reported in the *Epistola Alexandri de situ Indie* (ed. 1706, p. 33), as found in Vincent, *Spec. Hist.* IV. 58, and in the romances based on it.

88/27 *Mancy*: i.e. Manzi, the kingdom of southern China conquered by the Mongols from Cathay in the north in 1276. Odoric (p. 457) locates it in *Indiam superiorem* which here encompasses the whole of southern Asia excluding the subcontinent, cf. note to 69/26 above and the tripartite division of Marco Polo. Odoric reports the beauty of the women but only 'Mandeville' calls the land *Albanye* (a name formed on *albus* 'white') which he has perhaps identified with the medieval Albania, the ancient kingdom in the eastern Caucasus inhabited by Scythians, whose white hair is reported by Vincent, *Spec.* I. 69.

89/7 *Latorym*: i.e. Canton. Odoric (p. 458) calls the province *Censcala* and Marco Polo (p. 142) *Kan-giu*, properly Kuang-tong 'the province of Kuang', of which Canton is the capital. The form here reflects *Cartan* in Jean le Long's translation (Cordier p. 263) of Oderic, who says that the city is three times the size of Rome (not Paris). The large birds are the Guinea-geese (*anser cygnoides*) and the white hens are silk-fowl (*gallus lanatus*) which Odoric (p. 461) places in *Fuco* 'Fu-chow'. He says that the crown of the married women is *unam magnam barile de cornu*.

89/17 *loyrys*: i.e. *loutres* 'otters' which Vincent, *Spec. Nat.* XIX. 89 reports are used to catch fish. But Odoric (p. 462) says that tame *mergi* 'divers, cormorants' are used here.

89/21 *Cassay*: Odoric's *Camsay* 'city of heaven' (p. 463) and Marco Polo's *Quinsai*, i.e. Hang-chow (p. 143). Both report the circuit to be 100 *milliaria* and the bridges to number 12,000. Odoric calls the wine *bigin* (ultimately the Mongol *darasun*, which Rubruck p. 178 calls *terracina* 'rice wine'). Marco Polo describes it as a distillation of rice grains well spiced and potent. The monastery of Buddhist monks was on a lake on the west of the city. On the practice of summoning the beasts to eat see Moule, *Quinsai* (1957), pp. 34–5. Only 'Mandeville' says that the bell and platter were silver.

90/21 *Chibence*: Odoric's *Chilenfo* (p. 467), i.e. Chin-ling-fu and later Nanking. He says that the walls are 40 *milliaria* in circuit and that it has 360 bridges. The numbers given here are scribal corruptions inherited by 'Mandeville'.

91/3 *grete ryuer*: Odoric's *Thalay* (p. 468), which is *ta-le* 'the sea', the name the Mongols gave to the Yang-Tse. Odoric says that at its most narrow its width is seven miles.

91/5 *Pegmans*: i.e. pygmies, reported by Odoric. But apart from the diminutive Kuku-Kuku, a warrior tribe in the eastern highlands of New Guinea, there are no pygmies in Asia. Marco Polo reports that in Basman monkeys are tricked out as pygmies, and this may be Odoric's source. 'Mandeville' exaggerates Odoric's description, making them marry at six months, cf. De Vitry (p. 1112) at three years and Augustine, *De civitate dei* XVI. 8 at five years. Odoric follows Augustine.

91/13 *Menke*: Odoric's *Mencu* (p. 470), apparently Ming-chou, later Ning-po, but this city is near the coast south of Hang-chou and east of the Yang-Tse. Odoric says that the junks are washed with a white resin. Marco Polo, who describes the junks in detail at the beginning of Book III, says that they are coated with a mixture of lime and oil as a water-proofing. The common practice was to lime the bottoms with burned sea-shell and to seal the sides with chundruz gum and fish-oil.

91/17 *Caromosan*: Odoric's *Caramoram* and Marco Polo's *Kara-moran*, the Mongol 'Black River', cf. the Chinese Huang-ho 'Yellow River'. See Pelliot I. 182–3.

91/18 *Catay*: on the name, first recorded in the West in 1221, see Pelliot I. 216–29. The description of Cathay in lines 18–25 is not found in Odoric, but otherwise, with additions from Haiton reported in subsequent notes, the description of the Great Khan is taken from him. The merchants from Venice are presumably the Polos who pioneered the overland route in 1250. The eastern trade was, however, largely carried by intermediaries by sea (along the route sailed by Odoric from Hormuz) and by land along 'the Silk Road' until its disruption by the Ottoman Turks in the late fourteenth century.

91/28 *Cadom*: Odoric's *Taydo* (p. 471) and the Mongol *ta-tu* 'great court', built by Kublai Khan in 1267. See Pelliot I. 140–3 and note to 102/4 below.

92/13 *panters*: Odoric (p. 472) merely reports that the red skins on the walls were the best in the world. 'Mandeville' takes his description from Vincent, *Spec. Nat.* XIX. 99 (col. 1436) which he elaborates. The hides were presumably treated Russian leather, cf. the musk-laden brown skins of the common panda.

92/19 *mountour*: called *magna pigna* by Odoric, i.e. a bejewelled drinking fountain similar to that reported by Rubruck (pp. 209–10) in the Mongol palace at Karacorum. *mountour* 'mound' is due to an earlier confusion of *pigna* 'jar' with *pinna* 'mount'. Cf. Pelliot II. 740–1.

93/6 *mannus foot*: i.e. the traditional long tail called the *ku-ku* which hung from the caps of Tartar wives of tribal leaders. See Rubruck p. 89 note 1.

93/21 *grete vyne*: this vine is reported in the *Epistola Alexandri de situ Indie* (p. 22) and in *Historia de proeliis* cap. 81 and thence in the Alexandrine romances. Vincent, *Spec. Hist.* LXXVII mentions something similar in the Temple of Solomon. 'Mandeville' adds the lists of precious stones here and in the next paragraph from the *Letter of Prester John* (p. 917) which reports them in the Indus.

94/12 *my felawis and Y*: Odoric (p. 474) reports that he stayed three years in Cathay, which prompted 'Mandeville' to his anachronistic claim here. The Tartar general Chin-san Bay-an completed the conquest of Manzi in 1279, as Marco Polo (p. 134) reports. The details of the Mongols' eating habits are taken from Carpini, printed in Vincent, *Spec. Hist.* XXIX. 78.

94/25 *somme seiþ þus*: the division of the world among the sons of Noah gave to the descendants of Shem (Genesis 10: 21–31) the land from the Mediterranean to the Indian Ocean including Lydia, Syria, Chaldea, Assyria, Persia, and Arabia, and to the descendants of Ham the country of Egypt. This spurious linking of Ham to the name Cham, instead of Shem, was commonplace. The origin of Chan is the Mongol *khán* 'lord'.

95/11 *viii. ȝere ago*: 'Mandeville' wrote 'eight score'. Vincent, *Spec. Hist.* XXIX. 69 (p. 1209) dates the election of Genghiz Khan to 1202 (cf. the historical 1206), so that 'Mandeville' writing *c.*1356 is roughly ten years out. The rest of the chapter is taken from Haiton ch. 16 except the superscriptions of letters and seals, for which see note to 97/27 below.

95/14 *vii. lynages*: Haiton lists the tribes as Tartar, Tangut, Oirat, Chelair, Sunit, Merkit, Tibet.

95/18 *an old man*: Genghiz, born *c.*1167, was about 39 when he was elected *khákán* 'Great Khan'. The name Genghiz is the Arabic form of Turkish *tengiz* 'ocean' and so 'universal'; see Pelliot I. 296–303. On the popular derivation from *temujin* 'blacksmith' see Rubruck p. 124 note 3. The white knight is the shaman Tab-tengri who, according to legend, rode to Tengri the sky-god worshipped by the Tartars to discover his will before the election; see R. P. Lister, *The Secret History of Genghiz Khan* (London, 1969), pp. 191–5, and P. Ratchnevsky, *Genghis Khan. His life and legacy*, trans. T. N. Haining (Oxford, 1991), and J. A. Boyle, *The Mongol World Empire 1206–1370* (London, 1977).

96/5 *Isakan*: the *yasa khan* 'ordinances of the khan' which Genghiz Khan completed in 1225. The law code was written on rolls in Uighur script and kept in the treasuries of the chief khans. The adoption of Uighur script and scribes by the illiterate Mongols followed the employment of an Uighur captive as tutor to the sons of Genghiz; see J. J. Saunders, *The History of the Mongol Conquests* (London, 1971), pp. 31–4. Their *God almiȝty* was Tengri whose mediation in human affairs required the services of a shaman. The organization of the Mongol army by decades was based on long-standing practice among the tribes of Central Asia.

97/9 *mounte Belyan*: the sacred mountain of Genghiz Khan's youth in the Mongol homelands below the Great Kentei Shan, the mountain range in the north of Outer Mongolia, was known as Burqan Qaldun (8494 ft. high). The *see* is Lake Baikal, and the legend reported here by Haiton perhaps records the first major campaign by Genghiz Khan against his western neighbours the Karakhitai in 1209, which began the conquest of Cathay, reported here as its result. The mystical importance given to the number nine by the Mongols is also reported by Marco Polo.

97/27 *his lettres*: the first inscription given here is perhaps derived from letters sent by the khans to the West, such as that from Guyuk Khan to Innocent IV in November 1246 which reads, in translation from the Persian, 'We by the power of the eternal Tengri universal khan of the great Mongol Ulus—our command': *Revue de l'Orient Chrétien* III (1922–3), nos. 1 and 2. Carpini reports the second inscription without *sigillum* as the style of letters (not the seal, as here) and the third as the seal. 'Mandeville' introduces the Western usage of great and privy seals.

98/10 *God allemyghty*: the Mongols allowed religious liberty to all faiths, but this tolerance did not embrace a belief in Christianity except in individual converts and the shamanist followers of Nestorian cults. Though Haiton, who arrived at the Mongol Court in September 1254 two months after Rubruck's departure, claimed that Mongke Khan was baptised by a bishop in his embassy, this is very doubtful. See Rubruck pp. 21–4.

98/16 *foure tymes*: Odoric (p. 479), to whom 'Mandeville' here returns, does say *quatuor magna festa* but describes only two, which is the proper number as Marco Polo attests (pp. 82–3), the khan's birthday and the beginning of the Mongol year on 1 February. Circumcision was unknown to the Mongols and since it is improbable that Odoric was so grossly misinformed, the error is perhaps due to a scribal misreading of *circuitus anni* or some such phrase as *circumcisionis* in an abbreviated form. Alternatively, Odoric may have used the Christian feast of the circumcision on 1 January as a phrase to describe the beginning of the Mongol year; cf. Pipino's version of Marco Polo (p. 89), *in die vero kalendarum februarii die scilicet primo anni sed in tartarorum computacione*. The naming of the two other feasts here is not the invention of 'Mandeville'; though the French Odoric (Cordier p. 378) has only *et les ii. autres pour son ydole*, some Latin manuscripts of Oderic (e.g. BL MS. Arundel 13 and Hakluyt's copy-text) name the four feasts.

98/26 *camocas*: Persian *kamkhā* 'damasked silk', a highly prized fabric, different from *camlet*, Arabic *khamlat* 'nap, pile', woven from hair of goat or camel. See Pelliot I. 143–50.

99/8 *philosofris*: i.e. the shamans, astrologers, and soothsayers also reported by Marco Polo. 'Mandeville' adds the list of their specialities.

101/18 *phisicyans*: Odoric (Cordier p. 371) numbers the physicians as 300 idolators, eight Christians, and seven Saracens. The khan's trust in the Christian physicians is an addition by 'Mandeville'.

101/26 *pylour of gold*: the pillar and the carbuncle, a ruby believed to emit light in darkness, are added by 'Mandeville' from the *Letter of Prester John*, perhaps with the ruby of the king of Ceylon in mind. Cf. note to 85/23 above.

102/4 *Saduz*: i.e. the Mongol *shang-tu* 'upper court', the summer residence of Kublai Khan and the modern Xanadu, lay north-east of *Chamathlac*, i.e. the Mongol *khan-baliq* 'city of the khan', which was largely replaced by *ta-tu* 'great court' built by Kublai Khan in 1267.

103/23–107/28 *In his lond*: the rest of this chapter on the customs of the Mongols is taken from Carpini with one addition from Odoric concerning Prester John's daughter. Odoric (p. 483) says that Prester John always marries the daughter of the Great Khan. The basis of this claim is that Genghiz Khan married the niece of the Nestorian Wang khan of the Keraits (d. 1203) after his conquest of the Keraits, and that Tulai, the youngest son of Genghiz Khan, married another niece, the Christian Sorghaqtani who became the mother of Mongke Khan and so an important figure (named by Carpini). *Tyak Chan* is Kuyuk Khan, visited by Carpini in 1247. Carpini lists only males of the dynasty apart from Sorghaqtani. *Baruch Chan* and *Charauk Chan* are Burakchin and Turakina, the second and third wives of Ogatai Khan (d. 1241), son of Genghiz and father of Kuyuk and brother of Tulai, and they are named in a somewhat confused context by Simon of Saint-Quentin, a member of the papal embassy in 1247, whose account is incorporated with Carpini's by Vincent of Beavais, *Spec. Hist.* XXXI–

XLII. The identification of Prester John with the khan of the Keraits is made by Odoric (p. 483) who adds *de quo non est centesima pars eius quod quasi pro certo dicitur de ipso*, cf. Rubruck p. 122.

105/3 *melk of meris*: called *kemis* by Marco Polo and *comos* by Rubruck who describes its preparation (pp. 81–2), from Mongol *qumiz* or *qimiz*. The nobles drank the clear fermentation and inferiors the dregs. Cf. *airag* and *arkhi*, modern Mongol terms for the fermented and distilled products of mare's milk.

105/21 *þe deeþ*: the funereal customs of the Mongols, including the account of the death of the Great Khan, is taken from Vincent, *Spec. Hist.* XXXI. 86 (p. 1214), and the account of the election of a new khan from XXXI. 32 where Vincent follows Simon of Saint-Quentin's description of Kuyuk's election in 1246. 'Mandeville' conflates this account with Haiton's description of the election of Genghiz in 1206 by the *seuen kyndes* (listed above at 95/14 note).

106/25 *lond of Catay*: 'Mandeville' now summarizes Haiton's Book I, a geographical survey of 15 countries of Asia, to which he adds only the final paragraph on *Ethiope* at 110/18.

106/26 *Trachie*: Haiton's *Tarsa*, the land of the Uighurs, which he identifies with the biblical Tarshish, traditionally the city of the Magi (Psalm 72: 10). Haiton's uncle Sempad reported after his visit to Karakorum in 1247 that some among the Tanguts, presumably the Uighars, were descended from the Magi, thus apparently confirming the identification: H. Yule, *Cathay and the Way Thither*, rev. H. Cordier (London, 1915), I. 162.

107/1 *Corasyne*: i.e. Persian *Kharizm* 'lowland', between the Aral and the Caspian Seas. The city of Kwarizm was rebuilt by the Mongols to replace Urghendj (on the old course of the Oxus, north-west of Khiva) which they destroyed in 1221.

107/3 *Comayn*: the land of the great steppe north of the Black and Caspian Seas. The river *Ethel* is the Volga.

107/14 *see Occyan*: properly the Great Sea, otherwise the Black Sea of which *Maure* is the Greek name from μαῦρος 'black'. See note to 64/17 above.

107/19 *Port de Feare*: properly *le pont de fer* 'iron bridge', the great gate which according to legend Alexander built at *Berbent* (otherwise Persian *darbend* 'barrier') to shut out the tribes of Gog and Magog. See A. R. Anderson, *Alexander's Gate, Gog and Magog and the Inclosed Nations* (Cambridge, Mass., 1932). But the city and the wall which guard the pass into Persia through the Caucasus were built by the emperor Khusrau I Anoshirwan (d. 579), not Alexander. *Sarachie* (confused by reference to *Ararach*, otherwise Mount Ararat, mentioned by Haiton after he has named Tabriz as the principal city of the region) is Sarai, city of the Golden Horde.

108/2–18 *Now haue I tolde ȝow*: 'Mandeville' interpolates this paragraph before resuming his summary of Haiton with the account of Persia. There are some differences. Haiton does not mention Turkestan here and says that the kingdom stretches northwards (not westwards) to the Caspian. He names Bukhara and Samarkand as the principal cities, both sacked by Genghiz Khan in 1220. He calls the Oxus here the *Physon* (which 'Mandeville' elsewhere calls the Ganges) and names Nishapur and Isphahan but not *Sarmasse*. This is probably not the royal city of Shiraz but a relic of an earlier corruption in the French text of Haiton used by 'Mandeville', cf. *Sarachie* at 107/19. See A. Gabriel, *Marco Polo in Persien* (Vienna, 1963).

108/30 *Cordynz*: i.e. Kurds. The two cities are Shiraz and Kermanshah, called Qurmissin by the Arabs. But Shiraz is not in Media, being roughly 400 miles south-east of Kermanshah. The vagueness of medieval geography permits Haiton, generally an accurate recorder, such latitude.

109/2–110/6 *Abyor*: i.e. Mount El'brus in the western Caucasus. The kingdoms are Abazia and Georgia, and the legend of the land of darkness called *Hamsem* by Haiton probably refers to Hamschen or Hampasi, a district between the Black Sea and the Balkhar Dagh mountains. Haiton specifies that the *olde stories* are histories of Armenia, and that *Saures* is the Persian emperor and persecutor of Christians, Shapur II (d. 379). The great plain of *Megoun* is the steppe of Mūghān, west of the Caspian and lying about the lower course of the river Kur, and the darkness which Haiton experienced was possibly a seasonal fog. Many similar tales of lands of darkness occur, ultimately based on accounts of the Arctic night; see Pelliot II. 621. The biblical quotation at 110/2 is Psalm 118: 23.

110/8 *cuntreez*: the provinces of Turkey reported by Haiton are in their uncorrupted forms Cappadocia, Isauria, Phrygia, Lydia, Bithynia, Pontus.

110/12 *Meselle*: i.e. Mosul, on the Tigris. The city on the Euphrates is Edessa, called *Ruha* by the Arabs and *Rages* by the crusaders. The two mountains are Mount Sinjar, west of Mosul, near the modern Zenjan on the caravan route to Tabriz, and an unidentified peak in the Djar-Bakr range along the upper Tigris. Their mention concludes the dependence on Haiton, the following definition of 'Ethiope' being added by 'Mandeville'. Cf. note to 106/25 above.

111/3 *Caldilhe*: *Cadelis* in Odoric (p. 482) and *Cauli* in Marco Polo (p. 69) is the medieval Kao-li, now Korea. Odoric did not see the *pepones* 'gourds' himself, being told of them by *personis fide dignis*. For the legend see H. Lee, *The Vegetable Lamb of Tartary* (London, 1887). The barnacle geese are an Irish myth reported in Vincent, *Spec. Nat.* XVI. 40 (col. 1181) and possibly told to Odoric by his Irish companion Brother James. The myth was rejected by Albertus Magnus (d. 1280), *De animalibus*. The following paragraph of exotic spices and huge grapes is taken from De Vitry (p. 1099).

111/17 *Vber*: the classical *ubera Aquilonis* 'breasts of the North Wind', otherwise the Caucasus, where Alexander the Great allegedly imprisoned the ten tribes of Israel. 'Mandeville' combines the accounts in De Vitry (p. 1096) and Vincent, *Spec. Hist.* IV. 43 and adds from *Mirabilia mundi* the story of the fox. See A. R. Anderson, op. cit. in note to 107/19 above and *Viator* 22 (1991) 162. The coming of Antichrist was sometimes foreseen in the Mongol invasions.

112/5 *queene of Ermonye*: properly queen of the Amazons. Cf. note to 68/17 above. She is the classical Penthesilea, named Pencesolya in Von Diemeringen's German translation of *Mandeville's Travels*.

112/29 *Bakarie*: i.e. Bactria. The wool-bearing trees and the monsters are part of the Alexander legend, severally reported by De Vitry (p. 1100), Vincent, *Spec. Nat.* XVI. 90 (col. 1210), and the *Epistola Alexandri de situ Indie* (pp. 29, 55).

113/16 *Prestre Ioon*: the legends of Prester John have two strands, the older and perhaps original myth of *ya Ethiopia Negus* 'emperor of Ethiopia' and the myth of the Christian ruler of Central Asia. For 'Mandeville' Prester John is the lord of Central Asia. In this function Prester John is first reported by Otto von Freisingen, *Chronicle* before 1158. His informant was the Syrian bishop of Gabala who claimed that Prester John had won a victory over Medes and Persians; in fact, the victory of the Turkish khan Ye-lu-ta-shih (emperor of Qara-Khitan founded *c.*1125) in 1141 over the Seljük sultan Sanjar, the paramount ruler in south-western Asia. On 27 September 1177 Pope Alexander III wrote to Prester John whose existence had apparently been authenticated by the fabulous *Letter of Prester John*, a forgery in circulation by *c.*1165, which describes him as the Christian ruler of the three Indias and of immense power and wealth. This forged *Letter of Prester John* is the main source used by 'Mandeville' in his description of this prince. He was, more precisely, identified with the khan of the Keraits by Rubruck (pp. 122–3) and Odoric (p. 483) who both report that the reality did not match the legend; see note to 103/23 above.

113/22 *Pentoxore*: a scribal distortion of *prestre Iehan* which in several manuscripts of Odoric (Cordier, p. 433 note *g*) has an earlier form as *Pretezoan* with many variants. The name *Penthexoire*, of which this form is a variant, recurs only in Jean le Long's translation of Odoric and in two Latin manuscripts (Wolfenbüttel MS 41, Bremen Stadtbibliothek MS b. 2) which were affiliated to le Long's Latin base.

113/22 *Nyse*: apparently *Suse*, named at 117/4 and in the *Letter* (p. 920) as the palace of Prester John. As Odoric reports (p. 417), this was the capital city of the Persian kings from Cyrus onwards. Its ruins, about 3 miles in circumference, are still visible at Sus on the river Choaspes north of the Persian Gulf. Once the biblical Shushan and the southern terminus of the

Royal Road of the Persians, when 'Mandeville' wrote it was the seat of a Nestorian bishop (as the *Letter* reports in grandiose terms). Later, at 118/19–20 'Mandeville' distinguishes two cities, *Nise* and *Suse*. Nysa, an Indian city visited by Alexander, is probably there confounded with the royal palace at Nishapur; see note to 108/2.

113/24–114/11 *many kynges*: the *Letter* reports 72 kings under his dominion, but otherwise 'Mandeville' concocts these reasons for the lack of contact with Prester John's empire. The dangers of the *adamaunde* are repeated from Odoric; see note to 72/26. Since the sea that washes the fabulous empire of Prester John must itself be fabulous, the *yle of treez* has no identifiable location. Both Odoric and Marco Polo report the nail-less ships at Ormuz in the Gulf. The growths are probably in origin the tangled trees and roots in tropical rivers or even the *sudd*, floating vegetation in the upper Nile which impedes navigation.

114/19–115/4 *Hermes*: i.e. Ormuz, previously reported at 72/16. The absurd founding by Hermes Trismegistos is recorded by Haiton, who also mentions *Soboth* (i.e. Cambay, north-west of Bombay) and the *papyniayes*. These birds are parrots, of which *pystake* is merely the Greek ψιττακός. The marriage alliance between Prester John and the Great Khan is repeated from Odoric (p. 483); see note to 103/23 above.

115/9 *cristene*: in the *Letter* Prester John asserts that he is a zealous Christian and is served by the Patriarch of St Thomas, the *protopapaten* of Samarkand, and the *archprotopapaten* of Susa. The widespread existence of the Nestorian Church in the Turkish and Mongolian lands is not in doubt; the Christian chronicler Bar Hebraeus (d. 1286) reports that the majority of the Kerait tribe had been baptised in 1007/8. But this Christianity was always nominal, and all the accounts of the friars (Carpini, Rubruck, Odoric) stress the degeneration of their practice and belief to levels of barbarism. See Rubruck pp. 22–4, and C. F. Beckingham and B. Hamilton (eds.), *Prester John, the Mongols, and the Ten Lost Tribes* (Aldershot, 1996). From this point 'Mandeville' follows the *Letter of Prester John* closely; see R. Hennig, *Terrae Incognitae* (Leiden, 1950), II. 438–41, 499–512.

115/16 *grete grauely see*: otherwise called the Sea of Sand, this phenomenon is widely reported, by Odoric (p. 419) among others as being one day's journey from Yezd, cf. note to 20/18 above. It has a stark reality, being the Takla Makan desert, a wilderness of pure sand extending 600 miles from east to west and 250 miles north to south and having dunes over 300 feet in height. It was the major hazard on the old caravan route of 'the Silk Road' after the merchants passed through the Great Wall at Jiuquan *en route* to Kashgar and the outer limits of the Persian empire. North of the desert is the mountain range of Tien Shan, and south that of Kunlun Shan. Both ranges have a high rainfall, supplying oases at their bases and so making the route passable. In that way the rivers from the mountain valleys do disappear into the sand, and the major water-course the Tarim at the foot of the Tien Shan is often dry. The other details reported here are fabulous: the edible fish, the river from Paradise named the Indus in some versions of the *Letter*, the precious stones, the regular torrent.

116/4 *treez*: the miraculous trees are part of the Alexandrine legend and are reported by De Vitry (p. 1100). 'Mandeville' may have found them and the horned wild men in his copy of the *Letter* (which attracted many interpolations). The fruit are of faery, not iron; a copyist has mistaken *faerie* as *fer*.

117/17 *septoun*: another scribal confusion. 'Mandeville' wrote *ly septisme . . . est de crisolite* (ed. Warner 136/33). Earlier in the list *dyasper* is a scribal invention, cf. *iaspre vert diaspre* 'deep green jasper'.

118/22 *Catolonabes*: properly *Sheikh-ul-Jibal* 'chief of the mountain'. 'Mandeville' takes this fable of the Old Man of the Mountains from Odoric (p. 488) who sites it in *Millistorte* adjacent to the empire of Prester John. Odoric's name is ultimately from the Arabic *mulāhidah* 'heretics'; see Pelliot I. 785. Hasan i Sabbah broke away from orthodox Islam in 1096 and established his murderous sect at Alamut in the El'brus mountains. The power of the Assassins in Persia was broken by Hulagu in 1256 and in Syria by Baibars in 1273 by the destruction of the mountain fortresses. See B. Lewis, *The Assassins. A radical sect in Islam* (London, 1967). 'Mandeville' considerably embellishes Odoric's description of this earthly Paradise with a richness akin to the *Letter of Prester John*. The *maner of drinke* at 119/23 was in fact the drug hashish, whence the Assassins acquired their European name.

120/15 *valey enchaunted*: 'Mandeville' takes this marvel from Odoric (pp. 491–2) and, as with the story of the Assassins, inflates it with his fantasies. Stories of demons met by travellers in Central Asia are known from the seventh century and have some basis in the awesome sounds of desert winds and the bones of pack animals who died along the caravan routes. All the friars who journeyed to the Great Khan report such tales and experiences. Carpini mentions the skulls and bones lying on the ground like cattle-dung as he passes through the lands of the Qangli and the Cumans (pp. 112–13, cf. Rubruck pp. 128–9); his remarks echo those of the Chinese historian Hsuan-Tsang, *Ta-T'ang-Si-Yu-Ki* 'Memoirs on Western Countries' after 645 that travellers across the Takla Makan desert find nothing to guide them but the bones of beasts and men and the droppings of camels. Rubruck (p. 166) records his experience of such tales when crossing the snow-covered Tarbaghatai range.

Odoric's account is altogether more colourful, *aliud terribile magnum ego vidi*, possibly tinged by memories of terror and fantasies. His valley is seven or eight *milliaria* in length with a river of 'delights', no man who enters lives, it is full of noise and bones of the dead, there is a crag resembling a fearsome human face (perhaps a Buddha sculpted in rock), and from the top of a sand dune he could see vast quantities of gold and silver which were the illusions of devils. He mentions no place but since he was then somewhere in Tartary his adventure is likely to have been in a valley leading down to 'the Silk Road' as it crosses the Takla Makan desert. His *flumen deliciarum* is presumably a translation or distortion of a local name for that river valley. Tombs and pictographs are found in Mongolia. In summer the Orkan valley, on the upper reaches of which Genghiz Khan established Karakorum, has pasture, flowers, and sweet water, and T. Severin, *In search of Genghis Khan* (London, 1993) p. 127 reports an ancient graveyard of collapsed and robbed tombs in a side valley of the Orkan within a day's ride of Karakorum (visited by Marco Polo but not by Oderic).

Among the more imaginative details added by 'Mandeville' to Odoric's description are the entry to Hell, the features of the devil's face, the loss of four companions, and the inclusion of *ii. frere Menours of Lumbardy* in the company. This last reference to Odoric and his Irish companion Fr James is inspired to deflect any suspicion of forgery in a reader of Odoric. The melodramatic inflation of this account exceeds anything else in the book.

122/4–17 *biȝonde þat valey*: 'Mandeville' here begins a catalogue of monstrous and marvellous peoples, copied largely from Vincent but with several other sources, whose placing at this point depends on their location within the empire of Prester John. The giants are found in the *Epistola Alexandri* (p. 41) 24 cubits tall, and in Vincent, *Spec. Hist.* IV. 15 (col. 2392, where the source is the *Epistola*) 33 cubits tall, and are called the *Ichthyophagi*. Neither reports the long-tailed sheep (*ovis laticaudata*) recorded by Marco Polo in Kerman and perhaps here confused with the yak recorded by Odoric.

122/15 *preciouse stonus*: properly *pupillas geminas* 'double pupils' which became *gemmas* in the manuscript of Vincent, *Spec. Nat.* XXXI. 124 (col. 2391) used by 'Mandeville'. The women are the Bithiae of Scythia.

122/22 *gadlibiriens*: properly the Augylae in Libya reported by Vincent, *Spec. Hist.* I. 88 (p. 33). 'Mandeville' wrote *Cadebiriz* (ed. Warner 140/47), and a previous sequence of scribal variation *Augyles–Cagiles–Cadiles–Cadibes* is well within the possibilities of transmission. Vincent took his account from Solinus XXXI. 34 who misreported Herodotus IV. 172; the last records the practice of the Nasamones who visit the Libyan oasis of Augila and share the favours of the bride among the wedding guests. In the same paragraph Vincent describes the snake-eating troglodytes. 'Mandeville' has conflated and embellished these two accounts into a unique fantasy and glossed the scribal distortion *Cadebiriz* as a French word *cassecous* 'foolhardy persons' instead of the vulgar *cuintebrise* or *quadebrise*. Marco Polo (pp. 112, 115 in Pipino's version) reports two similar tales: in the province of Kain-du men offer their womenfolk to strangers, and in Tibet virgins are offered to travellers before they are married.

123/6 *Anoþer yle*: the women who weep at birth, ultimately the Thracians of Herodotus V. 5, and the king chosen by election, ultimately a ruler of Ceylon reported by Pliny VI. 89, are taken from Vincent, *Spec. Hist.* I. 89.

123/30 *grete plente of folk*: the ancient Britons reported by Caesar, *De bello gallico* V. 12, 14, whom 'Mandeville' found in Vincent, *Spec. Hist.* I. 91 without recognizing their identity.

124/10–31 *cokadrylles*: the catalogue of beasts which begins here has several sources. The crocodile is reported by Vincent, *Spec. Nat.* XVII. 106 (col. 1302). The cotton shrub is described by De Vitry (p. 1099). The giraffe, Arabic *zarāfa*, found only in Africa, is recorded by Vincent, *Spec. Nat.* XIX. 9 but the name *girsant* is taken from Boldensele's *jiraffan* (p. 40). The chameleon is also found in Vincent, *Spec. Nat.* XIX, 6 (col. 1386). The spotted swine and the white lions are reported by Vincent, *Spec. Hist.* IV. 5 (p. 132), where the rhinoceros is called *odontatyrannum* in a description taken from the *Epistola Alexandri*; the two forms here *lonhorans* and *toutes* are corrupt variants of the single name. 'Mandeville' reports all these beasts without embellishment.

125/1–126/8 *anoþer yle goode and grete*: the land of Brahmans is reported by Vincent, *Spec. Hist.* IV. 66–71. 'Mandeville' may also have used the *Epistola Alexandri* and De Vitry (p. 1108) and the *Historia de proeliis* (Loeb ed., p. 223). The river *Thebe* is the classical *Tiberoboam* (called *Tabobenus* in the *Historia*), otherwise the Hydaspes, which marked the eastern limit of Alexander's invasion of India. The letters which allegedly passed between him and Dindymus the Brahman ruler, reported by Vincent, are part of the Alexandrine legend.

126/9–127/13 *Synople*: the land of the *Gymnosophistae*, the Greek term for the Brahmans, adjacent to the land of the *Oxydracae* in the Punjab who opposed Alexander's invasion. De Vitry (p. 1108), Vincent loc. cit., and the *Historia* loc. cit. report their exchange with Alexander. De Vitry makes them one people. As with earlier claims, the final paragraph extolling the virtuous pagans (supported by quotation of Hosea 8: 12, John 10: 16, Acts 10: 15) is added by 'Mandeville'. See G. Cary, *The Medieval Alexander* (Cambridge, 1956), pp. 91–5.

127/14 *alle feþeris*: the translator's French text read *toutz pennez* instead of the better *toutz pelluz* 'all rough' (ed. Warner 147/31). These wild men are reported by Vincent, *Spec. Hist.* IV. 55, which follows the account of the Ichthyophagi in the *Epistola Alexandri*. Cf. note to 122/4 above.

127/18–29 *Renemare*: properly the Buemar in India by which Alexander camped after he had seen the golden idols of Hercules and Liber, which is reported by Vincent loc. cit., again following the *Epistola Alexandri*. 'Mandeville' applies to the river the breadth of the camp. The same source records the legend of the trees of the Sun and the Moon which foretold Alexander's death by poison in Babylon, first recorded in the Pseudo-Callisthenes *c.* AD 200. The wild beasts which allegedly prevented 'Mandeville' and his companions from visiting these trees are also in Vincent and the *Epistola*, but the elephants there are white and red (not blue).

127/30 *Pytan*: properly the land of the Trispithami recorded by Vincent, *Spec. Hist.* I. 93, who are ultimately the Astomi of Pliny VII. 25 inhabiting the upper reaches of the Ganges. 'Mandeville' has conflated them with the Pygmaei described by Vincent immediately afterwards. Cf. note to 91/5 above.

128/10 *Prestre Ioon*: this account of the origin of Prester John's name has no known source and is probably an embellishment by 'Mandeville' of the explanation of the style given in the *Letter of Prester John* (p. 924). The name appears to pre-date its appearance in the West before 1158 (see note to 113/16 above), and in early Portuguese reports of the emperor of Ethiopia has the form *Preciosus Ioannes*. The last part of this style is thought to be the Amharic *žan* 'lord'; see M. C. Marinescu, 'Le Prêtre Jean. Son pays. Explication de son nom', *Bulletin de la section historique de l'Académie Roumaine* 10 (1923), 73–112.

128/27 *many cristen men*: i.e. Nestorians. Cf. note to 115/9 above, and Rubruck pp. 22–4. Nestorius was condemned at the Council of Ephesus in 430, and thereafter the practices of his followers in the Persian empire and beyond developed differently from those of the Roman and Orthodox Greek churches.

129/8 *Tabrobane*: i.e. Ceylon, as described by Vincent, *Spec. Hist.* I. 79 (p. 28). 'Mandeville' does not recognize that he has already described the country as *Sylha* following Odoric, who followed Marco Polo. See note to 87/20 above. Vincent's source is ultimately Pliny VI. 79–89, and the name is derived from Sanskrit *Tamraparni*.

129/17 *Orelle and Argete*: the fabulous mineral isles of Chryse and Argyre, reported by Vincent, loc. cit., who follows Pliny VI. 80. The reference to Canopus there (VI. 87) was part of the report by a Ceylonese embassy to Rome which has been distorted in transmission. Canopus, the brightest star in the sky after Sirius, is not visible above 37° North (i.e. visible at

Alexandria but not at Athens) and does not eclipse the other stars. Cf. note to 77/26 above. 'Mandeville' fails to recognize that he has already reported this star as the *Anteryke* in discussing the rotundity of the world.

129/21 *hulle of gold*: the legend is reported by Vincent, *Spec. Nat.* XX. 134, ultimately from Herodotus III. 102. It has a factual basis. In the Karakoram mountains between India and Pakistan marmots (*Arctomys Himalayanas*, called 'mountain ants' in Persian) burrow to a depth of three feet to a gold-bearing stratum of sand and throw up the spoil, which the local Minaro people still refine.

130/14 *derk lond*: presumably a reference to the Arctic winter reported by Marco Polo and others, but the geography is a confusion. The east at the beginning of the earth suggests a flat world (perhaps taken from an early source), which is then confounded with the east of geography and the rotundity of the world which 'Mandeville' has emphatically endorsed earlier, cf. note to 81/20 above.

130/24–131/21 *wise men*: as at 81/20, these are the authorities from which 'Mandeville' takes his description, viz. Comestor (col. 1067), De Vitry (p. 1098), Vincent, *Spec. Hist.* I. 63, Isidore XIV. 3. 2. The last reports that the wall of Paradise is of fire, and the moss here is either an alteration of the type 'Mandeville' frequently makes for greater verisimilitude or the result of an earlier scribal distortion. All these authorities report the four floods of Earthly Paradise (which ultimately depend on Genesis 2: 10) and explain the northward flow of the Nile as a subterranean diversion. The explanation of the names of the rivers is fanciful, including the king *Gangeras* who is ultimately Gundoforus king of the Indians reported in the *Letter of Prester John* (p. 917).

131/22 *no man lyuynge*: the difficulties of reaching Earthly Paradise were commonly seen as insurmountable in the Middle Ages. Cf. the *Iter Alexandri ad Paradisum*, ed. J. Zacher (Ratisbon, 1859), pp. 20–1 and M. Lascelles, 'Alexander and the Earthly Paradise', *Medium Aevum* 5 (1936), 31–41. The report of the fierceness of the waters may owe something to the cataracts of the Nile which supposedly in some accounts led to an Earthly Paradise located in 'Ethiope'.

132/9 *Cassoun*: Odoric's *Cassan* (p. 484) and Marco Polo's *Kenjanfu*, cf. the Arabic *Kenchan*, which denotes the city of Si-nganfu and the province of Shensi under its government. Odoric follows Marco Polo closely. See Pelliot II. 814. Polo says that the governor (not the king) was Mangkola, the third son of Kublai (d. 1294), for whom see M. Rossabi, *Khubilai Khan. His life and times* (Berkeley, 1988).

132/20 *Ryboth*: Odoric's *Tibot* (p. 484), i.e. Tibet. Though Odoric claims to have visited the country, his account is dependent on others (though not, in this instance, on Marco Polo pp. 112–14). See B. Laufer, 'Was Odoric of Pordenone ever in Tibet?', *T'oung-Pao* 15 (1914), 405–18. The principal city is Lhasa and is accurately described. The country does not, however, produce wine or corn, and the use of tents and the avoidance of blood-letting are Tartar customs. The *Lobassy* is perhaps Persian *bakhshi* 'mendicant' (whence modern *bakhsheesh*) and so 'Buddhist monk'. Cf. Tibetan *gya-tso* (Mongol *ta-le*, whence modern *dalai*) 'ocean' and so 'universal' and the Tibetan title *'p'ags-pa* 'eminent one' which distinguished the Sa-skya hierarchs who ruled Tibet 1270–1340 after Kublai Khan installed Pags-pa Gya-tso 'universal eminent one' as sovereign lama; the style *dalai lama* and the belief in priestly re-incarnation were adopted after 1476. The Tibetan treatment of the dead father is reported by Carpini (pp. 60–1) and Rubruck (p. 158) and perhaps reflects the use of the human skull in lamaist rituals.

133/27–134/19 *a grete kyngdome*: Odoric (p. 486) merely reports that while he was in Manzi he passed the palace of a rich man whose sybaritic life was a wonder, and that he was one of four such men in the province. Odoric here follows Marco Polo's description of the *faghfür* 'emperor' of China (cf. Arabic *facfur* and Persian *baghbur* 'son of heaven', the Chinese imperial title) before the Tartar conquest in 1276 whom he identifies as one of the nine (not four) viceroys of the Great Khan. He adds the details of the palace and the long fingernails of the wealthy and the bound feet of their ladies. Marco Polo's *faghfür* in 1269 was the Sung emperor Tu-tsong, generally regarded by Chinese historians as a tyrant.

134/24–135/18 *God of kynde*: 'Mandeville' reverts to his ideas about the essential piety of the Tartars and their subjects, which perhaps reflects some awareness of their religious tolerance of other faiths and their worship of the single god Tengri. The imperfect knowledge of the Bible and the Trinity is specifically related to the Nestorians. The *two manere of aungels* are καλόν 'good' and κακόν 'evil', and 'Mandeville' may have had in mind the Platonic term *cachodemon* which was revived by William of Conches, *Philosophia* (PL 90. 1131), and was used by Vincent and other major encyclopaedists in their discussion of angels.

136/5 *hamwarde to Rome*: this interpolated story of submission of the book to the Pope at Rome occurs only in the Defective Version and its conflations and in one Latin manuscript written in England, printed in the *Bodley Version of Mandeville's Travels*, EETS OS 253 (1963), p. 175. Since the Pope did not return to Rome from Avignon until 1377, 'Mandeville' could not have written it *c.*1356. Papal approval was a common claim for authenticity, used by Haiton among others, and the anachronism suggests that the English translation was made some years after 1377; the alleged signs of French origin in the expanded passage in the Cotton conflation *c.*1400, reported by K. Sisam, *Fourteenth Century Verse and Prose* (Oxford, 1921), pp. 239–40, are very doubtful. The *book vpon Latyn* which the English translator mentions was possibly Higden's *Polychronicon*, the most respected 'authority' in England at that time and cited in the Latin interpolation *c.*1485 but rare on the Continent. The term *mappa mundi*, like that at Hereford Cathedral *c.*1330, was also used for a book containing maps with descriptive matter, like that presented to the Pope in 1321; see C. Kretschmer, *Die Weltkarte der Vatican* (Berlin, 1891) and BL MS Additional 27376. Both references suggest that the English interpolator was an educated man, possibly aware of the world-map which Higden added to his chronicle *c.*1350. *Mappemondes, A.D. 1200–1500*, Monumenta Cartographica Vetustioris Aevi (Amsterdam, 1964) catalogues all medieval world maps known to be extant. By a teasing coincidence Jean le Long, elected abbot of St Bertin 24 March 1365, met Urban V (d.1370) at Avignon.

136/26 *Explicit Iohannes Maundeuyle*: it is now possible to extend the conclusions of *Sir John Mandeville* (Aldershot, 1993) pp. 23–24 in these directions:

1. The Continental Version is the original version, of which Biblioteca Trivulziana MS. 816 (dated 1396) is a good copy. The Insular Version derives from a copy of the Continental Version carried into England *c.*1365.
2. the author was a Benedictine and probably studied at Paris (like Jean le Long *c.* 1345) where he had the opportunity to learn of the translations of Odoric, the Carpini extracts in Vincent, and the *Directorium* of Jean de Vignay (d. *c.*1342) and the cosmographical treatises and theories then current.
3. detailed analyses of the ways in which the author adapted his sources (especially Boldensele and Odoric in Jean le Long's translation) reveal the nature of the book.

These conclusions are explored in *Mandeville Matters* (forthcoming).

# TEXTUAL COMMENTARY

Here are recorded readings from the Insular Version which reveal the origins of the Middle English translation known as the Defective Version and explain some of its cruces. Also noted here are some Middle English readings which may be due to a scribe and not the translator.

The Insular Version is extant in twenty-three manuscripts classifiable into three subgroups: see *Scriptorium* 18 (1964), 38–54. It is edited by G. F. Warner, *The Buke of Iohn Maundeuill*, Roxburghe Club (Westminster, 1889), who prints his text from subgroup 1 and adds collations from one manuscript from both subgroups 2 and 3. It is evident, from readings cited below which are marked by an initial asterisk, that the Middle English translator used a manuscript more closely related to subgroup 2, which did not have the variant readings of subgroup 1 and subgroup 3; the last developed in France in or before 1402 and is excluded by time and place as well as its textual variations from a direct relationship to the Defective Version, though its lost common ancestor was affiliated to subgroup 2.

It is equally evident that none of the four manuscripts of subgroup 2 now extant nor any of the lost manuscripts of that subgroup which lie behind the three Latin translations known as the Harley, Ashmole, and Leiden Versions was a close affiliate of the translator's Insular manuscript. Quite apart from the crucial absences of the 'Egypt Gap' and the story of the book's submission to the Pope at Rome (absences common to all Insular manuscripts), several minor variant readings in these four manuscripts do not correspond with the Middle English translation. These four manuscripts have two independent lines of descent from their common ancestor. First, Bodleian MS Addition C 280 and BL MS Sloane 1464 (which lacks Warner's text 141/44–142/43). Secondly, Leiden MS Vossius Latin F 75 and BL MS Sloane 560 (which lacks Warner's text 27/26–53/32, 64/37–68/38, 146/36–151/32 due to loss of leaves after ff. 13, 18, 52). Overall, the Middle English translation reflects more closely the text of the first pair, but some forms of exotic names and occasional variant readings elsewhere reflect the text of the second pair. It would therefore appear that the translator's manuscript was superior in the scribal tradition of subgroup 2 to any of the four extant manuscripts of that subgroup.

In this Commentary these sigils are used for the Insular manuscripts and edition:

S MS Sloane 1464 (also Warner's S, lacks 1 leaf)
T MS Addition C 280
U MS Sloane 560 (16 leaves lost)

V MS Vossius Latin F 75
W Warner's edition
Z the hypothetical manuscript of the translator.

Z is not invoked when the relevant reading is extant, and the readings of S, T, U, V are not cited when they agree with the citation of W's printed text. An asterisk after f. indicates that the relevant folio is lost. In this Commentary 'subgroup' always refers to the Insular text unless preceded by 'ME'. The direction 'See note' refers to an entry in the literary Commentary. Many of the ME readings and omissions cited below could have arisen within the Insular or Defective scribal traditions, especially those of roman numerals, forms of exotic names, omissions by eyeskip, and simple errors like *cros* alongside *corps* and *la porte* alongside *le port*. Because the Defective Version is an abridged translation, comment is limited to the ME words and phrases of its printed text and does not comprehend the numerous omissions of words, phrases, clauses, and sentences in the more extensive Insular Version unless they impinge directly on the ME text.

5/9 *two and þirty*: cf. *vintisme et secunde* W 3/17, the palmary reading, and note to 136/1 below.

6/15 *ile towun*: Z *male ville*, cf. the better *Malleuille* (now Zemun) W 4/28.

*6/17 *goþ*: *vient* (S f. 4, T f. 16), cf. *gist* (U f. $3^{v}$, V f. $1^{v}$) and the better *naist* 'rises' W 4/29.

*6/30 *ygildid*: *de cupre dorrez* (S f. 4, T f. 16, U f. 16), cf. *couere dor* 'covered with gold' W 435 and V f. $2^{v}$.

7/21 *whiche is here ywrite þus*: not in M of subgroup 1 nor in ME subgroups 2–5 and no equivalent in W. Cf. 9/21 below.

8/1 *cros*: *corps* 'body' W 5/27.

8/26 *foure*: *trois* 'three' W 6/35. The error recurs at 26/18.

8/29–30 *and of þilke . . . saued*: cf. *quant larbre cresseroit et porteroit fruit adonqes serroit son pierre garry* W 6/36–7 (STUV omit *cresseroit et*. V f. 2 omits *fruit*). The translator has paraphrased and expanded his text.

9/19 *þe Iewis*: *Ieneueys* (S f. $6^{v}$, T f. $17^{v}$) and *Ianewys* (U f. $4^{v}$, V f. 4) and *Sanowys* W 6/45, properly the Genoese. A similar error occurs at 15/8.

9/20 *somme of gold*: cf. *bosoigne dargent* 'need of gold' W 6/45 (ST add *qil auoit*).

9/21 *þat is to seie ruysches*: no equivalent in W and only found in ME subgroup 1. Cf. 7/21 above. Perhaps a scribal interpolation.

10/70 *noþer no hows þat hit is ynne*: in W 7/34 this phrase is part of the preceding clause.

11/14 *many oþere*: *mult dautres gentz et la pais de* W 8/34.

12/17 *Ermogynes*: *Hermes* W 9/40. See note.

13/21 *þe grete see*: so ME subgroups 2–5, cf. Egerton Version 10/17 *þe Grekes see*. Either term is possible, cf. W 10/38 *les latins* for the whole clause.

14/2 *priueþ þilke þat beþ worthy*: *priue quant il troeue ascune cause* 'dismisses (them) when he finds any cause' W 10/45.

14/13 *þe ȝate*: *le port* 'the port' W 11/29.

14/15 *Grete*: cf. ME subgroups 2–5 and Egerton Version 10/17 *Greke*. S f. 11 has *la mer vert* (cf. the better *la meer vers* W 11/30). Perhaps the translator wrote *grene*.

*15/7 *Grece*: *Grece* (S f. 12, T f. 20), cf. the better *Crete* W 12/3, and *Dorete* and *de Orete* (U f. 7, V f. 4).

*15/8 *Ionas*: *Ianoais* and *Ionoais* (S. f. 12, T f. 20$^{v}$), cf. *Isaneneys* and *Ianewys* (U f. 7, V f. 4) and the better *Ianeweys* 'Genoese' W 12/37. A similar error occurs at 9/19.

15/27 *kniȝt*: Z *chiualer*, cf. the better *chiual* 'horse' W 12/45.

17/1 *vynes*: *vins* 'wines' W 14/26.

17/4 *by a place*: *deleez la goulf de Cathalie* 'beside the gulf of Satalia' W 14/27. Perhaps the translator is abridging or Z was corrupt.

17/14 *flowe aboute* : Z *reuola* 'flew over', cf. the better *remua* 'shook' W 14/33.

17/30 *Bernard*: *Barnabe* W 14/41.

18/10 *by londe . . . also*: cf. *per meer vers Ierusalem* W 15/34.

18/28 *Saphen oþer Sarepte oþer Sydonis*: *Serphen en Sarepte de Sidoniens* W 15/42, properly *Sarphen que est Sarepta Sydoniorum* of Vincent of Beauvais. S. f. 15, T. f. 22 read *Sarophen ou Sarapte*.

*18/29 *Ionas þe prophete*: *Ionas þe prophete* (S f. 15$^{v}$, T f. 22$^{v}$), cf. *Helyas la prophete la resusita il Ionas le filz a femme veue* 'there the prophet Elias raised Jonas the widow's son' W 15/43.

19/3 *Agenor*: omitted in ME subgroup 1, and ME subgroup 2 has several variants (2A *Ateles*, 2B *Ateldes*, 2H *Achelles*, 2C and 2M *Achilles*). *Agenor* W 15/45 is the palmary reading, with variants S f. 15$^{v}$ *Achens*, T f. 22$^{v}$ *Athans*, U f. 8$^{v}$ and V f. 5 *Achilles*. The Egerton form is *Achilles*, cf. Cotton *Agenor*.

20/23 *þe strong*: *le fort* W 17/20. Since 2C and some manuscripts of ME subgroup 3 read *le fort* (see p. xxi fn. 1 above), the translator may have preserved the French form.

*20/23 *londe*: *terre* (S f. 16$^{v}$, T f. 23$^{v}$, U f. 9$^{v}$, V f. 6) cf. the better *tetre* 'mound' W 17/21.

20/25 *many þousande*: *mult des milers* (S f. 17 and T f. 23v and U f. 9 *muliers*, V f. 5 *millers*) cf. the better *mult des meillours* 'many of the better' W 17/21.

*22/11 *he holdeþ Calaphes*: *il est Califfe* 'he is Caliph' W 18/41. The forms *Caliphes* (S f. 18v, T f. 24v) and *Calaphes* (U f. 9v) occur alongside *Califes* (V f. 5v).

*22/11 *to þe sowdan*: cf. *soudan en lour langage* (S f. 18v, T f. 24v, U f. 9v, V f. 5v) 'sultan in their language'. All manuscripts of subgroup 1 except MS Bodley 841 f. 9v omit *soudan* W 18/41.

22/12 *Roys Yles*: the phrase marks the beginning of the 'Egypt Gap'. Without the lacuna the Insular text reads *est tant a dire come roi Il y soleit auoir v. soudans* 'that is to say king There are five sultans' W 18/42. The first quire of the translator's copy or an ancestor ended *roi Il y s*, the second quire was lost, the third quire began *et est celle vallee mult froide* 'and this valley is very cold' W 32/37. All extant Insular manuscripts avoid this lacuna.

23/25 *vale*: cf. *cite* W 34/29 which places it at *ii. bonnes lieus*, not *xii. myle* from Beersheba. The ME subgroup 1 omits *þe vale of*.

23/29 *þer dwellid geauntis: la habitoient adonques ly geant* 'there dwelt still the giant' W 34/31. But the Continental Version (ed. Letts, p. 263) gives *les Iaians*. See note to 15/8 above.

25/2 *broþer*: *filz au frere* 'nephew' W 35/31. Either Z *frere* or a deliberate correction, cf. Genesis 13: 8, 11, and 14: 14, 16 where Abraham refers to his nephew as 'brother', a hebraism for 'kinsman', cf. ME *cousin*.

25/19 *a perilous way*: Z *chemin perilleux*, cf. the better *chemin par plainz* 'a way through plains' W 35/41.

25/28 *blamed wiþ wrong*: *encouplez a tort* 'falsely accused' W 35/45. An idiomatic translation, cf. Hoccleve, *Complaint of the Virgin* 133.

26/18 *ferþe*: *trois* (S f. 36, T f. 32, U f. *), cf. the better *xiii*me 'thirteenth' W 36/32.

28/13 *Mercaritot*: *Karitot* W 38/35. Perhaps the preceding *seint* was misread as *seme* (such confusion is possible in S f. 39) and thence partly attracted to the proper name. Cf. 2A f. 12 *M'charitot*.

*28/19 *Turkes*: W 38/30 adds *et des Tartariens*, omitted in S f. 39.

28/22 *xl.*: *vii*xx '140' W 38/32.

29/2 *to breke þe ston in pecis oþer poudre*: *prendre de la piere ou piece ou poudre* 'to take either a piece or dust of the stone' W 38/40.

29/11 *þe cros: celle roche* 'this rock' W 38/48. The translator or a scribe has omitted the previous sentence, and the ME reading (not in ME subgroup 1) is uncertain, though it makes good sense.

30/15 *assent*: *le sen* 'the direction' W 39/44.

30/21 *of Constantynople*: *Constantine* W 39/48.

30/22 *bridel*: *frein* 'bit' W 39/48. Perhaps an acceptable translation.

30/26 *vnto wel lowe in Ethiope*: *iusques bien parfonde en Ethiope* (S f. 42 and T. f. 39 *Egipte*, U f. *) 'almost as far as the centre of Ethiopia' W 40/29.

31/3 *þurȝ cristine men*: Z *par cristiens gentz*, cf. the better *par la pruesse de eaux* 'by their bravery' W 40/32.

31/13 *Benet*: *Augustyn* W 40/37.

31/22 *prestis*: *prestres indiens* 'Malabar priests' W 40/40.

*32/12 *Vatyns*: *Vatins* (S f. 43, T f. 40; U f. * and V f. 13 omits the reference), cf. the better *Latins* W 41/26.

32/21 *wiþ his grete seel*: no equivalent in W but perhaps summarizing the sentence W 41/33–6 omitted in translation.

*32/31 *prepoues*: *prepuce* (S f. 44, T f. 40v, U f. *, V f. 13), cf. the corrupt *presente* W 42/28 which appears in all manuscripts of subgroup 1 except MS Bodley 841 f. 22v.

32/32 *kyng Charlis . . . Parys*: *Charles ly chauues . . . Poitiers* (S *Peiters*, T *Peicers*, U*, V *Peyters*) *et puis a Chartres* 'Charles the bald . . . Poitiers and then to Chartres' W 42/28.

33/3 *þat*[2]: *qi* W 42/30. The translator or a scribe has introduced the following *And*, upsetting the syntax.

*34/2 *xxiiii.*: *xxiiii* (S f. 44v, T f. 41), cf. the better *xiii* W 42/43.

34/4 *comeþ*: *entroit* 'used to come' W 42/43.

34/16 *of . . . of*: both prepositions are otiose, presumably carried over by the translator from the preceding phrase *les tables des x. comandementz* W 43/29.

34/23 *iiii. figures and viii. names*: *vii. figures des nouns* 'seven figures of the names' W 43/32.

34/25 *þei hadde*: *il y auoit* 'there was' W 43/34

35/2 *Iacob held stille þe aungel*: *detenoit vn angel Iacob* 'an angel held Jacob still' W 43/36.

35/4 *in þis roche*: *sur celle roche* 'on this rock' W 43/38.

35/27 *set seynt Iame*: *getteront seit Iake* (S f. 46v *Iame*) 'threw Saint James' W 44/31.

36/1 *dwelliþ*: *demorrerent* 'dwelt' W 44/36.

41/4 *a litel cite*: *vne bele cite mes elle est toute destruite et ore nad qe une petite vilette* W 48/47.

42/12 *Alsiled*: *Alfetide* W 50/38. None of the minor scribal variants (S f. 54

*lalfetide*, T f. 47$^{v}$ *daffetide*, U*, V f. 16 *dalfetide*) resembles the ME form which is probably not due to the translator.

42/13 *þe watir is stynkyng*: in the Insular text W 50/39 and in ME subgroups 2–5 the previous paragraph follows. Cf. note to 87/28 below.

*43/18 *in þe entree of*: *entre* 'between' (S f. 56), cf. the better *outre* W 52/30 n. 11. Subgroup 1 omits the sentence.

*43/24 *Real Mount*: *roial Mont* (S f. 56, T f. 48$^{v}$, U*, V f. 16$^{v}$), cf. the corrupt *roialment* 'royally' in some manuscripts of subgroup 1 W 52/37.

*44/9 *Rama*: i.e. Ramah, as in S f. 56$^{v}$. Cf. W 52/42 *Rama et*.

44/17 *it is yclepid Neople*: this repetition of line 14 occurs in W 53/26 and 52/44.

45/17 *Iacobys welle*: *la fontaigne Iol* 'the fountain of Jol' W 54/23, properly the bath of Job.

46/7 *columba*: *coluber* 'serpent' W 54/40.

46/13 *þe Chane of Galile*: *la caue de Galile* 'the cave of Galilee' W 55/26, properly Chana in Galilee. The error recurs in the Wife of Bath's Prologue 11, perhaps copied from here.

*46/30 *þe blood*: *le sang* (S f. 60$^{v}$, T f. 51$^{v}$), cf. the better *le saut* 'the leap' W 56/32.

48/3 *ȝeode oure lorde drie foote*: *sur cel mer passa nostre seigneur* 'on this sea our lord walked' W 57/39.

48/20 *monkes*: *nouns* 'names' W 58/43. Z *moignes*.

50/1 *vndirneþe*: Z *desous*, cf. the better *dessure* 'above' W 60/27.

50/2 *Greguroys*: *Gregeois* 'Greeks' W 60/27.

50/15 *Iosiac*: *Isaac* W 60/37.

50/23 *Gardemarche*: *Sardenak* W 61/30. Manuscripts of ME subgroups 2–5 have *S*- forms like *Sardemarche*, and 2C has a conflated reading *de Sarmany þe which is clepid Gardmarch*.

51/6 *Darke*: *Arke* W 61/43, properly Archas (otherwise Villejargon) on the coast of Syria.

52/11 *lyknes*: *umbres* 'shadows' W 62/44, translated 'cloudes' in Egerton Version. Perhaps the translator here wrote *þyknes*.

52/13 *Cheynay*: *Emaux* W 62/46, i.e. Emmaus.

53/5 *þe Lay*: *le Lay* W 63/37. This confusion of *le lac de Nicaea* and the river Sangarius is apparently inherited from the source, Albert of Aix.

53/6 *Mornaunt*: *Noir Mont* W 63/37, i.e. the Black Mountains of Albert of Aix.

53/7 *þe better*: Z *meliour*, cf. the better *le menour* 'the less' W 63/39.

54/3 *Cambre*: *la Chaunlee* W 64/34, i.e. *Camela* of De Vitry, otherwise the ancient Emessa (modern Homs). Cf. S f. 70, T f. 59 *lachmulos*.

54/6 *þe londe of Flagame*: *la terre de Flagamie* 'the land of Flagam' W 64/36 and *le tor de Flagham*' 'the tower of Flagham' (as in the Continental Version, ed. Letts p. 300), near Haifa, otherwise *le tor de Destroit*.

*55/13 *Gasten*: *Garaston* (S f. 71, T f. 60), cf. the better *daresten* 'of Silistria' W 65/26.

55/27 *þei kepiþ hem*: Z *ils garnent* 'they provide for themselves' cf. the better *ils sarment* 'they arm themselves' W 65/34.

60/18 *fiȝte*: Z *combatre*, cf. the better *baretter* 'to cheat' W 69/36.

*64/27 *kynge*: *rois* (S f. 81, T f. 64), cf. the better *portz* 'port' W 73/32.

65/16 *desperuer*: *del Esperuier* 'of the Sparrowhawk' W 73/41. But subgroup 2 (except V) reads *del empereur* 'of the emperor' (S f. 81, T f. 64$^{v}$, U f. 21).

66/12 *þe lady grauntid hym*: this phrase joins two different stories (of the poor man's son and of the knight Templar) by scribal eyeskip, cf. *la dame ly ottroia . . . la dame luy ottroia* W 74/32–4. The omission does not occur in any Insular manuscript.

67/23 *xxv. myle*: *xxv. lieues* W 76/21, i.e. 25 Continental leagues or approximately 50 English miles.

67/29 *Cosara sone*: *filz de Gosra* (S f. 82$^{v}$, T f. 66), cf. the better *filz Are de Gosra* W 76/29, properly Jobab, son of Zerah of Bozrah (Genesis 36: 33).

68/3 *and sithen kyng of Isau*: *apres le roi Esau* 'after the king Esau' W 76/33. Probably a ME scribal confusion.

*83/14 *leeuys of þe same tree*: *des foilles* (S f. 103), *de propre foilles* (T f. 80$^{v}$) 'its own leaves', cf. the better *ses propres fiens* 'their own dung' W 94/41.

87/28–88/23 *þan men . . . þe see*: this passage is uniquely displaced in ME subgroup 1 and omitted in ME subgroups 2–5. In all Insular manuscripts W 98/29 this description of *Sylha* 'Ceylon' follows that of the Nicobar Islands which in the ME text ends at 86/13. Smaller dislocations of text are noted at 42/13 and 114/25.

88/9 *oþer naddris*: *des serpents et des grosses sangsues* 'snakes and large leeches' W 98/36. The translator may not have known *sangsues*.

88/13 *of an oynement made þerfore*: *del iucz de lymons* 'of the juice of lemon' W 98/39. Z *del oignement* or the translator's response to a badly written phrase.

89/26 *bygoun*: *Bigon* W 102/34.

90/6 *cliket*: *clokette* 'little bell' W 102/40. Perhaps the translator read *cliquet* 'latch of a gate'.

90/23 *whiche is a grete lord as Y haue seid bifore*: *qar est mult belle cite et mult abundante de touz biens* 'which is a very fine city full of goods of all kinds' W 103/35. The words occur at the end of a chapter, and the distance of the ME phrasing from the Old French perhaps reflects the translator's invention before a lacuna.

92/21 *mountour*: *montour* 'mound' W 106/32. The translator apparently did not recognize the meaning of the OF word. Cf. note to 134/17.

93/24 *alabance*: *alabaundines* 'almandines' W 107/41. The ME form perhaps depends upon a lost Insular variant, cf. the preceding *cremaus* for *grenaz* 'garnets'.

93/26 *onices*: *onices* 'onyx stones' W 107/42. All ME manuscripts read *quices* except 2C which may be an intelligent correction, rather than the translator's reading. *gerandys* is from OF *geracites* (Lat. *hieracites*) 'a stone of the colour of a hawk's neck'.

94/19 *ete no fleische as we do*: *mangent sans mappe* (ST *nape*) *sour les genilz* 'eat without a cloth on their knees' W 108/42.

95/11 *viii.*: *viii. xx* '160' W 110/30.

99/11 *astrolaberis*: *astrolabes* 'astrolabes' W 115/34. The plural suffix *-eris* recurs in *chasteryneris* 132/15 for *chasteigns* 'chesnuts' W 152/34.

*99/12 *coles brennyng*: *charbon ardentz* (S f. 123$^{v}$, T f. 96$^{v}$, U f. 40, V f. 38 has lacuna), cf. the better *charbouncles argentz* 'silver charbuncles' W 115/35.

103/17 *goþ þei home aȝen to here place*: *ly emperers dit a sez religious qils se retrahent* 'the emperor orders these religious to withdraw' W 120/37.

103/18 *defoule*: Z *defolez*, cf. the better *confolez* 'entangled with', unless the translator here and in the previous phrase interprets his text somewhat freely.

105/4 *melk*: *miel* 'honey' W 123/30. The translator may have written *mel*, but elsewhere renders this *hony*. Cf. 2B *mylette*.

106/26 *Tartary*: *Trachie* W 125/31, properly the land of the Uighars which marches westwards to Tangut. See note.

112/5 *Ermonye*: *Amasonie* W 131/40. Like *Egipt* and *Ethiope*, a common scribal confusion.

114/25–115/2 *þis emperour . . . litel*: this paragraph is misplaced. In the Insular text W 135/34–7 and in ME subgroups 2–5 it follows the grunting savages at 116/12. Cf. the textual note to 87/28 above.

116/8 *yrun*: Z *fer*, cf. the better *faierie* 'faery' W 135/31.

116/26 *vessel ful of gold . . . precious stones*: *vessaile dargent ouesque nobles ioyaux dor et des pierres precriouses* 'vessel of silver with rich inlays of gold and precious stones' W 135/45. The ME expansion naming seven types of precious stones is found only in ME subgroup 1.

117/15 *grene iasper anoþer of dyasper*: *iaspre vert diaspre* 'deep green jasper' W 136/34. The translator has mistaken the past participle as a noun.

117/17 *anoþer of septoun*: *et ly septisme* 'and the seventh' W 136/34. Unless Z had a corrupt variant, the translator has mistaken the adjective as a noun.

118/1 *his wyf but prys at iii. certeyn sesouns in þe ȝere*: *ses femmes qe iiii.* (ST *iii.*) *foitz en lan solonc les iiii. saisouns* 'his wives only four times in the year according to the seasons' W 136/39.

118/18–20 *And he haþ . . . Suse*: in the Insular text W 136/40 and in the ME subgroups 2–5 this sentence occurs at 118/2. Cf. other dislocations noted at 86/12 and 114/25 above.

119/1 *stories*: *museries des histoires* 'depictions of stories' W 137/36.

*122/22 *gadlibiriens*: *Gadiberiz* (S. f. 152, T f. 113), cf. the more common *Cadebiriz* W 140/47. See note.

124/18 *girsant*: *gerfaucz* 'giraffe' W 142/42, ultimately the Arabic *zarāfa*.

124/29 *lonhorans . . . tontes*: *loherans . . . odenthos* W 143/27. The names are corrupt variants of the fabulous beast called *odonta vel dentem tyrannum* in the *Epistola Alexandri* quoted by Vincent of Beauvais, *Spec. Hist.* IV. 54, possibly an inflated account of the rhinoceros.

*126/9 *Synophe*: *Sinosople* (S f. 153, T f. 117), cf. the better *Gynsonophe* W 145/42, the Gymnosophists of Alexandrine legend.

127/14 *alle feþeris*: Z *toutz pennez*, cf. the better *toutz pelluz* 'all rough' W 147/31.

*127/18 *Renemare*: *Renemar* (S f. 153$^{v}$, T f. 117$^{v}$, U f. 54, V f. 49), cf. *Buemar* W 147/33, the river marking the easternmost point of Alexander's invasion of India.

133/20 *lete make clene*: cf. *fait mettre cuyre* 'causes to be cooked' W 153/40.

133/27 *þe kyng*: *vn bien riche qi est ne prince ne duk ne admiralz ne conte* 'a very wealthy man who is neither prince nor duke nor admiral nor count' W 153/45. Unless Z had *roi* for *riche*, the translator has collapsed the meaning.

134/17 *palace*: *mouster* 'mound' W 154/37. At 92/21 the translator retained the OF form *mountour*, which is apparently the same word as *mouster*. The Egerton Version (ed. Warner, p. 154) has *palace*, which supports the emendation here, cf. the Cotton Version (ed. Hamelius, p. 208) *toothill* 'mound'.

135/20 *m$^{l}$.ccc.xxx$^{ti}$. and tweye*: cf. *mil ccc.xxii$^{de}$* cf. W 155/43.

136/1 *m$^{l}$.ccc.lx and sixe*: cf. *mil ccc.lvi$^{me}$* W 155/47. The dates in the Cotton

Version are 1322 and 1356 (as in the Insular Version). The Egerton Version has 1332 and 1366 (as in the Defective Version).

136/3–15 *And for as myche . . . poyntes*: this passage does not occur in any extant Insular manuscript. *Pace* K. Sisam, *Fourteenth Century Verse and Prose* (Oxford, 1921), p. 240 who comments on the expanded passage in the Cotton conflation, the interpolation may be due to the translator. He followed an Insular manuscript of subgroup 2, and the Cotton conflator expanded his ME base (a Defective manuscript of subgroup 1) by reference to an Insular manuscript of subgroup 1; and the precise position of both these lost Insular manuscripts within their scribal traditions is known. The absence of any trace of such an interpolation in either Insular subgroup, or in any of their Latin translations (except one very late copy based on the Defective passage) whose points of origin within the Insular scribal tradition are also known, is a strong argument against an Insular origin. Moreover, the more popular appeal of the English translation is more in keeping with the invention of such a story.

## A NOTE ON THE TRANSLATION

Both the translator's Insular manuscript and his own fair copy are lost, and comment is thus tentative. For the greater part the translation is a close competent literal rendering. There are very few mistakes of meaning in word or syntax. In some places, however, the phrasing is abridged and very occasionally this compression affects the sense. This approach to the translation suggests the possibility that the translator may himself have been responsible for the several more substantial omissions of text (excluding, of course, the 'Egypt Gap'). The assumptions of date and dialect, *c.*1385 Lincolnshire, are feasible on present knowledge but require substantiation. There are no clues to the translator's identity.

# APPENDIX:
## Extracts from the manuscripts

Here are given twelve extracts from Pynson's print and each manuscript of subgroups 2, 3, 4, and 5 which are used to determine their affiliation in the Introduction. The manuscripts are described in *Trans. Edinburgh Bibl. Soc.* IV, part 5 (1966), 169–210. There are collections of microfilm at Edinburgh and at Oxford.

Extract 3 marks the 'Egypt Gap'; extract 7 the place where the Hebrew alphabet has been lost in subgroups 3, 4, 5; extract 8 immediately precedes the names and figures of the Saracen alphabet; extract 9 marks the place where the account of the rotundity of the world has been omitted; extract 10 the place where the Latin version of the Dindymus letter is interpolated in subgroup 5. The other extracts mark smaller points of scribal divergence from the common substance which have been used to illustrate the affiliation of the manuscripts.

The manuscripts are presented in the sequence of their subgroups. In the headnotes any Mandeville text now bound with other texts not originally associated with it is designated part of the modern volume, and any Mandeville text once part of a larger volume now dismembered is designated *membra disjecta*. All chapter divisions are unnumbered and without rubric unless otherwise stated. The presence or absence of marginalia and an estimate of date and dialect of the Mandeville text are noted.

Within the extracts scribal contractions are silently expanded, and arabic numerals separated by a solidus refer to page and line of the text of this edition.

PYNSON'S PRINT *c.*1496 [BL pressmark 6173] 2P

72 pp. Black letter, Pynson's type 2. His device type 3 at end. Unique copy lacks two bifolia (title-page and sigs. A8; C1 and C8). 18 unnumbered and (except sig. d6$^{v}$) unrubricated chapters.

1. Aii$^{r}$ Iohn Maundeuyle knyght. Thoughe it so be that I be nat worthy that was borne in englonde in the towne of saynt Albone and passed the see in the yere of the Incarnacion of oure lorde iesu crist M.CCCxxxii on the day of saynt Myghell

2. Aii[v] wyth good company and of many lordes . . . and thoroughe the castell of Newburgh and by the ille towne that is towarde the ende of hungry

3. biv[r] also he holdethe Calaphes that is a greate thynge to the Soudan that is to say amonge theym Roys Ile and this vale is full colde

4. ci[v] and other kyngdoms many vnto welle lowe in Ethyope

5. di[r] Also two myle fro Ierico is flom Iordan. and ye shall wete the dedde see departeth the londe of Indee and of araby and the water of that see is full bytter . . . and some men call that lake the lake of the alphitedde

6. dii[r] a stronge castell that men call Carras or Sermoys. That is to say Reale mount in frenche

7. dii[v] in this countre dwelle many Iewes paynge tribute as crysten men done. and if they woll wete the letter of the Iewes they ar suche and the names of their letters as they call them. Alpha. for a beth. for b [*rest of names and figures follow*]

8. eiii[v] therfore larchesleuyn whan he receueth theym seyth thus

9. fiii[v] Theder brynge marchauntes their children to sell and those that are fatte they ete theym. and the other kepe they tyll they be fatte and than are they eten. Besyde thys Ile is an Ile that men call Somober

10. i iv[r] We haue a kinge amonge vs nat for to law ne deme no man. for there is no trespassoure among vs but all only to lere vs to be obedyent to him and so may thou nought take fro vs but oure gode peas

11. i iv[r] Another Ile is there that is called Synople . . . alysaunder was gretly astonyed of this answere

12. kiii[v] I Iohn Maunduyle that went oute of my countre and passed the se the yere of oure lorde a M ccc.xxxii. and I haue passed thorowe many londes and Iles and countrees and nowe am come to rest I haue compyled this boke and do wryte it the yere of oure lorde M.ccc.lxvi. at xxxiii. yere after my departynge fro my countre

LOST LEAVES contained text corresponding to 13/6–14/23; 28/3–29/24; 39/29–41/5.

BL MS ARUNDEL 140 part 1 2A

ff. 5–40. Leaf lost after ff. 5, 15. 1400–25. North Essex. 21 chapters, numbered. Marginalia.

1, 2 [*lost*. f. 5$^{v}$ *ends* fruyt þorough þe which 4/11, f. 6 *begins* in hys hond And men seiþ þer 6/31]

3. f. 10$^{v}$ also he haldes Calaphes þat is a grete þynge to þe soudeyne þat is to say amonge heme Roys ils and þis valle is fulle colde

4. f. 13$^{v}$ and oþere kyngdomes many vn to welle laugh in Ethiope

5. f. 16$^{r}$ Also two myle fro Ierico is flome Iordane And ȝe schalle wite þat þe deede see departys þe londe of Iude and of Arabie and þat see lastes fro Sora to Arabie and þe watyr of þe see is full byttere . . . And some men calle þat lake the lake of Alphtedde

6. f. 16$^{v}$ a stronge castelle þat men calle Carras or Sermoys þat is to say royalmont in ffrenche

7. f. 17$^{r}$ And in þis contree dwellez many Iewes payand trybute als [f. 17$^{v}$] crysten men do and if ȝe wille wytte þe lettres of Iewes þei are soche and names of þe lettres als þei calle hem $^{a}$Alpha $^{b}$beth [*names and characters follow*]

8. f. 22$^{r}$ þerfor Archetriclyne when he resceues ham says þus

9. f. 27$^{r}$ thedir brynge merchauntz þeire childre to selle And þois þat are fatte þei ete heme and oþere kepe þei and fede heme to þei be fatte and þene þei are etyn Bysyde þis ile is an ile that men calle Somobere

10. f. 38$^{v}$ we haue a kynge a mong vs noght for to saue nor deme no man for þeir is no trespasour a mong vs but alle only to lere vs to be obedyent to hym and so may þou noght take frome vs bot oure good pees

11. f. 38$^{v}$ Anoþer Ile is þeir þat is callede Synophe wheyr also are good folke and trewe . . . and Alysaundre was gretly stonnede of þis answer

12. f. 41$^{r}$ I Iohan Maundevyle þat wente oute of my contre and

passede þe see þe ȝeere of oure lorde m[l]. ccc. lxvi at xxxiiii. yeere aftre my departynge fro my contree

UNIQUE LACUNA f. 28[r]
þe acord is noght fro þis ile men goes to an Ile þat men calle Nacumerane [*om.* 85/16–22]

BL MS ROYAL 17 B. xliii part 1 2B
ff. 112. Leaf missing after f. 115. 1400–25. Hereford–Monmouth borders. Marginalia. 21 chapters.

1. f. 5[v] I Iohan Maundevyle a knyȝt þey hit be noȝt worthy that was bore yn Ingelonde in the towun of seynt Albon and passed the see yn the yere of the yncarnacioun of oure lord Ihesu crist m[l]. ccc. xxxii on the day of seynt Mychel
2. f. 6[r] with goude companey and of many lordes . . . and þorow the castel of Neuborewe and by the ile towun that is toward the ende of hungrye
3. f. 20[r] also he haldeþ Calaphes þat ys a grete þyng to þe soudan þat ys to say amonge hem Roys Ils and þys vale is ful colde
4. f. 27[v] and oþer kyngdomes many vn to lawthe yn Ethyope
5. f. 38[r] Also two myle from Ieryco ys flome Iordane and ye schulle wyten þat þe dede see departeþ londe of Iudee and of Arrabye and þat see lasteþ from Sora to Arabye and þe watur of þat see ys ful byttere . . . and som men calle þat lake [f. 38[v] ] þe lake of Alphytedde
6. f. 40[r] a wel stronge castelle þat men clepen Carras or Sermoys þat ys to say real mount yn frensche
7. f. 42[r] yn þys countre dwellyn wounder many Iewes and payeþ here trybute as crysten men doþ and yf ye wylle wyte þe letteres of Iewes þay ben ful wonderful And the names of þe letteres as þay clepen hem [a]alpha [b]beth [*names and figures follow*]
8. f. 56[r] larches leuen whanne þat he resseyueþ hem seyen þus
9. f. 70[r] þyder bryngeþ marchaundes heere chyldren to sylle and þees þat ben wel fatte þey eten hem and þe oþer þat ben but leene þey kepen hem tylle þat þey ben fatte

and þenne þey eten hem also And bysyde þys ile ys an ile þat men clepen Somobere

10. f. 108r Wee han a kynge amonge vs nouȝt for to deme no man for þare ys no trespassoure amonge vs but only to lere vs to ben obedyente to hym and so myȝt þow take fram vs but oure goude pees

11. f. 108r A noþer ile ys þare þat men clepen Synople . . . Alysaundre was gretely stunyede of þys aunswere

12. [*lost.* f. 115 *ends* no more of marueyles þat, *with catchwords* ben þare 135/24]

UNIQUE INTERPOLATION f. 70r

And also þere ys an ile a grete way a þys halfe þat men moten come to by see [f. 70v ] þat ys lxxiii. dayes iorne from þens þat men clepen þe ile of hogge þat peeple þere ys haþ þe body after a man and þe hede after an hogge And þere ben noon wymmen but as þey comen oute of oþer iles And whanne þat þey lyggen by hem fleschly as a man auȝt to doon by wymmen þenne þey þat same tyme wollen wrote wiþ heere moosel as swyn doon yn erþe vn tylle þey han oute hure herte blood And þenne ben þe wymmen dede And þenne mote men turne ayen euen northe est xli dayes iorne and þare ben wondur many iles and dyuersytees of men so wondurful þat þer ne nys no man þat me wolde þere of leue þey þat I tolde ffor yn somme ben men lyke vn to foules þe heede þe body best þe legges man and also many oþer dyuersyteez þe whyche y ne wulle not telle for þer ys noon þat wolde hyt lyue and also seldon comeþ eny yn þees landes þere or neuere and þere for wul no man hyt leue and þere for I wul speke of oþer landes where þat dyuerse men ben inne and men of þees landes here han ben inne

## BL MS ROYAL 17 C. xxxviii 2C

ff. 61. Lacks 1 leaf after f. 60, another after f. 61. Double-columned, with 110 tinted drawings, mostly in lower margins. 1400–25, early. Hampshire or West Sussex. Tabula and 22 chapters, numbered and rubricated.

1. f. 7vb Iohan Maundeuyle knyght thow y be nought worthi that was bore in Engelond in the toun of seynt Albones and passed the see in the ȝer of the incarnacioun of oure

lord Ihesu Crist Mi[l].ccc.xxxii. vppon seynt Michelis day

2. f. 8ra in company of greet lordes and other good companye . . . and thorgh the castel of Newbow by the same toun that is toward the eynde of Hungrie

3. f. 16rb and many oþer londes he holdeþ on his hond And the mount of seynt Katerine is moch heyr þan þe mount Moyses

4. f. 20va and oþer kyngdomes many in to Ethiope and in to Ynde þe lasse

5. f. 25ra and ȝe shal vnderstande þat þe dede see departeþ þe lond of Inde and of Arabye and þat see lasteþ fro Sara in to Arabie and þat water of þat see is ful better . . . som men callen þat water þe lake of alle fetida

6. f. 26ra a strong castel þat men callen Garras oþer Sermoyns þat is to say ryal mount in frenshe [*omits further phrase*]

7. f. 27ra In þis contre dwelleþ many iewes paynge tribute as cristen men doþ And if ȝe wole ywite þe letteris of iewes þey beþ soche And þes beþ þe names of her letters as þey callen hem Alpha beth [*names follow*] Now shal ȝe haue þe figures [*characters follow*]

8. f. 34ra þerfore larchesleuen þat is receyuour of cristen men when he receyueþ hem he seiþ þus

9. f. 40ra þyder bryngeþ marchauntes her cheldren to selle And þo þat ben fatte þey ete hem And þe oþer þey kepe and fede hem tylle þey ben fatte and þen þey ete hem In þis lond noþer in many oþer aboute [*account of rotundity of world follows*]

10. f. 58ra We haue a kyng among vs noȝt for lawe ne for demyng of no man for þer is no trespas among vs but al onlich to lere vs and to be obedient to hym And so myȝt þow noȝt take noȝt fro vs but our good pees

11. f. 58ra Anoþer Ile þer is þat is ycalled [f. 58rb] Synople wher also beþ good peple and trywe . . . kyng Alisaundre was gretly astoned of þis aunswer

12. f. 61rb Y Iohan Maundeuyle knyght þat wente out of my contre and passide þe see þe ȝer of our lord

Mi[l].ccc.xxxii. and y haue ypassed þorgh many londes contrees and iles and am now come to reste y haue compyled þis book and lat write it [f. 61[va]] þe ȝer of our lord Mi[l].ccc.lxvi. at xxiiii. ȝer after my departyng fro my contre ffor Y was trauelynge xxxiiii. ȝer

BL MS HARLEY 2386 part 2 (ff. 74–130) 2D

ff. 57. Leaf missing before f. 74. After 1470. Devon. Marginalia. 21 chapter divisions, numbered to C XI.

1. f. 74[r] [I] Iohan Maundeuylle knyht of alle I be nouht worþy þat was borny [*sic*] in engelonde in þe town of seynt albon and passed þe see in þe yere of our lord Ihesu crist a M [*blank space for three letters*] xxxii on Myhel masse day

2. f. 74[r] with gode compony of lordys The secunde chapitre . . . and throw þe castelle of Neuburghe men passe by þe ryuer of Danubie [*no ref. to* ile town]

3. f. 84[r] and he holdyth Calapes þat ys a gret thyng to þe Sawdan þat ys to saye a mong ham Rodys yle and hyt stondyth in a valy þat ys rygth colde

4. f.89[v] and othere kyngdomys yn to well longe yn Ethyopye

5. f. 96[r] fro Ieryco iii myle ys to þe dede see þat whych departydth þe lond of Indee and Arabye and þe see lastyth from Sore to Arabie And þe water of thys see is full beter . . . some men clepyth þat lake þe lake of Alphyded

6. f. 97[v] a stronge castell þat men clepyth Carras yn sermoys þat ys to saye [*blank space*] mont [*rest omitted*]

7. f. 98[v] yn þis contry dwllyth [*sic*] meny Iewys owndere trybutt as crystyn men dothe and yef þou wolte wete þe lettrys of Iewys thay bythe suche and þe namys of þe letterys as thay clepyth ham [a]Alpha [b]beth [*names and characters follow*]

8. f. 107[r] he þat is larchelyuen whane he reseuys tham sayth thus

9. f. 112[v] thay brynge hire chyldryn to sylle to marchandis thes ben fatte thay ete ham and there kepe thay tyll thay be

fatte and than beth thay etyn And there beth meny other gret iles of þe which hit were to moch to tell al

10, 11. [*omitted in larger lacuna* f. 126v]

12. f. 129v I Iohan Maundeuyle knyght þat went out of my contryz and passhdy [*sic*] þe see þe yere of oure lord m ccc xxxii and haue passyd thrugh meny contryz and londys and now ys come to reste y haue complyd þis boke and lat wret hyt þe yere of oure lord m ccc lxvi at xxxiiii after my departyng from my contrye

UNIQUE LACUNA f. 126v
and thay wolle chaste þe Olyfante and sley hym and þer beth meny oþer bestes of whch [*sic*] hyt were to long to wret and þer is anoþer hylle þat men calle [f. 127r] Pytan [*omits* 125/1–127/29]

BL MS HARLEY 3954, item 1 2H
A holster book. ff. 68. Slightly abridged, with 100 tinted drawings and 38 blank spaces awaiting artist. 1425–50. Norfolk. Marginalia. 21 chapters; only viii, xiiii, xx numbered.

1. f. 2r I Ion maundeuille kynth off al it be so þat I be not worthy þat was boryn in Ingelond in þe toun off seynt albone and passyd þe see þe ȝer off þe incarnacioun of owre lord ihesu crist Ml. CCC. XXXII. on myhelmesse day

2. f. 2r with good cumpanye of many worchepful lordys . . . thour þe castel of Newbergh and be þe euylton þat is to ward þe ende of hungerye

3. f. 11r also he haldyth Calaphes qwyche is a gret þing to þe sowdon þat is to say among hem Roys Ils And þis vale is ful cold

4. f. 15v And oþer kyngdomis many vnto þe vale off Ethyope

5. f. 19r And to myle fro Ieryco is flum Iordan [f. 19v] And ȝe xul vndirstonde þat þe ded see departyth þe lond of Indee and þe lond of arabye And þat see lestyth fro sora to Arabye And þe water of þat see is wol byttre . . . sum men clepyn þat lake þe lake of alphyted

6. f. 20v a strong castel þat is clepyd Carras or ellys sermoys þat is to seyn in frenhs þe mount real [*rest omitted*]

7. f. 21$^{r}$ in þis cuntre dwellyn many Iewys vnder tribut as crysten men do And if ȝe wyl knowyn þe lettrys of Iewys þis be þei þat folwyn Alpha beth [*names and characters follow*]

8. f. 27$^{v}$ þerfore þe larchesleuen qwan he reseyuyth hem seyth to hem þus

9. f. 38$^{r}$ Thydyr bryngyn marchauntis chyldre for to selle and þei ben fatte þei etyn hem and if þei be lene þei fedyn hem fatte and etyn hem [*tinted drawing*] And þer ner is an Ile þat is clepyd Somober

10. f. 62$^{v}$ We han a kyng among vs nowth ffor to demyn ne to Iugyn men for we han no trespassowrys but only to techyn to ben obedyent to hym And so may yow nowth takyn fro vs but owre good pes

11. f. 63$^{r}$ Anothyr Ile is þere þat men clepyn synaphe qwer also be good folk and trewe . . . kyng alysaundre was gretly astonyid of þis answere

12. f. 69$^{r}$ I Ion Maunduile knyth þat went owt off Ingelond and pasyd þe see þe ȝer of owre lord M$^{l}$. CCC. XXXIIII. And haue pasyd þour many londys and Iles and cuntres And now am comyn to reste I haue compylyd þis bok and don wretyn it þe ȝer of owre lord M$^{l}$. CCC. xlxvi. at þe xxxiiii. ȝer affter þe partyn fro my cuntre

## HUNTINGTON LIBRARY MS HM 114 2M

ff. 131–84. Leaf lost after ff. 137, 138. f. 146 top half torn. 1425–50. Essex. No marginalia. Almost 100 short chapters.

1. f. 131$^{v}$ I Iohan Mawdeville knyght born yn þe touun of seynt Alboun in Inglonde passid ouere þe see toward þe holy londe in þe ȝeer of our lord Ihesu Cryst M$^{l}$. CCC. in the day of seynt Michelle

2. f. 131$^{v}$ in cumpanye of grete lordis . . . þurgh þe castelle of Newborough and by þe yle Tourne þat goth to þe ende of hungrye

3. f. 138$^{v}$ also he holdiþ in his hondis þat is to sey Calaphes [*end of leaf.* f. 139 *begins*: wondir wele and þey do grete worschip 24/6]

4. f. 142r and othir kyngdomys meny in to þe tyme he fellyd þe lawes of Ethiopye

5. f. 147r Also ii myle from Ierico is fflom Iordane and ȝe shal vndirstonde þat þe reed see lastiþ fro Sora to Arabye and þat watir is ful bytyr . . . some clepe þat lake Alphidete

6. f. 148r a castelle þat men clepe Carras and in frensshe mount ryalle

7. f. 149r yn this cuntre dwelle meny iewes vndir tribute as done crystyn men Also ȝe schul vndirstonde thes bene her lettres and [f. 149v] and þe names of þe lettres as þei clepyn hem Alpha ha [*names and characters follow*]

8. f. 155v [*omits ref., reads* wikkydnesse and þer for þer is no god 63/17–19]

9. f. 161v þei bryng her childryn to market to selle as men do pygge or lambe goos or capoun and þo þat be fat þei sle hem and þo þat be lene þei kepe hem til þei be fat The londe of Somobre wher men be markyd with a hoot yryn þere is anoþer londe þat men clepe Somobre

10. f. 179v we have no kyng among vs to deme no man ne to do lawe but þer is no trespassour among vs but we be obedyent to hym þat we byleve on and so may þou take noght from vs but our good pees

11. f. 179v þer is a noþer Ile þat men clepe Sinople wher be good folk and trewe . . . kyng Alisaundre was gretly astonyd of this answere

12. f.184r I Iohan Maundevyle þat went oute of Inglonde and passid þe see þe ȝeer of our lord Ml. ccc. xxxii. haue passid thurgh meny londis yles and provynces and now am y come to reste Also y haue compiled þis and writyn hit þe ȝeer of our lord a Ml. ccc. lxvi. and atte þe xxxiii. ȝeer after my departyng out of Inglonde

BL MS ADDITIONAL 33758 3A

ff. 50. Complete. 1450–75. Berkshire. No marginalia. 13 chapter divisions.

1. f. 3v I Iohan Maundeuyle knyȝt ȝof alle y be not worþi þat whas born in Englond in the towne of seynt Alban and

passyd þe see in the yere of the incarnacion of oure lord Ihesu criste m. ccc yere in the day of seynt myȝhelle

2. f. $4^{r}$ with goode company of many lordes . . . and þrou þe castelle of Newbron and by the yle Turne þat is to þe ende of hungry

3. f. $11^{r}$ also he holdes Calapes that ys a gret thynge to þe saudan that ys to say a monge Roys yles and þis vale [f. $11^{v}$] ys fulle colde

4. f. $15^{v}$ and oþer kyngdoms many vnto he felle low into Ethiope

5. f. $20^{r}$ Also ii. myle from Ierico is flom Iordan and the falle of the dede see departyþ the londe of Ynde and of Araby and the whater of that see ys fulle better . . . and some men calle it the vale of Alpheted

6. f. $21^{r}$ a stronge castelle that men callen Gallas or Sert Moyr þat ys to say yn affryth yn englysch a kyngly hille

7. f. $22^{r}$ yn þat contree dwellen many Iewes payng tribute as cristen men don and that is here wylle wyth here lettres the Iewes are suiche as the namys are as thay callen the alphabe

8. f. $28^{v}$ therfore larceflemayn whan he receyuyth ham sayþe thus

9. f. $34^{v}$ þeder brynge marchaundes her children to selle and these children þat are fatte þay ete and þe other children þat are not fatte thay fede ham welle and kepe ham tenderly telle they be fatte and thanne they ete tham Besyde þys yle þer ys anoþer yle þat men callen Somebere

10. f. $48^{r}$ we haue no kynge amonge vs but only to obey to god and so may þou nouȝte take from vs but oure goode pes

11. f. $48^{r}$ Another yle ys there þat cleped ys Synople . . . and Alysaundre was gretely stondyd yn this answere

12. f. $50^{v}$ Y Iohan Maundeuyle knyȝte þat went oute of my contree and passed the see yn the yere of our lorde a þousande and $iii^{c}$ and after my departynge at xxxiiii yere from my contre Y came ayene

UNIQUE LACUNA f. 29
[*omits the characters but not the names of the Saracen alphabet, leaving half line blank and reading*] these are the namys now here schulde be the figurs

INITIAL RUBRIC f. 3
Here begynnith the boke of Maundeuyle knyȝt that techyþ the weyes to Ierusalem and of the meruelis of ynde and of the londes of Prestre Iohun and of the grete Chane and of constantynople and of many oþer contreys

## BODLEIAN MS RAWLINSON B 216 ff. 131–61 3B

Double-columned, with the *Brut*. 1425–50. 21 chapters. Marginalia, cropped. SE Midlands.

1. f. 131va I Iohan Mavndevyle knyght ȝif al y be nouȝt worthi that was bore in Engelonde in the tovne of seint Albon and passed the see in the yeer of the incarnacioun of oure lorde Ihesu criste a thousand and thre hundred yeer on the day of seint Mighelle
2. f. 131va with good companye of many lordys . . . and þorgh the castelle of Newbowre and be the Ile turne that is to the ende of Hungry
3. f. 135vb and also he holdeth Calaphes that is a gret thing to þe soudan yt is to seye among Royeys ylys and þis vale ys riȝt colde
4. f. 138rb and many oþer kyngdoms an fille lowe into the cuntre of Ethyope and into Inde þe lasse
5. f. 141ra Also ii. myle fro Ierico ys flome Iordon and the falle of the dede see departeþ þe lond of Iude and of Arabye and the water of þat see ys wel bytter . . . some men clepen hit þe lake of Alohetede
6. f. 141va a stronge castel þat men clepen garras or sersmoys þat is to seye a rial movnte in a frych in englissh a kyngleche hille
7. f. 142ra in þis cuntre dwellen many iewes paying trybute as cristen men doon and it is the wil whiche as þe namys ben they clepen hem alphabe

8. f. 146ra þerfore larteslauyn whan he shalle resseyue hem to þat feiþ he seyde þus

9. f. 149va Thider bringen marchauntz children to selle and þos þat ben fatte þey ete and þe oþere þey kepe and fede hem til þey be fatte and þan þei ete hem Beside þis ile is an ile þat men clepe Somobere

10. f. 158va we haue no kyng amonges vs nouȝt to lawe ne deme no man for here nys noo trespassour among vs but al oonelyche obedyent to god and so þou myȝt nouȝt take fro vs but oure goode pees

11. f. 158vb Anoþer ile is þer there þat men clepen senople and þere ben also goode men . . . kyng Alisaundre was gretliche astonyed of this answere

12. f. 161ra I Ioon Mavndeuyle þat went out of þe londe of Englond fro þe cuntre and þe tovne of seint Alboun the yeer of oure lord m[l] ccc and at þe xxxiiii[ti] yeer after þat I departed fro my cuntre I come aȝein

UNIQUE INTERPOLATION f. 139ra

And therfore ȝif [*sic*] Iulianus apostate ȝaf leeue the Iewys to make aȝein the temple but ȝe shul wite that Vaspasyan lay at þat citee viii ȝeere er þe Iewys were gete and whan they seye þat they shoulde be wonne þey ete alle here Iuely for no man shulde haue hem and þan þe women eten her children and there was a Iew þat helede Vaspacyan of his cardyacle and had his lyf þerfore

UNIQUE INTERPOLATION ff. 135vb–6ra

Ȝe shulle vnderstonde that to the mount Synay ys an abbey of religious of monkys þat lyuen in grete abstinence and right pore lyf and þat abbey is right high and strong and welle walled and here gatys stronge made with iren for drede of wilde beestys In that abbey liggiþ the bonys of seint kateryne in a faire toumbe of alabastre and aboute þe heye auter there is the busshe þat god stoode in whan he spake with moyses whan he be toke him his lawe writen [f. 136ra] in two tablys of stone And þat busshe is ȝit as fresshe as it was þat day And pylgryms seyn that the toumbe of seint katerine rennyth oyle but thei sein here wille ffor I have be there and sey hem for the bonys lyggith in alabauster and a litel scots dewe rist vpon the bonys and the prelat ȝaf me therof for gret loue as moche as two peny weyȝt But whan he takithe oile ther of he sterith the bonys with a spadure of siluer and in that abbay is a meruayle ffor every monke a lampe brennyng hath with oyle and whan he shal deye he shal wite by his lampe for ever as he drawith to deth the light of his lampe with drawith here liȝt And whan he is dede the lampe goth oute by him self And whan her abbot deyeþ they do synge a masse on the hie auter and while the masse is a doing they shalle wite who shalbe abbot of her bretheren ffor whan the masse is doo they fynde a scrowe writen ther on his name who it shalbe and þan they reyseyven him with gret dynete and make him her prelat And vpon seint katerynes nyȝt the bryddes of that cuntree bryngn to that place in her mouth a braunche of olyue tree in significacioun of offryng as men seyn and therof thei make oyle to her lampes and for here mete þat hem nedeþ for al that yeer And sithen fowles of vnresonable kynde don so moche worschippe to þat holy virgyn moche more shulde men worschepe þat ben of resonable kynde in the honoure of god the place of seint katerine

INITIAL RUBRIC f. 131$^{ra}$
Here begynneþ þe book of Iohan maundeville knyght techith the weyes to Ierusalem and þe mervailes of ynde and of the londis of preter Ion and of the grete cane and of Costantyn the noble and of many other cuntrees

## BODLEIAN MS RAWLINSON D 100 3C

ff. 73. Leaves lost before f. 1, after ff. 28, 50, 57, 68, 72, 73. Lower half of f. 27 lost. 1425–50. Worcestershire. 14 chapter divisions survive. Marginalia by second scribe ff. 32$^{v}$–73$^{v}$.

1, 2 [*lost*. f. 1 *begins* lond or elles to hy erryngge þat þey haue nede of 18/17]

3. f. 3$^{v}$ also he holdeþ Calaples þat is a gret þnge [*sic*] to þe sawdan hit is to sey among Roys yles and þis vale is ful cold

4. f. 10$^{v}$ and oþer kyndames monye vnto he destreyzed lawe in Ethiope

5. f. 19$^{r}$ Also ii. myle from Ierico is flym Iordane and þe falle of þe dede see departed þe lond of Iude and of Arabye and þe water of þat see is ful bitter . . . and som men callon hit þe lake of Alphatedde

6. f. 20$^{v}$ a strong castelle þat men callon Sarras or sermoys þat is

to seyn in Englyche [f. 21$^{r}$] a ryol moynt in a fryth a kyngliche hul

7. f. 22$^{v}$ in þat contre dwellon mony Iewes payynge tribute as cristene men don and hit is þe wille with þe lettres of þe Iewes þey beþ sucche as þe names are as þey calle hem Alpha be

8. f. 33$^{v}$ therfore larchesleuyn when he resseyueþ hem seyþ þus

9. f. 46$^{v}$ þyder brynge marchaundes childron to selle and them at are fatte þey ete and oþere kepe þey and fede hem tyl þey be fatte and then þey ete hem Bysyde þys yle ys an yle þat men calle Somobere

10, 11, 12 [*lost.* f. 73$^{v}$ *ends* and he haþ iii longe hornes in hys forhed bitynge as sharpe as eny swerde 124/30]

## BODLEIAN MS DOUCE 109 3D

ff. 73. Leaf lost before f. 1, f. 2 misbound as f. 29. 1425–50. SE Midlands. No marginalia. 15 chapter divisions.

1. [*lost.* f. 1 *begins* pepulle þat wille pulte her bodyis 4/23]

2. f. 1$^{v}$ with meny grete lordis [f. 1$^{v}$ *ends* þe lond Bugres and 6/22]

3. f. 11$^{v}$ and many oþer londis he holdith in his honde and also he holdith Calaphes þat is a grete þynge to þe Sowdaun it is to seie amonge Ieyis ylis and þis vale is fulle colde

4. f. 18$^{r}$ and othir kyngdomis vnto þe tyme þat he distroyid þe lawe in Egipte

5. f. 24$^{r}$ Also two myle fro Ierico is flom Iordan and þe fallyng of the depe see þat departith þe londe of Inde and [f. 24$^{v}$] of Arrabie and þe watir of þe see is fulle bitter . . . and summe men clepen it þe lake of Atheltede

6. f. 25$^{v}$ a strong castel þat men clepen Garras or Sers moys þat is to seie a rialle mounte and on a faire hille and a worschipfulle hille

7. f. 27$^{r}$ in þat contre dwellen many Iewis that payen tribute as cristen men and it is clepid the welle of Iewis to ben clepid as þe namys ben as þay clepen Alphabe

8. f. 36v and þerfore lerth he his bileue whane þay resseyuen hym he seith þus

9. f. 44v thidir bryngen merchantis childir to selle and þoo þat ben fatte þay eten and þoo þat ben lene þay kepe stille tille þay be fatte Biside þis yle is an yle þat men clepen Samobre

10. f. 67r we haue no kyng among vs forto doon lawe noþer deme no man for þere is no trespacere amonge vs but we ben obedient to hym þat made alle þyng and so þou mayste take no þyng fro vs but oure good pees

11. f. 67r an oþer yle þer is þat is clepid Synople where also ben good men and trewe . . . alisaundir was gretely astonyid in þis answere

12. f. 72v y Iohan Maundeuyle þat wente oute of my cuntre and passid þe see in þe ȝere of oure lord a Ml CCC and aftir þe xxxiii [ȝe]re of my departynge fro my cuntre y come a[ȝen]

TOKYO, TAKAMIYA MS 63 (kindly checked by owner) 3L
ff. 116. Lacks 1 leaf. 1400–25. West Riding. No marginalia. 21 chapter divisions.

1. f. 2v Ion Maundewile knyȝte alle if I be not worthie was borne in Ynglonde in þe toune of seynt Albane and passede þe see in þe ȝeer of þe incarnacion of our lorde Iesu Criste M ccc on þe day of saynt Michel

2. f. 3r with goode company of lordes . . . and by þe yle turne þat itt es ȝett on hende of Hungery

3. f. 17r and also he haldes Calaphes and þat is a grete thynge to þam itt is to say amange þame royes iles and þis vale is full calde

4. f. 25r and oþer kyngdoms many to he hade fordone þe lawe of Ethiope

5. f. 35v also ii. myle fra Ierico is flome Iordane and þe fallynge of þe dede see departise þe lande of Inde and of Arabie and þe water of þatt see is fulle bitter . . . summe men calles itt þe flome of deuels [*omits ref. to* Alphatede]

6. f. 36v a strange castelle þat men calles Carras þat is to say a riale mounte in ynglise

7. f. 38v in þat contre duellys many Iews þat pays tribute as cristen men dos and itt is þe wille of þe Iews to be callyd as þer names er as þai cale þam alphab

8. f. 53r þarfor larcheslene when he resaues þame he says þus

9. f. 66r marchandes brynges þider childer for to selle and þai þat er fatte þai ett þame and þe lene þai kepe stille to þai be fatte besyde þis ile is an ile þatt men calles Samober

10. f. 105v we haue na kynge amange vs to do law nor to dem na men for þar is na trespasour amange vs bott we be obedient to gode and so may þu nott take fra vs bott our gode peese

11. f. 106r [*unrecorded*]

12. f. 116r I Iohan Mawdewelle þat went oute of my contre and passyde þe see in þe ȝer of oure lorde m and ccc and efter þe xxxiiii ȝeer efter my departynge fra my contree I come agayne

EXCISION AFTER f. 102
whar is many ewille wommen and felle and þai haue preciose stannes in þar een and [f. 103r] make ioy of þar dede þai say when he is borne he is made to haue sorow [*omits* 122/15–123/14]

## RUGBY SCHOOL MS 3R

ff. 38. Leaves lost after f. 8. 1425–50. SE Midlands. Marginalia. 22 chapter divisions. Readings 10 and 12 conflated from subgroup 1.

1. f. 1v I Ion Maundeuile knyȝt þouȝ Ye be vnworþi þat was born on Engelon in þe toun of seynt albon and passed þe see in þe ȝeer of oure lord ihesu Crist m. ccc on þe day of seint Miȝhel

2. f. 1v wiþ many lordes in good companye . . . and þourȝ þe castel of Neweborwe and bi þe hille Tune to þe ende of hungarie

3. f. 8r also he holdeþ Calaphes þat is a gret þing to þe Sauden hit is to sai amonge hem Rois Iles And þis valei is ful cold

4, 5, 6 [*lost.* f. 8v *ends* for þe holi patriakes liggeþ þere And þei soffre 24/7, f. 9r *begins* doþ it gret worschep 45/12]

7. f. 9r in þis contre duelleþ many iewes payng tribut al as cristen men doþ And if ȝe wolle wite þe letres of iewes þei buþ siche Alpha Betha et cetera [*no names or characters*]

8. f. 14v and þerfor larchessenyn when he reseyueþ hym saiþ þus

9. f. 19r þeder bryngeþ marchandes hir children to sille and þese þat ben fatte þei ete ham and oþere þei kepe tille þei be fatte and þanne þei eten hem Bisidis þis yle is an yle þat men calle Somober

10. f. 33r We haue a kyng amonge ous not for to iugge no man for þer is no trespas amonge ous bote al onliche to lere ous to be obedient to him And so maist þu nouȝt take fro ous bote oure gode pees

11. f. 33r [*omitted in larger lacuna*]

12. f. 36v and Y Ion Maundevile knyȝt þat went oute of my contre and passed þe see þe ȝeer of oure lord a Ml. CCC. and xxxii and Y haue passed þourȝ meny contreis and iles and now Y ham come to reste Y haue compeiled þis book and lette write hit þe ȝeer of oure lord a M. CCC. and l and vi and xxiiii ȝeer after my departyng out of my contre for Y was in traueling xxx ȝeer and four

LACUNA f. 33r (as in subgroup 1)
he sente to ham þat þei scholde kepe wel hire gode maners and haue no drede of hym for he wolde not dere ham And þouȝ þei haue not þe articles of oure feiþ þei troweþ þat god is wel pa[f. 33v]ied of hire livyng [*omits* 126/9–26]

TCC MS R. 4. 20 3T
ff. 172. Complete, with *Siege of Thebes*. 1425–50. SE Midlands.

1. f. 2r I Iohan Maundevile knyght al though I be not worthy þat was born in Englonde in the toun of seynt Albone passede the see in the ȝeer of the Incarnacioun of oure

lord Ihesu crist M CCC XXXII [f. 2^v] on the day of seynt Mighel

2. f. 3^r with good cumpanye and with many lordis . . . and thorough the castel of Newborough and by ile toun that is the eende of Hungarye

3. f. 15^v many other londis he holdith in his hondis And also he holdith Calaphes it is a gret thing to the Sowdan it is to say among hem Royes iles and this vale is ful oolde

4. f. 22^r and other kyngdomys many oon vnto Weltlawe in Ethiopie

5. f. 29^v also ii. myle from Ierico is the fflum Iordane and thou shalt wite that the deed see departith the lond of Iude and of Arabie and that see lastith fro Sora to Arabie and the watir of þat see is ful bittir . . . and sum men callen that lake the lake of Alphetid

6. f. 31^r a strong castel that men callen Carras in Sermoys that is to seye royale mount in frynch in english a kyngly hille

7. f. 32^v in this cuntre dwellen manye Iewis that paien tribute as cristen men done and yf ye wole wite of the lettres of Iewis þei ben such and the names ben as they callen hem

8. f. 43^v and therfore largesleum whanne he resseyueth hem seith thus

9. f. 53^r Thidre bringen marchauntes her children to sille and tho that ben fatte they eten hem and othere kepen they and fede til they ben fatte and thanne ben they eten Biside this ile is an ile that men callen Somobre

10. f. 79^v we haue no kyng amonge us nought [f. 80^r] for to lawe ne deme no man for there is no trespassour amonge us but al oonly to lerne to be obedient to hym and so maist thou nought take fro vs but oure goode pees

11. f. 80^r Another Ile is ther and that is callid Synophe where also ben goode folk and trewe . . . [f. 80^v] . . . And Alysaundre was gretly stoneyd with this answer

12. f. 86^v I Iohan Maundeuyle that wente out of my cuntre and passide the see the yeer of oure lord a thousand and three hundrid and two and thritty and haue passid

thorough many londis and ilis and cuntreis and now is comen to rest I haue compilid this book and let write it the yeer of oure lord a thousand and thre hundrid and thre score and sixe at iiii and thritty yeer aftir my departyng fro my cuntre

## BODLEIAN MS ADDITION C 285 4A

ff. 88, complete. 1400–25. SE midlands. Margins severely cropped. 9 chapter divisions.

1. f. 2$^{r}$ I Iohan Maundeuyle knyȝt þogh I be noght worþ þat was borne in Engelonde in þe toun of sent albone and passed þe see in þe ȝer of incarnacioun of oure lorde ihesu crist a M. CCC. on þe day of sent Michel
2. f. 2$^{v}$ with good company of many londes . . . þorgh þe castel of Norwborw and by þe Ile turne þat is to þe ende of hungry
3. f. 12$^{r}$ and also he holdeþ Calaphes þat is a gret Citee þing to þe soudan þat is to saye among þise yles and valeyes it is ful colde
4. f. 17$^{r}$ and oþere kyngdomes many vnto þe feld lawe in ethiope
5. f. 23$^{r}$ also tuo myle fro ierico is þe fflum Iordan and þe vale of þe dede see departede þe londe of þe Inde Arabie and þe water of þe see departed þe fflum and þe [f. 23$^{v}$] fflum is ful bitter . . . and some callen þat lake of alfebe
6. f. 24$^{r}$ a stonge [*sic*] castel Carras or Cersmoys [f. 24$^{v}$] þat is to say a real mount in africh in englys a kynglike hille
7. f. 25$^{v}$ in þis countre duelle many iewes payande tribute as cristene men done and it is alle here wille of þe iewes to calle hem after here names as alphabe
8. f. 33$^{v}$ þanne here larcelin whan he receyuede hem saiþ þus
9. f. 41$^{v}$ þider come marchauntz and bringen children to selle and þese þat are fatte þay ete and þe oþere þey kepe til þay ben fatte and þanne are þey eten Biside þis Ile is anoþer Ile þat men callen Sombre
10. f. 64$^{r}$ we haue no kinge amonge vs for to lawe vs ne deme vs

for þer is no trespassour among vs but al only to be obedient to him and so may þou noght take fro vs but oure goode pees

11. f. 64[r] anoþer Ile is þere þat is called synople . . . alisaundre was gretly astoneyed with þis answere

12. f. 69[v] I Iohan Maundevyle þat wente out of cuntree and passede þe see in þe ȝere of oure lorde a M. CCC. and at xxxiiii ȝere after my departyng of my cuntree I come aȝein

INITIAL RUBRIC f. 1
Here bigynneth þe book of Iohan Maundevyle þe knyght who techeþ þe weyes to Ierusalem to Inde to þe grete Cane and to the Soudan and to Prester Iohanes lande and of many oþere meruayles and als [dyuerse] contrees and naciouns as þe booke telleþ

## MANCHESTER, CHETHAM'S LIBRARY MS 67111 4C

ff. 82, complete. 1400–25. NE Midlands. 21 chapter divisions. No marginalia.

1. f. 2[va] I Iohan mawndevyle knyght ȝiff all y be nought worthy that was born in yngelond in the toun of seynt albon and passed the se in the ȝere of the incarnacioun off oure lord ihesu crist mill. and ccc ȝere on the day of seynt mighell

2. f. 2[vb] with good companye off many lordes . . . and thouf the castel off newburgh and be the yle turne that ys to the ende of hungry

3. f. 14[rb] And also he holdes Calaphes that ys a gret thyng to the Saudan Among those yles And this vale ys ful cold

4. f. 21[ra] manye vnto he felde lawe in Ethiope

5. f. 26[va] Also ii myle fro ierícho ys flum Iordan and the fal at the dede se departes the lond of Inde and of Arabye and water of that se ys ful bitter . . . som men calles that the lake of Alferede

6. f. 27[vb] a strong castelle that men calles Garras or Sersmoys that ys to say a real mount in a frith in englisch a kynglik helle

7. f. 29[va] in this contre dwelles manye Iewes payende tribut as

cristen men dos and hit ys the wylle with the lettres of the iewes thay are swilke as the names are als thay calle hem alphabe

8. f. 41[va] therfore larcesleuyn when he ressayueth hem seis thus

9. f. 51[vb] Thider bringe merchaundes chylder to selle and those that er fatte thay ete and other kepe thay and fede theym to thay be fatte and than ar thay ete Be[f. 52[ra]]side this yle ys on yle that men calles Somobere

10, 11. [*omitted in larger lacuna* f. 78[vb]]

12. f. 79[ra] y Iohan Maundevyle þat wente out of my contre and passed the see the ȝere of oure lord mill ccc and xxxiiii after my departynge fro my contre y com agayn

UNIQUE LACUNA f. 78[vb]

men don hem after that thay haue don Ther ar manye other contres and maruayles þay y haue spoke nought off ne sen and tharfore y can nought speke of hem propirly [*omits* 123/30–135/18]

INITIAL RUBRIC f. 2[ra] (badly affected by damp)

Here begynneth the book of Iohn Mawdevyle knyght the whilk techeth the right way to ierusalem fro dyuerse contres and of the meruayles of ynde and of diuersite off the contres off the grete chane off the sawdon off babyloyne off Prester Iohn off the emperor of ynde and many other kyndomes yles and lordschipes as ȝe schal here in this . . . book that have . . . and first y schal deuyse the holy londe

CUL MS Gg. 1. 34, part 3 4G

ff. 87, complete. 1450–75. Isle of Ely. Margins cropped. 13 chapters. Reading 1 conflated.

1. f. 4[r] I Iohan Mavndevile knyht yif all it be that i be nowht worthi that was born in England in the town of seynt Albonis and paste the see in the yere of owre lord Ihesu Crist M[l]. CCC xxxii at Myhelmasse day

2. f. 4[v] with greet cumpanye of lordis . . . and thorghw the castell of Neweburgh and men passiht by

3. f. 15[r] manye othir londis he holdis in his hond and also he haldis in his hand Calaphes and that is a greet [*sic*] to

the sowdan but amonggis this hillis and thise valeyis it is full cold

4. f. 21[r] and othir kyngdomis manie vnto Ethiope

5. f. 29[r] Also ii. myle from Ierico is the flum Iordan And in the falle of the deed see departis the lond of Ynde and Arabye and into that watir rennis the flum and it is fulle betir . . . and swm men callyn hit the lake of Alphebe

6. f. 29[r] And ther been ii. stronge castellis that men callyn Carras and Sermoys that is for to seye a ryalle mount on Afryght and that [MS that that] is a kyngly hille

7. f. 30[v] and in this cuntre dwell manye iewys payingge tribute as cristin men doon [*rest omitted*]

8. f. 39[v] and than the wardeyn that shalle resseyve hem he seyis thus

9. f. 48[v] thedir comys marchauntis with childrin and they bryngge theym thedir for to selle and thoo that ben fatte they eete and thoo that been lene they kepe theym tille they been fatte and thanne they eete theym Besyde this ile is annothir ile that men calle Cvmbere

10. f. 75[v] we haue no kyng amongis ws with no lawe for to governe ws no forto deme ws for ther is noo trespasovr amongis ws but alle only to be obedient to god and to pees And so may thow nowt take froo ws but owre good pees

11. f.75[v] Annother Ile ther is there that men calle Synople wher are as good folk and trewe [f. 76[r]] . . . kyng Alexandre was gretely asstonid in this anssweryngge

12. f. 81[v] I Iohan Mavndeuyle that wente owt of my cuntre and paste thee see in thee yeer of owre lorde Ihesu Crist a m[l]. ccc and attee the xxxiiii.yeer after my departyng froo hens owte of my cuntre I come ageyn heder

UNIQUE CORRECTION f. 32[v]
seven lines added to bottom margin by another hand correcting a lacuna of text 48/11–15

PRINCETON UNIVERSITY MS TAYLOR 10 *membra disjecta* 4P ff. 42, complete. *c.*1420. Worcestershire. No marginalia. 8 chapter divisions. Reading 10 conflated.

1. f. $1^{vb}$ Iohun Mawndeuyle kny3t of alle nou3t worþ þat was boren in Ingelond in þe towne of seynt Albones And passed þe see in þe 3ere of þe carnacioun of owre lord ihesu crist a $m^{l}$. and ccc. 3ere on þe day of seynt Michael

2. f. $1^{vb}$ wiþ good company of mony lordes . . . and callen Newborowy And by þe yle turne þat is to þe ende of hongry

3. f. $8^{ra}$ also he holdeþ Calaphes þat is a gret þynge worþe to þe sowden And amonge his yles is fulle cold

4. f. $11^{rb}$ [*omitted in larger lacuna* 30/22–31/4]

5. f. $15^{ra}$ Also ii. myle from Ierico is flum Iordan in þe valeys of þe dede see departeþ þe lond of Iude And arabye and þe water of þe flom is ful bytter . . . sum men clepeþ yt þe lake Alphobe

6. f. $15^{vb}$ a stronge castelle þat men clepeþ carreo or sersemoys þat is to sey A real mount in a fryth in Englyssh a kyngly [f. $16^{r}$ ] hulle

7. f. $16^{vb}$ and in þis contre duellen mony iewes payng tribute as cristen men doþ [*rest omitted*]

8. f. $20^{vb}$ [*omitted in larger lacuna*]

9. f. $25^{rb}$ þydeþ [*sic*] comeþ marchaundus and bryngeþ chyldren to selle and þo þat beþ fatte þey ete and þe toþer þey kepe tylle þey be fatte and þen buþ þey i ete Besyde þis yle is anoþer yle þat men clepeþ Sombre

10. f. $39^{ra}$ Quid potest sufficere cui totus mundus sufficere non potest . . . We haue no kynges among vs nou3t for to lawe vs ne deme vs And þer is no mys[f. $39^{rb}$]doer among vs but alle only to be obedyent to god and to pes and so may þou from vs no take but owre good pees awey

11. f. $39^{rb}$ Anoþer yle þer is þat is cleped synople where ben alle goode folke and trwe . . . Alysaunder was gretly astonynd with þis ansuere

12. f. $42^{va}$ I Ioon Mawndeuyle þat ȝede out of my contrey and passud þe see in þe ȝere of oure lord a þowsaund þre [f. $42^{vb}$] hondred and foure and þrytty ȝer after my departynge fro my cuntre And com aȝeyn

UNIQUE LACUNA f. $20^{vb}$

And so þey þat schulde be turned to god by good ensample to Ihesu crystes feyþ buth drawe away þorow euel lyuynge And þerfore hit is ful longure fro Marrok yn þe see of spayne [*omits* 61/20–64/16]

INITIAL RUBRIC f. $1^{ra}$

Here bygynneþ þe booke of Ion Mawndevyle a knyȝt of wayes to Iherusalem to Iwde to þe grete Cane Also to Preter Ionus lond and to oþer mony a meruelles þat y wolle telle as hit comeþ to mynde as god wolle sende grace

## BODLEIAN MS TANNER 405 4T

ff. 41. Leaves lost after ff. 24, 37. 1425–50. SE Midlands. No marginalia. 10 chapter divisions survive.

1. f. $2^r$ I Iohan Maundevyle knyght yf y vnworthi be was borne in Englond in the toun of seynt Albons passed ouer þe see in þe yere of oure lord a $M^l$ CCC on þe day of seynte Michelle

2. f. $2^v$ with companyes of god men of dyuerse nacyouns . . . thorow the castelle of newborgh by that ile turne to the lond of þe ende of hungrye

3. f. $12^r$ many oþer landis he haldeth in his hand with Calaphes þat is a grete thyng to þe sowdan Amonge these iles and valeys hit ys fulle colde [f. $12^v$]

4. f. $17^v$ and oþer kyndomes many vnto Ethiop

5. f. $23^r$ And iii. myle fro Ierico ys flom Iurdan and þe vale of the dede see departeth þe londe of Inde And of Arabye . . . somme calle hit þe lake of Alphede

6. f. $24^r$ a stronge castelle ycalled Carras or Sermoys Affrythe in Englyssche

7, 8. [*lost.* f. $24^v$ *ends* þe montes þere was grete worschip 45/6]

9. f. $25^r$ Thider comen marchauntis to selle children and tho tho

[*sic*] þat ben fatte þey eten They [*sic*] oþer that tyl tyme þey be fat þey kep hem There bysyde is the hylle of Comober

10. [*lost.* f. 37v *ends* Ther inne groweth trees bygynnye 116/4]

11. [f. 38 *begins* ffor they haue neuer no tempeste 125/16] . . . Tho he was astonyd of the wordes

12. f. 41r I Iohan Maundevyle wente oute of my cuntre of Englond in the yere of oure lord ml. ccc and xxxiii yere and come home ageyn into Englond

UNIQUE ADDITION f. 41v

Also there ys a Cuntrey that when any man or womman dyen The next of hur kyn or her children welle hyre oþer folk to make sorow and lamentacyoun for hem so that þey wolle alle to drawe her here and hedes and alle for scracche hem selfe in þe ffase or body And with gret noyse cryeng orribly And who þat maketh most orryble he schalle haue best for his labour And best be alowd euer after of this kynred

INITIAL RUBRIC f. 1

Here bygynneth tbe boke of Iohn maundevyle kny3te of Englond y borne at Seynte Albons tellynge of þe weyes goyng in to Ierusalem And many oþer meruailes þat he sawh in dyuerse cuntreys

## DUBLIN, TRINITY COLLEGE MS E. 5. 6 part 1 5D

ff. 54. Leaf lost after f. 53, ends imperfectly. 1425–50. Lincolnshire. Marginalia. 9 chapter divisions survive.

1. f. 2r I Iohan Maundevile kny3t 3if alle I be no3t worthy þat was borne in Ingelonde in þe toun of seint Albon and passede þe see in þe 3ere of þe incarnacoun of oure lorde Ihesu Crist a mil. ccc. 3ere on the day of seint Michel

2. f. 3r with gode companye of many londes . . . and þurgh þe castelle of Newbourgh and by þe ile turn þat es to þe on ende of Hungry

3. f. 11v and also he holdes Calaphes þat es a gret þinge to þe Soudan And sothe to saie amonge þise iles and valeies es fulle colde

4. f. 16[r] and other kyngdomes many vnto þe ffeldelawe in Ethiope

5. f. 21[r] Also ii. mile from Ierico es þe fflome Iordan and þe falle of þe depe see departes þe londe of Iude and Arabie and þe water of þe see departes þe fflome þat es ful bitter . . . and sum calle þat þe lake of Alphebe

6. f. 21[v] a strong castelle þat men calle Carras in Sermois þat es to saie a rialle mounte in Affrike in Englissh a kyngli hille

7. f. 22[v] in þis countre duelle many Iewes and paie tribute as cristen men done And it es alle þair wille of þe Iewes to calle þaim after þaire names as Alphabe

8. f. 28[v] and þaire larcelyn when he ressaiues þaim sais thus to þaim

9. f. 36[v] þider comes marchauntz and bringes children to selle And þise þat es fatte þai ete and þe other þai kepe tille þai be fatte and þan er þai eten Biside þis ile es another ile þat men calle Sombre

10. f. 51[v] quid potest sufficere homini cui totus mundus sufficere non potest . . . we haue no kinge be lawe vs demynge ne sentensynge for we passe nouȝt processe of lawe but alle onlie ben obedyent to god and acorde and pees and so þou myȝt nouȝt haue of vs but oure pees Fare welle

11. f. 52[r] Another ile es þere þat men calle Symple . . . and Alisaundre was gretlie astoned in his answere

12. [*lost. The last legible clause on* f. 54[v] *reads* And as the prestis of oure contre syngeþ subuenite sancti dei 133/3]

NAT. LIB. OF SCOTLAND ADVOCAT. MS 19. I. II part 1 5E ff. 69. Lacks leaves after ff. 2, 10, and ends imperfectly. 1450–75. SE Midlands. 28 chapter divisions. Marginalia.

1, 2 [*lost.* f. 2 *begins* men passyn thorowe þe lond of Epynteres 6/23]

3. [*lost.* f. 10 *begins* of them there ys made a fayre chirche 20/4]

4. f. 14$^{v}$ and othyr kyngdomys many onto the feld lowe in Ethiope

5. f. 21$^{r}$ Also ii. myle fro Ierico in þe fflom Iordon and þe falle of þe depe see departith þe lond of Ind and Arabie and the watyr of þe see departyth The fre fflom þat is fulle bitter . . . and sum men calle þat þe lake of Alphabe

6. f. 22$^{v}$ a stronge castelle þat men calle Carias in Sermois that ys to saye a ryalle mount in Afrike in Englissch a kyngely hille

7. f. 23$^{v}$ and in this cuntre dwelle many Iewes and pay tribute as cristen men don and yt ys here wille to be clepid after here namys as Alphabe

8. f. 33$^{v}$ and her latery wanne he resceyvyth hem seth þus

9. f. 42$^{v}$ and thedyr comth marchandys and brynge chyldryn to selle And tho þat be fat they ete and þe oþer they kepe tylle thay be fatt Besyde þis ile ys [MS. ys ys] anothyr ile þat men calle Sombre

10. f. 67$^{v}$ quid potest sufficere homini cui totus mundus sufficere non potest . . . we haue no kynge be lawe us demyng ne sentensyng for we passe not processe of lawe but alle only be abedyent to pes and to good acorde and soo þou myȝt not haue of vs but our good pes Fayre wille

11. f. 68$^{r}$ And there ys an othyr Ile that men calle Symple . . . [f. 68$^{v}$] . . . Alysaundre was gretly astonyd in thys aunsswer

12. [*lost*. f. 69$^{v}$ *ends* of good ffeyth and of good lawes and they haue prestes to synge messe 128/27]

BODLEIAN MS LAUD MISC. 699 5L

ff. 92, complete. *c.*1425. SE Midlands. 14 chapter divisions. Marginalia.

1. f. 2$^{r}$ I Iohan Maundevile knyght though I be not worthi that was borun in Engelond in the touune of seynt albon and passed the see in the yere of the incarnacoun of oure lord Ihesu Crist a M$^{l}$. CCC. ȝere on the day of seint Michell

2. f. $2^{r}$ with good company of mony londes . . . through the Castell of newebrough and by the Ile Turnee that is to þe ende of Hungree

3. f. $12^{v}$ and also he holdeth Calephes þat is a gret thyng to the Sowdan and sothe to seie amonge these Iles and valeyes is ful colde

4. f. $18^{r}$ and other kyngdoms many one to the felde lowe in Ethiope

5. f. $25^{r}$ Also two mile fro Iericho is þe flom Iordan and the fall of the depe see departyth the flom that is ful bittyr . . . sum men call þat the lake of alphabe

6. f. $26^{r}$ a strong Castell þat men call Carias in Sermoys þat is to sey Ariall mount in affric in englisse a kyngely hill

7. f. $27^{v}$ in this cuntree dwelle many Iewes and þey [*sic*] tribute as cristen men done and it is here willes to be clepyd aftyr her names as alphabe

8. f. $36^{v}$ and here larcery whan he resceyuyth hem seith þus

9. f. $45^{r}$ theder comyth marchandes and brynge children to selle and that [*sic*] ben fatte thei ete and the other thei kepe tille þei be fatte Bysydyn this Ile is an other Ile þat men callen Sombree

10. f. $70^{r}$ quid potest sufficere homini cui totus mundus sufficere non potest . . . we have no kyng by lawe vs demyng ne sentencyng ffor we passe not by processe of lawe but alle onely be obedyent to pees and to good acorde and so thou myght not have of vs but oure good pees

11. f. $70^{v}$ there is an other Ile that is Called Symple . . . Alysaunder was gretly astonyd in þis answere

12. f. $77^{r}$ I Iohan Maundevile that went oute of mye Contree and passed the see in þe yere of oure lord god a $M^{l}$ CCC and after the xxxiiii yere of my departyng fro my Contre I came ayene

BODLEIAN MS RAWLINSON D 652 *membra disjecta* 5R

ff. 36. Leaves lost after ff. 1, 20, 33. 1425–50. SE Midlands. Marginalia. 12 chapter divisions survive.

1. f. 1v — I Ihon Maundevyle knight if al I be not worthi þat was born in Ingelond in þe toun of seynt Albon and passed þe see in þe ȝeer of þe Incarnacoun of oure lord Ihesu Crist a Ml CCC. ȝeer on þe day of seynt michel

2. f. 1v — with good compaignye of many londes . . . [*ref. to* ile turne *on missing leaf*]

3. f. 6v — and also he holdeþ Calaphes þat is a gret þing to þe Soudan and soth to seie amonge þise Iles and valeyes is ful cold

4. f. 9v — and oþere kyngdomes many vnto þe ffeldelawe in Ethiope

5. f. 12v — Also ii. myle fro Ierico is þe flom Iordan and þe falle of þe depe see departeþ þe londe of Inde and Arabie . . . some calle þat þe lake of Alphebe

6. f. 13r — a strong castel þat men calle Carras in Sermois þat is to seie a rial mount in affrik in englessh a kyngli hille

7. f. 14r — in þis contre duelle many Iewes and paie tribute as cristen men doo and it is alher wille of þe Iewes to calle þaym after þair names as Alphabe

8. f. 17r — þair Cartelyn whenne he ressaiues hem seis thus to þaim

9. f. 21v — þidir comeþ marchauntz and bringe children to selle and þo þat ere fatte þei ete and þe oþer þei kepe til þei be fatte and þan er þey eten Biside þis Ile is anoþer yle þat men calle Sombre

10, 11 — [*lost.* f. 33v *ends* euery of her wyues schal be comune 124/5. f. 34r *begins* þe mone but in þe laste quarter In þis ile is a gret hulle of gold 129/19]

12. f. 36r — I Iohun Maundewile þat wente oute of my contre and passed þe see in þe ȝere of oure lord Ml CCC and atte xxxiiii wynter after my departynge fro my Contre y come ageyn

## BL MS SLOANE 2319 5S

ff. 42. ff. 4–5 reversed, 17 and 30 misbound. Leaves lost before f. 1, after ff. 8, 9, 12, 16, 22, 28, 42. 1450–75. SE Midlands. 5 chapter divisions survive. Readings 4, 5, 8 conflated.

1, 2, 3 [*lost*. f. 1$^{r}$ *begins* annis proximus fui generacionis 29/33]

4. f. 1$^{v}$ and other kyngdoms monye vnto Ethiope

5. f. 8$^{r}$ and two myle fro [f. 8$^{v}$] Ierico is flom Iordan and in the vale of the deede see departeth the lond of Iude and Arabie and the water of the see that departethe the flom Iordan that is fulle bitter . . . some calle it the stynkyng flom of the deuele [*omits ref. to* Alphebe]

6, 7 [*lost*. f. 9 *begins* and ther maad folk of Ebrewe 44/7. f. 10$^{r}$ *begins* myle and ther oure lorde 47/15. f. 13$^{r}$ *begins* and eche man shal haue 56/22]

8. f. 16$^{r}$ and than her warden when he receyueth hem he saith thus

9. [*lost*. f. 18$^{r}$ *begins* benedicite bot thai saie noght sothe 66/26]

10. f. 42$^{r}$ quid potest sufficere homini cui totus mundus sufficere non potest . . . we haue no kyng bi lawe vs to deme ne sentensyng for we passe noght the processe of lawe bot onely ben obedient to god pees and acorde and so thou shalt noght mowe haue of vs bot oure good pees

11. f. 42$^{r}$ An other Ile ther is that is called Symple wher ben also good folk and trewe and of ful good feithe . . . And Alisaundre was gretelie astonyed of her aunsewere

12. [*lost*. f. 42$^{v}$ *ends* this was doon that men 127/10]

UNIQUE LACUNA f. 20$^{v}$
men fynd elues like the fairest creatures of the worlde [71/26–73/24]

# GLOSSARY

This select glossary gives forms and meanings of words not immediately recognizable in modern English. Citations are generally of the first occurrence. *ȝ* is alphabetized after *g*, and *þ* after *t*. The prefix *y-* indicating a past participle is disregarded in the alphabetical arrangement. An asterisk indicates that the following form is emended or adopted from a manuscript which is not the base manuscript, Queen's College Oxford MS 383.

**acord** *n.* amity 4/28
**acordiþ** *pr. 3 s.* agrees 127/4; ***acordede** *p. 3 pl.* 121/9
**adamaund** *n.* loadstone 70/14
**adoun** *adv.* down 22/18
**aferd** *pp.* afraid 57/17
**aforse** *pr. 3 pl.* force 60/17; **aforsed** *pt. 3 s.* 67/4
**alabance** *n.* almandine, a garnet from Alabanda 93/24
**albespine** *n.* white hawthorn 10/3
***alegge** *pr. 3 pl.* read 49/3
**almysdede** *n.* act of charity 60/22
**alondy** *inf.* land 57/14; **alondiþ** *pr. 3 s.* 52/1
**alsoone, als soone** *adv.* immediately 17/15
**amatyst** *n.* amethyst 94/7
**angriþ** *pr. 3 s.* vexes 130/24
**aparayle** *inf.* decorate, dress, repair 76/24; **aparayld** *pp.* 68/13
**apayd** *pp.* satisfied 125/18
**apperiþ** *pr. 3 s.* appears 42/6; **apperide** *pt. 3 s.* 31/11
**apposid** *pp.* examined 10/1
**appul** *n.* apple 6/31
**araye** *n.* state 98/15
**arere** *inf.* raise 47/22; **arerid** *pt. 3 s.* 47/27
**arise** *pp.* arisen 47/21
**arke** *n.* wooden coffer 34/13
**arwis** *n.* arrows 105/7
**aryueþ** *pr. 3 s.* arrives 64/26
**asaye** *inf.* test 38/14; **assayed** *pr. 3 s.* 30/17, *pp.* 30/6
**asayle** *inf.* attack 71/4
**askes** *n.* ashes 42/10
**asoile** *inf.* absolve from sin 12/26
**aspye** *inf.* find out 23/32
**assay** *n.* test 71/20
**assemble** *n.* gathering 4/25
**assent** *n.* judgment 30/15
**astroloberis** *n.* astrolabes 99/11
**atempre** *adj.* temperate 118/20
**auenture** *n.* hazard 121/9
**auȝte** *pr. 3 pl.* ought 4/9
**autere** *n.* altar 11/17
**avowtrie** *n.* adultery 35/11
**axe** *n.* ash, cinder 13/29
**axeltree** *n.* axle 79/11

**bachelere** *n.* knight bachelor 119/14
**barliche, barly** *n.* barley 34/27
**bate** *n.* discord 85/13
**baþ, baaþ** *n.* bath 36/6
**baþed** *pt. 3 s.* bathed 36/17
**benes** *n.* beans 54/24
**benesoun** *n.* blessing 100/27
**beof** *n.* beef 27/11
**beost** *n.* box 34/22
**bere** *inf.* bear, carry 45/5; **bare** *pt. 3 s.* 25/6; *pt. 3 pl.* 18/24; **ybore** *pp.* 27/19; **bore** *pp.* 17/30; **berynge** *pr. ppl.* 54/24
**beryng** *n.* birth, carrying 27/17
**besily** *adv.* carefully 25/15
**bigge** *inf.* buy 72/17; see **by**
***biggyd** *pr. 3 pl.* built 41/7
**bigile** *inf.* beguile 60/18
**bigynnere** *n.* founder 19/1 n.
**bihedid** *pp.* beheaded 44/32
**bihoting** *n.* promise 101/4
**bitoke** *pt. 3 s.* gave 26/30
**blamed** *pp.* accused, reproved 25/28
**blewe** *adj.* blue 45/26
**bodeliche** *adv.* in shape 120/24
**boisch** *n.* bush 96/25
**boon** *n.* bone 104/15
**boordys** *n.* edges 117/9
**bordis** *n.* trestle tables 18/8
**bordure** *n.* border 92/26
**brede** *n.* breadth 108/22
**breeþ** *n.* breath 86/26
**breke** *inf.* smash 140/3 29/2

**brenne** *inf.* burn 30/31, *pr. 3 pl.* 69/4; **brend, brent** *pp.* 30/30; **brennyng** *pr. ppl.* 26/3
**briddes** *n.* birds 85/1
**bridel** *n.* bridle 30/22
**brigge** *n.* bridge 6/22
**broode** *adj.* broad, wide 48/1
**broþ** *n.* broth 54/26
**buglis** *n.* oxen 113/11
**bullis** *n.* documents 76/4
**buske** *n.* bush 88/3
**by, bye** *inf.* buy, redeem 3/19; **bouȝtist** *pr. 2 s.* 47/11; **bouȝte** *pt. 3 s.* 4/3; **bouȝt** *pp.* 39/9

**cacche** *inf.* chase 4/15; see **chace**
**calamele** *n.* drink made from sugar-canes 63/4
**calenge** *inf.* claim 4/18
**camakas, camocas** *n.* rich silken fabric 98/26
**camelyouns** *n.* chameleons 124/22
**canel** *n.* cinnamon 82/25
**cane** *pr. 3 pl.* know 112/1
**cannes** *n.* canes 83/26
**carie** *pr. 3 pl.* carry 50/13
**castel** *n.* castle 15/14
**catel** *n.* possessions, property 4/4
**cesid** *pp.* possessed 4/13
**cesterne** *n.* reservoir 36/15
**chace** *inf.* chase 23/12
**chace** *n.* chase, pursuit 96/27
**chaleys** *n.* cup 40/1
**chambrere** *n.* handmaid 62/16
**Chanens** *n.* Canaanites 28/27
**chanouns** *n.* canons 31/14
**charbuclis, charbugle** *n.* carbuncle(s) 101/27
**chasteyneris** *n.* chestnut trees 132/15
***chepe** *n.* trading 114/2
**cheritrees** *n.* cherry trees 14/18
**chese** *n.* cheese 13/30
**chese, chesiþ** *pr. 3 pl.* choose 123/18; **ychose** *pp.* 56/27
**chesyng** *n.* election 123/18
**cipres** *n.* cypress 34/8
**claperes** *n.* dens 90/8
**clef** *pt. 3 s.* clove, split 35/8
**yclensid** *pp.* cleansed 127/10
**clepe** *pr.1 pl.* call 8/19; **clepiþ** *pr. 3 pl.* 6/11; **clepid** *pt. 3 s.* 27/27, *pt. 3 pl.* 24/22, *pp.* 3/12; **yclepid** *pp.* 9/10
**cliket** *n.* clapper 90/6
**closed** *pp.* enclosed 45/7
***closet** *n.* room 46/24
**cloþyngis** *n.* robes 34/20
**clowis** *n.* cloves 82/15
**clustre** *n.* cluster 111/15
**clyft** *n.* fissure 35/8
**coaguleþ** *pr. 3 s.* crystallizes 68/10
**coerboyle** *n.* stiffened leather 105/9
**cocadrilles** *n.* crocodiles 87/30
**coles** *n.* coals 42/10
**comyne** *adj.* common 16/2
***commyners** *n.* commoners 90/14
**condyt** *n.* pipe, conduit 27/27
**coniured** *pt. 3 s.* charged, demanded 57/11
**conseyued** *pp.* conceived 36/10
**cornilyn** *n.* cornelian 117/16
***costage** *n.* expense 51/25
**costand, coosting** *pr. ppl.* sailing by the coast of 53/11
**couenable** *adj.* suitable 49/20
**couent** *n.* fraternity 90/5
**coueytyse** *n.* greed, avarice 120/22
**counsayl, counseil** *n.* advice, counsel, secret 11/12
**counseyl** *n.* council, meeting 11/19
**counterfetis** *n.* images 93/6
**cours** *n.* current 131/26
**coursere** *n.* charger 15/23
**cremaus** *n.* garnets 93/24
**crestal** *n.* crystal 9/18
**crisolites, *crysolites** *n.* quartz stones 93/26
**croice, croys** *n.* cross 7/13
**croppen** *n.* crupper 124/20
**cubetis** *n.* cubits (approx. 20 inches long) 9/13
**cumpas** *n.* circle 28/30
**cuntenaunce** *n.* face 121/1
**cowpes** *n.* cups 101/8

**debatis** *n.* disputes 71/1
**deceyt** *n.* trick 120/6
**dedly** *adj.* mortal 13/25
**defaute** *n.* fault, lack 4/12
**defaute** *adv.* through the fault of 71/22
**degrez** *n.* steps, degrees of the compass, degrees of rank, steps 31/22
**deliþ** *pr. 3 s.* practices 71/2; **delte** *pt. 3 s.* 57/8
**delites** *n.* pleasures, delights 56/18
**deme** *inf.* judge 45/23; **demyd** *pp.* 25/30

**deol** *n.* grief 28/15
**deope** *adj.* deep, profound 18/4
**departid** *pp.* divided 4/27
**depaynted** *pp.* painted 26/10
**dere** *inf.* annoy, harm 10/7, *pr. 3 pl.* 121/6
**deseyuyng** *pr. ppl.* deceiving 39/7
***despeyre** *n.* despair 39/3
**deuer** *n.* duty, obligation 65/29
**deynte** *n.* choice morsel 133/22
**dichis** *n.* ditches 18/4
**diȝte** *inf.* adorn, make 125/30; **diȝteþ** pr. *3 pl.* 55/1; **ydiȝt** *pp.* 9/18
**discomfitid** *pp.* conquered 34/15
**disherite** *inf.* disinherit 4/21
**dispende** *inf.* spend 51/23
**dome** *n.* judgement, verdict 13/10
**douȝty** *adj.* valiant 15/21
**doute** *n.* doubt, fear 48/6
**dowfe** *n.* dove 8/13
**drauȝt** *n.* shot 102/12
**drawe** *inf.* draw, tear, pull out 83/28; **drowe** *pt. 3 pl.* 32/13; **ydrowid** *pp.* 83/23
**dremynges** *n.* dreams 71/1
**drenchid** *pp.* drowned 48/4
**drie** *adj.* dry, withered 25/4
**dried** *pt. 3 s.* withered 25/7
**dromundaries** *n.* dromedaries 50/14
**drunkeschip** *n.* drunken stupor 27/4
**dryue** *inf.* drive, herd 80/31; **droof** *pt. 3 s.* 81/4, *pt. 3 pl.* 81/7; **dryuen, ydryue** *pp.* 24/24
**dyasper** *n.* a calque, see note 117/16

**eeris** *n.* ears 99/23
**eftsoones** *adv.* again 10/12
**egle** *n.* eagle 113/4
**eir** *n.* air 3/11
**eires** *n.* heirs 5/2
**eiren** *n.* eggs 13/30
**elde, *eelde** *n.* age 14/20
**ellis** *adv.* else 22/21
**emperice** *n.* empress 93/13
**encense** *inf.* make sweet-smelling 76/19
**enclyne** *pr. 3 pl.* bend, kneel 32/25; **inclynand** *pr. pl.* 32/27
**enflawmed** *pp.* inflamed 4/20
***englentere** *n.* sweet briar 10/15
**engyn** *n.* device 119/2
**ensample, sample** *n.* example 57/20
**ensensours** *n.* censers 34/24
**entres** *n.* doorways 36/16
**esementis** *n.* rooms 91/16
***eyere** *n.* heir 50/16

**fadid** *pt. 3 pl.* died, withered 25/8
**fallyng yuel** *pr. ppl.* + *n.* epilepsy 25/16
**faste** *adv.* forcefully 10/4
**fayrie** *n.* land of spirits 65/20
**fecche** *inf.* fetch 40/19
**fel** *n.* skin 75/27
**fel, felle** *adj.* savage 36/24
**feld** *n.* field 24/30
**fele** *inf.* feel 11/27
**felliche** *adv.* fiercely 18/2
**fer** *adv.* far 66/24; **ferrer, ferþer** *comp. adv.* 79/21
**ferd** *pp.* afraid 57/10
**ferþe** *adj.* fourth 26/18
**ferþermore** *adv.* farther 37/15
**fey** *n.* faith 29/29
**ficchid** *pp.* fixed 29/26
**figuris** *n.* letters 45/31
**firre, fuyre** *n.* fire 21/24
**fisician** *n.* doctor 50/20
**fisyk** *n.* medicine 50/21
**flixe** *n.* dysentry 69/20
**floodes** *n.* rivers 64/13
***floreschede, florischid, floryst** *pp.* adorned with flowers 25/28
**floridous** *adj.* adorned with flowers 25/27
**flouris** *n.* flowers 118/27
**foly** *n.* lust 17/6
**fooles, voles** *n.* foals 130/2
**forbode** *pp.* forbidden 13/27
**forȝat** *pt. 3 s.* forgave 18/25
**forsoþe** *adv.* truly 15/1
**forwery** *adj.* very weary 131/29
**fosse** *n.* ditch 20/9
**fownes** *n.* fawns 124/27
***freses** *pr. 3 s.* freezes 51/9; **yfore** *pp.* 107/11
**frount** *n.* foreheed 87/7
**fulfille** *inf.* complete, endow 111/24; **fulfilde** *pt. 3 s.* 37/8, *pp.* 75/6
**fulle** *imper. pl.* fill 78/10
**fylth** *n.* impurities 123/10
**fyneþ** *pr. 3 pl.* refine 70/9

**gart** *pt. 3 s.* caused 60/8
**gastelich** *adv.* in supernatural form 47/17
**geaunt** *n.* giant 23/29
**gedre** *inf.* gather 88/11; **gederiþ** *pr. 3 pl.* 106/9; **gederid** *pp.* 22/16
**gederyng** *n.* confluence 131/11

**gentel** *n.* well-born 90/13
**gentry** *n.* mark of gentility 134/9
**gerandys** *n.* geracites (onyx stones) 94/1
**gerfaucons** *n.* falcons 101/14
**getiþ** *pr. 3 pl.* beget 87/21; **gate** *pr. 3 s.* 62/16, *pt. 3 pl.* 24/21; **ygete** *pp.* 46/19
**getyng** *n.* begetting 118/2
**ygildid** *pp.* gilted 6/30
**gilty** *adj.* guilty 25/32
**girdyng** *n.* girdling 49/31
**gladloker** *comp. adv.* more gladly 122/8
**goost** *n.* spirit 59/24
***gostely** *adv.* spiritually 59/30
**graue** *inf.* dig, bury 112/26, *pr. 3 pl.* 84/24; **grauen** *pp.* 22/15
**graynes** *n.* seeds 8/26
**greez, gres, greces** *n.* steps 26/19
**gret, grette** *pt. 3 s.* wept 23/27
**gretelich** *adv.* greatly 133/17
**greue** *inf.* injure, offend 8/6; **greued** *pt. 3 s.* 26/25
**grises** *n.* swine 27/8
**ground** *n.* base, bottom 29/28
**gurdel** *n.* girdle 40/29
***gurdes** *n.* gourds 111/4

**ȝate** *n.* gate 14/13
***ȝeldith** *pr. 3 pl.* yield 54/24
**ȝeode** *pt. 3 s.* went 15/29
**ȝeueþ** *pr. 3 pl.* give 22/28; **ȝaf** *pt. 3 s.* 22/20
**ȝhe** *affirm. part.* yes 125/9
**ȝokid** *pp.* yoked 113/8
**Ȝole Eue** *n. + n.* Christmas Eve 13/20
**ȝolewe** *adj.* yellow 45/26
**ȝong** *adj.* young 17/6
**ȝowþe** *n.* youth 74/20

**halewid** *pp.* sanctified 3/5
**halewis** *n.* saints 49/28
**halp** *pt. 3 s.* helped 122/1
**hardeliche** *adv.* fiercely 83/29
**hardy** *adj.* fierce, foolhardy 15/18
**hare** *poss. pron.* theirs 40/15
**hauen** *n.* harbour 17/21
**hauk** *n.* hawk 65/19
**heele, hele** *n.* salvation, health 8/24
**heeliþ** *pr. 3 s.* heals 71/8; **heelid** *pt. 3 s.* 57/23
**heer** *n.* hair 40/26
**helid** *pp.* roofed 32/17
**hemelokis** *n.* hemlock nettles 55/9
**heo** *pron.* she 15/14
**herburȝ** *n.* lodging 40/23
**herburwid** *pt. 3 s.* lodged 40/21; *pp.* 84/24
**here** *pron.* her 15/14
**heris** *poss. pron.* theirs 14/8
**heuynes** *n.* misery 123/14
**hiȝe** *adj.* high 19/27; *comp.* **heiȝer** 24/14
**hiȝt** *pr. 3 pl.* promise 105/19, *pp.* 4/12
**honest** *adj.* respectable, clean 94/18
**hongyng** *n.* overhang, slope of a hill 24/4
**hool** *adj.* whole, healed 36/18
**yhouselyd** *pp.* given the Eucharist 121/14
**hud, yhudde** *pp.* hidden 30/20
**hure** *pron.* her 16/16
**hure** *poss. adj.* her 9/11
**hure** *inf.* hear 5/4; **huyreþ** *imp.* 43/11
**hureris** *n.* listeners 136/22
**hurne** *n.* corner 36/5
**hy** *pron.* they 12/18
**hydous** *adj.* hideous 15/25

**iasper** *n.* jasper 92/30
**iȝe, iȝen** *n.* eye(s) 40/25
**ilke** *adj.* each 62/10
***inewght** *n.* enough 111/15
**iogelouris** *n.* jugglers 101/4
**ionqes, ionques** *n.* rushes 9/21
**iourney** *n.* journey, a day's travel 21/8
**iouste** *inf.* joust 101/9
**ioustyng** *n.* jousting 12/4
**ipotaynes** *n.* hippopotami 112/32
**iuggid** *pp.* condemned 38/28

**kembid** *pt. 3 s.* combed 15/31
**kepere** *n.* governor 62/4
**kernels** *n.* battlements 25/24
***keruande** *pr. ppl.* cutting 106/17
**keuered** *pp.* covered 37/28, *pt. 3 s.* 130/28
**kittiþ** *pr. 3 s.* cuts 42/9, *pr. 3 pl.* 134/3
**knaue** *n.* boy, male 69/2
**kunne** *pr. 3 pl.* know (how to) 49/3; **kan** *pr. 3 pl.* 134/29
**kunnyng** *n.* understanding 81/8
**kyn** *n.* lineage, tribe 24/29
**kynde** *n.* nature, tribe 23/18
**kyndely** *adj.* natural 13/11
**kyndeliche** *adv.* naturally 85/6
***kyrnelled** *pp.* castelated 24/5

**laithe** *adj.* loathsome 68/14
**lambre** *n.* amber 86/2

**lappe** *pr. 3 pl.* wrap 45/25; **lappid** *pp.* 45/8
**laueris** *n.* larks 101/14
**lawe** *n.* moral code 3/8
**lay** *n.* religion, moral code 100/28
**led, leed** *n.* lead 32/17
**leeue, leue** *n.* permission 21/4
**leeues** *n.* leaves (of a tree) 25/6
**lemman** *n.* lover, concubine 27/15
**leosiþ** *pr. 3 s.* loses 71/22
**lere** *inf.* learn, teach 50/21, *pr. 3 pl.* 122/10; **lerid** *pt. 3 s. 35/10; pp.* 56/26
**let** *pt. 3 s.* caused 32/32
**letonyes** *n.* litanies 77/20
**lette** *inf.* hinder, refrain from 86/13, *pr. 3 pl.* 114/2
**lettrid** *adj.* educated 57/27
**leynten** *n.* Lent 13/18
**leue** *n.* leave, farewell 22/26
**leuer** *comp. adj.* rather, preferable 18/9
**lewid** *adj.* lay 49/29
**licour** *n.* liquid 104/16
**ligge** *inf.* lie 60/24; **liggeþ, *lyggen** *pr. 3 pl.* 24/7; **liggyng** *pr. ppl.* 7/25
**liȝt** *n.* light 35/9
**liȝtneþ** *pr. 3 s.* lights 29/7; **liȝted** *pt. 3 s.* 59/18; **liȝt** *pp.* 29/6
**liȝtlich** *adv.* easily 59/27
**likyng** *adj.* pleasant 23/20
**liþ** *pr. 3 s.* lies 10/27, *pr. 3 pl.* 52/16
**liyf, lyf** *n.* life 29/9
**loke** *n.* lock 78/15
***lokkide** *pp.* locked 111/26
**lokid** *pt. 3 s.* looked 15/31
**lombe** *n.* lamb 111/6
**loofes** *n.* loaves 41/17
**louteþ, lowtiþ** *pr. 3 s.* inclines, bends in homage 103/10
**lybardis** *n.* leopards 101/2
**lyft** *adj.* left 29/5
**lymes** *n.* limbs 70/28
**lynages** *n.* tribes 95/14
**lynnen** *adj.* linen 23/17

**maces** *n.* nutmeg flowers 82/25
**maigne** *n.* force, **priue maigne** *adj.* + *n.* bodyguard 102/15
**malisoun** *n.* curse 27/5
**manase** *inf.* threaten 7/9
**marchal** *n.* marshal 118/14
**marche** *n.* borderland 43/23
**marchiþ** *pr. 3 s.* shares common boundary, extends to 6/7
**mareys** *n.* marshes 55/16
**marmesetez** *n.* monkeys 90/4
**Massydoynes** *n.* Macedonians 28/18
**mastyfs** *n.* hounds 74/10
**mastyk** *n.* mastic gum 14/17
**maunde** *n.* maundy 13/5
**maundementis** *n.* commandments 60/5
**mawgree** *prep.* despite 15/26
**mawmet** *n.* idol 77/2
**mawmetrie** *n.* idolatry 135/18
**mede** *n.* reward 41/12
**medlid** *pp.* mingled 29/12
**meke** *adj.* meek 57/4
**mekeliche** *adv.* meekly 126/32
**mele** *n.* meal, corn 83/11
**melk** *n.* milk 26/25
**membre, menbre** *n.* limb, genitals 8/23
**menours** *n.* Minorites 121/10
**mere, meere** *n.* mare 130/2
**merþe** *n.* mirth 133/4
**mesel** *n.* leper 43/16
**metyng** *n.* meeting 73/27
**meyntene** *inf.* confirm 135/18
**Miȝghelmasday** *n.* Michaelmas Day 5/9
**mirre** *n.* myrrh 26/15
**mo** *adj.* more 21/27
**mokk** *n.* muck, dung 55/1
**morwe, morwenyng** *n.* morning 16/8
***mountour** *n.* mound 92/19
**mouþ, mowþis** *n.* mouth(s) 16/10
**mowe** *pr. 1 pl.* may 12/32
**moyst** *adj.* damp 11/30
**myche** *adv.* much 22/14
**mychel** *n.* stature 91/7
**myne** *n.* mine 70/9
***mynystrede** *pt. 3 s.* administered 44/8
**mysdoers** *n.* sinners 7/10
**mysdoyng** *pr. ppl.* sinning 28/21
**myss** *n.* mice 54/28
**mystre** *pr. 3 pl.* need 76/23
**mystrowand** *pr. ppl.* unbelieving 33/29

**naddris, *neddyrs** *n.* serpents 73/1
**nakers** *n.* kettle-drums 120/18
**nama** *adv.* + *adj.* no more 47/28
**name** *n.* reputation 85/13
**naysche** *adj.* soft 70/6
**neiȝest, nexte** *sup. adj.* next 52/7
**neode** *n.* need 18/17
**neodeful** *adj.* needy 66/10
**nere** *adj. and adv.* near, nearby 14/22
**netelis** *n.* nettles 55/9
**nombrid** *pp.* numbered 96/9

**nonnes** *n.* nuns 50/24
**norischaunt** *adj.* nourishing 63/13
**norische** *inf.* nourish 73/14, *pr. 3 pl.* 85/4; **ynorischid** *pp.* 70/16
**notes** *n.* nuts 70/14
**nouȝt, noȝt** *adv.* not 7/7
**nygromancye** *n.* necromancy 99/9
**nyȝ** *ad.* almost 9/1
**nys** *pr. 3 s.* is not 24/33

**obeschaunt** *adj.* obedient 11/13
**oker** *n.* usury 13/14
**olyf, olyue** *n.* olive 7/26
**olyfauntz** *n.* elephants 84/7
**onelich** *adv.* only 6/2
***onices** *n.* onyx stones 93/26
**ony** *adj.* any 3/25
**onys, oonus** *adv.* once 13/12
**openeþ** *pr. 3 pl.* reveal 58/26
**openly** *adv.* widely 3/25
**or** *conj.* before 29/32
**ordynetly** *adv.* temperately 125/19
**ordeyne** *inf.* order, regulate 98/23; **ordeind** *pp.* 98/23
**ordris** *n.* ordinations 128/19
**orient** *adj.* brilliant 86/1
**orisoun** *n.* prayer 100/27
**orlagis** *n.* time-pieces 119/2
**oþer** *conj.* or 3/26
**oþer** *adj.* other 13/15
**ouerlappid** *pt. 3 s.* enveloped 109/27
**ouertwert** *adv.* crosswise 7/24
**ouertwert** *n.* cross-piece 8/11
**oure** *n.* hour 74/17
**owe** *pr. 1 pl.* ought 4/17
**oynementis** *n.* ointments 72/21

**paas, pases** *n.* paces 26/11
**pans** *n.* pence 39/5
**panters** *n.* panthers 92/13
**papyniayes** *n.* parrots 101/15
**passage** *n.* crusade, way 5/4
**paupiouns** *n.* hunting lynxes 17/30
**pauy** *inf.* pave 18/5; **ypaued** *pp.* 32/17
**pawmes** *n.* palms 127/15
**payed** *pp.* satisfied 43/11
**payems, payen, peynym** *n.* pagan(s), Saracen(s) 31/1
**payned** *pt. 3 pl.* took pains 29/2; **peyned** *pp.* tortured 29/14
**payntures** *n.* paintings 135/11
**pece** *n.* piece 7/23
**pegmans** *n.* pygmies 128/2
**peny** *n.* penny 33/8
**perles** *n.* pearls 86/1
**perischid** *pp.* pierced 83/19
***perydes** *n.* chrysolites 94/9
**pesyn** *n.* pea(s) 84/25
**pilour, piler** *n.* pillar 7/10
**pitous** *adj.* pitiful 28/15
**plat** *adj.* flat 87/13
**pledyng** *n.* pleading at law 70/30
**plenerliche** *adv.* more fully 5/17
**police** *inf.* polish 71/11; **polyschid** *pp.* 71/13
**poudre** *n.* dust 11/31
**pouert** *n.* poverty 68/2
**prepous** *n.* prepuce 32/31
**prest** *n.* priest 86/19
**preyseþ** *pr. 3 pl.* value 92/17
**prime** *n.* prime, 9 a.m. 65/8
**pris, prys** *n.* value 71/24
**priue** *adj.* secret, private 85/27
**priueþ** *pr. 3 s.* deprives 14/2
**profitable** *adj.* useful, fertile 69/10
**profre** *inf.* offer 84/21
**puriþ** *pr. 3 pl.* refine 129/22
**pursue** *inf.* chase, search for 112/23; **pursued** *pt. 3 s.* persecuted 109/19
**pynaclis** *n.* spires 25/24
**pyromacie** *n.* pyromancy 99/10
**pysmyres** *n.* ants 129/21

**quarels, *qwarelle** *n.* fight(s), battle(s) 83/30
**quere** *n.* choir 26/8
**queynte** *adj.* cunning 121/22
**queyntise** *n.* cunning 129/25
**quike** *adj.* living 14/30

**rad** *pp.* read 56/15
**ratouns** *n.* rats 54/28
**rayed** *pp.* adorned 87/31
**rederis** *n.* readers 136/22
**reede** *adj.* red 17/2
**rekened** *pp.* reckoned 82/7
**relyf** *n.* remnant (of meal) 90/5
**remenaunt** *n.* remnant 75/9
**remewiþ** *pr. 3 pl.* shift 9/29
**renneþ** *pr. 3 s.* runs 6/18
**rentes** *n.* tributes 133/29
**reod** *n.* reed 7/12
**repreuys** *n.* reproofs 3/10
**reproue** *inf.* find fault with 81/21
**rerid** *pt. 3 s.* raised, resurrected 18/29, *pp.* 40/26

**resceyue** *inf.* receive 51/2; **resceyueþ** *pr. 3 s.* 63/18; **reseyuede** *pt. 3 s.* 35/5
**rewe** *n.* line, row 90/9
**riȝtwys** *adj.* righteous 39/7
**ripeþ** *pr. 3 pl.* reap 129/11
**roos** *pt. 3 s.* arose 29/8; **rise** *pp.* 31/12; **rysen** *pp.* 38/2
**roseris** *n.* rose trees 26/3
**rote** *inf.* rot 8/2
**ruysches** *n.* rushes 9/22
**rynde** *n.* bark 83/19
**rys** *n.* rice 114/24
**ryueryng** *n.* hawking 92/10

**sacres** *n.* hawks 101/15
**saffres, safires** *n.* sapphires 94/8
**salme, psalme** *n.* psalm 65/4
***Samaretyns** *n.* Samaritans 44/23
***Samaritane** *adj.* Samaritan 44/16
**samen** *adv.* together 22/16
**sardyn** *n.* sardonyx 117/9
**saueliche** *adv.* safely 86/11
**sauour** *n.* smell 52/21
**sautere** *n.* Psalter 26/22
**sawdeour** *n.* soldier 21/29
**schaftmountes** *n.* arrow-lengths, cubits 20/9
**schankis** *n.* shanks, legs above the knee 72/19
**schaue** *pp.* shaven 49/29
**scheep** *n.* sheep 4/26
**scheephurd** *n.* shepherd 4/26
**scheld** *n.* shield 23/15
**schellis** *n.* shells 84/23
**schere** *pr. 3 pl.* cut 71/15
**schere þorsday** *adj. + n.* Maundy Thursday 13/5
**scheþe** *n.* sheath, scabbard 35/4
**schoon** *n.* shoes 33/27
**schrift** *n.* confession 49/15
**schryue** *inf.* confess 48/25; **yschryue, schryue** *pp.* 48/32
**schuldris, *scholdres** *n.* shoulders 68/17
***ischutte** *pp.* shut, locked 38/12
**schyneþ** *pr. 3 s.* shines 56/4; **schenyng** *pr. pp.* 20/10
**sclaundre** *n.* slander 13/16
***scloys** *n.* sledges, sleighs 55/24
**scolle** *n.* skull 133/24
**se** *inf.* see 12/5; **sauȝ** *pt. 3 s.* 16/13; **ysey, seye, seiȝe, yseie** *pp.* 9/23
***see, sege** *n.* seat, siege 90/23
**seeke, sike** *adj.* sick 8/21
**semple** *adj.* simple 60/21
**semplesse** *n.* simplicity (of mind) 63/17
**sensure** *n.* censer 102/28 n.
**septoun** *n.* a calque, see note 117/17
**Sermoys** *n.* Arabic, Saracen 43/24
**yset** *pp.* pledged 4/5
**siche** *adj.* such 4/9
**sikerly** *adv.* surely 60/12
**sille, sillen** *pr. 3 pl.* sell 13/14
**siþen, siþþe** *adv.* afterwards 16/22
**skile** *n.* reason 49/18
**skirtes** *n.* shirts, dresses 94/21
**sle** *inf.* kill 105/15; **sleeþ** *pr. 3 pl.* 105/10; **slow** *pt. 3 s.* 27/3; **slawe, slayn, sleiȝe** *pp.* 46/31
**slides** *n.* sleighs 54/23
**smyteþ** *pr. 3 s.* smites 133/5; **smot** *pt 3. s.* 35/3; **smyte** *pp.* 37/19
**snewe** *pp.* snowed 55/17
**solace** *n.* joy 106/6
***solace** *inf.* entertain 94/5
**sond** *n.* sand 88/3
**sondy** *adj.* sandy 21/8
**sooþ, soþe** *adj.* true 30/2
**sorwe** *n.* sorrow 28/13
**soþfast** *adj.* devout 60/21
**soude** *n.* treaty 69/7
**sowdan** *n.* sultan 21/3
**sowkedist** *pt. 2 s.* sucked 18/24
**sowpe** *pr. 3 pl.* sup 54/26
**spede** *pr. 3 pl.* fare, prosper 73/27
***sperrede** *pp.* shut 111/27
**spores** *n.* spurs 104/10
**spounge** *n.* sponge 7/11
**sprenglyng** *pr. ppl.* flashing 120/29
**springe** *pr. 3 pl.* sprinkle 75/13
**springe** *inf.* grow 116/5; **yspronge** *pp.* 114/14
**springyng** *n.* source 131/10
**stagis** *n.* tiers 12/4
**staleworþ** *adj.* brave 71/8
**staleworþly** *adv.* vigorously 6/19
**stank, *stange** *n.* pond 34/9
**stap, stappis** *n.* step(s), footprint(s) 32/6
**staunche** *inf.* satisfy 12/33
**stedis, *steedes** *n.* places 6/3
**stenyd** *pp.* stoned 32/2
**stere** *inf.* stir, move 36/17; **steriþ** *pr. 3 s.* 20/15; **sterid** *pt. 3 s.* 39/15; **stirand, stiring** *pr. ppl.* 47/9
**steryng** *n.* stirring 36/18
**sterre** *n.* star 26/18
**stewe** *n.* stove 56/1

**stiȝe** *n.* ladder 34/30
**stok** *n.* stem, main beam 7/25
***stoniede** *pp.* astonished 128/26
**storid** *pp.* provided 106/4
**strangly** *inf.* strangle 85/5; **straungelid** *pp.* 85/8
**straunge** *adj.* foreign 4/19
**strayte** *adv.* tightly 72/21
**stretis** *n.* streets 40/6
**streyt** *adj.* narrow 60/20
**strokis** *n.* sparks, strokes 101/11
**stryues** *n.* strifes, fights 71/1
**sugetis** *n.* subjects 4/7
**suster** *n.* sister 37/1
**sute** *n.* suit 99/4
**swete, swote** *adj.* sweet 63/13
**swolewe** *inf.* devour 46/8
**swolough** *n.* gulf 20/18
**symylacris** *n.* fantastic images 73/3

**table** *n.* board 7/26
**tabres** *n.* tabors 120/16
**targe** *n.* shield 85/28
**tartaryns** *n.* cloths of Tartary 106/23
**teeþ** *n.* teeth 15/26
**tempre** *adj.* temperate 70/1
**tempre** *inf.* mix 83/15
**terrestre** *adj.* earthly 64/11
**tetys** *n.* teats 18/24
**til** *conj.* until 15/29
**til** *prep.* to 4/12
**tilieþ** *pr. 3 pl.* till 23/8
**tilyng** *n.* tilling 27/13
**title** *n.* inscription 8/11
**tobroke** *pp.* broken 9/28
**toome** *adj.* empty 103/17
**topaces** *n.* topazes 93/25
**torn** *n.* revolution 72/6
**tour** *n.* tower 53/29
**trapping** *n.* horse armour 105/9
**trauayl** *n.* journey, labour 81/3
**traueile** *inf.* labour 27/12; ***trauayled** *pp.* burdened 71/9
**tree** *n.* wood 8/22
**tresorie** *n.* treasury 12/16
**tresoun** *n.* malice, evil 35/18
**trespace** *n.* sin 48/29
**trespassouris** *n.* sinners 4/8
**treuþe** *n.* faith 21/19
**triacle** *n.* salve, remedy 83/16
**trist** *n.* trust 121/12
**troone, trone** *n.* throne 77/16
**trouble, trowble** *adj.* disturbed 20/15
**trouble** *inf.* disturb 126/6; **troublid** *pp.* 70/4
**trowe** *inf.* believe 58/4; **trowiþ** *pr. 3 pl.* 5/26; **trowyng** *pr. ppl.* 4/16; **trowid** *pt. 3* 8/10
**trumpes** *n.* trumpets 34/27
**tunge** *n.* tongue 8/28
**turned** *pt. 3 s.* converted 48/23, *pp.* 49/7
**turtlis** *n.* turtle doves 35/26
**twengid** *pt. 3 pl.* stung 123/1
**twey** *adj.* two 22/21 n.
**twoname** *n.* second name 44/1
**tygris** *n.* tiger 131/19

**þank** *n.* thanks 89/13
**þankid** *pp.* thanked 60/11
***þeire** *adv.* there 42/1
**þekkid** *pp.* strengthened 28/27
**þeof** *n.* thief 7/17
**þerf** *adj.* unleavened 12/3
**þicke** *adj.* thick, muddy 45/19
**þies** *n.* thighs 76/14
**þilke** *demon. adj.* those 11/29
**þinkeþ** *pr. 3 s. impers.* seems 81/21; **þouȝt** *pt. 3 s.* 16/11
***þois** *demon. adj.* those 41/7
**þonder** *n.* thunders 10/7
**þouȝt** *pt. 3 pl.* thought 3/23, *pp.* 80/26
**þraldome** *n.* servitude 95/12
**þurȝ** *prep.* through 4/11

**vnccioun** *n.* anointing 13/7
**vndoynge** *n.* ruin 66/13
**vndren** *n.* mid-morning 72/24
**vryn** *n.* urine 74/29

**veel** *n.* veal 27/11
**yvengid** *pp.* avenged 120/6
**veniaunce** *n.* vengeance 42/10
**venym** *n.* poison 83/13
**verrey** *adj.* true 30/14
**vers** *n.* biblical verse 7/21
**veuer** *n.* vivarium 76/20
**viage** *n.* voyage 4/29
**vikery** *n.* vicar 12/25
***vilanye** *n.* ill-repute 87/3
**visage** *n.* face 82/16
**vitaile** *n.* foodstuffs 22/28
**vois** *n.* voice 17/11
**vowtid** *pp.* vaulted 12/6
**voyde** *adj.* empty 130/3

**waast** *n.* desert 87/29
**waast** *adj.* desolate 20/2
**waische** *pr. 3 pl.* wash 13/22; *pp.* 39/1; **woische** *pt. 3 s.* 40/25
**wake** *inf.* to awake 62/27; **wakid, woke, wook** *pt. 3 s.* 65/27
**wanhope** *n.* despair 76/1
**wastid** *pp.* laid waste 41/5
**wawes** *n.* waves 115/18
**wayke** *adj.* vulnerable 31/30
**wedde** *n.* pledge 9/19
**wende** *pt. 3 s.* thought 57/11, *pt. 3 pl.* 96/23
**weies** *n.* routes 5/25
**werche** *inf.* work 27/12
**werching** *n.* work 111/22
**were** *pr. 3 pl.* wear 49/31
***were, werre** *n.* war 66/7
**werriours** *n.* fighters 69/7
**wery** *adj.* weary 31/28
**wexe** *inf.* grow 25/12
**wham** *relat. pron.* whom 9/11
**wheolis** *n.* wheels 55/24
**whider** *conj.* whither 4/27
**wit** *n.* intelligence 81/21
**wite** *inf.* know 11/3; **woot** *pr. 3 s.* 4/27; **wot** *pr. 1 s.* 45/10; **witen, wote** *pr. 3 pl.* 60/17; **wiste** *pt. 1 s.* 35/1; **wist** *pt. 3 s.* 61/8
**woke** *n.* week 115/27
**wond, woned** *pp.* accustomed 6/31
**woo** *n.* woe 46/11
**wordelich, wordly** *adj.* worldly 4/28
**wreþþe** *n.* wrath 122/16
**wrooþ** *adj.* angry 62/26
**wrouȝt** *pp.* made 29/25

**ymage** *n.* image, statue 7/10
**ymage** *pr. 1 s.* give as illustration 81/23
**ynow** *adv.* enough 60/17
**yren, yrun** *n.* iron 41/31
**yss** *n.* ice 55/23
**yssche** *pr. 3 pl.* hiss 85/19

# INDEX OF PERSONS AND PEOPLES

# INDEX OF PLACES